American Education

American Education

SIXTH EDITION

Joel Spring

State University of New York
College at New Paltz

McGraw-Hill, Inc.

New York St. Louis San Francisco Auckland Bogotá Caracas
Lisbon London Madrid Mexico City Milan Montreal New Delhi
San Juan Singapore Sydney Tokyo Toronto

This book was developed by Lane Akers, Inc.

This book was set in Palatino by Better Graphics, Inc.
The editors were Lane Akers and Larry Goldberg;
the production supervisor was Leroy A. Young.
The cover was designed by Carol Couch;
the cover art was designed by Jane Sterrett.
R. R. Donnelley & Sons Company was printer and binder.

AMERICAN EDUCATION

1 2 3 4 5 6 7 8 9 0 DOC DOC 9 0 9 8 7 6 5 4 3

ISBN 0-07-060551-3

Library of Congress Cataloging-in-Publication Data

Spring, Joel H.
    American education / Joel Spring.—6th ed.
        p.   cm
    Includes bibliographical references (p.   ) and index.
    ISBN 0-07-060551-3
        1. Education—Social aspects—United States.   2. Education—
Political aspects—United States.   3. Educational equalization—
United States.   4. Education and state—United States.   I. Title.
LC191.4.S684   1994
370'.973—dc20
                                                        93-8342

About the Author

JOEL SPRING, professor of education at the State University of New York–College at New Paltz, received his Ph.D. in educational policy studies from the University of Wisconsin. His father was born a citizen of the Choctaw Nation in Indian Territory prior to the abolishment of the Choctaw government and the creation of Oklahoma. Professor Spring's current interest in Native American culture and history is a reflection of his Indian background.

Professor Spring is the author of many books including *Images of American Life: A History of Ideological Management in Schools, Movies, Radio, and Television; Wheels in the Head: Educational Philosophies of Authority, Freedom, and Culture from Socrates to Paulo Freire; The American School, 1642–1993* (now in its third edition); and *Deculturalization and the Struggle for Equality: A Brief History of the Education of Dominated Cultures in the United States.*

Contents

Part Two
POWER AND CONTROL IN AMERICAN EDUCATION

Chapter 10   **The Politics of Curriculum, Instruction,
            and Textbooks**   232

Chapter 11   **The Courts and the Schools**   258

Preface

THE MODERN VERSUS
THE POSTMODERN TEXTBOOK

On American soil, the modern textbook was born in the seventeenth century with the publication of the *New England Primer*. The authoritarian methodology of the book set the tone for future textbooks. Students were required to memorize and recite phrases such as, "In Adam's fall we sinned all." The book was not designed to entertain, but was organized for memorization. Students probably found themselves nodding off to sleep as they tried to concentrate on the book's dull prose. It would almost seem that the birth of the modern textbook was accompanied by a license to torture students.

Things got worse by the twentieth century. At least earlier textbooks were not contaminated by a false sense of being scientific and by the managerial approaches of modern corporations. In their quest to be scientific, educators stripped textbooks of language that did not fit into preconceived word lists. Adding the final touch to making modern textbooks the most boring reading in the world, publishers introduced concepts of team management to the writing process. Individual authorship was replaced with teams of technical writers working under the direction of an editor. The author supplied the ideas and the book was written by the team. Created in this manner, textbooks sunk to their lowest levels.

The postmodern textbook breaks with these traditions. While still being concerned with instruction, the postmodern textbook avoids an authoritarian approach to knowledge and a format designed for memorization of content. In "From the Ivory Tower to the Bottom Line: College Textbook Publishing from an Editor's Perspective," Naomi Silverman outlines five characteristics of the postmodern textbook.[1] First, the postmodern textbook is concerned with creating a dialogue between the student and the text. While information and data are transmitted to the reader, on another level the meaning of the text is in the interaction between the reader and the text. Second, postmodern textbook writers do not claim they are presenting an "authoritative, neutral, objective, unchanging source of knowledge." In fact, a problem with modern textbooks is that they appear to be presenting truth to the reader when an official canon of truth does not exist in most fields of knowledge. Third, the postmodern textbook is viewed as an original piece of scholarship as opposed to a compendium of supposedly objective information. Authors provide their own interpretation and synthesis of material. Fourth, the postmodern text places knowledge in a context through the discussion of a history of ideas and the impact of social and political forces on the material. And last, the author is concerned about telling a story through the introduction of anecdotal and narrative material. The postmodern textbook provides the student with the opportunity for critical thinking and intellectual enjoyment.

My revision of *American Education* reflects Silverman's ideas regarding the postmodern textbook. The book is organized to raise questions in the mind of the reader and create a dialogue with the text. The goal is to have the reader think about the material—not to memorize for a multiple choice test. Most sections of the book contain my original interpretations of the material. Rather than a separate section on the history of education, I have woven historical material into each chapter. The historical background provides a context for understanding the ideas and information being presented. And finally, I use a narrative style in many chapters with a reliance on anecdotal material. My goal is to have readers think about the field of education and derive intellectual pleasure from engaging in a debate with the text.

CHANGES IN THE SIXTH EDITION

Multicultural Education

Based on my experience teaching undergraduate courses in multicultural education, I added a new Chapter 6, "Multicultural Education," to the Sixth Edition of *American Education*. In teaching multicultural education I found it useful to distinguish between the educational problems confronting immigrants and those confronting cultures that are dominated by American-European culture, such as Native Americans, African Americans, Mexican Americans, and Puerto Ricans. Consequently, Chapter 6 opens with a section discussing the experience of new immigrants which is followed by a discus-

[1] Naomi Silverman, "From the Ivory Tower to the Bottom Line: College Textbook Publishing from an Editor's Perspective," *Perspectives on Textbooks and Society*, edited by Philip Altbach et al. Albany, N.Y.: State University of New York Press, 1992.

sion of the educational problems confronting dominated groups. The remaining sections discuss possible educational solutions facing new immigrants and dominated groups including: "Ethnocentric Education," "Issues of Language," "Bicultural Education," and "Multicultural Education."

Inequality of Educational Opportunity

Issues involving segregation and second generation segregation are now discussed in Chapter 5. In addition to my previous discussion of the struggles for equal educational opportunities by African Americans, I have added to Chapter 5 sections titled: "Native Americans," "Mexican Americans," and "Students with Special Needs."

Education and the Job Market

The discussion of the relationship between education and the social structure in Chapter 4 was updated by eliminating dated material on social mobility and income, and replacing it with discussions of the labor market in the 1990s and the interconnection between education, the new labor market, and the global economy. In addition, Jonathon Kozol's *Savage Inequalities: Children in America's Schools* generated a great deal of discussion about the inequality of educational opportunities between school districts. Consequently, I added a section to Chapter 4 on "Savage Inequalities." And, because of the recent debate on eliminating tracking, I added to Chapter 4 a section titled: "Should Tracking and Ability Grouping Be Abolished?"

The Profession of Teaching

Besides updating material on teachers and teaching, I added a section to Chapter 2 on recent changes in the professional model of teaching titled: "Teachers as Researchers and Scholars." I finely tuned material in other sections of Chapter 2 to produce two new sections titled: "The Working Conditions of Teachers" and "Teacher Burnout." Reflecting current trends that affect classroom practices, I added two new sections to Chapter 10 titled: "National Standards" and "Critical Pedagogy."

Restructuring and the Politics of Education

Restructuring continues to be the magic word in school reform, and, consequently, I added to Chapter 7 a section on "Charter Schools" which, in combination with previous sections on "Site-Based Management" and "Choice," rounds out a discussion of the issue. Because of the recent criticism of the educational bureaucracy, I refined existing material in Chapter 7 to produce a new section titled: "The Educational Bureaucracy." Also, in response to the restructuring agenda, I added two new sections to Chapter 8 on "The Politics of State Education" and "The Nationalization of State Policies."

With the election of President Bill Clinton in 1992, I had to change my discussion of educational goals for the 1990s in Chapter 1 and on national educational politics in Chapter 9.

Teacher Liability

Recent court decisions were added to Chapter 11 along with a new section on "The Liability of Teachers."

Joel Spring

American Education

PART ONE

The School
and the Social Order

The Purposes of Public Schooling

"They should stick to teaching these babies that $1 + 1 = 2$, instead of what daddy and his boyfriend are doing in the bedroom," shouted Neil Lodato, a construction worker, outside his daughter's school in Queens, New York. Lodato was joined by other parents protesting the 1992 requirement that their local elementary school teach tolerance toward gays and lesbians. "I learned about [gay couples] on the street, that's where she should too," Lodato screamed. Diane Kirsten, the mother of a second grader, was one of the few parents in the crowd supporting the requirements of the new 443-page multicultural curriculum guide called "Children of the Rainbow." Kirsten told a reporter that the hysteria over the new curriculum was caused by "fear and anger and homophobia."

Across town, the Chancellor of the New York City school system, Joseph Fernandez, was trying to decide what to do with the rebellious Queens school district. Raised on the streets of New York, Fernandez admitted in his autobiography that as a teenage dropout in Harlem he frequently snorted and injected heroin. Wanting to save other children from the past he experienced, he dedicated his career to school reform. Previous to the "Children of the Rainbow" controversy, he was embroiled in a struggle over the distribution of condoms in high schools as a means of preventing the spread of AIDS. The condom distribution plan was bitterly protested by religious groups that opposed birth control and by groups wanting the schools to emphasize sexual abstinence.

The "Children of the Rainbow" curriculum was originally planned to increase tolerance between the large number of cultural groups living in New York City. Many interest groups, including those representing the gay and lesbian community in New York City, pressured the school system to have their concerns represented in the new curriculum. Consequently, the authors of the 443-page volume included one small section of less than a page which recommends that as early as the first grade students should be introduced to different family structures, including "two-parent or single-parent households, gay or lesbian parents, divorced parents, adoptive parents, and guardians or foster parents." In addition, teachers were asked to present students with "the positive aspects of each type of household." Among the books recommended for use in the classroom were *Daddy's Roommate* and *Heather Has Two Mommies*. Both books show pictures of gay couples, including a drawing of two men in bed.

Standing on top of a truck outside Fernandez's office, Mary Cummins, the president of the local Queen's district board of education, led a demonstration against the curriculum. "It is bizarre," she said, "to teach 6-year-olds this [referring to the gay and lesbian content of the curriculum]. Why single out [homosexuals] for respect? Tomorrow it will be skinheads." Religious beliefs were given as the main objections to teaching tolerance toward gay and lesbian families. Catholic, Pentecostal, and Baptist churches along with Orthodox synagogues protested that homosexuality was a sin and it should not be tolerated. Some parents thought first graders were too young to be introduced to the topic of gay and lesbian lifestyles. Others thought that these were issues better left to the family and that schools should focus on teaching reading, writing, and arithmetic. Criticism even came from those who supported building tolerance for gay and lesbian lifestyles. Well-known political activist Kenneth Toglia, who himself was raised in a lesbian household, objected to the book *Heather Has Two Mommies*. "You never," he said, "call your mother's friend mom."

The controversy swirling around "Children of the Rainbow" highlights the issues involved in the purposes of public schooling. One of the current goals of many public school systems is to instill tolerance in students. This is certainly the goal of "Children of the Rainbow." Of course, not all members of society define tolerance to include gays and lesbians, and many do not even accept the goal of instilling racial tolerance. In general, most of the goals of public schooling create some form of controversy. For instance, some people argue that the purpose of schools is to instill moral values in children, while others argue that moral education should be a function of the homes. Traditionally, public schools were charged with the duty of educating good citizens. But some religious groups object to the inclusion of flag salutes and recitations of the Pledge of Allegiance in the school curriculum because they consider it a worship of graven images and therefore a violation of the precepts of the Bible. In addition, there is the problem of who defines good citizenship. While public schools are given the goal of educating good workers, there is a dispute over whether this means training students to be compliant employees or to be active union members. The political and economic content of schooling is disputed by people with differing political and economic philosophies. Every goal of public schooling has the possibility of creating some form of public controversy.

The protest over "Children of the Rainbow" highlights the potential conflict between public and private goals for education. Public goals for education are announced by agencies of the government. In this case, the public goal of building tolerance for gay and lesbian families was given by the

Board of Education of New York City. On the other hand, private goals are the reasons parents have for sending their children to school. Parents who threatened to withdraw their children from school because of "Children of the Rainbow" rejected the public goal given by the Board of Education. The next section of this chapter will deal with the differences between public and private goals for public schools. In the remaining sections of the chapter, I will discuss the controversies involved in the major *political, social,* and *economic* purposes of education. Among other things, this discussion will provide a brief history of the schools and an understanding of the multiple roles of public schools in contemporary society.

PUBLIC VERSUS PRIVATE GOALS

A great deal of confusion and conflict can occur over the difference between public and private goals in education. A parent might send his or her child to school to learn basic intellectual skills while considering moral and social training a function of the home. On the other hand, the school might assume the responsibility of producing moral, socially responsible citizens. This situation has the potential to create conflict between the parents and the school over the content of moral and social training, and the goals that should control the education of the child.

If the school in question is a public school operated by the government, then the problem becomes even more difficult. Government-operated schools by their very nature have the responsibility of carrying out the wishes of the general public and not those of private individuals. This means that the education of a child in a public school is subordinate to the general educational goals of the government. The public school serves public purposes.

The fact that the public school serves public purposes is inherent in the very idea that governments should establish and operate educational systems; government educational systems were set up to serve public—not private—goals. How the goals were established is a political question, and will be linked to concerns about social and political stability, reform, and economic development. Therefore, parents who send their child to a public school to achieve purely intellectual goals might be frustrated and concerned about both the time spent on government goals for education and the content of those goals. Certainly, in the history of American education one of the greatest arenas of conflict has been between private moral and religious beliefs and the values taught in the public schools. Other issues have also created bitter dispute. Educating children in public schools for citizenship has always been an area of conflict, a conflict concerned with content and purpose. Similar conflicts occur over the use of public schools to pursue economic goals.

Although private goals are subordinate to government goals in public schools, they cannot simply be dismissed. It is important to understand them because of the potential conflict between private goals and public schools, and because of the larger issue of whether the public schools serve the interests of the individual.

One of the more recent surveys of private goals was conducted by John Goodlad for his study, *A Place Called School.* Goodlad surveyed the educational goals held by students, teachers, and parents, and divided them into vocational, social, intellectual, and personal goals. These categories differ slightly in meaning from those used in the remainder of this chapter to describe the public goals of schooling. Goodlad defines *vocational* to mean preparation for work; *social* to mean preparation for the social life of a complex society; *intellectual* to mean academic skills and knowledge; and *personal* to mean development of individual responsibility, talent, and free expression.

The most striking conclusion one reaches in looking at the results of Goodlad's survey is the difference between private and public goals. The dominant public goals for education in the twentieth century are economic. These economic goals include preparation for work, the control of the labor market, and economic development. In Goodlad's survey, *vocational* is the word closest in meaning to *economic* and it was chosen as the least important goal by teachers and parents. All teachers in elementary, middle, and high school grades selected vocational as the least important goal after intellectual, personal, and social goals. Parents of elementary and middle school children selected vocational goals last, and parents of high school students chose vocational as third, after intellectual and personal goals. High school students, on the other hand, selected vocational as the most important goal, whereas it was the second choice for middle school students.

Nothing gives greater evidence of the potential conflict between public and private goals than the fact that the number-one goal of teachers and parents is intellectual. Students maintain this as their number-one goal until high school, when it moves into second place after vocational. This means that the majority of parents send their children to school primarily to learn academic skills and knowledge. Although on the surface this seems reasonable and a commonsense conclusion, it is in conflict with the major public goals that have been used to justify the establishment and maintenance of public schools. In fact, parents rank personal goals as second in importance, leaving social and vocational at the bottom in relative importance.

The differences between public and private goals should be kept in mind by the reader as she or he studies the following pages. What the public official wants the school system to achieve can be entirely different from what the individual citizen wants. Also, differing attitudes and perceptions can develop about what is happening within public school systems.

The following discussion of the public goals of schooling is divided into political, social, and economic goals. In general, political goals refer to the attempts to use educational systems to mold future citizens, maintain political stability, and shape political systems; social goals include attempts to reform society, provide social stability, and give direction to social development; and economic goals involve the use of the public school system to sort and select talent for the labor market, develop human capital, and plan economic development. However, the reader should be aware that these categories often overlap. For instance, the goal of eliminating poverty through schooling can be considered both an economic and a social goal.

THE POLITICAL PURPOSES OF SCHOOLING

The most important political goals of public schooling are *educating citizens, selecting future political leaders, creating a political consensus, maintaining political power,* and *socializing individuals for political systems.* These political goals can be both a source of political freedom and a means of exerting political oppression. A totalitarian state can use its educational system to exert political control over its population while other governments might use their educational system to teach citizens how to use their political rights.

Most modern governments use public schools to *educate future citizens.* This purpose of education can mean different things depending on the nature of the political organization. For instance, in Nazi Germany during the 1930s, schools were enlisted in a general campaign to produce citizens who would believe in the racial superiority of the German people, support fascism, and be willing to die at the command of Hitler. Racial biology and fascist political doctrines were taught in the classroom; patriotic parades and singing took place in the school yard. The lesson learned from the experience of schools in Nazi Germany is that one must carefully evaluate the citizenship-training function of public schools. Citizenship training is not necessarily good, nor can it exist apart from a general political philosophy.

In America early proposals for public systems of education reflected a variety of concerns about the establishment of a republican form of government. One of the major worries expressed immediately following the American Revolution was the *selection of political leaders* for the new government. Since hereditary nobility and monarchy would no longer be bases for leadership, a question arose about who would be the leaders of a republican government. Revolutionary leader Benjamin Rush proposed in the late eighteenth century the establishment of a national university and a requirement that all government officials hold a degree from that institution. Rush argued that one should no more allow quacks to practice politics than one would allow quacks to practice medicine. President George Washington proposed a national university before Congress as a means of training political leaders and creating a common national culture by bringing together within one institution students from all areas of the country.

One of the arguments against Washington's proposal for a national university as a training ground for political leadership was the charge of elitism. (Current criticism of reliance upon educational institutions as sources of political and social leadership makes the same charge.) Critics of Washington's proposal felt that a national university would be training leaders who would view themselves as "better" and more important than the general public. These educated leaders would not necessarily represent the interests and welfare of the general public. The hereditary aristocracy might be replaced by an aristocracy of the educated. If none but the rich had access to higher education, then the rich could use higher education as a means of perpetuating and supporting their social status.

One answer to the charge of elitism is the concept of a meritocracy. This idea permeates our existing educational institutions. A meritocracy is a social system in which all members are given an equal chance to develop their abilities and rise in the social hierarchy. In a meritocracy the school is often viewed as the key institution for training and sorting citizens. One of the earliest and most elaborate proposals for a society based on the selectivity of education was Plato's *Republic.* In Plato's utopian proposal each generation was trained in music and gymnastics, and from each generation the most talented were selected for further education as guardians. The most talented guardians were educated to be philosopher-kings. An educational system functioning in this manner, Plato believed, would result in the ruling of society by the wisdom of philosopher-kings.

One of the earliest proposals in the United States to create an educational system designed to select and promote talent into a social hierarchy was made by Thomas Jefferson in 1779 in a proposed *Bill for the More General Diffusion of Knowledge.* Jefferson's plan called for three years of free education for all nonslave children. The most talented of these children were to be selected and educated at public expense at regional grammar schools. From this select group the most talented were to be chosen for further education. Thomas Jefferson wrote in *Notes on the State of Virginia,* "By this means twenty of the best geniuses will be raked from the rubbish annually, and be instructed, at the public expense. . . ."

The details of Jefferson's plan are not as important as the idea, which has become ingrained in American social thought, that schooling is the best means of identifying democratic leadership. This idea assumes that the educational system is fair in its judgments and that its basis for judgment has some relationship to the role for which students are being selected.

Fairness of selection in education assumes that the individual is being judged solely on talent demonstrated in school and not on other social factors such as race, religion, dress, and social class. As will be discussed in later chapters, these factors have been related to performance in school. If, for example, the educational institution tends to favor an individual from a particular religion or social class, then it would tend to select and promote that particular individual in school and, consequently, in the social hierarchy.

This situation could result in a democratic elitism in which certain groups would be favored in school, and the social power of their class perpetuated through the school. If all members of society were taught to believe that the school selected fairly and only those selected by the educational system could lead society, then all members of society would accept the social hierarchy perpetuated by the educational system. Acceptance of this situation might obscure other inequalities in society. For instance, if the educational system favored those with wealth, then all members of society might come to accept differences in wealth as differences in talent as determined by educational institutions.

Another debatable issue is the assumption of a relationship between talented performance in an educational institution and performance in a social role. There might not be any necessary relationship between the skills and attitudes required for good academic performance and those required for good occupational and social performance. The best medical doctor might not be the one who received the highest grades in medical school; the best politician might not be the one who received the highest grades in political science courses. Of course, this depends on what one means by the "best doctor" or the "best politician." The important issue is whether one believes that the skills required to succeed in an educational institution are the best skills for a particular social role.

The differences between these approaches are reflected in the differences between Thomas Jefferson and Horace Mann, who is often called the father of American education. Jefferson proposed a very limited education for the general citizenry. The three years of free education to be provided to all children were to consist of training in reading, writing, and arithmetic, with reading instruction given in books on Greek, Roman, English, and American history. Jefferson did not believe that people needed to be educated to be good citizens. He believed in the guiding power of natural reason to lead the citizen to the correct political decisions. The political education of the citizen was to come from a free press; the citizen would judge between competing political ideas found in newspapers. The only requirement was that the citizen know how to read.

Interestingly, while Jefferson wanted political opinions to be formed in a free marketplace of ideas, he advocated censorship of political texts at the University of Virginia. These contradictory positions reflect an inherent problem in the use of schools to teach political ideas. There is always the temptation to limit political instruction to what one believes are "correct" political ideas.

Horace Mann, on the other hand, believed that a common political creed had to be instilled in all citizens. Without this *political consensus* a democratic society was doomed to political strife and chaos. Mann developed these ideas and his reputation as America's greatest educational leader while serving as secretary of the Massachusetts Board of Education from 1837 to 1848. Mann began his career as a lawyer; he dedicated his life to public schooling when, he claimed, he realized that schooling was the key to the reform of society.

Horace Mann lived during a period of great political tension and fear that the extension of suffrage would lead to violence and mob rule. Mann believed that political and social order could be maintained if all citizens accepted a common set of political values. These values were to be taught in a common public school and would provide a political consensus or framework in which democracy would function. For Mann the important idea was that all children in society attend the same type of school. This was what was meant by "common." It was a school common to all children. Within the common school, children of all religions and social classes were to share in a common education. Basic social disagreements were to vanish as rich and poor children, and children whose parents were supporters of different political parties, mingled in the schoolroom.

Within the walls of the common schoolhouse were to be taught the basic principles of a republican form of government. Mann assumed that republican principles existed that members of all political parties could agree upon, and therefore, these principles could be taught without objection. In fact, he argued against the teaching of any politically controversial topic because of its potential for destroying the public school. The combination of common schooling and the teaching of a common political philosophy was to create the political consensus that would make it possible for a republican society to function. Political liberty would be possible, according to Mann's philosophy, because it would be restrained and controlled by the public school.

One of the many problems in Mann's philosophy, and a problem that has plagued public schools in the United States since the nineteenth century, is the assumption of the existence of common republican principles upon which all citizens agree. Since the nineteenth century, there have been continual pressures and controversies about the political philosophy to be taught in the public schools. Conservative political groups, such as the American Legion and the Daughters of the American Revolution, have throughout the twentieth century put pressure on local public schools to avoid teaching what these organizations consider "left-wing" ideas. On the other hand, liberal organizations and particularly labor unions have attempted to influence the schools to teach their particular political doctrines.

There has also existed a tradition of strong dissent to a public system of education teaching political doctrines. Some people argue that the teaching of political doctrines is a method of *maintaining the political power* of those in control of government. As far back as the late eighteenth century, English political theorist William Godwin warned against national systems of education because they could become a means by which those who controlled the government could control the minds of future citizens. Godwin wrote in 1793, "Their views as institutors of a system of education will not fail to be analogous to their views in their political capacity: the data upon which their instructions are founded."

Another problem with Horace Mann's vision of a democratic consensus built upon the common school is that American public schooling has never been common to all children. All races, religions, and social classes have not mingled within a single common school. Racial segregation continues to exist in American public schools even after massive efforts at desegregation in the 1960s and 1970s. A variety of religious groups, including the Amish and Catholics, have maintained a tradition of parochial schools in opposition to the secularism of the public schools. Children in wealthy suburbs attend private schools, or public schools that are quite different from those in poorer school districts. Mann's dream of the common public school has never come into existence in the United States.

The way in which Horace Mann hoped to reduce tension between social groups in American society was by *socializing children for the political system.* This learning was to take place in school through social interaction, not through the specific content taught in the classroom. In the case of the common school, a reduction of tension between groups was to be primarily a result of the intermingling of students and not of textbook learning, class recitation, or lectures by the teacher.

It has been argued that socialization in the school is one of the most powerful means of political control. The very fact of having an entire generation in an institution where they are required to cooperate and obey rules is considered by some people to be a preparation to cooperate and obey the rules of the government. Johann Fichte in Prussia in the early nineteenth century asserted that schools would prepare the individual to serve the government and country by teaching obedience to the rules of the school and developing a sense of loyalty to the school. He stated further that students would transfer their obedience to the laws of the school to obedience to the constitution of the country. What was even more important, according to Fichte, was that interaction between students, as well as loyalty and service to the school and fellow students, would prepare the individual for service to the country. The school was a miniature community in which children learned to adjust their individuality to the requirements of the community. The real work of the school, Fichte said, was in shaping this adjustment. The well-ordered government required that the citizen go beyond mere obedience to the written constitution and laws. Fichte believed that the child must be adjusted to see the government as something greater than the individual, and must learn to sacrifice for the good of the social whole.

Fichte also advocated the teaching of patriotic songs, national history, and literature to increase the sense of dedication and patriotism to the state. This combination of socialization and patriotic teachings, he argued, would produce a citizen more willing and able to participate in the army and, consequently, would reduce the cost of national defense.

In the United States the combination of patriotic exercises and development of loyalty to the institution of the school began to appear in the 1890s. It was during this period of large-scale emigration from Southern and Eastern Europe that the public schools became heavily involved in what were called "Americanization" programs. Americanization involved teaching the immigrant the laws, language, and customs of the United States. Naturally, this involved the teaching of American songs and customs. With the coming of World War I, the Pledge of Allegiance, the singing of patriotic songs, participation in student government, and other patriotic exercises became a part of the American school. In addition, the development of extracurricular activities led to an emphasis on school spirit. The formation of football and basketball teams, with their accompanying trappings of cheerleaders and pep rallies, was supported with the idea that these activities improved school spirit and, consequently, service to society.

The involvement of the American public school in the teaching and development of patriotism has created problems for a democratic society with a variety of religious, ethnic, and political groups. Some religious groups object to pledging allegiance to the flag because it involves worship of a "graven image." The U.S. Supreme Court ruled in 1943 in *West Virginia State Board of Education v. Barnette* that expulsion from school of children of Jehovah's Witnesses for not saluting the flag was a violation of their constitutional right to freedom of religion. Some teachers view patriotic exercises as contrary to the principles of a free society. In a later chapter that deals with the rights of teachers (Chapter 11) there is a lengthy discussion of the court cases dealing with academic freedom and loyalty oaths; conflict between patriotism and students' rights is also dealt with in that chapter.

Alongside the role of patriotism in a democratic society is the question of service to the country. Is it good in a democratic society to place service to society above service to oneself? Or should the individual demand that institutions in a democratic society be designed to serve the individual?

The problems inherent in using public schools as a means of political control in a democratic society are not easily resolved. One of the central questions is who or what group should determine the kinds of political teachings and political socialization in the schools. This question leads directly to the issue of who controls American education (discussed in later chapters). It may be that the attempt to use the school as a means of creating a political meritocracy or a political consensus or a sense of patriotism is contradictory to the ideals of political liberty.

THE SOCIAL PURPOSES OF SCHOOLING

The major social purposes of education are *social control, improving social conditions,* and *reducing social tensions caused by economic inequalities.* The idea of using the school as a means of *social control* was first explicitly stated by American sociologist Edward Ross in the 1890s. Ross referred to education as an inexpensive form of police. He divided social control into external and internal forms. Traditionally, he argued, internal forms of control had centered on the family, the church, and the community. The family and church had worked on the child to inculcate moral values and social responsibility to ensure social stability and cohesion. In modern society, Ross declared, the family and church were being replaced by the school as the most important institution for instilling internal values. Ross saw reliance on education as a means of control becoming characteristic of American society. More and more, the school was taking the place of the church and the family. "The ebb of religion is only half a fact," Ross wrote. "The other half is the high tide of education. While the priest is leaving the civil service, the schoolmaster is coming in. As the state shakes itself loose from the church, it reaches out for the school."

One of the things heard constantly throughout the twentieth century is that the family and religion are collapsing, and thus the school must pick up the pieces. Whether these two institutions have in fact collapsed is debatable, but the argument has been used to justify the continued use of the school to solve problems.

The school has been used in a variety of ways in the twentieth century to *improve social conditions.* The very act of requiring school attendance has been viewed as a means of reducing juvenile delinquency. The development of summer schools in the late nineteenth and early twentieth centuries was justified as a means of keeping youths off the streets. Once they were off the streets, it was hoped that the moral and social influence of the school would keep them from future acts of crime and from the use of tobacco and alcohol. In later years, the schools would assume the burden of eliminating traffic accidents through driver training; improving family life through courses in modern living and home economics; and eliminating drug abuse, venereal disease, and a multitude of other social problems through health education.

The hope of improving society through public schooling has almost become an article of American faith. Horace Mann believed it was the key to solving all social problems. He argued that past societies had experimented with different forms of government and laws in an attempt to stop crime and that they had all failed. The answer, Mann said, was in the proper training of young children so that they would not desire or perform criminal acts. Mann even suggested with a certain amount of utopian hope that America might see the day when the training at the schoolhouse would make it unnecessary to enforce the law.

For some twentieth-century Americans, the school became the symbol and hope for the good society. This hope is best illustrated by a story told to kindergartners in the early part of the century about two children who bring a beautiful flower from their school class to their dirty and dark tenement apartment. The mother takes the flower and puts it in a glass of water near a dirty window. She decides the flower needs more light to expose its beauty. The mother proceeds to wash the window, which allows more light into the apartment and illuminates the dirty floors, walls, and furniture. The added light sends the mother scurrying around to clean up the now-exposed dirt. In the meantime the father, who is unable to keep a steady job because of a drinking problem, returns to the apartment and is amazed to find his grim dwelling transformed into a clean and tidy home. The transformation of the apartment results in the father's wanting to spend more time at home, and less time in the tavern. The father's drinking problem is solved, he is able to maintain a steady job, and the family lives happily ever after.

This story characterizes the hope that the moral influence of the school would reach out into the homes and neighborhoods of America. One unanswered question, and a question that is inherent also in the earlier discussion of political control, is this: Whose moral and social values will permeate the American school? Horace Mann argued that there were certain moral values that all religious groups could agree upon and that these shared values would become the backbone of the moral teachings of the school. A variety of religious groups have disagreed with this idea from the time of Mann up to the present. The largest single religious group to dissent and establish its own system of schools was the Catholic church. The argument of Catholic church leaders was that all education by its very goal of shaping behavior was religious and that it was impossible for a public institution to claim that it could satisfy the needs of all religious groups. Even if the public school eliminated all religious and moral teaching, this alternative could not be accepted because education would then become irreligious.

Even more important than the question of whose social and moral values should permeate the school is the question of whether the school should be involved in attempts at social reform or improvement. One reason schools have gotten involved with so many social problems is that the school is the most available institution and the one least likely to affect other parts of the social system. For instance, alcoholism might be the product of boredom with monotonous work, deteriorating urban conditions, family traditions, or a variety of other factors in the social structure. To turn to the school to solve the problem of alcoholism through health classes is to say the problem is one of individual training and is not related to factors in the social structure. It is easier to give a health course than to change job conditions, improve urban environments, or manipulate family traditions. Of even greater importance is the fact that the school is less threatening than such direct changes. Changing job conditions involves confronting the whole organization of industry and the conflicting interests of unions and business.

The school is often the safest and least controversial way of planning for social improvement. A politician in the state legislature or in the local community can call for social reform through the school and thereby give the appearance of doing good without antagonizing any community interests. From this standpoint it can be argued that reform through the school is the most conservative means of social reform.

This has been one of the charges made against the schools' attempt to end poverty in America. Since the nineteenth century, a purpose of schooling has been *reducing social tensions caused by economic inequalities*. Using the school to eliminate poverty is considered a means of reducing tensions between social classes in American society. In 1964 and 1965 the federal government, under the leadership of President Lyndon B. Johnson, launched a massive War on Poverty with the passage of the Economic Opportunity Act and the Elementary and Secondary Education Act. Both President Johnson and the congressional legislation placed primary emphasis upon the role of education in ending poverty. The theoretical support for government action came from the Council of Economic Advisers.

Within this theoretical framework, lack of education was seen as one element of a series of social factors that tended to reinforce the condition of being poor. An inadequate education restricted employment opportunities, which caused a low standard of living and, consequently, poor medical care, diet, housing, and education for the next generation. This model of poverty suggested that one could begin at any point in the set of causal relationships and move around the circle of poverty. The improvement of health conditions, for instance, would lead to fewer days lost from employment, which would mean more income. Better income would mean improved housing, medical care, diet, and education. These improved conditions would mean better jobs for those of the next generation.

The idea that the poor were locked into a circle of poverty led to the belief that a culture of poverty existed. Within this framework modern technological society had left the poor behind, and once they were caught in the circle of poverty, a culture of poverty developed that helped to perpetuate social conditions. The War on Poverty was to be a war to destroy a culture by attacking a number of social conditions. Government action was directed toward housing, diet, and health care; but the greatest importance was placed on education to begin the chain reaction that would end poverty.

The War on Poverty program included Head Start programs, special funding of programs in local schools for the culturally disadvantaged, job-training programs, bilingual education, minority education, and a host of other special programs. Head Start programs were based on the premise that children of the poor were culturally disadvantaged with regard to learning opportunities, when compared to the children of the middle and upper classes. Head Start programs were therefore to provide early childhood education, which would give the poor a "head start" on schooling and allow them to compete on equal terms with other children. Job-training programs were based on the assumption that the cure for teenage and adult unemployment was job training. Special reading programs were developed for the so-called culturally disadvantaged because it was argued that poor reading ability was the most important reason for the failure of the poor in school. Bilingual and minority education programs were developed because it was argued that public education tended to discriminate against the culture of minority groups, which resulted in the failure of these groups in school. All these programs were to contribute to the ending of poverty in the United States.

More than a decade later, poverty had not ended in the United States, and serious doubts were expressed about the role of schooling in ending it. Some argued that the War on Poverty's educational programs had never really been given a chance because of inadequate funding by the government and mismanagement by federal bureaucrats. Others insisted that better educational programs could be encouraged and that to develop them would require more time and research. Still others felt that the school could accomplish nothing because of community and family influences on the child.

Most important for our discussion of the social purposes of schooling is the charge that was made that emphasis upon education was one way of avoiding basic economic problems. The educational component of the War on Poverty assumed that if you educated the poor, they would be able to get jobs and achieve higher income levels. The one flaw in this thinking is that job training does not necessarily increase salaries. Society might always need people for menial tasks, and increased schooling might only result in educational inflation whereupon the nature of jobs did not change but educational requirements increased.

This became one of the problems of the early 1970s when the labor market was flooded with college graduates, and scholars with doctorates were driving taxicabs and cooking in small restaurants. In this situation the occupational structure did not expand to meet the increased educational training of the labor force. The response of educational institutions was to reorganize for more specific career training and call for more limited educational aspirations. The important lesson in this situation was that the nature of the labor market was more important in determining employment than was the amount of education available to the population. In terms of social reform it seemed to indicate that education alone would not solve the problems of poverty and that more direct changes had to be made in the organization of labor and the structure of the American economic system.

In the 1980s and 1990s, value conflicts resulting from the use of schools to solve social problems are most clearly evident in discussions about AIDS education. These discussions often pit those who believe in a strong moral code to control sexual behavior against those who believe in the right of free sexual activity between consenting adults. Those who believe in a strong moral code tend to support AIDS education programs that advocate sexual abstinence outside of marriage and take a strong line against homosexual activities. Those at the other end of the value spectrum emphasize educational programs that teach safe sexual procedures and advocate the dispensing of condoms in public schools.

In fact, issues surrounding sex education are often the most volatile. In the 1980s, heated discussions occurred concerning the establishment in New York City of the Harvey Milk High School for homosexual teenagers. Some members of the community objected because it seemed to condone homosexuality, while others supported the idea because they believed homosexual teenagers needed help in establishing an identity. Similar controversies occur concerning homosexual teachers. Some people argue that homosexual teachers are not more likely to impose themselves on children than heterosexual teachers. Others fear that homosexual teachers will serve as a model for students inclined toward homosexual behavior. Those supporting gay rights believe homosexuals have as much right to teach as heterosexuals and should be role models for homosexual teenagers.

Controversy over sexual values plagues attempts to deal with such social problems as out-of-wedlock pregnancies among teenagers. For instance, consider the differing and controversial approaches to problems of teen pregnancies exemplified by Baltimore's program of offering long-term contraceptives to its students and the federally sponsored teen chastity programs. Under the Baltimore plan announced in 1992, school-based health clinics offer to surgically implant the long-term contraceptive Norplant in female students. The immediate reaction of religious groups was that birth control devices promote promiscuity and the emphasis in school programs should be on abstinence. On the other hand, advocates of the program say that it is unrealistic to think that schools can limit teenage sexuality by teaching abstinence.

At the opposite end of the spectrum of solutions to increasing teenage pregnancy is the federally funded teen chastity program. Under this program, the federal government sponsored Teen Choice and other groups advocating chastity as the solution to teenage pregnancy. The objections to this program have come from the American Civil Liberties Union (ACLU) which claims that the material sponsored by the federal government is full of religious statements and therefore is a violation of the First Amendment requirement of separation of church and state. The ACLU submitted as evidence a federally sponsored pamphlet advising teenagers to "pray together and invite God on every date." Teen Choice and other federally funded programs recommend a curriculum called "Sex Respect," which says "God is supreme . . . God does exist." While the ACLU criticized this program because of its religious content, defenders argued that there was only limited reference to religion in the programs and that religious values were an important means of promoting chastity.

In general, the concern about teenage pregnancy and the spread of AIDS has increased debate about sex-education courses. The focus of this debate is the moral content of the subject matter, contraceptives, and abortion. Some community members believe that the primary goal of a sex-education course should be to influence youth not to engage in sexual activities. Usually these members of the community do not want the schools to teach about contraceptives and abortions, because they believe that having information about them increases sexual activity. This group believes that the primary way of reducing unwanted teenage pregnancies is to convince youth to avoid intimate sexual contact.

On the other hand, some members of the community believe that a sex-education course should be designed to prepare youth for sexual activity by teaching about contraception and sexually transmitted diseases. This group usually believes that youth will continue to engage in sexual activity and that the best means of avoiding unwanted pregnancies is to provide teenagers with adequate information about contraception.

I have described the major range of opinions about sex education found in communities, but there are also other positions that can be taken. For instance, some community members might believe that sex-education courses should include discussions about improving and enhancing sexual relationships. This represents the extreme opposite position from that which supports sex education as a means of preventing sexual contact. There are also those who want sex-education classes to provide arguments against contraception and abortion.

The dream of American education as the panacea for America's social ills continues to be plagued with questions of whose social and moral values and goals should be in the schoolhouse, and whether the panacea of education is just a way of avoiding more direct and controversial approaches to social problems. These questions remain unanswered, but American educators still tend to share Horace Mann's hope that the school will be the heart and salvation of American society.

THE ECONOMIC PURPOSES OF SCHOOLING

The most important arguments given for the support of public schooling are that education *increases national wealth* and *advances technological development.* The contribution of the school to economic growth can occur in two distinct ways. One is the *socialization* of the future worker into the modern organization of industry. It is contended that the school, the first formal public organization encountered by the child, provides the preparation and training needed to deal with other complex social organizations. Within this argument the school is viewed as one of the important elements in the modernizing of underdeveloped countries from traditional agricultural societies to modern industrial societies. The second way the school might help economic growth is through the *sorting* and *training* of the labor force. By "sorting" is meant the identification of individual abilities and interests and the determination of the best type of individual training and future employment.

The goal of *socialization* for the workplace is found throughout the history of American education. One of the arguments given in the nineteenth century in support of marching, drill, and orderliness in schools was preparation for the coordination and orderliness required in the modern factory. Lining up for class as well as marching in and out of the cloakroom and to the blackboard were activities justified in terms of training for factory assembly lines.

Several important questions arise regarding the use of the school as the socialization agent for the workplace. Is it the proper role of the school to act purposely to instill certain attitudes and habits, as preparation for future employment? Such socialization might create a static society in which the worker is prepared only for existing or known work organizations. More important, whose ideas on proper preparation for work should be included in the planned socialization of work? Employers will naturally suggest the development of work attitudes and habits that will maximize their profits, but these attitudes and habits might not be in the interest of the worker. At one time a common tenet of the Protestant ethic was that hard, steady, and faithful performance of work would result in steady promotion and increase in salary. Labor unions contended that this was an ethic designed to persuade the worker not to fight, through unionization and the strike, for higher wages and better working conditions. Like the issues of political control and social reform, the issue of socialization in the schools for the workplace calls into question whose values and attitudes will be instilled in the students.

Concern about the sorting and training of the labor force is directly related to the development of vocational education and vocational guidance. Vocational guidance as a function of schooling developed in the United States in the early part of the twentieth century as part of a general reform movement to create a more efficient society. It was argued that one of the most inefficient aspects of society was the distribution and selection of human resources. Strikes and worker dissatisfaction were seen as resulting from people being in jobs that did not interest them and for which they had no aptitude. In addition, human resources were not being fully developed to meet the needs of the labor market.

The early emphasis in vocational guidance, and certainly one of its lasting purposes, was the identification of student interests and abilities and the matching of those interests and abilities with an educational program that would lead to a suitable vocation. The vocational guidance counselor was envisioned as the link between school and industry. The counselor would determine the needs of industry in terms of labor shortages and surpluses. This information would be used in the development of educational programs and the vocational counseling of students.

This general goal for vocational guidance counselors has never been achieved because of the difficulty of training enough people to staff all the junior and senior high schools in the country with counselors who possess expertise in labor-market analysis, work analysis, testing, educational programming, and psychology. Also, predicting the future needs of the labor market is very difficult and not easily adapted to educational programming. In addition, within the profession of counseling a tension developed between counseling for improvement of psychological problems and interpersonal relations, and counseling for vocations. During the depression of the 1930s, as the job market retreated, counselors got more and more involved in student psychological problems. During the 1950s the National Manpower Council and the Carnegie Corporation placed pressure on the federal government to support training of guidance people that would emphasize vocational guidance and labor-market analysis. It was believed that guidance had to get out of therapy and back into manpower planning.

During the 1970s vocational guidance expanded its role in manpower planning and vocational training as it became part of career education. Career education was born in the early 1970s as a response to apparent dissatisfaction with the educational system and the large numbers of unemployed college graduates. Career education brought together vocational guidance and vocational education and attempted to resolve one of the major controversies in vocational education.

This traditional controversy has centered on whether vocational education should provide the future worker with a broad set of skills and knowledge or whether it should prepare the worker for a specific vocation. The controversy originated at the beginning of the twentieth century when unions were suspicious that vocational education would destroy apprenticeship programs. Unions worked hard to assure both their involvement in vocational education and that vocational education should be training for broad sets of skills and not narrow specialization. In educational ranks there was controversy about whether vocational education should be located in specialized institutions or in a general high school. The National Education Association in 1918 supported the development of comprehensive high schools with both college preparatory and vocational programs. It was felt that comprehensive high schools, with all students under one roof, would contribute to a sense of national community and that separate institutions would separate people and cause a breakdown of society.

During the late 1950s the role of vocational guidance in a comprehensive high school was reiterated in a widely circulated report by James Conant on *The American High School Today.* The 1959 report, written for the Carnegie Corporation, called for the consolidation of small high schools so that a greater variety of subjects could be offered within one comprehensive school. The courses of study within the school were to be more closely geared to the future vocational destination of the student. Conant argued that the heart of the school had to be the vocational guidance person, who would measure skills and interests and arrange an educational program that would provide the student with marketable skills. Educational administrators were to maintain contact with the local employment situation and assess educational needs in terms of the local labor market. Conant even made the recommendation, which never became a reality, that all high school graduates be given a wallet-size record of their subjects and grades, which could be presented on demand to any employer.

In 1971 and 1972, in response to unemployment problems and the supposed breakdown of American education, the U.S. Office of Education initiated conferences and projects in career education. Like a fast-moving brush fire, career education entered the public schools of the United States. Within one year the Office of Education could claim the participation of 750,000 young people.

Career education places vocational guidance at the center of academic planning and learning. During the elementary and junior high school years, career education is to be a subject-matter field that acquaints students with the world of work and the varieties of occupations available. After studying and preparing for an occupational choice in these early grades, the student upon entering high school is to begin preparing for entry either directly into an occupational career or into higher education. Career education as a subject-matter field means learning about all the different occupations available in the labor market and the interests and abilities associated with these occupations. Career education or vocational guidance, like science and arithmetic, is something to be studied as a formal subject.

The process of acquainting the student with a variety of occupations supposedly answers the charge that vocational education at the public-school level restricts future vocational choice by segregating students in a particular educational program. In addition, under a policy of career education other school subjects are made more relevant because the student supposedly is able to see the relationship between present learning and a future occupation.

A question central to career education (and to the political and social purposes of schooling) is whether career education should be a function of public schooling. For instance, a realistic problem in career education is the school's ability to acquaint students with all possible occupations and at the same time teach the required subjects. The curriculum of the public school is extremely cluttered. One proposal suggests that subjects such as reading, writing, and social studies be taught using career-education material. But this would mean that a student's contact with other literature, and with conflicting economic, political, and social ideas would be greatly reduced.

It is also questionable whether social scientists have developed the necessary methods for accurately predicting future labor needs and rapidly organizing vocational training material to meet these needs. Even if the available methodology were to make this possible, would it be desirable? Using the school as a key element in controlling the labor market assumes that the best economy is planned and managed, and that the existing economic system is the best. This assumption contradicts the traditional laissez-faire economics of the United States, which is based on the premise that the best economic system is one controlled by the natural forces of the free marketplace. Critics of the existing economic system could argue that career education would be an educational system designed to maintain the power of the existing economic structure.

Also, career education does not change the nature of the labor market; it only eases the transition from school to the existing occupational structure. It does not mean that workers will receive higher pay or better working conditions. All that career education can promise is the hope that less time will be spent finding a job and that the entry-level job will be related to an individual's interests and abilities. The danger lies in viewing career education as a way to solve basic economic problems in the United States.

In the 1990s, the central focus of national purposes for education is economic. The concerns of the 1990s are with international economic competition with Germany and Japan, and educating the work force. A discussion of these issues will be the focus of the next section.

NATIONAL GOALS FOR THE 1990s

"We live in a world," President Clinton argued during his second television debate with George Bush and Ross Perot, "where what you earn depends on what you learn." Similar to his predecessors Ronald Reagan and George Bush, President Clinton sees the primary goal of education to be economic. Along with his secretary of labor, Robert Reich, whose ideas on education and the labor market I will discuss in Chapter 4, President Clinton is interested in improving the skills of American workers through improved educational programs. The major differences between Clinton and his predecessor George Bush are the issues of choice and equity. As I will discuss in more detail in Chapters 7 and 9, Bush supported public funding of parental choice of a private school, while Clinton favors limiting parental choice to public schools. Also, Clinton places higher priority than Bush did on assuring that all students have an equal opportunity to receive a quality education and attend college. Despite these differences, President Clinton agrees with the Bush administration's efforts to create national standards for education. As I will discuss in more detail in Chapter 10, it is believed that national standards on what students should learn will improve student achievement.

One reason for the general similarity between the educational goals of the Clinton and Bush administrations is the work of the National Governors' Association. The Bush administration worked cooperatively with the National Governors' Association to plan education goals for the year 2000. Both Clinton, as governor of Arkansas, and his secretary of education, Richard Riley, former governor of South Carolina, were active in the formulation of the educational goals of the National Governors' Association. In his acceptance speech, Secretary Riley alluded to the bipartisan work of the National Governors' Association: "We must . . . continue to work for achieving the national education goals which Governor Clinton, certainly, has worked and provided leadership in, and we must do it together in a bipartisan way."

The six goals originally agreed upon by the National Governors' Association are: (1) All children will start school ready to learn; (2) high school graduation rate will be at least 90 percent; (3) students will demonstrate competence in critical subjects; (4) U. S. students will be the first in the world in mathematics and science achievement; (5) every adult will be literate and have skills to compete in the economy; (6) schools will be free of drugs and violence.

The major focus of the goals for the year 2000 is economic competition in international trade. A series of reports issued in the 1980s called upon the schools to solve problems in international economic competition. In 1983 the federal government's National Commission on Excellence in Education issued a report, *A Nation At Risk,* that declared: "If only to keep and improve on the slim competitive edge we still retain in world markets, we must rededicate ourselves to the reform of the educational system for the benefit of all." In language designed to frighten the reader into supporting more money for public education, the commission warned, "If an unfriendly foreign power had attempted to impose on America the mediocre educational performance that exists today, we might well have viewed it as an act of war."

Also in 1983, the Task Force on Education for Economic Growth established by the Education Commission of the States issued its report, *Action for Excellence,* which linked improved schooling to economic development. The task force primarily was composed of state governors and heads of American corporations. The report of the task force warned of America's declining position in world markets as a result of increased productivity and efficiency of foreign industry. The answer to these problems, according to the report, was improved schooling to make the American labor force more efficient. The task force stated, "It is the thesis of this report that our future success as a nation—our national defense, our social stability and well-being and our national prosperity—will depend on our ability to improve education and training for millions of individual citizens."

Influenced by his secretary of labor, Robert Reich, President Clinton is giving particular attention to improving the skills of the general work force. Job training is an important focus of this effort. Clinton believes that this emphasis is essential for making the U.S. economy more competitive and improving the economic opportunities of the American worker. As I discuss in Chapter 4, Reich draws a direct relationship between the type of education provided by schools and the placement of the worker in the labor market. He believes that many workers will be trapped in low-paying jobs unless their employment skills are improved. Also, Clinton believes the children of the poor require a greater opportunity to receive a quality education and attend college.

Clinton ties his program of providing equality of educational opportunity to community service. In his plan, students requiring loans to complete their college education can pay them off through some form of community service. The idea of requiring community service as part of an educational program began during World War I, and it has reappeared as a concept throughout the rest of the twentieth century. Supporters of community service claim that it will educate youth for social service. Critics of the program argue that participants would be paying for their education by working at low wages on government projects.

The strong emphasis on the economic purposes of education by the Clinton administration and the National Governors' Association continues the trend of closely linking education to the needs of the business community. In fact, by the 1990s it was assumed by many Americans that business was a natural partner in the control of schools. No one seemed to blink at the statement issued by Bush and the National Governors' Association that, "Parents, businesses, and community organizations will work together to ensure that schools are a safe haven for all children." Why would business be considered a logical partner in this objective? Why was there no mention of unions or churches? In fact, why was there no mention of participation by all the citizens who pay taxes to support schools?

The extensive and often unquestioned involvement of business in American schools increased at a rapid rate since the 1980s. Along with the work of the Bush administration and the National Governors' Association, business involvement made economic purposes the number-one priority of public schools. A February 1, 1990, article in the business section of the *New York Times* opened, "When it comes to reforming the nation's schools, these days the leading radicals are likely to be wearing pin-striped suits and come from oak-paneled board rooms rather than the ivy-covered walls of academia." After detailing business involvement in shaping the curriculum, managerial methods, and organization of the nation's schools, the article states, "The impetus behind the corporate embrace of education reform is concern about the quality of the American labor pool."

Business involvement in schools raises a number of issues. It is not necessarily true that what is good for American business is good for American schools and students. The primary concern of business is the maximization of profits. This can mean several things with regard to public schools. First, a major business expense is taxes. Businesses have a stake in reducing taxes, including taxes that support public schools. A major criticism of the Bush administration's educational policies and the educational reform efforts in many states is that they have not been accompanied by increased spending on education. In fact, there might be a trend to shift the financial support of schools from corporate taxes to sales taxes and lotteries. This could mean that middle and lower income groups could be paying an increasing percentage of public school expenses while business could be paying a decreasing percentage.

Questions can also be raised regarding financial donations made directly by businesses to public schools. Often, adopt-a-school programs involve some kind of business contribution to an adopted school. Obviously, a direct donation to a public school gives the contributor some influence over school programs. On the other hand, if the same money came to the school through taxes there would be greater public determination of school programs. If businesses have the money to give to schools, they have enough money to be taxed to support schools. Giving money directly to schools increases business influence over education at the expense of control exercised by citizens through the government.

Business profits also depend on the quality and expense of workers. As I discussed in the previous section, while businesses want educated workers, they also want workers who are compliant and loyal to the company. Should the public schools emphasize the development of habits that will meet the requirements of business?

Also, business has a stake in keeping down wages. Wages often depend on the supply of labor. From the standpoint of business, the ideal situation for hiring is a large pool of applicants that will allow business to pay the lowest wages and select the best worker. Obviously, this situation does not help the worker. For example, in the 1950s business put pressure on the schools to educate more scientists and engineers and by the late 1960s there was a surplus of scientists and engineers, causing low wages and unemployment. This situation worked to the advantage of the employer but not the employee.

LIBERALS, CONSERVATIVES, AND CRITICAL THEORISTS

Political beliefs are directly related to opinions on educational issues. For instance, consider the controversy about elementary report cards in a community divided between conservative and liberal factions. In this particular community, as reported by Donald McCarty and Charles Ramsey in *The School Managers: Power and Conflict in American Public Education,* liberals favored a card that simply reported "satisfactory," "unsatisfactory," and "excellent," based on a child's potential learning rate. Conservatives wanted a card that gave grades of "A" through "F," based on percentage test scores. In this particular situation, *liberal* refers to a set of beliefs that stress economic cooperation along with competition and that the government should take positive steps to assure equality of opportunity. *Conservative* refers to a set of beliefs that see the economy prospering through competition and reduced government aid. Liberal support of a report card based on a student's potential learning rate reflects the belief that schools should actively support the capabilities of each student and provide equal opportunity to achieve. On the other hand, conservative defense of the use of letter grades reflects a belief in the importance of promoting competition and rewarding the best.

This example of the division between liberals and conservatives over report cards is reflected in national educational policies. In general, liberal beliefs have their greatest impact on the educational platforms of the Democratic party, while conservatives are influential in the Republican party. (Given the confused nature of American party politics and the lack of ideological clarity of the major parties, many different political beliefs, of course, creep into the discussions of each party. But it can be said with some certainty that liberal beliefs are dominant in the Democratic party and conservative beliefs are dominant in the Republican party.) *Critical theory* is a recent movement among American intellectuals; its impact on American politics, at least at the time of the writing of this book, cannot be clearly discerned. As a set of political beliefs, the major impact of critical theory is in academic discussions about educational policies.

Let us begin by discussing the relationship between liberal political beliefs and political policies. Twentieth-century liberalism is characterized by a belief in the positive role of government in assuring social justice and regulating the economy. While believing in private ownership of the means of production, liberals argue that the government should manage and regulate the economy to protect against economic depressions and assure that corporations work for the public good. Also, liberals are characterized by a belief that government should take an active role in protecting the rights of minorities and in assuring equal opportunity in the economic system.

Liberal educational concerns are a direct reflection of these political beliefs. Liberals tend to favor strong government intervention to assure equal opportunity for minorities and the poor. They support federal funds for educational programs to help the disadvantaged. In keeping with their belief in positive government intervention, liberals favor federal programs that support special educational programs for the disadvantaged and the minorities, and federal intervention to protect minority rights. In general, liberals favor a curriculum designed to meet individual needs. Often this has meant having the schools offer a variety of educational programs that students can select according to individual needs and goals. The individualization of the curriculum reflects a general concern with humanpower planning that is designed to match educational programs with labor market needs.

In contrast to liberals, conservatives believe in the "negative state"—that is, an absence of government control—with a free market as the primary regulator of the economic system. Consequently, conservatives want to minimize government regulation and interference in the economy. While recognizing the importance of minority rights, conservatives believe that minority rights are best protected by the courts with minimum government intervention. In fact, conservatives argue that most government programs primarily benefit government bureaucrats and provide only minimum aid to the poor and minority groups. Conservatives argue that the best hope for the poor and minority groups is through self-advancement in a free-market economic system. While conservatives would minimize government intervention in the economy, they tend to support law to regulate personal morality.

In keeping with their philosophy of the negative state and in contrast to liberals, conservatives oppose federal support and regulation of public schools. During the Reagan years of the 1980s, conservatives supported a reduction of the federal role in education and an increased role for state and local governments.

Conservatives are critical of education programs designed to meet individual differences and want all students to study the same core curriculum. Reflecting their concern with morality, conservatives believe that a core curriculum will teach moral values and will be a source of educational excellence. They argue that the needs of the labor market can best be met through school-business partnerships, where school leaders learn the employment needs of the business community. Also, conservatives believe that the best hope for minority and immigrant groups is to learn English and to be socialized into American culture. Consequently, they oppose educational programs that emphasize minority languages and cultures.

Critical theorists find fault with both liberal and conservative positions on the economy and education. From the perspective of critical theorists, the debate about the positive versus the negative state is really a debate about different forms of economic exploitation. On the one hand, they argue, large corporations use government regulation as a means of maintaining economic monopolies. Within this framework, government intervention and regulation can sometimes be a means of increasing the advantages of business in the marketplace. On the other hand, critical theorists argue, corporations demand less government intervention and regulation of the economy when the actions of government are hurting profits.

For critical theorists the key to economic and social justice is democratic struggle. While recognizing that some forms of government regulation and intervention are to the advantage of ruling elites, critical theorists believe that economic and social justice can be achieved by democratic movements working through government. Critical theorists believe that history is the continuous expansion of political, economic, and social rights as a result of struggle against oppression. Their view of history is optimistic and hopeful, but this optimism and hope depends on people continuing to fight against oppression and economic exploitation.

Given this optimistic view of history, critical theorists emphasize an education for democratic empowerment, which simply means giving students the knowledge and skills they need to struggle for a continued expansion of political, economic, and social rights. Of utmost importance is making students aware that they have the power to affect the course of history and that history is the struggle for human rights. Critical theorists accept the importance of government regulation and intervention to protect equality of educational opportunity. In fact, they would argue that equality of educational opportunity is one of the achievements of the civil rights movement in the United States in the 1950s and 1960s.

The educational concerns of critical theorists can be understood by comparing their ideas regarding a core curriculum with those of conservatives. Conservatives want a core curriculum as a means of teaching a common moral code to maintain social order and as a means of improving academic standards and intellectual skills. Critical theorists, however, might instead support a core curriculum organized to teach students that they have the power to shape history and one that will give students the skills and knowledge to participate in shaping that history.

The consideration of liberal, conservative, and critical theorist positions on education is meant to show the relationship between political values and educational purposes. In summary, the purposes of education are determined by political processes and political beliefs, and the purposes of education affect the profession of teaching, the content of schooling, and the organization of schools.

EXERCISES

This chapter has focused on the major political, social, and economic purposes of education. Throughout the chapter questions have been raised about these purposes and about the continuing problems they cause for public education in the United States. In a discussion group or in essay form present your ideas on the following issues:

1. Who or what group should determine the political teachings and political socialization in public schools?
2. Should public schools be used to create a political meritocracy?
3. What citizenship training should public schools provide in a democratic society?
4. Who or what group should determine the moral and social values to be taught in public schools?
5. What social problems do you think the schools are best able to solve?
6. What do you think should be the relationship between the school and social reform in a democratic society?

7. What do you think should be the relationship between the school and the economic system?
8. Should the focus of public schooling be on career education, or should occupational choice and training be a direct function of the labor market?

SUGGESTED READINGS AND WORKS
CITED IN CHAPTER

Asseso, Laurie. "Teen Chastity." *Compuserve Executive News Service,* no. 2120 (17 February 1991). This article discusses the ACLU's objections to the federally sponsored teen chastity programs.

Barbanel, Josh. "Under 'Rainbow,' a War: When Politics, Morals and Learning Mix." *New York Times* (27 December 1992): 34. This lengthy article discusses the politics and objections to the inclusion of gay and lesbian issues in "Children of the Rainbow."

Berlowitz, Marvin J., and Frank E. Chapman. *The United States Educational System: Marxist Approaches.* Minneapolis: Marxist Educational Press, 1980. This collection of articles provides an introduction to Marxist interpretations of the education system in the United States.

"Clinton Text." *Compuserve Executive News Service,* no. 0501 (22 December 1992). This article contains the acceptance speech of Secretary of Education Richard Riley.

Conant, James. *The American High School Today.* New York: McGraw-Hill, 1959. A major study of the conditions and goals of the American high school. This book had an important impact on shaping the future direction of the high school.

Cremin, Lawrence. *The Republic and the School.* New York: Teachers College Press, 1957. A good selection of Horace Mann's writings taken from his reports to the Massachusetts Board of Education. A good introduction to the social and political purposes of American education.

Ehman, Lee H. "The American School in the Political Socialization Process." *Review of Educational Research* 50 (Spring 1980): 99–119. A summary of studies on the political socialization of American school children.

Goodlad, John I. *A Place Called School.* New York: McGraw-Hill, 1984. A detailed study of what actually happens in American schools. Goodlad uses a great deal of data to analyze the functioning of the American educational system.

Holmes, Steven. "School Reform: Business Moves In." *New York Times* (1 February 1990): D2, D8. A good survey of business involvement in public schools.

Jordan, Mary. "School Guidance on Gays Has N.Y. Parents Divided." *Compuserve Executive News Service Washington Post* (8 December 1992). This article on controversy surrounding the gay and lesbian sections of "Children of the Rainbow," includes the quotes used in the text from Neil Lodato, Diane Kirsten, and Mary Cummins.

Katz, Michael. *The Irony of Early School Reform.* Boston: Beacon Press, 1968. An important study of the early relationship between social reform and education.

Lazerson, Marvin, and W. Norton Grubb. *American Education and Vocationalism: A Documentary History 1870–1970.* New York: Teachers College Press, 1974. A good collection of documents dealing with vocational education and the relationship between the school and the economy.

Lee, Gordon. *Crusade Against Ignorance: Thomas Jefferson on Education.* New York: Teachers College Press, 1961. A collection of statements by Jefferson on education with a good introductory essay.

McCarty, Donald, and Charles Ramsey. *The School Managers: Power and Conflict in American Public Education.* Westport, Conn.: Greenwood, 1971. This book discusses the liberal and conservative divisions over report cards.

National Commission on Excellence in Education. *A Nation at Risk.* Washington, D. C.: U.S. Government Printing Office, 1983. The report and recommendations of this commission had a major impact on discussions about the American school.

Perkinson, Henry. *The Imperfect Panacea: American Faith in Education, 1865–1965.* New York: Random House, 1968. A study of attempts to use the school to solve major social problems in the United States.

Portner, Jessica. "Baltimore Plan to Offer Teenagers Norplant Raises Ethical, Medical, Legal Questions." *Education Week* (16 December 1992): 1, 13. This article discusses the Baltimore plan to provide Norplant contraceptives in school clinics.

Rodman, Hyman, Susan Lewis, and Saralyn Griffith. *The Sexual Rights of Adolescents.* New York: Columbia University Press, 1984. This book provides information on the legal, social, and psychological aspects of adolescent sexuality.

Silverman, Gary. "Governors Urge Using Peace Dividend for Education." *Compuserve Executive News Service UPI* (26 February 1990). Discusses the passage of the resolution supporting the use of savings from peace dividend to support the educational goals for the year 2000.

Task Force on Education for Economic Growth. *Action for Excellence.* Denver: Education Commission of the States, 1983. Recommendations that were made by a task force composed primarily of state governors and leading business people.

Task Force on Teaching as a Profession. *A Nation Prepared: Teachers for the 21st Century.* New York: Carnegie Corporation of New York, 1986. Important report calling for restructuring of the teaching profession and the establishment of a national teacher certification board.

"Text of Statement on Education Goals Adopted by Governors." *Education Week* (7 March 1990): 16. Complete text of the national goals agreed to by President Bush and the National Governors' Association.

Timpane, Michael. *Corporations and Public Education.* Report distributed by Teachers College, Columbia University, 1981. This was a study conducted for the Carnegie Corporation on the growing links between public schools and business.

"Transcript of 2d TV Debate Between Bush, Clinton and Perot." *New York Times* (16 October 1992): 12–14. Transcript contains Clinton's campaign promises regarding education.

Tyler, Ralph W. "The U.S. vs. the World: A Comparison of Educational Performance." *Phi Delta Kappan* (January 1981). This article provides a summary of the data collected by the International Association for the Evaluation of Educational Achievement.

Walker, Reagan. "Accord on Goals Hard to Attain, Executives Find." *Education Week* (31 January 1990): 1, 13. A discussion of the process leading to agreement on national goals for the year 2000.

Welch, William. "Governors." *Compuserve Executive News Service AP* (27 February 1990). Welch discusses the negative reaction of Democratic governors to President Bush's unwillingness to increase federal funding of public schools.

CHAPTER 2

The Profession of Teaching

During the 1990s, the profession of teaching is being transformed by a variety of factors. As I will discuss in this chapter, there is an increasing possibility that national certification of teachers will occur as a result of the establishment in the late 1980s of the privately controlled National Board for Professional Teaching Standards. In addition, many states are granting teaching licenses to some applicants who do not study the normal teacher education curriculum. Also, teachers are being affected by the restructuring of American schools. Many states and local school districts are implementing different forms of site-based management. Site-based management gives more power to individual schools to control school budgets and curriculum. Often, site-based management requires teachers to participate in governing the school and planning the curriculum and, consequently, gives them more power over policy issues.

Other changes initiated in the 1980s will continue to affect the teaching profession. Foremost is the development of career ladders for teachers. Traditionally, classroom teachers could only progress in their careers by leaving the classroom and becoming school administrators. As I will discuss later, a career ladder allows teachers to progress through different professional levels while remaining in the classroom.

Similar to other justifications for educational reform in the 1990s, the transformation of the teaching profession is considered necessary by some people for improving the ability of the United States to compete in world markets. One important report that has guided changes in the profession of teaching, *A Nation Prepared: Teachers for the 21st Century*, links the improvement of schools and the economy with the reform of teaching. To achieve improvement in the American economic system, the report states, "the key to success lies in creating a profession equal to the task—a profession possessed of well-educated teachers prepared to assume new powers and responsibilities to redesign schools for the future." As will be discussed in more detail later in this chapter, the report recommends sweeping changes in teacher education, certification, and their roles within schools.

   This chapter discusses these changes in the profession by first considering the rewards and dissatisfactions of teaching. It is important to consider
why people enter and remain in teaching before making sweeping changes in
the profession. The chapter will then explore the concept of professionalism
in education, career ladders, national certification, and, lastly, teacher education. Two other important aspects of teaching—teachers' unions and teacher
politics—will be discussed in Chapter 3.

THE REWARDS AND DISSATISFACTIONS
OF TEACHING

Many of the proposed reforms of the teaching profession emphasize the
importance of salaries and status in attracting people to the profession, but
actual studies of teacher satisfaction consistently suggest that interacting with
students provides the greatest reward for teachers. The issues of teacher
salaries and status are more clearly highlighted in comparisons between
American and Japanese teachers. A 1987 report prepared for the U.S. Office
of Education, *Japanese Education Today,* states that, in general, Japanese educators have a much higher status in their society than educators in the United
States. For instance, elementary school principals in Japan have a higher
status than department heads of large corporations, public accountants, and
authors. And, surprisingly when compared with the United States, elementary-school teachers in Japanese society have a higher status than "civil and
mechanical engineers, white-collar employees in large firms, and municipal
department heads." University professors were ranked above physicians and
just below court judges and presidents of large corporations.

   According to the report, a Japanese high school teacher with a bachelor's
degree had a starting salary 15 percent higher than that of a starting white-
collar worker with a similar degree and 12 percent higher than the starting
salary of an engineer. The report states, "First-year teacher salaries are generally higher than those of other professions such as businessmen, engineers,
pharmacists, etc." In contrast, *A Nation Prepared: Teachers for the 21st Century*
reports that the median weekly income of American teachers was slightly
below that of mail carriers and slightly above that of plumbers. Ranking above
American teachers in median weekly earnings were attorneys, engineers,
chemists, systems analysts, and accountants.

   Low salaries continue to be source of complaint among U.S. school
teachers despite the fact that as of 1992 increases in teachers' salaries out-
paced inflation for ten of the previous eleven years. In 1992, the average
teacher's salary in the United States reached an all-time high of $34,213. As
indicated in Table 2.1, there is a great deal of variation between states in the
average teacher's salary, with Connecticut having the highest average of
$47,510 and South Dakota having the lowest average of $24,495.

   While salary remains an important issue, teachers rate interaction with
students as the most important source of job satisfaction. A major complaint

TABLE 2.1 Highest and
Lowest Average Teacher's
Salary by State, 1992

HIGHEST	
Connecticut	$47,510
Alaska	43,800
New York	43,335
New Jersey	41,027
Michigan	40,700

LOWEST	
Idaho	26,345
New Mexico	26,244
North Dakota	24,495
Mississippi	24,368
South Dakota	23,291

Source: This table was adapted from
Michael Blood, "Teachers Salaries,"
Compuserve Executive News Service AP,
no. 1455 (27 August 1992).

about the organization of American schools is that the organization itself
interferes with the relationship between students and teachers. For example,
Dan Lortie, whose study *Schoolteacher: A Sociological Study* is the most complete report on the social world of the teacher, surveyed teachers in Dade
County, Florida, and found that the reward from teaching identified most
often by teachers was "knowing that I have reached students and they have
learned."

For the purposes of his study, Lortie divided teacher rewards into extrinsic, psychic, and ancillary. Extrinsic rewards are those associated with salary
and community status. Psychic rewards are associated with the psychological
satisfaction derived from the job. Ancillary rewards refer to security of position, summer vacation time, and freedom from competition.

Of the more than 5,800 teachers included in Lortie's survey, over 76 percent gave top priority to the psychic rewards of teaching. Only 11.9 percent
selected extrinsic rewards, and 11.7 percent chose ancillary rewards. The
choice given teachers with regard to psychic rewards ranged from the "knowing that I have reached students . . ." statement to "chance to associate with
other teachers." "Knowing that I have reached students . . ." was selected by
86.1 percent of the teachers as the most important psychic reward. The
second choice, "chance to associate with children or young people," was
selected by 8 percent of the teachers in the survey.

An aspect of psychic rewards that Lortie did not include in this particular
survey, but to which he has given reference throughout his study of American schoolteachers, is the psychic reward experienced by teachers through
the exercise of creative autonomy in the classroom. It has been estimated that
teachers make over two hundred decisions an hour in their classrooms. These
decisions range from curricular and teaching problems to behavioral problems. Compared to the routine of some factory and office jobs, the autonomy

and creative decision making required of teachers attracts many individuals to the profession. This particular psychic reward has also led to conflict when administrators and other agencies outside the classroom have attempted to control the behavior of teachers. This threat to the independence of teachers may be one of the reasons for the rapid growth of teachers' unions.

The ancillary rewards of teaching are also attractive to many individuals. The most popular ancillary reward is the time for extended vacations and travel provided by the long summer vacation and other school holidays. Second to vacation time is the security of income and position. In most states teacher tenure laws provide a security not often found in other jobs. Of course, school closings and financial crises can threaten this security for many younger teachers.

John Goodlad, in *A Place Called School,* provides a somewhat different picture than Lortie's. In Goodlad's sample 57 percent of the major reasons for teaching centered around the desire to teach, while only 15 percent of the reasons were related to liking children. Because of the differences between questions asked by Goodlad and Lortie in their surveys, it is difficult to compare their results. The desire to teach can be considered a desire to interact with students. But, on the other hand, the desire to teach does reflect a greater concern with subject matter as opposed to simply interacting with students. Goodlad also found a higher level of satisfaction among teachers than one would have suspected from the current criticism of the profession. In his sample, 74 percent felt their "career expectations had been fulfilled," and 69 percent said they would again "select education as a career."

Goodlad found that "personal frustration and dissatisfaction in the teaching situation" was the major reason teachers left teaching. Conflicts with fellow teachers, administrators, and students ranked low as reasons for leaving the profession. Even low pay was not given as a major reason except insofar as it was related to a general sense of dissatisfaction. Goodlad argued that even though interest in money was not a major reason given by teachers for entering the career of teaching, it was given as the second reason for leaving it. Goodlad writes:

> We might speculate that, anticipating rewards intrinsic to the work, teachers begin with a willingness to forego high salaries. However, when confronted with the frustration of these expectations, the fact that they sometimes are paid less than the bus drivers who bring their students to school may become a considerable source of dissatisfaction as well.

Another source of frustration for teachers is their relations to parents. In 1990 and 1991, Louis Harris and Associates conducted a survey of teachers' attitudes. Seventy percent of the teachers surveyed reported positive experiences with their students and almost 60 percent reported positive relations with other teachers. On the other hand, only 50 percent reported that their working relationship with school principals was productive. The lowest percentage of teachers expressing satisfaction was with relations with parents. Only 25 percent reported finding their relations with parents to be cooperative and supporting.

With regard to the factors contributing to a person leaving teaching, the Harris survey found that the most often cited reason was lack of parental support. The next most often cited reason was low salary. In addition, the survey found that 20 percent of new teachers felt that they were very likely to leave the profession within their first five years of teaching.

THE WORKING CONDITIONS OF TEACHERS

Descriptions of working conditions highlight teachers' frustrations with their interaction with students and other teachers, and with the after school employment required because of low salaries. Ernest Boyer and Theodore Sizer sketch vivid portraits of teachers that provide an understanding of the factors contributing to teachers' dissatisfactions. Theodore Sizer's description of a day in the life of high school English teacher Horace Smith is one of the finest pieces of educational literature. Sizer provides sympathetic insight into the life of a twenty-eight-year veteran of teaching who still cares about his work but is constantly forced to compromise his instructional ideals with the realities of public school teaching.

Sizer assures the reader that Horace's compromises are not the result of unusually poor working conditions. In fact, the reader is often reminded that Horace Smith teaches in a suburban school where conditions are far superior to those faced by teachers in central-city school systems. Sizer is also realistic. He recognizes that all jobs involve compromises between ideals and realities. But, he feels, the compromises required in teaching require more than ordinary adjustments to the realities of work. The compromises required in teaching not only shatter ideals but cheat students of opportunities to learn.

Horace Smith is proud and committed to his job. His day begins at 5:45 A.M. with a brief breakfast and a forty-minute drive, bringing him to school by 7:00. He heads directly for the teachers' lounge, where he enjoys a cup of coffee and a cigarette before the beginning of his 7:30 class. The teachers' lounge is portrayed as a warm setting in which there is the smell of old cigarette smoke and a continual card game being played by groups of teachers during their off hours. It is the one haven in the school where teachers can meet and share daily events and professional concerns.

His three junior-level classes for the day are reading *Romeo and Juliet*. As a veteran teacher who has spent many years teaching *Romeo and Juliet*, he moves his classes quickly through the drama, anticipating their difficulties and avoiding distracting issues. His second-bell class is excused for an assembly, which allows him to return to his coffee cup in the teachers' lounge. His fourth-bell class is a senior advanced-placement class that is studying *Ulysses*. On this particular day, thirteen of the eighteen seniors are attending a United Nations week at a local college. Sizer describes Horace's annoyance at losing the teaching days but also his feeling of gratefulness at being able to avoid teaching, thus allowing his students time to read. In addition to his five classes, Horace has a preparation period and a lunch hour.

The final bell ends the school day at 2:00 P.M. After conversations with students, he collects his papers, leaves his classroom at 2:30, and goes to the auditorium. Horace is faculty adviser to the stage crew, for which he earns an extra $800 a year. For that small amount he puts in about four hours a week—and many more hours than that in the ten days before a performance. After stopping in the auditorium he drives to his brother-in-law's liquor store where he works behind the counter in the stockroom from shortly after 4:00 P.M. until 6:30. His salary from the school system is $27,300, and the work at the liquor store adds another $8,000.

He eats dinner at 7:45 and then spends an hour grading papers. This is followed by several phone calls from sick students wanting assignments and students wanting to talk about the upcoming stage production. Finally, Horace ends his day by drifting off to sleep after the 11:00 news.

Horace's compromises are in the shortcuts he must take in order to deal with his busy day. He knows that he should be assigning his students a weekly essay of a page or two. But with a total of 120 students (central-city teachers often have more than 170 students) he is realistic and only assigns one or two paragraphs. Even with these short assignments, he estimates that grading and writing comments will take fifteen to twenty minutes of his time per student. This still involves roughly thirty hours of grading. Again, Horace is realistic about his time and takes shortcuts in grading to reduce the time per student to five minutes. This means that even with reducing the assignment from a short theme to one or two paragraphs, and cutting corners while grading, Horace still must devote ten hours a week to grading.

He must also take shortcuts in class preparations. He has taught some of his classes before, whereas others require more preparation. But even when classes are studying the same material, the differences among students require separate lesson plans. Horace recognizes that he should spend many more hours on preparation but again compromises and spends only about ten minutes per class on preparation.

His shortcuts in grading and preparation, along with his teaching, administration, and extracurricular drama work give him a forty-two-hour week. If he didn't cut corners there would be another twenty hours of grading and possibly another six hours for preparation, which would mean a sixty-eight-hour week. On top of this is the time spent by Horace in his brother-in-law's liquor store trying to add to his inadequate salary. And, of course, there are the three full days he spends during Christmas vacation writing letters of reference for his students.

Lost in all these commitments is the time that should be used for reading professional journals and new literature, and to do those things that renew the life of the mind. As Sizer describes the situation, Horace hides his bitterness toward the critics who demand from teachers more scholarship and intellectual involvement. And, in the end, the students are as cheated as Horace's ideals.

In *High School,* Ernest Boyer provides similar descriptions of teachers who are overwhelmed by course loads and are forced to seek outside employment to add to their meager salaries. In many ways, Boyer paints an even grimmer picture of a high school teacher's life. His teachers have five to six classes a day with three different levels in a course. The different levels mean that more of the teachers' time is required in order to review subject matter and prepare for class. In addition, many teachers are assigned classes for which they have had no training. For instance, a social studies teacher might be assigned a science or mathematics course, which means endless hours of preparation. Added to this is the time spent on grading papers, preparing lesson plans, and counseling students.

Boyer found that a great deal of a teacher's time is spent on clerical and administrative chores. Many of these extra duties are nothing but babysitting and security tasks such as supervising hallways, lunchrooms, and student activities. Boyer found widespread complaints about clerical chores resulting from endless requests from both the school administration and the central administration of the school district. Also, teachers must keep elaborate student attendance records and send written reports to school counselors.

A great deal of a teacher's time is spent counseling students. Boyer gives the average pupil-to-counselor ratio in the United States as 319 to 1. This means there is little hope for the average student to find a counselor who has enough time to deal to any great extent with personal, academic, and career problems. This means students often turn to teachers for help. This creates a bind for many teachers because the better and more popular teachers often have the greatest demands on their time.

A feeling of isolation among teachers was also found in the high schools visited by Boyer. Teachers spend very little time in the company of other adults. Contact with other adults usually occurs only at lunchtime or during preparation periods in the faculty lounge. This situation gives teachers few opportunities to discuss common problems, professional issues, and intellectual topics with other teachers.

Teachers are also frequently without a permanent classroom, which means they are without their own desk: most move from room to room carrying all their material. Many schools, particularly in central cities, are poorly maintained and have dirty windows and floors. In addition, there is often a shortage of school materials, and teachers dip into their own pockets to buy supplies.

For Boyer, a teacher's working conditions are made even more intolerable by a lack of public recognition and reward. Boyer argues, using the previously mentioned research by Dan Lortie, that the primary satisfaction for teachers comes from psychic rewards. But he finds little evidence of these rewards in high schools of the 1980s. First, students have a negative attitude toward school. Boyer cites statistics that in 1980, 73 percent of high school teachers stated that student attitudes toward learning had a negative effect on teacher satisfaction from teaching. Second, there is a lack of respect from other adults outside of teaching. The teachers Boyer interviewed reported a subtle disrespect for teachers by many adults. A number of teachers even avoid mentioning to other adults the nature of their occupation. One teacher, who works as a meat cutter during the summer, was told by a fellow butcher who discovered he was a teacher, "Man, that's a dead-end job. You must be a real dummy."

Although Sizer and Boyer spent their time analyzing the life of the high school teacher, many of their conclusions can also apply to elementary school teachers. Elementary school teachers also feel time pressure in their class preparations and grading. They also feel the grim climate of isolation from adults, poor physical environment, and lack of community respect. They also must seek extracurricular school and summer employment to fill the gap left by inadequate salaries.

Table 2.2 provides a list of the rewards and dissatisfactions expressed by teachers in the studies cited in this chapter. This list provides an understanding of the causes of teacher burnout discussed in the next section.

TEACHER BURNOUT

The list of dissatisfactions in Table 2.2 provides a good guide to the causes of *teacher burnout*. The symptoms of teacher burnout are periods of depression and an extreme dissatisfaction with teaching, to the point of finding it difficult to get up in the morning and go to work. It can be the cause of excessive fatigue resulting from depression and stress. Teacher burnout does not always result from the same circumstances. For instance, a salesperson for a book publishing firm recently came to my office and, after discussing the texts her company had for sale, she told me, "I quit teaching last year to take this job. I am a product of teacher burnout. I just couldn't face those students again." She had taught in a wealthy suburban district with comparatively good working conditions and few disciplinary problems. Another burnout case was a teachers' union leader in an inner-city school who declared, half in

TABLE 2.2 Summary List of the Rewards and Dissatisfactions of Teaching

Rewards	Dissatisfactions
1. Interaction with students	1. Disinterested and violent students
2. Teaching	2. Administrative interference with teaching
3. Interaction with colleagues	3. Isolation from colleagues
4. Autonomy	4. Bureaucratic interference with autonomy
5. Long summer vacations	5. Low salaries
	6. Uninvolved parents
	7. Large class sizes
	8. Too heavy a course load in middle and secondary schools
	9. Low status of profession

jest, "I warn all teachers to take an extra pair of underwear to school because of the fear caused by student violence."

One way of understanding teacher burnout is to consider it in terms of Lortie's survey of rewards. If the primary rewards of teaching are psychic, what happens when those psychic rewards are withdrawn? Except for the flexibility of schedules and long vacations, there is little left in a low-salaried, careerless profession. In terms of Lortie's survey, if a student resists learning and does not care about school, then the major satisfaction in teaching no longer exists. When this lack of reward is combined with threats of student violence and problems of student discipline, it seems reasonable for teachers to burn out and either become bitter or quit teaching.

Burnout is not a phenomenon peculiar to teaching. People in other occupations also become frustrated and bored and seek career changes. What is distinctive about teacher burnout is that it may be intrinsic to the educational system. Students are not rewarded by the system for demonstrating a joy of learning. The educational structure is built on accumulating course credits and years of instruction in order to get a degree or pass on to another level of instruction. Classes filled with students who are there because the law requires their presence or because they want a degree do not constitute ideal educational circumstances. Teachers are often trying to figure out how to make students learn, while students are trying to figure how to get by with the minimum effort. This situation cannot maximize teachers' psychic rewards.

In recent years the satisfaction teachers have gained from autonomous decision making and creativity has been threatened by expanding bureaucratic structures and attempts to control teacher behavior in the classroom. These changes may have led to greater unionization by teachers as they have attempted to restore their autonomy and ability to influence educational policy.

The growth of bureaucratic structures in education can be illustrated as follows: Consider the expansion in the twentieth century of the hierarchical administrative staff in education. According to the *Digest of Education Statistics*, in 1919–1920 there was a single supervisor or principal for every thirty-one teachers, librarians, and other nonsupervisory instructional staff. During the 1920s, educational administration began to professionalize and expand so that by 1929–1930 there was a principal or supervisor for every twenty-two teachers, librarians, and other nonsupervisory instructional staff. This trend continued so that by 1973–1974 the ratio was 1 to 16.

As teachers experienced an expanding bureaucratic structure they also found their schools and school districts becoming larger. The 1940s saw a major national effort to reduce the number of school districts and increase the size of schools. Reducing the number of school districts was achieved by consolidating existing districts into larger units. The general purpose of school consolidation was to provide more services to students. It was argued that the larger the school district, the more opportunity there was to provide specialized programs that could not be offered in smaller districts.

The major school consolidations occurred from the 1940s to the mid-1970s, when the number of school districts was decreased from 101,000 to 16,300—a dramatic reduction of 83.8 percent in thirty years. By the late 1970s the rate of decline in the number of districts had slowed to 250 consolidations a year.

At the same time that school districts were consolidating, the numbers of administrative staff, instructional staff, and students were increasing. The combination of school district consolidation and more complex hierarchical administrative structures resulted in increasing the distance between the leaders of a school district and the classroom teacher. For example, it became much more difficult for a teacher to have direct contact with a superintendent and school board members. Yet this sort of contact between a teacher and administrative leaders can often result in the teacher's having some influence over educational policy.

As teachers found themselves working in larger bureaucratic structures they increasingly turned to unionization as a means of influencing educational policy. (Chapter 3 discusses in detail the organization and objectives of teachers' unions.) It should be noted that there is no way to prove that expanded bureaucratic structures caused teachers to form and join unions. All that can be argued is that teachers' unions provided a formal organizational mechanism by which teachers could influence educational policy. Teachers' unions are concerned not only with salaries and benefits, but with a wide variety of issues including curriculum content and textbooks.

Joining a union and/or a professional organization can be a means by which a teacher can increase his or her sense of self-worth and also influence educational policy. Every area of teaching has some organization that publishes journals dealing with developments in curriculum and teaching methods and that attempts to influence school policy at state and national levels. Usually the professional organization has an annual national convention at which policies affecting the particular teaching field are discussed and formulated. For instance, the National Council of Teachers of English has spent many sessions and has devoted many pages of its journal to the vital issue of censorship. In a similar manner, professional organizations in the social studies, mathematics, science, vocational education, art, physical education, and other fields work actively to spread new knowledge among their members and protect the interests of the profession.

Professional organizations and unions can be an important means by which teachers can increase their rewards from teaching. Obviously, unions provide a possible means of increasing external and ancillary rewards. Professional organizations in particular subject-matter areas can provide increased psychic rewards by enhancing a teacher's sense of control and autonomy.

The knowledge gained through active participation in a professional organization can also be a means by which a teacher can counter the increasing intrusion of bureaucratic structures in the classroom. It is important to understand that this intrusion is not inherently wrong. A problem arises because the intrusion can reduce the important psychic rewards from teaching by limiting the autonomy and creative decision making of teachers. When there are no significant increases in salaries and few external rewards, this intrusion can seriously contribute to teacher burnout and to an increased number of teachers changing careers.

Dan Lortie argues that the best protection teachers have against the loss of autonomy is through claims of expert knowledge. This means that the more knowledge teachers have of their subject matter, methods of teaching, and educational policy, the better they are able to protect their power in and control over the classroom. From this standpoint, active participation in a professional organization and keeping abreast with new knowledge in the field are the best means teachers have of assuring personal satisfaction from their work.

THE PROFESSIONALIZATION OF TEACHING

A much-discussed issue in education for over a century is whether teaching is a profession. One of the difficulties in resolving this issue is that *professionalism* can be defined in a variety of ways. For example, some people argue that teaching is not a profession because teachers do not control entrance into the field; nor do they control teaching practices, salaries, and working conditions. Arguments such as these often compare teaching to the medical profession. Medical doctors through their professional organizations control medical-school education, licensing, medical practice, working conditions, and fees. If this comparison defines professionalism, teaching is not a profession. Professional teacher organizations do not have the power that professional medical organizations have.

But defined in narrower terms, teaching is a profession. For the purposes of this text, *profession* is defined as an occupation requiring expert knowledge that justifies a monopoly of services granted by government licensing. The ability to gain a government license is dependent on the applicant's demonstrating this expert knowledge, either by passing an examination or by completing special training courses in an educational institution. In the teaching profession this usually means graduation from a college or university and a claim to expert knowledge based on courses taken in departments or colleges of education. Teacher licenses are usually granted by the government on the basis of fulfilling certain educational requirements. In a growing number of states there is the added requirement of passing a state examination.

The term *profession* also involves a set of ethical standards based on service to the client of the profession. In other words, a teacher's primary ethical responsibility must be to the client, namely, the student. (In a similar manner, doctors and lawyers must serve their patients and clients.) If a teacher's primary responsibility is to serve the student, then the teacher must assume responsibility for maintaining the knowledge and skills that can provide the student with the best possible education. In addition, the teacher must be willing to defend and fight for teaching conditions that enhance learning opportunities.

There is a difference between ideal definitions and reality. Some doctors and lawyers are more interested in increasing their incomes than serving their clients. And some teachers lose sight of the fact that their primary responsibility is to serve students. This can easily happen in school systems where teachers are bombarded with administrative tasks and record keeping. Every teacher facing five classes of forty students thinks primarily in terms of how to make the job manageable. When teachers have to struggle to survive, they can often forget where their primary service should be directed. In a school where a heavy emphasis is placed on discipline, a teacher may lose sight of the fact that the primary goal of an educational institution is to teach students and not to maintain orderly classrooms.

The other reality facing teachers at present is the low status of their profession compared with other professions. This low status is rooted in historical conditions that have reduced both economic rewards and the status of the teaching profession. One can argue that those responsible for the mind of the child and its future development, such as teachers, should receive compensation comparable to those responsible for the body of the child, such as doctors. This argument can be made even more forcefully for educational specialists—reading specialists, special-education teachers, and teachers with other specialized training. When one considers the number of years of training needed to acquire this specialization, the gap in salary between educational specialists and other professionals is out of proportion to the differences in their training.

It is important for teachers to understand how education became professionalized so that they can participate in changes that may enhance the status of the teaching profession. The present conditions surrounding the profession of education are not the result of historical accident but of certain policies and developments. Teachers can serve their students and increase their own external and psychic rewards by working to enhance their professional status.

The first step in the professionalization of education in the United States was the establishment in 1839 of a teacher training institution in Lexington, Massachusetts. Called a *normal school,* this institution was designed primarily to train teachers for the elementary grades. The establishment of the school gave recognition to the fact that certain teaching skills can be *taught* to prospective teachers. The normal school emphasized not only subject matter but also methods of teaching.

A major problem in the early professionalization of teaching was that it accompanied the increasing recruitment of women into teaching. Women in the nineteenth century were inexpensive and stable members of the work force; they were second-class citizens in both the political and economic arenas. Willard S. Elsbree, in *The American Teacher: Evolution of a Profession in a Democracy,* quotes the Boston Board of Education in 1841 as it discusses why there should be an increased number of women in teaching. States the board:

As a class, they [women] never look forward, as young men almost invariably do, to a period of legal emancipation from parental control, when they are to break away from the domestic circle and go abroad into the world, to build up a fortune for themselves; and hence, the sphere of hope and of effort is narrower, and the whole forces of the mind are more readily concentrated upon present duties.

Horace Mann, a common-school leader and the person mainly responsible for the founding of the first normal school, wrote in 1846: "Reason and experience have long since demonstrated that children under 10 or 12 years of age can be more genially taught and more successfully governed by a female than by a male teacher." He went on to state that as more and more schools experimented with the use of female teachers, opposition to their entry into teaching would decrease. Elsbree reports that from the 1830s up to the Civil War, increasing numbers of women entered teaching through training in the normal schools. And the Civil War, with its demands for manpower in the military, completed the evolution of elementary school teaching from a male occupation to a primarily female occupation. For example, Elsbree states that in Indiana the number of male teachers in all grades dropped from 80 percent in 1859 to 58 percent in 1864; in Ohio the number of male teachers went from 52 percent in 1862 to 41 percent in 1864.

The second-class citizenship of women in the nineteenth century made it possible to keep teaching salaries low and contributed to the continuing low status of teaching as it became professionalized. In many school systems male teachers received higher salaries than female teachers. In the twentieth century, in spite of the struggle by women teachers for equal salaries, the low status of the profession continued because of changes in teacher-certification laws.

Nineteenth-century teachers were usually certified by taking an examination administered by the employing school system or the county board of education. Licensing, or the granting of certificates to teach, was based primarily on examination and not on the number of education courses taken. Elsbree reports that in 1898 only four states had centralized certification or licensing at the state level. The rest of the states gave the certification power to local districts and counties. By 1933 forty-two states had centralized licensing at the state level; the primary requirement for gaining a teacher certificate was the completion of a certain number of courses in teacher education and other fields.

The centralization of certification and the dependence on teacher-education courses led to a rapid expansion of normal schools and colleges of education in the early part of the twentieth century. State certification laws and expanded training in education completed the professionalization of teaching. Since 1933 this pattern of professionalization has continued, with the elimination of most normal schools and the expansion of college and university departments of education. Course requirements in most states have generally increased and there has been a greater monitoring of teacher-education programs. By the 1970s some states had added state teaching examinations as part of the certification requirement.

One would assume that with the increased professionalization of teaching there would have been an increase in the status of teachers. The problem was that as teaching became more professionalized, its status was linked to the status of its professional training.

On some college campuses, taking courses in education is viewed as a form of "intellectual slumming." Dan Lortie in his previously mentioned study found teachers referring to their education courses as "Mickey Mouse" courses, and he never found a teacher who complained that education courses were too difficult. The status of the education faculty also is often not as high as that of other faculty members. In *To Be A Phoenix: The Education Professoriate,* Arthur Powell and Theodore Sizer (at the time dean and associate dean, respectively, of the Harvard School of Education) portray the professor of education as a "gentle, unintellectual, saccharine, and well-meaning . . . bumbling doctor of undiagnosable ills, harmless if morosely defensive. He is either a mechanic . . . or he is the flatulent promoter of irrelevant trivia."

Some authors argue that the status of the education professoriate is a result of the recruitment that occurred when education faculties expanded in the early part of the century. Many faculty members were recruited directly from teaching or public-school administration. They often lacked the academic and scholarly background of other faculties on college campuses. Once on campus they tended to concentrate only on problems dealing directly with classroom practice rather than with a broader concept of learning in a modern society. The narrow focus of education faculties has often contributed to the low academic status of departments of education.

It is difficult to pinpoint exact reasons for the low status of the education professoriate, but the consequences of that status are evident. Obviously, the lack of prestige of training in education contributes to the low prestige of the profession and probably influences the relatively poor economic rewards received by teachers as compared with other professionals. A claim to rigorous training and specialized knowledge is one of the most important ingredients in maintaining the status of a profession.

In addition to the effect of lack of rigorous training on status and income, this lack also affects psychic rewards. Dan Lortie found that teachers not only consider education courses "Mickey Mouse," but also do not perceive their preparation as conveying anything special. There is no sense of shared ordeal among teachers as there is among graduates of medical and law schools. Many teachers do not feel honored by having graduated from college or university departments of education.

How much the lack of prestige in the training and the lack of shared ordeal contribute to teacher burnout is difficult to measure. On the surface it seems that a teacher who had negative feelings about his or her training, who gained little status from that training, and who taught in a world of decreasing psychic rewards, would be prone to burnout.

It is evident from the previous discussion that an important way of increasing economic and psychic rewards for teachers is to upgrade the quality of professional training. Higher academic standards, requiring more rigorous training and more selectivity among applicants for teacher education, will help increase teacher rewards and status. They will create among teachers the sense of shared ordeal and the sense of shared technical culture.

From the standpoint of upgrading the status of the teaching profession, it is essential for teachers to become involved in influencing and controlling teacher education. An important function of a professional is to participate in the quality and training of those entering the field. For many years, teachers have failed to fully realize the importance of this involvement to their economic and psychological well-being. Becoming a professional means continuous study of and interest in new knowledge in the field, in addition to a concern for and involvement in the training of new entrants into the profession.

In recent years, the reform movement in teaching has been attempting to increase professionalism by creating career ladders and new professional roles. In addition, teachers are gaining greater control over the certification process to enter the profession. This is a key element in the development of a profession. The next two sections will discuss career ladders, the role of master teachers, and national certification. All of these are important efforts in the continuing professionalization of teaching.

CAREER LADDERS AND MASTER TEACHERS

An important issue is the "careerless" nature of teaching. As I discussed in the introduction to the chapter, "careerless" in this case means the lack of advancement possibilities for classroom teachers. Other careers usually hold out the hope of advancement within the organization or through individual entrepreneurial skills. An office worker can move through the hierarchy of the organization, and a professional can attempt to increase income through his or her own ability.

Traditionally, when teachers entered the classroom there was no possibility of advancement except to leave the classroom and be trained as an administrator—or to get out of the education profession completely. Most teachers could not increase their income by superior teaching or service. In fact, merit pay is often opposed by teachers because of its potential abuse. Career ladders and master-teacher plans attempt to correct the problem of the careerless nature of teaching and the lack of rewards for superior teaching by providing different career levels. One way of understanding this idea is to compare it to university teaching. Traditionally, universities hire new faculty members as assistant professors. After a period of five to seven years the faculty member applies for tenure and a position as an associate professor. Once promoted to associate professor, the faculty member might be promoted to professor if he or she demonstrates superior qualities in teaching or scholarship. Each advancement in rank provides increased recognition and rewards.

The same basic idea underlies proposals for career ladders and master-teacher plans. A teacher might be hired as an apprentice teacher and after a number of years of receiving satisfactory evaluations be promoted to the rank of regular teacher and receive tenure. Later, if the teacher if considered superior, that teacher might be promoted to master teacher. It is important for the reader to understand that this is only a simple example. Some proposals are more complex and involve added duties for the master teacher. These will be discussed later in the text.

In addition to overcoming the problem of the careerless nature of teaching, master-teacher and career-ladder proposals are supposed to solve the problems inherent in traditional methods of compensating teachers. The traditional salary schedule for teachers allows for increases in pay with each year of service and for added academic degrees from universities. Under a traditional pay plan all beginning certified teachers with a bachelor's degree receive the same base salary. For each year of service after the first year, salaries increase by a fixed percentage. Under this method of payment a teacher receives an automatic salary increase with each year of service. In addition, a teacher can increase his or her salary by earning more college credits. Usually, the earning of a master's degree results in an increase in salary in addition to the automatic yearly increase. Also, there are usually increases for earning an additional fifteen hours beyond the master's degree and for earning a doctoral degree.

One of the major complaints about the traditional method of compensation is that it is not based on the ability of teachers to teach. This became a heated issue in the early 1980s when everyone admitted that teachers were underpaid but many felt that salaries should be increased only for superior teachers. This is the reason for proposals for career ladders and master teachers. These plans are considered as replacements for the traditional salary schedule.

Another plan for providing additional compensation without changing the traditional salary schedule is that of merit pay. With merit pay, superior teachers would be identified and would receive an additional salary increase over their automatic yearly increase in salary. But merit-pay plans have been bitterly resisted by teachers because of the problem of setting criteria for superior teaching. This is also an issue with career ladders and master-teacher proposals. Teachers fear that school administrators will use merit pay to reward only personal favorites and those who are compliant with administrative orders. There is also the real difficulty of defining and evaluating superior teaching.

Most proposals for career ladders include extra duties for teachers, including supervising other teachers during their probationary years and planning curriculum. Traditionally, teachers have been confined to classrooms, extracurricular activities, policing chores, and committees established by the school principal. Supervision of new teachers introduces a role traditionally assumed by the administration. It adds an administrative function to the role of teaching. Participation in planning curriculum adds another dimension to the role of teaching.

Adding responsibilities and extending the months of the teaching contract are criticized as not providing an actual increase in compensation but only additional pay for additional work. It would, however, be possible to have the category of master teacher include additional compensation without adding extra work. In the university system, promotion from assistant to associate or full professor does not entail any additional responsibilities. Similar criticisms can be made of the extended contract year. Why not just increase salaries without requiring additional months of work?

How the issues of compensation and extra duties are distributed is exemplified by the career ladder introduced in Tennessee in 1984. Under the original plan, the Tennessee legislature established five levels in the career ladder, with additional compensation ranging from $500 to $7,000 per year. The first level is for new teachers on probationary status who receive state certification after receiving positive evaluations. Teachers who receive certification become apprentice teachers for three years and receive a yearly supplement of $500. Apprentice teachers are evaluated each year and by the third year must receive tenure and be promoted to Career Level One teachers or lose their jobs. Career Level One teachers are certified at this level for five years and receive an annual supplement of $1,000. Teachers at this career level assume the additional duties of supervising student teachers and probationary teachers.

Under this plan a teacher might remain at Career Level One for his or her entire teaching career. Promotion to Career Level Two requires evaluation by the state, using Career Level Three teachers from outside the district of the teacher being evaluated. If the teacher is promoted to Level Two, he or she receives an annual pay supplement of $2,000 for a 10-month contract and $4,000 for an 11-month contract. Career Level Two teachers are given the additional responsibilities of working with remedial and gifted students, along with supervising apprentice teachers. The evaluation procedure for Level Three is similar to that of Level Two. Level Three teachers receive an additional $3,000 for a 10-month contract, $5,000 for an 11-month contract, and $7,000 for a 12-month contract. In addition to the duties added for Level Two teachers, Level Three teachers also conduct evaluations of teachers who are on other career levels.

An important issue in career ladders is teacher participation in evaluation of other teachers. Traditionally, evaluation of teachers has been conducted by school administrators. Teachers complained for years about this system and they argued that if teachers are truly professionals they should be evaluated by their peers. The Tennessee legislation incorporates this idea by using Level Three teachers for evaluation. Also, most master-teacher proposals give senior teachers the added duty of participating in teacher evaluations.

The issue of method of evaluation is more complex. The debate on this issue ranges across several dimensions. First is the problem of whether teachers should be evaluated on the basis of their performance in the classroom or the performance of their students. The difficulty of using student performance is the range of abilities existing among students and between classes of students. Some students, because of a variety of factors, including family background and intelligence, might learn faster than other students. It would be unfair to evaluate a teacher of students with rapid learning abilities against a teacher of students with slow learning abilities. Also, most evaluations of students are conducted by using standardized tests. Systems using student performance as a means of teacher evaluation run the danger of teachers directing their efforts mainly toward preparing students to do well on performance tests.

If teacher performance becomes the basis for evaluation, then there will be a set of problems arising from the need to define good teaching. Historically, there has been an almost continuous debate dating from the nineteenth century over whether teaching is an art or a science. Obviously one's position on this issue would be reflected in the teaching qualities one would consider in evaluation. In recent years there has been a debate between those who believe that good teaching is composed of measurable competencies, and those who believe that good teaching is a product of experience that is displayed in reaction to a variety of classroom situations.

It is the issue of compensation that causes the greatest difficulty for career ladders. In 1990, Vilma Leake, president of the teachers' union in Charlotte-Mecklenburg, North Carolina, expressed the desire of her organization to dismantle the school district's career ladder. The district received national recognition in 1984 as one of the first systems to adopt a career ladder. In addition, the North Carolina Association of Educators voted overwhelmingly in January, 1990, to fight any expansion of career-ladder plans in the state.

Wage issues are the major reason these North Carolina teachers' organizations are resisting spending state money on extending career-ladder plans to all state school districts. In 1990, the estimated cost of expanding the career-ladder program was from $150 million to $400 million a year. From the perspective of the teachers' organization, the money used for administering the program could be used for increasing all teachers' salaries. David Bingham, president of the Professional Educators of North Carolina, expressed his worry about the "bloated" bureaucracy used to administer the plan.

The troubles in North Carolina highlight the fact that salaries are the central and continuing issues regarding career ladders. Career ladders can be used to spend less money on teachers' salaries by only rewarding those in the upper rungs. Teachers' organizations are very aware of this possibility. Only by providing adequate compensation to all teachers will state and local school systems be able to convince teachers to support the concept of career ladders. But as state governments encounter increasing financial problems in the 1990s, the issue of compensation will probably continue to dominate discussions of career ladders.

Career ladders represent one aspect of the current attempt to improve the profession of teaching. Another idea for increasing the status of teaching is national certification. And, like career-ladder plans, national certification has been attacked by teachers' organizations.

NATIONAL CERTIFICATION

The current efforts to establish national certification of teachers began in 1986 when the Task Force on Teaching as a Profession, working under the auspices of the Carnegie Forum on Education and the Economy, proposed changing the basic structure of the teaching profession. Its recommendations included the formation of a national certification board, which was then established in 1987 as the National Board for Professional Teaching Standards.

The justification for national certification included economic need and a shortage of qualified teachers. As discussed in Chapter 1, the task force report, *A Nation Prepared: Teachers for the 21st Century,* is premised on the belief that America can no longer compete in mass-production goods in world markets. Consequently, the report argues, the nation must shift its economy to emphasize knowledge-based industries. In this context, the schools must stop teaching repetitive skills needed in mass production and start teaching all students higher order thinking. According to the report, the old educational requirements needed for a mass-production economy could be packaged in texts, and teachers could be trained to use those texts. A knowledge-based economy, according to the report, requires students who are intellectually prepared to deal with a nonroutine world and unexpected events. The report argues that the training of students in higher order skills requires abandoning traditional textbook teaching and developing new teaching strategies. These new teaching strategies require a teacher who no longer uses routine teaching methods, but constantly adapts to different learning situations. This is why, at least in the eyes of the Carnegie Forum, the key to changing the schools to meet the requirements of a knowledge-based economy is the reform of the profession of teaching.

The report describes the teacher needed for a knowledge-based economy as one who is highly creative and has the ability to constantly learn as new knowledge becomes available. In the words of the report, these new teachers "must think for themselves if they are to help others think for themselves, be able to act independently and collaborate with others, and render critical judgement. They must be people whose knowledge is wide-ranging and whose understanding runs deep."

The Carnegie Forum believes the teacher shortage provides an ideal opportunity to change the profession of teaching and, as a result, adapt the schools to the requirements of a knowledge-based economy. The report's figures show that in 1985 the demand for teachers was roughly equal to the supply of teachers. In the 1990s, the report projects an increasing demand and a decreasing supply.

It is important to understand the reasons for this projected shortage of teachers because it provides insight into the challenging demographic patterns in teaching. One reason for the projected increase demand for teachers is increasing teacher retirements. When the baby boom ended in the 1970s and classrooms were closed because of decreasing student enrollments, school systems stopped hiring many new teachers and fired many young teachers. Consequently, the average age of teachers increased. Between 1976 and 1984, the number of teachers with 15 years of experience increased from 27 percent to 44 percent. During the same period, the number of teachers under 34 years of age declined from 53 percent to 37 percent. Because of retirements from the more experienced teachers, some school districts will be replacing over half their teachers between 1986 and the early 1990s. Adding to the problem of teacher retirements is an increase in school populations as the children of baby boom parents enter school.

As a result of these factors, the Carnegie Forum projects an increase in annual demand of from 115,000 new teachers in 1981 to 215,000 by 1992. From 1986 to 1992 it is estimated that 1.3 million new teachers will be hired in American schools.

The problem of demand is intensified by the fact that more job opportunities are available now to women and minorities. Women, who we have previously noted traditionally dominated the ranks of teaching, are now finding more rewarding opportunities in other careers. For instance, in 1966 the intended occupation of almost 40 percent of freshmen women in college was education, while less than 5 percent intended to enter business. By 1976 the percentages were about equal, and after that year more women began to select business over education as a career. By 1985, more than 20 percent of first-year college women planned a career in business, while less than 10 percent planned to be teachers. In addition, the number of minority teachers is declining.

Besides the issue of supply, the Carnegie Forum is also interested in the quality of future teachers. If a knowledge-based economy requires a more intellectual teacher than a mass-production economy, then the academic qualifications of teachers must increase. Traditionally, education students have been academically poorer than other college students. And, according to the report, the academic qualifications of teachers dropped dramatically between 1973 and 1983. In 1973, the average verbal score on the Scholastic Aptitude Test (SAT) for college-bound high school seniors was slightly more than 440, while the average score for those intending to major in education was less than 420. By 1983, the average score for those intending to enter education programs dropped to less than 400, while the average score for all college-bound seniors dropped to 430. In addition, the number of potential teachers graduating from high school academic programs has been declining. In 1974, 25 percent graduated from general high school programs and in 1982 this increased to 34 percent. And in 1974, 7 percent of education majors graduated from high school vocational programs; by 1982 the figure was 8 percent.

While the teacher shortage offers the opportunity for changing the profession by hiring large numbers of new teachers, there is the potential for a decrease in the academic qualifications of teachers. The problem for the Carnegie Forum is attracting students to careers in education and assuring that these new students have high academic qualifications.

One hope for improving the quality and the status of the profession is, according to the Carnegie Forum, national certification. To achieve this goal, the Forum organized in 1987 the National Board for Professional Teaching

Standards consisting of sixty-four members, the majority of whom are teachers. The goal is to create a national teaching certificate that would be in addition to the current licensing of teachers by individual states.

Under the plan, states would continue to issue licenses to ensure that prospective teachers meet the minimum standards established by state laws, and to signify that the holder is not a danger to public safety and the safety of a client. The national certificate would indicate that the holder meets the standards established by the profession itself. The purpose of a national certification board, then, is to establish standards for the profession of teaching and to certify that individuals meet these standards.

One of the first tasks of the National Board for Professional Teaching Standards is the creation of a test that would qualify candidates for the national certificate. In addition, the board must establish prerequisites for certification. This is the issue that has generated the greatest controversy.

The issue of prerequisites has pitted educators against politicians and corporate interests. Currently, many politicians and corporate leaders favor dropping the requirement of graduation from an accredited teacher-preparation program for earning a state license. Consequently, in the prerequisites for national certification announced in July, 1989, the board offered the opportunity for national certification to any person with a bachelor's degree and three years of successful teaching experience. There was no mention of requiring graduation from an accredited teacher-preparation program. The board argued that such a requirement would be counter to its "fundamental orientation toward performance rather than toward design standards."

Gary Sykes, a consultant to the board and an assistant professor of education at Michigan State University, argued that the decision reflected the funding problems encountered by the board. The board is not a creation of government and depends on external funding. It must raise at least $50 million to develop assessment methods for certification. Sykes is quoted in the January 17, 1990, issue of *Education Week* as saying that, "The sentiments among corporate leaders and politicians in favor of relatively relaxed entry standards into teaching certainly influenced the board's votes."

Obviously, educators, particularly those associated with teacher-training programs, were appalled by this decision. In September, 1989, the American Association of Colleges of Teacher Education denounced the actions of the board. In January, 1990, the directors of the largest teachers' union, the National Education Association, announced that it would do its best to ensure that national certification would require both a state license and graduation from a teacher-education program.

In the 1993–1994 school year, the National Board for Professional Teaching Standards conducted assessments for certification of teachers of English-language arts to children in early adolescence. This initial assessment was part of a broader plan to field test assessments in a network of schools and districts in nineteen states. As originally planned, this initial assessment includes a written test of content knowledge, a three-part portfolio exercise, and exercises given at an assessment center. The portfolio exercises include a

planning and teaching segment where the teacher is asked to keep over a
three-week period videotapes, student work, classroom handouts, and other
material. This segment of the portfolio is used to determine a teacher's ability
to plan and conduct teaching sessions. For the second part of the portfolio,
student learning, the teacher keeps folders tracking the learning of two
students. And the last segment of the portfolio is a videotape of the teacher
and students engaged in a discussion of a piece of literature.

One of the important questions regarding this assessment is who should
do the judging. At the summer 1992 meeting of the Board it was decided that
only classroom teachers would be allowed to do the assessing. This is an
important advance in the professionalization of education. Professionalism is
often defined in terms of its members controlling access to the profession.
Teacher control combined with national certification, it is hoped, will enhance
the profession of teaching in the public's eyes. This view of the importance of
national certification was reiterated by Carole Scala, a teacher in Orlando,
Florida, who is quoted in a September 16, 1992, issue of *Education Week*: "This
[national certification] will give our profession the credibility it's lacking. The
public needs concrete proof that we're a profession."

TEACHER EDUCATION

In 1992, when the two largest teacher-training institutions in Maryland, the
University of Maryland and Towson State University, approved the abolition
of the undergraduate major in teacher education, they were following the
lead of criticism of teacher education begun in the 1980s. At the heart of this
criticism is the argument that American schools failed to meet the nation's
economic needs because of poorly trained and anti-intellectual teachers. The
cry of the 1980s was that teachers, particularly elementary school teachers,
needed a stronger academic background. Consequently, teacher-training institutions around the country began to require that elementary school teachers earn a liberal arts degree before entering a teacher-training program.
Maryland educators reacted to this reform movement by requiring a liberal
arts degree before entering a fifth-year professional training program in
education.

These important changes reflect the relationship between the goals of
education, and the content and organization of teacher training. This relationship can be found in the 1983 report that sparked the current ongoing changes
in teacher education, *A Nation at Risk*, which links a declining economy to
mediocre schools. A major cause of poor schools, the report argues, is poor
teaching training. The report complains that elementary school teacher candidates spend 41 percent of their course time in education courses. In addition,
the report expresses concern that too many "teachers are being drawn from
the bottom quarter of graduating high school and college students."

In 1992, these themes appeared again in the report of the American Association of State Colleges and Universities, *Teacher Education for the*

Twenty-First Century. But, what is different in this 1992 report as compared to *A Nation at Risk* is a requirement for "multicultural proficiency." The association's report calls for the education of "teacher-scholars," who have a strong liberal arts education with an in-depth focus on subject matter and training in a professional school of education. The teacher-scholar, according to the report, should have a knowledge of methods of instruction, human development, learning theories, affective skills, and, of course, subject matter. The requirement for proficiency in multicultural education reflects the goals for education in the 1990s. As I will discuss in Chapter 6, multicultural education is an important theme of the 1990s.

As these two reports indicate, the goals of education and social issues have a direct impact on teacher education. But, despite these pressures, there continues to be a certain logic to the requirements that must be met before a person becomes a teacher. It is logical that teachers know the subject matter they are to teach, the psychological and physical natures of those they plan to teach, the political and social structures of the institutions in which they will be teaching, the methods by which people learn, and the best methods for teaching a particular subject matter.

Most teacher-education programs include all of the above components. An introductory course on American education or educational foundations provides the future teacher with an understanding of the political and social contexts in which he or she will be working. Courses in educational psychology, human development, and theories of learning provide the prospective teacher with an understanding of the individuals to be taught. In addition, courses in methods of instruction prepare a would-be teacher to teach in particular subject-matter areas. General education requirements are designed to ensure that a teacher knows his or her subject matter well.

Teaching not only requires knowing the subject matter, the learner, and the political and social context of learning; it also involves skills that can be improved through actual practice. All teacher-education programs have some form of practice teaching that allows experienced teachers to aid prospective teachers in gaining teaching skills. Some teacher-education programs require observation periods before actual practice teaching. Other programs provide clinical experiences before or during practice teaching.

Although most teacher educators would agree that the preceding combination of knowledge and skill development should form the basic components of a teacher-education program, there are disagreements about the actual content of each component, the proportion of time that should be devoted to each area, and the additional knowledge and skills necessary for teaching. There are also general disagreements about the whole process of teacher training.

While there is a certain logic to requiring a prospective teacher to study certain courses before entering the classroom, there is still criticism of the whole process. In recent years, states have turned to teacher examinations as a means of improving the quality of teachers. As states turn to an examination system as a means of certification, the political struggle becomes extremely important. The results of that struggle can have grave consequences for both colleges and elementary and secondary schools. For instance, consider the issue of statewide testing of knowledge of subject matter. It is important to understand that knowledge is not neutral. In any discipline, competing factions claim to have the "right" interpretation or framework for understanding the subject. This is particularly true in subject areas like history, political science, sociology, economics, and psychology. It can even be true in the "hard" sciences and mathematics.

The important question regarding statewide testing is this: Who will determine the content and interpretation of the subject-matter area covered by the test? Tests by their nature can cover only part of a subject. There has to be some selection of the most important items to be covered on any examination. In addition, there has to be some value judgment regarding the correct answers to specific questions.

The issue of correct answers is particularly important if the examination is given in the form of multiple-choice questions. Multiple-choice examinations can be the most value-laden form of testing because the answers are determined solely by the authors of the examination. A student's response is limited by the specific choices on the examination and the interpretation by the author of the test as to what is the correct answer. For instance, consider the issue of inflation. Not only do economists disagree about the causes of inflation, but thinking about how to interpret the causes of inflation has shifted rapidly throughout the twentieth century. Even if you brought the leading economists in one state together, and they all agreed on important questions and the answers to those questions, there would still be the issue of whether their thinking represents the "right" thinking in the field. Those identified as "leading economists" might be no more than "established economists" in their field. Younger scholars might be preparing newer theories that would replace those held at present by the leaders. This situation is true in almost every field of academic study.

The issue becomes more important when one considers the potential consequences of a statewide examination on subject matter. First, there would probably be a tendency for colleges to teach for the examination. After all, colleges would be embarrassed if large numbers of their students failed the examination. Also, teacher candidates would want to be taught in terms of passing the examination. In other words, the content of the state examination could have a powerful influence on the content of courses in colleges and universities.

Second, if colleges begin to teach in terms of preparing students to pass a state examination, then what a college graduate knows about a field will be determined by the examination. This means that when that individual teaches, the content of his or her teaching will be strongly influenced by the state examination. This would not be a problem if knowledge were neutral and all people agreed upon what knowledge has most worth. But that is not the case, and state examinations could have a stultifying effect on the development of knowledge.

The same problem exists with any statewide evaluation of teacher performance. Educators do not agree about what makes a good teacher or about how to evaluate teaching. There are several schools of thought. Within any college of education one can find as many ideas about what constitutes good teaching as there are professors or education. What items are to be used in the evaluation of teaching performance or on examinations in pedagogy, and how answers are to be determined, is very important.

Issues involved in the control of content of evaluation are extremely important as greater centralization of teacher education occurs. It is also important to understand that this trend is the result of an attempt to improve the quality of teaching in the schools and create higher professional standards, which will result in higher status and greater rewards for teachers.

The flood of education reports that appeared in the 1980s recommended reforms that included increased selectivity of teacher-education candidates, more emphasis on general academic training, and incentives to attract more qualified candidates to teacher-education programs. *A Nation at Risk* recommended simply that "persons preparing to teach should be required to meet high educational standards, to demonstrate an aptitude for teaching, and to demonstrate competence in an academic discipline." In addition, the report urged that colleges of education be judged on the basis of the performance of their candidates and that grants and loans should be made available to attract outstanding students to teaching. These general recommendations were not accompanied by any specific plans for action.

The report of the Task Force on Education for Economic Growth, *Action for Excellence,* was also general in its recommendations. This report was intended to serve as a guide for governors in planning the educational policies of their particular states. The report called for financial aid to attract the most able people to teaching. More important, the report stated that the improvement of the academic knowledge of teachers and their teaching skills would require "a substantially restructured and renewed curriculum for teacher training, which would include the management and application of technology." In a general plea for action, the report called upon governors to improve the academic quality of teacher-education curriculum.

The Carnegie Foundation for the Advancement of Teaching's report, *High School,* provided more specific recommendations for carrying out the general improvement of teacher education. The author of the report, Ernest Boyer, recommended that the first two years of college training be devoted to the study of a core of common learning. The responsibility for this core curriculum would be in the hands of the liberal arts faculty. Admission to a teacher-education program would occur in the junior year of college, and admission would require a "B" average or better plus strong recommendations from two professors. The teacher-education program would be three years long, with the first two years (the student's junior and senior years) devoted to completing a major in an academic discipline and to classroom observation.

After studying a core curriculum and completing an academic major the prospective teacher would take teacher-education courses. Boyer is aware of the criticism directed at education courses. He writes, "While many speak disparagingly of teacher-education courses, we conclude there is important information uniquely relevant to teachers." Boyer believes that four areas of study should be part of the teacher-education curriculum. The first area is what the report calls "schooling in America." This course would be devoted to the history of education and current issues in education. The other three areas would deal with "learning theory and research," "teaching of writing," and "the use of technology." Boyer writes that "all teacher education students should study theories of learning, the ways teachers teach and students learn, and examine also the findings of current psychological and physiological research bearing on these themes." Boyer's emphasis on prospective teachers learning to teach writing reflects the general concern of the report with language instruction. The report argues that writing is not only an essential skill for self-expression, but is also an important means of teaching critical thinking. Boyer believes that all teachers should be prepared to teach students how to write better. Also prospective teachers should study educational technology, including computers, as a means of significantly improving classroom instruction.

In addition to the course work, Boyer recommends that the fifth year include classroom observation and practice teaching. He recognizes that teaching ability is dependent upon the type of experience that can only be gained in practice and in working with other experienced teachers, which is why he believes that practice teaching should be done with a team of teachers. The report also recommends that fifth-year teacher-education students should meet with outstanding arts and sciences "scholar-teachers" in a series of common learning seminars to "relate the knowledge of their fields to a contemporary political or social theme." Boyer expresses the hope that this seminar will help prospective teachers to relate to other disciplines and be able to teach a common core of learning to students in the schools.

A Nation Prepared: Teachers for the 21st Century, discussed in detail in the previous section, links raising standards in teacher education to increasing the status of teaching and, as a result, attracting more capable students to education programs. Basic to the report's program of restructuring teacher education is the replacement of undergraduate programs in education with graduate programs in education. While the report states that the national certification board will not establish national standards for teacher education, the authors do admit that their proposed evaluation techniques and standards for certification will have a significant effect on teacher education.

In general, *A Nation Prepared* advocates an undergraduate program devoted to a broad liberal education and a thorough study of the subject or subjects the student plans to teach. In keeping with the general trend toward a core curriculum, the report recommends an undergraduate curriculum that would provide rigorous study of history, government, science, literature, and the arts. The authors argue that elementary teachers need the same strong academic background as high school teachers because they have equal responsibility to impart our common culture and heritage.

Professional courses in education would be provided at the graduate level in a master-in-teaching degree program, to give teachers information about techniques of teaching, research on teaching, human development, and different learning styles. In addition, teachers seeking advanced certification would study philosophy of education, policies in education, and techniques of measurement.

The ideal two-year master-in-teaching degree program as outlined by the report would begin with a semester of courses on methods of instruction. During the second semester, students would perform an internship in teaching at a school with a diverse student population while taking several other graduate courses in education. In the following summer, students would take a full load of courses building on the teaching experience of the internship. Finally, students would spend the second year in residence at a school working under the guidance of a lead teacher.

The recommendations of the Task Force on Teaching as a Profession are guided by a medical school. The second year of graduate work in education places the student in residence at school, as a medical student spends a year in residence in a hospital. In fact, the report recommends that identification of *clinical schools* that would be analogous to teaching hospitals. These clinical schools would be models of the type of collegial environment advocated by the report.

Also recommending abolishment of the undergraduate education degree is the 1986 Holmes Group report, *Tomorrow's Teachers*. Originally organized in 1983 as a coalition of twenty-three deans from major research institutions in education, the Holmes Group expanded by 1987 to include representatives of ninety-four leading universities. It advocates a strong undergraduate education in the subject-matter areas each individual plans to teach. Graduate training in education, the report proposes, should focus on subject-matter-oriented studies of teaching and learning that integrate research on cognitive psychology.

As many teacher education programs rush to fifth-year models, many states are adopting plans for alternative forms of certification that could eliminate all accredited teacher education. As discussed in the previous section, the National Board for Professional Teaching Standards in 1989 decided not to require teacher education as a requirement for certification. In the 1980s, New Jersey adopted a plan in which state licensing would require a college degree, experience gained through teaching, and training programs offered in local school districts. This plan meant that prospective teachers did not have to take courses in an organized college-based teacher-education program.

The arguments for alternative routes to licensing that would bypass teacher-education programs are, in part, based on a traditional attitude that educational training is anti-intellectual. In addition, it is argued that many talented people are kept out of teaching careers because they do not want to subject themselves to education courses. And, of course, alternative routes to teaching might increase the supply of teachers and decrease teachers' salaries.

According to the Center for Policy Research in Education's report, "State Education Reform in the 1980s," by 1986, twenty-three states offered alternative routes to certification. Most of these were designed to facilitate the entry into teaching of liberal arts graduates. In the words of the report, "The proliferation of alternative routes to certification, however, may signal a smaller role for teacher colleges in educating prospective teachers."

Teachers' unions fear the possibility of alternative routes to certification reducing salaries. As mentioned previously, this is why the National Education Association objected to the National Board for Professional Teaching Standards dropping the prerequisite of graduation from an accredited teacher-training program for gaining national certification. But to fully understand this issue and the direction of the teaching profession, one must understand the workings of teachers' unions and teacher politics. This is the topic of the next chapter.

TEACHER AS RESEARCHER AND SCHOLAR

When the report *Teacher Education for the Twenty-First Century* calls for the education of "teacher-scholars," it is reflecting a current trend in the professional development of teachers. The concept of *teacher as researcher* and *teacher as scholar* refers to the active research by teachers into their own classroom practices. In the past, teachers were often treated as passive objects by college professors who believed they could tell teachers the best means of improving their teaching. In addition, there was a tendency to promote "teacher-proof" classroom materials. Teacher-proof materials were to be so highly structured that they could not be misused by poor teachers. Basically, teacher-proof material turned the teacher into a technician whose major function was to implement someone else's teaching methods and materials.

In contrast to teacher-proof material, the model of teacher as researcher and scholar assumes that classroom teachers are the best persons to do research on classroom methods and materials. In addition, the model assumes that part of the satisfaction of teaching involves the development of new methods of instruction and new classroom materials. In this model, the teacher assumes the responsibility of judging his or her own teaching methods, experimenting with and evaluating new methods, and actively exploring new methods of instruction by working with other teachers and seeking advice from university researchers and scholarly publications. The model also assumes that teachers are scholars of the material they teach. Through their own scholarly pursuits, teachers develop their own classroom material rather than rely upon others.

One of the arguments supporting the idea of teacher as researcher and scholar is that teachers are the best source of information about teaching and that their shared experiences provide a method of improving instruction. In *Creating Spaces and Finding Voices: Teachers Collaborating for Empowerment*, Janet Miller provides an example of the importance of teachers relying on their own experience and abilities to develop teaching strategies, or what Janet Miller calls "finding their voices." In the book, which is a narrative about a group of teachers exploring their own experiences in teaching, Miller tells the story of "The Carton of Knowledge." In this story, a new teacher of a college course receives a carton of lesson plans and classroom material from the previous teacher of the course. Initially, the new teacher unpacked the carton and tried to replicate the teaching of the previous teacher. After the teacher's initial attempts to use the material from the carton, she realized that her perspective on the course was quite different from that of the previous teacher. In addition, she was angry with herself for so willingly trying to follow the previous teacher's methods rather than expressing herself through her own materials and methods. She realized that most teachers and students are treated as passive objects who receive their wisdom from others. But passivity leads to poor teaching because teachers lose enthusiasm and creative energy, and their understanding of the subject matter is clouded by the imposition of someone else's ideas.

The development of the model of teacher as researcher and scholar depends on teachers sharing experience. For instance, in *Teacher Lore: Learning from Our Own Experience*, teachers analyze their own classroom experiences and share them with other teachers. The editors of the book, William Schubert and William Ayers, argue that most teachers reflect on their own experiences and constantly monitor their teaching. Through this reflection, teachers are constantly improving their instructional practices and classroom materials. It is this active research on the part of teachers, they argue, that can provide the basis for improving the teaching of all teachers. The key to this process is giving teachers confidence in their own work and the opportunity to share it with others.

CONCLUSION

The profession of teaching has changed greatly since the nineteenth-century model of teachers as paragons of morality. The current emphasis on teacher as researcher and scholar reflects the growing control of the profession by teachers. Teachers are no longer passive objects; they are actively involved in improving their professional status and in improving teaching methods. As I will discuss in the next chapter, an important factor in current trends in professionalism is the power of the two teachers' unions.

EXERCISES

1. Students should interview teachers regarding the rewards and dissatisfactions they gain from teaching. Compare the results of these interviews with a classroom survey on why students want to be teachers.
2. Working in small groups, students should devise their ideal plan for the professionalization of teaching. In developing this plan, the following

questions should be considered: Should there be local, state, or national certification of teachers? Who should control entrance into the profession? Should appropriate college courses in education be a requirement for entering the profession? Should national or state examinations be required of teachers? If examinations are required, then who should determine the content of the examinations? Should there be moral standards for entrance into the profession?

3. Working in small groups, students should devise an ideal curriculum for teacher education. Included in the discussion of this curriculum should be a consideration of whether or not education courses should be taught in a fifth-year program. Students should compare their ideal program to the one currently offered by their college.

SUGGESTED READINGS AND WORKS CITED IN CHAPTER

Blood, Michael. "Teacher Salaries." *Compuserve Executive News Service*, no. 1992 (27 August 1992). This article provides a summary of teachers' salaries for the 1991–1992 school year.

Borrowman, Merle. *The Liberal and Technical in Teacher Education: A Historical Survey of American Thought.* New York: Teachers College Press, 1956. This is the classic study of the debates that have surrounded the development of teacher education in the United States. The book provides the best introduction to the history and issues regarding teacher education.

Boyer, Ernest L. *High School.* New York: Harper and Row, 1983. This study conducted for the Carnegie Foundation for the Advancement of Teaching contains important descriptions of the work life of teachers and recommendations for the reform of teaching.

Bradley, Ann. "N.E.A. Assails Board's Policy on Prerequisites for Certification." *Education Week* (17 January 1990): 1, 11. This is an example of the National Education Association's concerns about alternative routes to teacher certification as supported by the National Board for Professional Teaching Standards.

————. "Pilot Test Offers a Glimpse of Board's Teacher Assessment." *Education Week* (16 September 1992): 1, 16. This article discusses the method of assessment used by the National Board for Professional Teaching Standards for English teachers in 1993–1994.

————. "Revamp Teacher Recruitment, Training, Continuing Education, Colleges Urged." *Education Week* (2 December 1992): 8. This article summarizes the report of the American Association of State Colleges and Universities, *Teacher Education for the Twenty-First Century.*

Elsbree, Willard S. *The American Teacher: Evolution of a Profession in a Democracy.* New York: American Book, 1939. Still the best history of the profession of teaching in the United States. Unfortunately it traces the professionalization of teaching only to the 1930s.

Goodlad, John. *A Place Called School.* New York: McGraw-Hill, 1984. This detailed study of American schools contains surveys and recommendations about the profession of teaching.

Holmes Group. *Tomorrow's Teachers*. East Lansing, Mich.: Holmes Group, 1986. Report on restructuring teacher education and the profession issued by an organization composed of leading research institutions in education.

Lortie, Dan. *Schoolteacher: A Sociological Study*. Chicago: University of Chicago Press, 1975. The most complete study of the social interactions and world of the American teacher.

Miller, Janet. *Creating Spaces and Finding Voices: Teachers Collaborating for Empowerment*. White Plains: Longman, Inc., 1990. This book explores the role of teachers as researchers.

National Commission on Excellence in Education. *A Nation at Risk*. Washington, D.C.: U.S. Government Printing Office, 1983. This important report contains recommendations for improving the quality of teachers and teacher education.

Olson, Lynn. "In North Carolina, Career-Ladder Plan Nears a Crossroads." *Education Week* (1 February 1989): 1, 14. This is an example of the criticism made by teachers' unions of career ladders.

"Panel Endorses Plan to Revamp Md.'s Teacher Education Programs." *Education Week* (16 December 1992): 2. Announcement of approval to eliminate the undergraduate teacher-education program in Maryland public colleges and replace it with a fifth-year program.

Phi Delta Kappan Special Issue: Reform in Teacher Education (October 1980). Articles by a wide range of authors on issues in teacher education.

Powell, Arthur, and Theodore Sizer. "Changing Conceptions of the Professor of Education." In James Counelis, ed., *To Be a Phoenix: The Education Professoriate*. Bloomington, Ill.: Phi Delta Kappa, 1969.

Richardson, Joanna. "Poll Finds Teachers' Relations with Parents Unsatisfactory." *Education Week* (16 December 1992): 10. This article reports the Harris survey on teachers' attitudes, particularly regarding the rewards and dissatisfactions of the job.

Schubert, William H., and William C. Ayers, eds. *Teacher Lore: Learning from Our Own Experience*. White Plains: Longman, Inc., 1992. This is a collection of analyses by teachers of their own teaching.

Sizer, Theodore. *Horace's Compromise: The Dilemma of the American High School*. Boston: Houghton Mifflin, 1984. This study of the American high school contains important insights into the problems encountered by teachers.

"State Education Reform in the 1980s." *CPRE Policy Briefs*. New Brunswick, N.J.: Center for Policy Research in Education, 1990. This reports provides a summary of information regarding the growth of alternative routes to certification.

Task Force on Education for Economic Growth. *Action for Excellence*. Denver: Education Commission of the States, 1983. This report by governors and corporate leaders contains recommendations that have influenced the actions of state governments regarding teachers.

Task Force on Teaching as a Profession. *A Nation Prepared: Teachers for the 21st Century*. New York: Carnegie Corporation of New York, 1986. Important report calling for the restructuring of the teacher profession and the establishment of a national certification board.

U.S. Office of Education. *Japanese Education Today*. Washington, D.C., 1987.

CHAPTER 3

Teachers' Unions and Teacher Politics

"We have for the first time, released all of our resources . . . both staff, as well as monetary, to do our member-to-member campaign on behalf of the Clinton-Gore team," stated Debra S. DeLee, the director of government relations for the National Education Association, in an interview in the October 14, 1992, issue of *Education Week*. Traditionally, the National Education Association (NEA), along with its rival union the American Federation of Teachers (AFT), supports candidates from the Democratic Party. During the 1992 presidential campaign, every state affiliate of the NEA assigned one person to coordinate the Clinton-Gore campaign, and seven people to help union members get out and vote for the Democratic ticket. In addition, Jerry L. Carruthers, a government-relations specialist for the NEA, spent several hours daily meeting with campaign leaders at the Clinton headquarters. The AFT assigned ten of the union's thirty-five national organizers to work for the Clinton-Gore ticket. In addition, some local affiliates paid for substitute teachers so that their political directors could devote their time to the Clinton-Gore campaign. One group of AFT teachers called the "Bush-Whackers" did their bit for the Clinton-Gore ticket by recording a cassette of anti-Bush songs titled "Ambush at the White House."

With the election of Bill Clinton, the NEA and the AFT hoped for a new day in the White House. As Maurice Berube points out in *Teacher Politics: The Influence of Unions*, both unions had a difficult time with the two Republican administrations. A story told him by the Washington lobbyist of the NEA compared the treatment of the two unions by the two major political parties. During the years that Democratic President Jimmy Carter occupied the White House, Dale Lestina, manager of NEA lobbying, would walk the six blocks from the NEA headquarters to the White House for early morning breakfasts with representatives of the administration. The NEA played a major role in President Carter's election campaign. In contrast, during the Republican administrations of Presidents Ronald Reagan and George Bush, telephone calls to the White House went unanswered and lobbyists from the NEA were not invited to frequent early morning breakfasts. The NEA had campaigned for the Democratic opponents of both Reagan and Bush.

The story illustrates the importance of national politics for teachers' unions. Both teachers' unions, the AFT and the NEA, actively participate in national elections. They work for both presidential and congressional candidates. Over the last two decades, a majority of their support has been given to candidates from the Democratic party. This has created a split between the two national political parties over teachers' unions. In general, Republicans tend to oppose the work of teachers' unions, while Democrats tend to be supportive. Of course, like other aspects of American politics these alliances can vary from state to state.

Besides working in election campaigns, both unions have full-time Washington lobbyists who try to ensure that federal legislation does not jeopardize the welfare of teachers. Also, both unions maintain lobbyists at the state level and work for candidates to the state legislature. At the local level, teachers' unions have increasingly supported and campaigned for candidates in local school board elections.

The involvement of teachers' unions in national, state, and local politics has made them a powerful political force. Their power may be increasing as local units of the unions begin to merge. In 1969, the local affiliates of the AFT and NEA in Los Angeles created the first merged local in the nation. In 1989, the second merged local was created when local affiliates of the AFT and NEA combined to create the United Educators of San Francisco. If the two unions were to merge at the national level, they would produce one of the most powerful organizations in American politics. But the history and politics of the two unions do not indicate that a merger will occur in the near future.

In the next two sections, I describe the differences in history and political style of the two unions. Following these descriptions, a case study of a president of a local teachers' union will provide an example of union activities in a school district. The chapter will conclude with a discussion of current trends in teacher politics.

THE NATIONAL EDUCATION ASSOCIATION (NEA)

Founded in 1857, the NEA adopted the goal of nationalizing the work of state education associations. This would be one of its major functions in the history of American education. The letter inviting representatives to the founding meeting states, "Believing that what has been accomplished for the states by state associations may be done for the whole country by a National Association, we, the undersigned, invite our fellow-teachers throughout the United States to assemble in Philadelphia. . . ."

The 1857 meeting in Philadelphia gave birth to an organization that in the nineteenth and early-twentieth centuries had major influence over the shaping of American schools and contributed to the nationalizing of the American school system. From the platform of its conventions and the work of its committees came curriculum proposals and policy statements that were adopted from coast to coast. Until the 1960s the work of the NEA tended to be dominated by school superintendents, college professors, and administrators. These educational leaders would take the proposals of the NEA back to their local communities for discussion and possible adoption. The NEA thus had an important nationalizing function through the sharing of information between school leaders from different parts of the country and through its recommendations and proposals.

Examples of the work of the NEA include its major role in the shaping of the modern high school. In 1892 the NEA formed the Committee of Ten on Secondary School Studies, under the leadership of Charles Eliot, the president of Harvard University. The Committee of Ten appointed nine subcommittees with a total membership of 100 to determine the future of the American high school. The membership of these committees reflected the domination of the organization by school administrators and representatives of higher education: Fifty-three were college presidents or professors, twenty-three were headmasters of private schools, and the rest were superintendents and representatives from teacher-training institutions. The work of the Committee of Ten set the stage for the creation in 1913 of the NEA Commission on the Reorganization of Secondary Education, which in 1918 issued its epoch-making report, *Cardinal Principles of Secondary Education.* This report urged the creation of comprehensive high schools offering a variety of curricula, as opposed to the establishment of separate high schools offering a single curriculum, such as college preparatory, vocational, and commercial. This report became the major formative document of the modern high school.

The NEA influenced the standardization of teacher training in the United States. The Normal Department of the NEA began surveying the status of institutions for teacher education in 1886, and debates began within the organization about the nature of teacher education. The official historian of the NEA, Edgar B. Wesley, stated in his *NEA: The First Hundred Years:* "By 1925 the training of teachers was rather systematically standardized." The work of the Normal Department of the NEA can claim a large share of the credit for this standardization.

NEA conventions and meetings also became a central arena for the discussion of curriculum changes in elementary and secondary schools. During the 1920s and 1930s large numbers of surveys, studies, yearbooks, and articles were published. In 1924 the Department of Superintendence began issuing what were to be successive yearbooks on various aspects of the curriculum at various grade levels. In 1943 the Society for Curriculum Study merged with the NEA Department of Supervisors and Directors of Instruction to form an enlarged department called the Association for Supervision and Curriculum Development (ASCD). ASCD is still recognized as the major professional organization for the discussion of curriculum issues.

After the passage of the National Defense Education Act in 1958, the NEA's leadership role in the determination of national educational policy was greatly reduced as the federal government became the major springboard for national policy. The NEA became an organization whose central focus was teacher welfare and government lobbying. This shift was a result of several developments: the emergence of the leadership role of the federal government, demands within the NEA for more emphasis on teacher welfare, greater democratic control of the organization, and the success of the AFT in winning collective bargaining for its members (thus serving as a model for the NEA).

In 1962, the activities of the NEA underwent a dramatic transformation when it launched a program for collective negotiations. This meant that local affiliates would attempt to achieve collective-bargaining agreements with local boards of education. This development completely changed the nature of local organizations and required a rewriting of local constitutions to include collective bargaining. Up to this point in time, many local education associations had been controlled by local school administrators, who used the local organizations to convey policies determined by the board and administration. Collective bargaining reversed this situation and turned the local affiliates into organizations that told boards and administrators what teachers themselves wanted.

Collective bargaining created a new relationship between locals of the NEA and local boards of education. Traditionally, local units of the NEA might plead for the interests of their members, but they most often simply helped to carry out policies of local school boards and administrators. Teachers bargained individually with the school board over salary and working conditions. With collective bargaining, teachers voted for an organization to represent their demands before the school board. Once selected as a representative of the local teachers, the organization would negotiate with the school board over working conditions and salaries. Many school boards were caught by surprise when their usually compliant local of the NEA suddenly demanded higher wages and better working conditions for all teachers.

The NEA's early approach to collective bargaining differed from that of the union-oriented AFT, which had pioneered collective bargaining in education. The NEA claimed it was involved in professional negotiating and not in union collective bargaining. Professional negotiation, according to the NEA, would remove negotiation procedures from labor precedents and laws and would resort to state educational associations, rather than those of labor, to mediate or resolve conflicts that could not be settled locally.

All pretense of the NEA not being a union ended in the 1970s, when the NEA joined the Coalition of American Public Employees (CAPE). CAPE is a nonprofit corporation composed of the National Education Association; American Federation of State, County, and Municipal Employees; AFL-CIO; National Treasury Employees Union; Physicians National Housestaff Association; and American Nurses Association. These organizations represent about four million public employees. The stated purpose of CAPE is "to provide a means of marshalling and coordinating the legislative, legal, financial, and public relations resources of the member organizations in matters of common concern." The most important of these matters "is supporting legislation to provide collective-bargaining rights to all public employees, including teachers."

By the 1980s, support of collective-bargaining legislation became one of many legislative goals of the NEA; the organization by this time was also directing a great deal of its energies to lobbying for legislation and support of political candidates. The turning point for the NEA was its endorsement of Jimmy Carter in the 1976 presidential election. This was the first time the NEA had supported a presidential candidate. After this initial involvement, the NEA expanded its activity to support candidates in primary elections. In 1980, the NEA worked actively in the primaries to assure the victory of Jimmy Carter over Edward Kennedy for the Democratic nomination. In 1984 and 1988, the NEA committed itself to the support of Democratic candidates for the White House.

At its 1992 convention, NEA took a strong stand against the increasing use of standardized testing mandated by government. The 1992 NEA resolution states, "The National Education Association opposes standardized testing that is mandated by a state or national authority." One traditional objection to mandated standardized tests is that teachers often teach to the test. In contrast, as I will discuss in the next section, the NEA's rival, the AFT, adopted in 1992 a policy statement that supported the idea of teaching to the test. In addition, NEA members strongly objected to the use of standardized tests to compare schools and school districts.

At its 1992 convention, the NEA called upon the federal government to provide more aid to local schools. In addition, the union announced its support of early childhood education programs from birth through age 8 and asked the federal government to implement fully funded programs through the public schools. Of course, early childhood programs operated by public schools would undercut efforts in the private sector and bring early childhood teachers under union contracts. Also, the NEA urged its locals to "seek an optimum class size of fifteen students in regular programs and a proportionately lower number in programs for students with exceptional needs." Small class sizes would improve the working conditions of teachers and, according to the union, improve student achievement. And, the NEA called for universal health care for children.

The NEA also took a strong stand on the issue of tracking. As I will discuss in more detail in Chapter 4, tracking refers to separating students into different academic curricula. For instance, high school students might be placed in a college bound track, general education track, or vocational track. One of the major criticisms of tracking is that it reflects socioeconomic and racial grouping. Children from poor families and racial minorities tend to be placed more often in vocational programs than children from wealthy parents who are more often placed in college bound tracks. The NEA resolution states, "The National Education Association believes that the use of discriminatory academic tracking based on socioeconomic status, race, or sex must be eliminated in all public school settings."

The evolution of the NEA from an association of educational organizations to a militant teachers' union is an important chapter in the political history of the United States. In recent years the NEA has emerged as the more socially concerned and militant of the two teachers' unions. By the 1980s, the NEA had become so politically active that its rival the AFT was accusing it of trying to be a political "kingmaker." In fact, the AFT claimed it had more interest in educational standards than the NEA. As I will discuss in the next section, the historical irony of the AFT's claim is that it originated as an organization representing the broad political and social interests of the working class. By the 1990s, the AFT lost most of its early labor union radicalism.

THE AMERICAN FEDERATION OF TEACHERS (AFT)

Unlike the NEA's origins as a national policy-making organization, the American Federation of Teachers (AFT) began in the struggle by female grade school teachers for an adequate pension law in Illinois. The first union local, the Chicago Teachers Federation, was formed in 1897 under the leadership of Catherine Goggin and Margaret Haley. Its early fights centered on pensions and teacher salaries. As a result of its success in winning salary increases, its membership increased to 2,500 by the end of its first year. In 1902, with the urging of famous settlement-house reformer Jane Addams, the Chicago Teachers Federation joined the Chicago Federation of Labor, which placed it under the broad umbrella of the American Federation of Labor (AFL).

From its beginnings, the AFT placed teacher-welfare issues and improving public education in the more general context of the labor movement in the United States. In an interview titled "The School-Teacher Unionized" in the November 1905 issue of the *Educational Review*, Margaret Haley declared: "We expect by affiliation with labor to arouse the workers and the whole people, through the workers, to the dangers confronting the public schools from the same interests and tendencies that are undermining the foundations of our democratic republic." Those "same interests" referred to in Haley's speech were big business organizations, against whom Haley felt both labor and educators were struggling. The early union movement was based on the belief that there was unity between the educators' struggle to gain more financial support for the schools from big business and labor's struggle with the same interests to win collective bargaining rights. Haley went on to state, "It is necessary to make labor a constructive force in society, or it will be a destructive force. If the educational question could be understood by the labor men, and the labor question by the educators, both soon would see they are working to the same end, and should work together."

Margaret Haley's comments highlighted the union's efforts to create mutually supportive roles between teachers and organized labor. On the one hand, teachers were to work for the interests of workers by fighting for better schools and working to remove antilabor material from the classroom. Teachers would fight to provide the best education for workers' children, while organized labor would provide the resources of its organization to support the teachers' struggle for improved working conditions and greater financial support for the schools. In addition, the type of education received by children in the schools would provide children with the economic and political knowledge needed to continue the work of the union movement, and teachers could also share their knowledge with the adult members of the labor movement. Teachers would also increase their political and economic knowledge through their association with the labor movement.

In December 1912, the newly established magazine of the union movement, the *American Teacher*, issued a statement of the beliefs of the growing union movement in education. First, the statement argued that the improvement of American education depended on arousing teachers to realize that "their professional and social standing is far too low to enable them to produce effective results in teaching." Second, it was necessary for teachers to study the relation of education "to social progress, and to understand some of the important social and economic movements going on in the present-day world." Third, it was believed that teachers could use their experience in teaching to adjust education to the needs of modern living. Fourth, in one of the earliest declarations for the end of sexism in education, the statement called for high-quality teaching "without sex-antagonism."

In 1915, union locals from Chicago and Gary, Indiana, met and officially formed the American Federation of Teachers. In 1916 this group, along with locals from New York, Pennsylvania, Oklahoma, and Washington, D.C., were accepted into the American Federation of Labor as the American Federation of Teachers. At the presentation ceremony, the head of the AFL, Samuel Gompers, welcomed the AFT to "the fold and the bond of unity and fraternity of the organized labor movement of our Republic. We earnestly hope . . . that it may . . . give and receive mutual sympathy and support which can be properly exerted for the betterment of all who toil and give service—aye, for all humanity."

It was not until 1944 that the AFT exercised any organizational control over a local school system. In 1944, the AFT local in Cicero, Illinois, signed the first collective-bargaining contract with a board of education. The form of the contract was that of a regular labor-union contract. It recognized the local as the sole bargaining agent of the teachers and listed pay schedules and grievance procedures. At the annual convention of the AFT in 1946 a committee was assigned to study collective bargaining and its application to school management. In addition, material was to be collected from trade unions on the education of shop stewards and union practices. With the introduction of collective bargaining, the AFT entered a new stage in its development.

The involvement of the AFT in collective bargaining led naturally to the question of teacher strikes. Since its founding, the AFT had had a no-strike policy. In 1946 the use of the strike as a means of supporting teachers' demands became a major issue at the annual convention. Those supporting the use of the strike argued it was the only means available to arouse an apathetic citizenry to the problems in American education. It was also the only meaningful leverage teachers had against local school systems. AFT members who favored retention of the no-strike policy argued that teachers were in a public service profession and that work stoppage was a violation of public trust. In addition, it was argued that a strike deprived children of an education and was counter to the democratic ideal of a child's right to an education.

The AFT maintained its no-strike policy in the face of growing militancy among individual locals. In 1947 the Buffalo, New York, Teachers Federation declared a strike for higher salaries. The strike was considered at the time the worst teacher work stoppage in the history of the country. Other local unions supported the strikers, with local drivers delivering only enough fuel to the schools to keep the pipes from freezing. The Buffalo strike was important because it served as a model for action by other teachers around the country. School superintendents, school board associations, and state superintendents of education condemned these actions by local teachers. The national AFT maintained its no-strike policy and adopted a posture of aid and comfort but not official sanction. As William Edward Eaton states in his *The American Federation of Teachers, 1916–1961*, "Even with a no-strike policy, the AFT had emerged as the leader in teacher work stoppages."

The event that sparked the rapid growth of teacher militancy in the 1960s, and contributed to the NEA's rapid acceptance of collective bargaining, was the formation of the New York City local of the AFT, the United Federation of Teachers (UFT). In the late 1950s, the AFT decided to concentrate on organizing teachers in New York City and to provide special funds for that purpose. After the organization of the UFT in 1960, there was a vote for a strike over the issues of a dues check-off plan, the conducting of a collective-bargaining election, sick pay for substitutes, 50-minute lunch periods for teachers, and changes in the salary schedules. On November 7, 1960, the UFT officially went on strike against the New York City school system. The union declared the strike effective when 15,000 of the city's 39,000 teachers did not report to school and 7,500 teachers joined picket lines around the schools. In the spring of 1961 the UFT won a collective-bargaining agreement with the school system and became one of the largest and most influential locals within the AFT.

During the 1960s, teachers increasingly accepted the idea of collective bargaining and the use of the strike. This was reflected in the rapid growth of membership in the AFT. In 1966 the membership of the AFT was 125,421. By 1981 the membership had more than quadrupled to 580,000. This increased membership plus the increased militancy of the NEA heralded a new era in the relationship between American teachers' organizations and the managers of American education. With the coming of age of the strike and collective bargaining, teachers in the NEA and AFT proved themselves willing to fight for their own welfare and the welfare of American public schools.

While the AFT did not support the Reagan and Bush administrations in the 1980s and early 1990s, they did adopt the view that one of the major purposes of education is to improve the ability of U.S. companies to compete in world markets. This goal is reflected in the AFT's policy statement, "U.S.

Education: The Task Before Us," adopted at its 1992 annual convention. The policy statement opens with a call for the better education of "citizens of a democratic society" and "productive workers of a world-competitive economy."

To accomplish these goals, the policy statement outlines an agenda for the future improvement of U.S. schools. First on the list is the creation of new types of schools, including the adoption of school-based management. As I discuss in more detail in Chapter 7, school-based management would involve teachers sharing power with administrators in the management of schools. Of course, this form of increased teacher power is an important item for the union. In addition, the statement calls for the exploration of new methods of instruction and the investigation of alternative forms of schools.

With regard to traditional schools, the union calls for less interference from outside lay people, such as boards of education. In other words, as I will elaborate on in Chapter 7, the union wants more control of schools by professional educators. The statement also supports the creation of a national curriculum, national tests, and examining new ways of separating students into different curricula. With regard to the issue of standardized tests, the union argues that with the creation of curriculum-based and challenging tests, "'teaching to the test' is a constructive way to spend class time." As I previously mentioned, the NEA is strongly opposed to mandated standardized tests.

And finally, the AFT's policy statement calls for more spending on education by pointing out that other countries spend more on elementary and secondary education than the United States. Recognition is also given to the wide disparities in income in the United States and, as I will discuss in Chapter 4, the extreme differences in spending per student between school districts. In addition, since health is an important factor in student achievement, the policy statement supports a national health care system.

While many of the policies in "U.S. Education: The Task Before Us" reflect current concerns such as national standards and tests, alternative forms of education, and a better work force, there are several policies that reflect traditional union interests. Obviously, a call for shared management in schools and for more spending on education reflects the traditional concern with giving teachers more power and improving the financial condition of education. While specific policies of the AFT will change over time, the real constants in union activities are the protection of teachers' rights, pay, and working conditions, and increasing union power and membership.

A CASE STUDY OF THE PRESIDENT OF A LOCAL TEACHERS' UNION

I wrote this case study after spending two months tagging along with Tom Mooney, president of the Cincinnati Federation of Teachers (AFT), as he worked in the union's offices and visited schools. He is a politically successful union president having continuously held his office from 1979 into the 1990s.

My case study portrays the political world of a local union leader who must spend time convincing teachers that the union can provide better wages, benefits, and working conditions. The sketch gives a picture of the internal political life of a teachers' union and the ways in which unions become involved in a variety of political activities.

Tom Mooney describes his youth as being propelled by political activism and a compulsion to become self-supporting. He breezed through high school and college and in 1974, at the relatively young age of 20, earned his diploma from Antioch College. During the period of his attendance, Antioch College was known for its politically oriented student body's support of social causes. While at Antioch, Mooney worked for the Farm Workers Union. As Mooney describes his entry into teaching at the age of 20, it was a classic case of being pointed toward a classroom and having to sink or swim. His college work did not prepare him for the realities of an inner-city junior high, nor did he receive much help from the school administration. He even had a difficult time understanding the language of the African-American students, who made up the majority of the school's population.

With hindsight, it seems natural for a young teacher like Mooney to become interested in teacher union activities. He claims that his major motivation at the time was low teacher salaries and the fact that the school system had fouled up the operation of the schools. Mooney argues that school systems have traditionally expected teachers to dress and act like members of the middle class but they have never provided a high enough salary to allow a teacher to achieve a middle-class lifestyle. From the perspective of a young inner-city teacher, the school system failed to provide decent working conditions and the services and supplies required to provide education to inner-city children.

His movement through the union organization was as swift as his high school and college career. During his first year of teaching, he had a chance to experience briefly a union position when he served as building representative for one week. The following year he transferred to another junior high school and joined the union's Educational Policy Committee. While on the committee, he wrote a critique of the superintendent's five-year plan for the school system. Mooney's report was adopted by the union as their official position. He became an area coordinator with the responsibility of coordinating union representatives from the various schools. When the Cincinnati Federation of Teachers conducted a major successful strike in 1977, he served on the union's bargaining team.

In 1979, when the president decided not to run for reelection, Mooney launched a campaign for the position. The major parts of his platform were building a united bargaining council and influencing school board elections. A united bargaining council, which was later achieved, would bring together other workers in the system (like school office workers) with teachers so that a united front could be presented to the Board of Education. As I will discuss later, attempting to influence school board elections is part of Mooney's general concern with increasing teacher power.

Mooney won the election in 1979 and he is still president at the time of the publication of this book. After the election, Mooney moved into the union offices in a building occupied by other trade unions. Mooney's office reflects a dedication to trade unionism and progressive politics. On the wall directly in front of his desk hangs a picture of union leader Big Jim Larken giving a speech to a group of workers in Dublin in 1913. On the top of a bookcase sits a picture of Mooney with Senator Edward Kennedy. A picket sign from the successful 1977 strike hangs on the wall.

Mooney sees improving working conditions for teachers and increasing teacher power as his most important job. To understand his position on teacher power, one must also understand his general philosophy with regard to social action. He believes that the key to social action is convincing people that they have the power to make a change and a difference. This means overcoming the apathy and sense of powerlessness that pervade modern societies. One way of convincing people that they can make a difference is to engage them in collective activity where they learn that working with others can bring about social and political change.

Mooney is concerned that teachers overcome a sense of powerlessness that has tended to dominate the profession. This can be accomplished by teachers learning through the collective work of the union that they can make a difference in the control and operation of a school system. This does not mean that the teachers' union can leap immediately into major attempts to exert control over the system. What must first take place is the gradual unfolding of awareness that greater influence is possible through collective action. One of the things Mooney claims he has learned since being in office is that things take time and that social and political goals require hard work and incremental steps.

This belief in social change through collective action based on incremental steps and a growing awareness of ability to affect social change is in Mooney's goals for teacher unionism. He feels that the union has accomplished major gains in salaries and working conditions, but that it needs to exert more control over educational policy. This he believes is the next stage in the gradual unfolding of "teacher power." Rather than stressing wage issues, the current union negotiating items center around policy issues.

Regarding the ultimate goals for teachers' unions, Mooney would like to see Teacher Building Committees sharing equal decision-making power with the principal. As I will discuss in Chapter 7, this is a trend in school organization. On a systemwide level, he would like to see the union sharing equal power with the Board of Education on issues involving educational policy.

Any discussion of teacher power leads to the issue of the potential conflict between the interests of teachers and the educational welfare of students. This issue is most often raised with regard to possible union protection of incompetent teachers, but it also includes union support of educational policies that might be detrimental to students.

The protection of incompetent teachers, Mooney argues, is a false issue usually raised by those who do not understand how school systems work. In the first place, most school systems put new teachers on an appraisal system for three or four years before giving them a permanent contract. Even after receiving a permanent contract, teachers can still be dismissed. According to Mooney, if incompetent teachers exist within a system, the guilt is on the shoulders of the administration and not the union. Clearly, continued employment of poor teachers has to be blamed on the inaction and failure of the school administrations to evaluate teachers adequately. The union's role in these situations is to assure that the appraisal system is fair and to provide the teacher with help. Mooney describes the dismissal process as adversarial, with the administration presenting its case and the teacher organizing his or her case, but the decision rests with the administration. If the union feels that a teacher is unfairly dismissed, it can find some means of appeal through arbitration proceedings or through the courts.

The variety of issues and concerns related to the growth of teacher power and unionism is reflected in the types of activities Mooney engages in as union president. There is no such thing as a typical day for a union president because of the cyclical nature of some issues and the way other issues will suddenly burst onto the scene. The issues that generally follow a cycle involve negotiations with the local school board and meetings over the school budget. When these occur, they generally absorb a majority of Mooney's time. Some issues can appear suddenly, like a challenge from the local branch of the NEA that required a special election for teachers to determine their bargaining agent. When this occurred, Mooney found the majority of his time was devoted to campaigning.

This range of activities requires that the union president maintain a constant awareness of political and economic issues affecting the schools, changes in school policies, union politics, and the needs of teachers. How these concerns blend together could be seen during a typical campaign day after being challenged by the local affiliate of the NEA. The NEA was able to collect enough signatures to require a special election to be called in which teachers could determine their bargaining agent.

On a typical day during the campaign, Mooney met with two groups of teachers at different elementary schools. The first meeting was scheduled during the first hour of school when teachers were free for their preparation period. It was held in the school library, with the head of the Teacher Building Committee acting as chairperson of the meeting. The other meeting was held informally in the teachers' lunchroom during their lunch break. In this situation, Mooney ran the meeting and answered questions from teachers.

Mooney's general strategy was to open meetings by emphasizing the benefits gained by the union. He was able to do this in an indirect manner by asking if the teachers had any questions about the new dental and medical benefits the union had negotiated with the school board. Mooney was guaranteed a stream of questions and an interest on the part of the teachers. After a lengthy discussion of these benefits, Mooney moved directly into a general campaign speech that emphasized the bargaining goals of the union and why a strong show of support by teachers in the coming election would strengthen the union's position at the bargaining table. Mooney was able to campaign by linking past negotiated gains with hope of future benefits.

Mooney's presence provided an opportunity for teachers to express their individual and collective problems. As a union leader and good politician, Mooney has a responsibility to respond and act on these concerns. At the school visited in the morning, teachers were upset by the conduct of their principal who, they complained, was often late to school and managed discipline poorly. In this situation, Mooney recommended that the Teacher Building Committee meet with the principal and express their concerns, and pressure the principal into making formal rules to handle the discipline problems.

Following the morning meeting at the first school, Mooney was invited to the classrooms of two teachers to discuss their individual problems. The first had a complaint about the way the principal was handling her evaluation. He had not explained any of the procedures nor given her any written information about the appraisal process. Mooney assured her that the union would send her information and have a union representative stop by and check on the matter. The other teacher wanted to join the union, but was hesitant about doing it in public. She was an older teacher who had never thought she would join a union. She wondered aloud why administrators made so much more money than teachers. After Mooney explained the payment of dues, she asked about the pension fund and the contribution made by the Board of Education. This led to a general discussion about retirement in which she voiced the opinion that teachers used to be able to teach thirty, forty, and sometimes fifty years, but that this was no longer possible because they could no longer stand the stress of the job.

At another school, Mooney greeted teachers on their lunch hour with discussions about benefits and the future election. The teachers did not have any general complaints about the school, but one did request a private meeting over a personal problem. The teacher's husband had been fired from his job just prior to requiring hospitalization. When he was fired, he lost his hospitalization insurance. She called the Board of Education and asked that he be put under her insurance plan and was guaranteed immediate inclusion over the telephone. It had not occurred and now the couple had a $5,000 hospital bill with one member of the family still unemployed. Mooney copied down the details of the problem and promised to check with the board and insurance company to see if anything could be done about the bill.

This combination of concerns with union survival, teacher welfare, and educational policy was expressed at a meeting of the union Educational Policies Committee. The major issue of the meeting, as I observed, was the organization of middle schools to replace existing junior high schools. Mooney had expressed a concern to me before the meeting that middle schools might be one way the school administration had for attacking the union. The argument was that the administration was planning to require that middle school teachers have elementary certification. In the past, junior high schools were staffed by teachers with secondary certification, who usually were new teachers waiting for a position in a high school. It was from this pool of young junior high school teachers that the union received its strongest support and most active participation. Middle schools staffed by older elementary teachers would eliminate, according to Mooney, this most active element in the city's teaching staff.

The meeting illustrated how teacher welfare issues, educational concerns, and union politics had to be balanced in dealing with the issue of the middle school. The major concern of the meeting was that most industrial arts and home economics teachers in the remaining junior high schools and middle schools would lose their jobs because there was no room in the planned schedule for those subjects. Of primary interest to the union was the protection of those teachers' jobs. In addition, the teachers composing the committee argued that students of that age needed those types of educational experiences. The task the committee felt it had to perform was the creation of an alternative schedule that would allow for the inclusion of those courses. The plan was to take this alternative schedule to the administration and try to achieve some modification of their plans.

One plan that the teachers developed did seem to work, but it required all teachers to increase their workloads with the addition of one extra class. Mooney rejected this plan because it would not receive support from other middle and junior high school teachers. Or, in political terms, it would put Mooney in a difficult position to advocate a change of that nature. The safest plan politically required the hiring of extra staff so that the number of classes could be expanded without requiring teachers to work an extra class. Though politically a sound plan, it had its major drawback in the fact that the school system was short of cash and had stated several times that it would not be hiring new staff.

Over issues of this type Mooney most often negotiates with members of the school administration rather than the Board of Education. From the perspective of his position, he has witnessed a real shift in power in recent years between the central administration and the Board of Education. Mooney argues that in recent years the board has given most of the power to the central administration. Consequently, the real power is in the hands of the middle managers who became stronger as the board became weaker. It is these middle managers, Mooney claims, who are now becoming the major adversaries of local union power.

The political picture that emerges from this case study is one where the union leader must attend to the welfare needs of teachers, protect teachers' jobs, and play politics with the school administration. In addition, the union leader must remain aware of any possible challenges to the union and to his or her position in the union. While this case study outlines the career route for Mooney from classroom teacher to president of the local teachers' union it does not deal with career opportunities within the union. For instance, a president of a local teachers' union might want to climb up the union career ladder by gaining a position in the state or national union organization. This would add another dimension to the president's life as he or she did battle with the union's internal political forces.

Tom Mooney's concern about protecting teachers' jobs and improving wages, benefits, and working conditions reflects the general principles that have guided the activities of teachers' unions. Whether the issue is organizing middle schools or national certification of teachers, the first question teachers' unions ask is how will it affect jobs, salaries, and working conditions. As I will discuss in the next section, this question defines the position of teachers' unions on most educational issues.

SALARIES AND TEACHER STRIKES

In 1990 a new era opened in teacher strikes. In the past, most union strikes were between local affiliates and school boards. In 1990, the strike arena shifted from the local level to the state level as teachers became more concerned with wage issues. This change followed the pattern of school funding in the 1970s and 1980s which, in part, shifted from local governments to state governments. When teachers of the 1990s want higher salaries they often go to state governments.

The recent surge of strikes for higher wages follows a period when teachers' unions were primarily concerned about extending their power over educational policy and influencing legislation. One of the startling facts about changes in teacher salaries is the relationship to teacher supply and demand. There was a national teacher shortage of varying degrees from the end of World War II to approximately 1967. During this period, the ratio of teachers' salaries to the average U.S. per capita income steadily increased. After 1967, the nation experienced a dramatic surplus of teachers resulting from declines in school enrollments. This resulted in a decline in teachers' salaries.

It was during this period of surplus teachers and declining salaries that there was an increase in union activity. As the availability of jobs declined, older teachers were concerned with protecting their jobs. Collective bargaining provided security through seniority rules and negotiated reductions in staff. These activities are important for older union members because when school districts are suffering budget problems it is cheaper to replace older teachers who earn more money with teachers who start at the bottom of the salary schedule. Therefore, there does seem to be a relationship between supply and demand, teachers' economic conditions, and increases in unionization.

So in the 1970s and early 1980s, unions were faced with the problem of school systems having little money and a membership who feared losing their jobs. During this period there was a reluctance on the part of teachers' unions to press for higher wages. Consequently, unions focused on noneconomic issues. A study conducted in the late 1970s by Lorraine McDonnell and Anthony Pascal documented the emphasis on noneconomic issues. For instance, they found an increase from 11 percent to 37 percent between 1970 and 1975 in the number of local teacher union contracts that had provisions for teacher layoffs. The other areas over which unions fight that the two researchers found were length of the school day, the right of teachers to exclude disruptive students, class size, and the number of teacher aides.

By the late 1980s and early 1990s these conditions changed. With a shortage of teachers in some areas and better economic times, the circumstances were ripe for a resurgence of teacher militancy over salaries. Of course, these conditions could change since it was reported in 1990 that enrollment in teacher-training programs increased by 61 percent between 1985 and 1990. This could result in a surplus of teachers by the middle of the 1990s.

Union militancy surfaced in early 1990 in Washington, Utah, and West Virginia. In early February, 1990, 13,000 teachers in 35 of Washington's 296 school districts announced they were planning a walkout for higher salaries. Eight thousand other teachers pledged to attend after-hour rallies and marches. The protest was planned by the state affiliate of the NEA, the Washington Education Association, to demand that the state surplus of funds be used to increase teacher salaries by another 10 percent. In 1989, the state legislature approved a 10 percent increase but the teachers' union demanded another 10 percent. In 1990, the average starting pay in Washington was $18,000 with the average pay for a teacher being $33,100.

Using the concern about economic competitiveness and the quality of teachers, Teresa Moore, spokeswoman for the 49,000-member union stated, low salaries have an "impact on national competitiveness, the ability to keep good teachers, and also an impact on how we can attract new people into the profession." Ignoring union demands for higher salaries, Governor Booth Gardner, who has called himself "the education governor," told a rally of school board members and administrators that while he is committed to creating a world-class education system there could be no salary increases because the state's $611 million budget surplus was a one-time phenomenon.

In Utah, the issue was the passage in the state legislature of a $38 million reduction in state taxes. Like Washington, Utah's state government was hardly in bad financial straits since it could afford a large tax reduction. On the other hand, the average teacher salary in Utah in 1990 was $22,621, and the state's teacher-student ratio of 25.4 to 1 was the highest in the nation. On February 16, 1990, a majority of the 16,000 members of the Utah Education Association (NEA) authorized their union board to call a strike. On February 19, teachers rallied in front of the state legislature demanding more spending for education. As a result of union activity, the state legislature granted a $1,000 salary increase for all teachers and a 4 percent increase in state money to local school districts.

Union actions in Washington and Utah set the stage for one of the largest and longest state teachers' strikes in history. The only previous strike of this nature was a three-week strike by Florida teachers in 1968. On March 7, 1990, two-thirds of West Virginia's 22,000 teachers walked off the job for what would be an eleven-day strike. The strike idled one-half of the 328,000 students in West Virginia schools.

Led by the 3,000-member West Virginia Federation of Teachers (AFT) and the 16,000-member West Virginia Education Association (NEA), teachers began their protests for higher salaries with a rally on February 15, 1990, which ended when state troopers were called in to restrain teachers as they pounded on the doors of the state legislature demanding higher pay. The average salary for West Virginia teachers was $21,904, ranking them 49th among other states. On March 2, teachers skipped school chanting, "Pay raise or strike." Twenty-one counties canceled classes, and pickets in one county turned away buses at three schools. A group of 5,000 teachers met at the state legislature where they were joined by members of the United Mine Workers and other unions. A group of 100 teachers surrounded Education and Arts Secretary Steve Haid screaming questions and complaints. At the rally, the president of the West Virginia Education Association, Kayetta Meadows, complained that while the state was not able to raise teachers' salaries, they were able to give raises of 5 percent to 25 percent to The Division of Highways engineers and they were considering raising state trooper salaries by $7,000 a year. In response to the governor's claim that there was no money for increasing teachers' salaries, she retorted, "Do they think we're so dumb that we can't read the paper, that we can't tell what's going on?"

As the strike continued into a second week, the state education superintendent closed all schools for a cooling off period. Governor Gaston Caperton urged county superintendents to fire all teachers who did not go back to work after the cooling off period. As the tension built, the state's attorney general's office issued a statement that the teachers were striking illegally and could be suspended or fired, and charged with misdemeanors. Pressured by threats of being fired or refusing to back union demands, some teachers crossed picket lines. In one county, it was estimated that 30 percent of the teachers crossed picket lines.

Lasting antagonisms developed between striking teachers and those who crossed picket lines. Strikers greeted teachers crossing picket lines with handouts and with demands that they honor the line. Jeanne Taylor, a home economics teacher who crossed a picket line, reported, "We drove slowly, we rolled down our window, we stopped and we listened to what the pickets had to say. We respect their view. It would be nice if they respected ours." After entering the school building, she said, "I cried . . . . the emotions are like a roller coaster. You're up and down. You're taking Maalox and Rolaids." Lois Swineford, a math teacher who crossed a picket line complained, "I haven't slept; I've had nightmares over this. It's hard to know what's right anymore."

On March 17, the two unions urged teachers to return to work after leaders of the state legislature agreed to call a special session to develop a long-range plan for the educational system and raise teachers' salaries. In addition, the unions were feeling pressured by a series of court decisions regarding back-to-work orders. After reaching an agreement with the leaders of the legislature, Kayetta Meadows, president of the West Virginia Education Association, told a news conference, "We've moved education to the fore-front, so it just isn't something that you pay lip service to during elections."

Of course, the strike caused bitterness between striking and nonstriking teachers. "I suspect there's a degree of animosity and maybe even bitterness for those who walked across the picket line," said Bob Brown, executive director of the West Virginia Federation of Teachers. "If they can live with themselves, we can live with them." Some schools actually held counseling sessions to try and reduce tensions between striking and nonstriking teach-ers. In one county, the local ministerial association sent counselors to the schools to help teachers work out their feelings.

While union actions in Washington, Utah, and West Virginia reflect concerns about wage issues, the 1992 strike by Detroit teachers highlights the potential conflict between school reform and union power. In 1992, the Detroit board of education adopted a policy designed to empower an individ-ual school if requested by its principal, 75 percent of its teachers, and its parents council. Rather than receiving the 70 percent of per pupil costs allocated to other schools, the empowered school would receive 92 percent. The rest of the per pupil expenditures are retained by the central administra-tion for special programs and administrative costs. In addition, the em-powered schools would be allowed to select their own teachers. Essentially, these empowered schools would function as independent schools in the Detroit system.

The Detroit teachers' union objected to the potential ability of empowered schools to violate provisions of the union contract. Also, the union objected to the autonomy granted empowered schools to hire their own teachers. The president of the Detroit union, John Elliot, argued that Detroit teachers prefer a centralized school system with the same rules applying to all teachers. From the union perspective, the creation of independent schools threatened the ability of the union to bargain for all teachers and the viability of a contract that specifies work rules and working conditions for all teachers in the system.

The bitter Detroit strike lasted for twenty-seven days and affected 170,000 students. In the final contract, the union agreed to the plan for empowered schools with the requirement that a vote of 75 percent of the teachers in an empowered school would be required to waive a limited number of contract provisions. To get waivers from other provisions of the contract would re-quire a formal review by the union. This agreement represents a compromise between the Detroit board's desire to free schools from the control of the central administration and the union's concern with maintaining its power.

The final settlement in the Detroit strike also highlights the bargaining process during contract talks. While the issue of empowered schools was the main reason for the strike, the union was also concerned with salaries, textbooks, and class size. While the union agreed with the board to accept empowered schools under specific conditions, the board agreed to a 4 percent salary increase, to spend $1 million a year to buy duplicate sets of textbooks, and to establish a committee to find ways to pay for reduction in class sizes.

The strike by the Detroit teachers' union emphasizes that unions are primarily interested in the welfare of their members and in maintaining union power. The power of the Detroit union was directly threatened by the creation of independent schools. Sometimes it is hard to focus on these basic concerns of teachers' unions because they constantly surround themselves with the rhetoric of educational reform and helping children. It is true that they are interested in reform and children. But their support of any educational issue is conditioned by their concern to protect their membership and the power of the union. Primarily, teachers' unions are interested in expanding their membership and gaining more power, increasing teachers' salaries, and creating better working conditions.

EXERCISES

1. Contact local members of the AFT and NEA about current goals and issues in local school districts. Inquire about the lobbying activities of both organizations at the state and national level. If possible, organize a class debate between representatives of both organizations.
2. In a group discussion or essay, discuss the current goals of the AFT and NEA. These goals can be found in the current NEA handbook and the most recent September issue of the AFT's *American Teacher.*
3. Contact local members of boards of education about their views concerning collective bargaining with the NEA and AFT. Ask what they think should be the role of teachers' organizations in American education.

SUGGESTED READINGS AND WORKS CITED IN CHAPTER

The best sources of current information about the NEA and AFT are the NEA *Handbook* and the AFT's *American Teacher.* Contact local offices of these organizations for more information about them.

Ammons, David. "Teacher Walkouts." *Compuserve Executive News Service AP* (13 February 1990). Report of the teacher walkout in Washington.

Aronowitz, Stanley. *False Promises: The Shaping of American Working Class Consciousness.* New York: McGraw-Hill, 1973. An important book for understanding why professionals, including teachers, are rapidly joining the union movement.

Berube, Maurice. *Teacher Politics: The Influence of Unions.* Westport, Conn.: Greenwood Press, 1988. This is a very good introduction to the contemporary politics of teachers' unions.

Bradley, Ann. "Contract Accord in Detroit Ends 27-day Teacher Strike." *Education Week* (7 October 1992): 13. This article describes the final settlement in the Detroit strike.

_____. "Politics, N.E.A. Style: Anti-Bush Rhetoric, Clinton Endorsement, an Alexander Attack." *Education Week* (5 August 1992): 12–13. This article describes the NEA's reaction to Bill Clinton.

_____. "Teachers in Detroit Strike Over Proposal for Flexible Schools." *Education Week* (9 September 1992): 1, 21. This article describes the reasons for the Detroit strike.

Dreyfous, Leslie, "Teaching Trend." *Compuserve Executive News Service AP* (22 March 1990). Report of the increase in enrollment of 61 percent in teacher-education programs between 1985 and 1990.

Eaton, William E. *The American Federation of Teachers, 1916–1961.* Carbondale: Southern Illinois University Press, 1975. A good history of the development of the AFT.

Formanek, Ray. "Teacher Strike-In School." *Compuserve Executive News Service AP* (13 March 1990). This article deals with the psychological problems encountered by teachers who crossed picket lines during the West Virginia strike.

Groutage, Hilary. "Utah Teachers." *Compuserve Executive News Service AP* (27 February 1990). Report of Utah teachers' protest over wages.

Henry, Tamara. "Restructuring Schools." *Compuserve Executive News Service AP* (5 March 1990). News story covering speech given by head of NEA to the National Press Club.

Kissel, Kelly. "Teacher Strike." *Compuserve Executive News Service AP* (17 March 1990). Announcement of agreement to end West Virginia teachers' strike.

"The 1992–93 Resolutions of the National Education Association." *NEA Today* (September 1992): 22–30. Resolutions adopted at the 1992 National Education Association convention.

Olsen, Lynn. "Unions Putting Time, Money, Energy to Task of Campaigning for Clinton." *Education Week* (14 October 1992): 1, 24. This article describes the involvement of the AFT and NEA in the Clinton campaign.

Urban, Wayne. *Why Teachers Organized.* Detroit, Mich.: Wayne State University, 1982. This excellent history of teachers' unions argues that the primary reason for the formation of these unions was protection of wages and seniority.

"U.S. Education: The Task Before Us." *American Educator* 16, no. 4 (Winter 1992): 19–30. This is the 1992 AFT policy statement.

Wesley, Edgar. *NEA: The First Hundred Years.* New York: Harper and Brothers, 1957. The main source of information, in addition to original sources, about the early years of the NEA. The controversy about the American Legion article is discussed on pages 316–18.

Wilson, Jill. "Teacher Strike." *Compuserve Executive News Service AP* (20 March 1990). Details tension after strike between striking teachers and those who crossed the picket line.

CHAPTER 4

The Social Structure and American Education

EQUALITY OF OPPORTUNITY

From the nineteenth century to the present America's democratic ideology has promised equal opportunity for all citizens. *Equality of opportunity* means that all members of a society are given equal chances to enter any occupation or social class. It *does not* mean that everyone will have equal incomes and equal status; rather all have an equal chance to compete for any place in society. Ideally, equality of opportunity should result in a social system in which all members occupy their particular positions as a result of merit and not as a result of family wealth, heredity, or special cultural advantages.

One way of thinking about equality of opportunity is as a race where everyone is competing for jobs and income. To provide equality of opportunity to compete in the race all participants should begin at the same starting line. During the actual running of the race, some people will end up leading while others will follow. In this model of equality of opportunity, education can either ensure that everyone begins on equal terms at the starting line or it can control the race to ensure that competition is fair. In the first instance, the concern is with ensuring that everyone has an equal education at the beginning of the race. In the second instance, the concern is with identifying and developing everyone's abilities while they are running the race. American schools have at different times taken both approaches to providing equality of opportunity.

The role of the school in the provision of equality of opportunity changed from the nineteenth century to the twentieth century. In the nineteenth century, the school was to provide everyone with an equal education or the same education, and the race for jobs and status was to be run after graduation from school. Equality of opportunity was to be a function of competition outside of the schoolhouse, with the starting line at the point of exit from the school.

In the late nineteenth and early part of the twentieth centuries it was argued that competition outside of school was not fair because of the possible influence of family wealth and other social factors. To make equality of opportunity fair, it was argued, the school had to play a greater role in identifying individual abilities. Students were separated according to their abilities, interests, and future occupations. They were placed in ability groups in classrooms and in different curricula according to their abilities and interests. The result was that students received unequal and different educations. Some students might graduate with vocational training and others with preparation for going to college. What this meant was that the school no longer provided an equal education with competition occurring outside of school. It provided instead an unequal education with competition for social positions taking place in the school. It was believed that standardized tests, teachers' judgments, and counselors could make a fairer decision about where a person could go in the social structure than could be achieved through competition outside of school.

A brief history illustrates the changes in the role of the school in the provision of equality of opportunity. In the common school of the nineteenth century, differences of social class and special advantages were supposed to disappear, as everyone was given an equal chance to get an equal education. This was one of the reasons for the support of common schools in the nineteenth century. During the 1830s, workingmen's parties advocated the establishment of publicly supported common schools and the end of the pauper schools that were the only free schools up to that time. It was asserted that with public schools for the poor and private schools for the middle class and the rich, education reinforced social differences and doomed the children of the poor to a perpetual lower-class status. Only common schools could provide for equality of opportunity.

The most extreme statements came from one faction of the New York Workingman's party. This group argued that sending students to a common school would not in itself eliminate differences in social background, because the well-to-do child would return from school to a home richly furnished and full of books, whereas the poor one would return to a shanty barren of books and opportunities to learn. School, in the opinion of these workingmen, could never eliminate these differences. Their solution was that all children in New York should be removed from their families and placed in state boarding schools where they would all live in the same types of rooms, wear the same types of clothes, and eat the same food. In this milieu, education would truly allow all members of society to begin the race on equal terms. This extreme solution to the problem did not receive wide support, and debates about it eventually led to the collapse of the New York Workingman's party.

In the late nineteenth and early part of the twentieth centuries, the development of intelligence tests was considered a means by which equality of opportunity could be made fairer. Some people argued that intelligence tests could be an objective measure that could be used to determine one's best place in society. The first intelligence test was developed in the early 1900s by the French psychologist Alfred Binet, who wanted to find a method of separating children with extremely low levels of intelligence from those with normal intelligence levels. The assumpton of the test was that an inherited level of intelligence existed and could be measured independent of environmental factors such as social class, housing conditions, and cultural advantages.

In the United States the movement to measure native intelligence spread rapidly because of its link to the ideology of equality of opportunity. The doctrine of native intelligence provided the premise that the role of the school was to eliminate all hindrances to the full development in individual intelligence. Individuals would be given an equal chance to develop their particular level of intelligence. Identifying a particular characteristic such as intelligence and recognizing that all members of society would achieve different positions in the social race because of differences in native intelligence seemed to give scientific validation to the arguments for equality of opportunity.

The movement to measure intelligence allowed for equality of opportunity and at the same time justified a hierarchical social structure, based on intelligence, in which all people were not equal. Within this framework democracy was viewed as a social system in which all people were given an equal chance to reach a level in society that corresponded to their individual level of intelligence.

The major problem in the link between attempts to measure native intelligence and to provide equality of opportunity is that levels of measured intelligence tend to be related to social class and race. That is, the poor and minority groups in the United States tend to get lower scores on intelligence tests than middle- and upper-class majority groups. In fact, it can be argued that the measurement of intelligence discriminates against certain social classes and minority groups.

Discussions about the relationship between the measurement of intelligence and discrimination center on whether an inherited native intelligence exists and, if it does exist, whether it can be measured. For instance, those who believe that an inherited level of intelligence exists and is measurable by tests state that the differences in measured levels of intelligence accurately reflect the conditions of society. Alfred Binet contended that the reason the poor did not do well on intelligence tests was because they did in fact have lower levels of intelligence and, moreover, that was why they were poor. More recently, psychologist Arthur Jensen argued that existing tests accurately measure inherited intelligence and that differences in performance by certain racial and social groups are accurate. On the other hand, there are those who believe in the existence of inherited intelligence but feel that the questions asked on existing tests reflect the cultural and social bias of the dominant middle class in the United States. The poor, and certain racial groups, perform poorly on existing tests because many of the test questions deal with things that are not familiar to those groups. Within this framework, the solution to the problem is the creation of an intelligence test that is free of any cultural bias.

Another approach to the problem is the complete rejection of the idea of inherited intelligence and the acceptance of the view that intelligence and abilities are primarily a result of environment. This is the famous "nurture-nature" debate. Those who see nurture as being more important argue that differences in measured intelligence between social and racial groups primarily reflect differences in social conditions. The poor grow up in surroundings that are limited in terms of intellectual training: an absence of books and magazines in the home; poor housing, diet, and medical care; and lack of peer-group interest in learning all might account for their poor performance on intelligence tests. This approach suggests that the school can act positively to overcome differences caused by social and cultural conditions.

Most recently, school programs have tried to overcome inequalities caused by differences in backgrounds. The argument for equality of opportunity is placed in the context of the culture-of-poverty argument described in Chapter 1. Through compensatory education and Head Start programs, schools attempt to end poverty and provide equality of opportunity by trying to compensate for unequal social conditions. Head Start and early-childhood education programs are designed to counteract the supposedly poor learning opportunities of the children of the poor, and compensatory education is designed to provide special instruction in reading and other skills in order to offset cultural and economic disadvantages.

Of fundamental concern in current discussions is whether the school can make any contribution to equality of opportunity. One issue is whether the school reproduces and reinforces the social-class structure of the United States. The other important issue concerns the degree of contribution the school makes to social mobility.

SOCIAL-CLASS DIFFERENCES IN EDUCATION

One major criticism of public schools is the apparent internal duplication of the social-class structure of society. Table 4.1 lists the educational practices discussed in this section that can contribute to the reinforcement of social class differences among students. Two methods that can separate students according to social-class background are tracking and ability grouping. *Tracking*, primarily a practice of the high school, separates students into different curricula such as college preparatory, vocational, and general. *Ability grouping* places students in different classes or groups within classes on the basis of their abilities. These abilities are usually determined by a combination of a teacher assessment of the student and standardized tests.

Often, the social-class background of students parallels the levels of ability grouping and tracking. That is, the higher the social-class background of the students, the more likely it is that they will be in the higher ability

TABLE 4.1 Educational Practices That Can Reinforce Social-Class Differences Among Students

1. Tracking

2. Ability grouping

3. Counseling methods

4. Teacher expectations

5. Unequal school expenditures

groups or a college-preparatory curriculum. Conversely, the lower the social-class status of the students, the more likely it is that they will be in the lower ability groups or the vocational curriculum.

Studies show the existence of this condition in the American public schools from the 1920s to the present. One of the first major studies of social-class differences in relationship to adolescent culture and the high school was conducted in a small town in Indiana by a team of sociologists headed by A. B. Hollingshead. Their findings, which they titled *Elmtown's Youth*, can still be found duplicated in many high schools throughout the country.

The Hollingshead study divided the population of Elmtown into five social classes as shown in Table 4.2. The tracks, or courses of study, at Elmtown's high school were college preparatory, general, and commerical. When the social-class origins in each track were determined, it was found that children from social classes 1 and 2 concentrated on college-preparatory courses (64 percent) and ignored the commercial course. Class 3s were found mainly in the general course (51 percent), with 27 percent in college preparatory and 21 percent in commercial. Class 4s slipped down the hierarchical scale of curricula; only 9 percent were in college preparatory, 58 percent were in general, and 33 percent were in commercial. Only 4 percent of class 5s were in the college-preparatory curriculum, whereas 38 percent were in commercial, and 58 percent in the general curriculum.

That the distribution of students in the various curricula of a school reflects social class does not in itself indicate a problem or that the school is responsible. Hollingshead found that social pressures from family and peer

TABLE 4.2 Social Class in Elmtown

1. Upper class, wealth primarily a result of inheritance

2. Income from profession, family business, or a salaried executive

3. Income from small businesses, farms, and wages from white-collar jobs in mines, mills, and public service

4. Income from blue-collar occupations in mills and mines

5. Income from unskilled, part-time labor and welfare

Source: Summarized from chapter 5 of A. B. Hollingshead, *Elmtown's Youth* (New York: John Wiley and Sons, 1949).

group contributed to the decision to enter a particular course of study. Upper-class parents tended to be more oriented to college, while lower-class parents thought in terms of training for jobs within their own particular social class.

Pressures outside the school existed to support the differences in social classes, but Hollingshead also found that the school, through a variety of methods, gave support to the differences in social class. Differences of response to a given educational situation tended to vary with the social class of the student. *Counseling methods* were found to reinforce social-class differences. For instance, the parents of students were counseled differently according to social class. Although children from social classes 2 and 3 received better grades than lower-class children, parents of social classes 2 and 3 were more often called to school to discuss the work of their children. The parents of lower-class children, however, were more often called to school to discuss the behavior of their children. This situation was paradoxical because not only did lower-class children tend to receive lower grades but they also tended to fail courses more often than children from the upper classes. Objectively, one would assume that if the school were acting free of social-class bias, parents of lower-class children would receive more counseling about schoolwork than about behavior.

In the situation described by Hollingshead, problems related to children of the lower social class tend to be considered behavior problems in school, whereas those related to the upper classes tend to be considered learning problems. Nothing so dramatically tells the story of institutional response to social class than the tale about the enforcement of the school lateness rule. Elmtown High School adopted a new tardy rule, which the principal and superintendent intended to enforce with vigor. The first violator of the tardy rule was the son of a class 1 family, who arrived late to school in his father's Cadillac. The student was told by the principal to report for detention after school. When the student did not appear for detention after school, the principal phoned the father, who brought the student back to school. The superintendent, nervous about offending the father, greeted the boy at the school door and had him sit for ten to fifteen minutes in his outer office before sending him home. The superintendent later stated that he did not want the boy to have to sit with the other students in the detention room.

The opposite response occurred that next day when a son of a class 4 family arrived late to school. The principal and superintendent made joking comments about the student's dress and statements about his father being a laborer at the local fertilizer plant. When school ended, the superintendent and principal roamed the halls, and when they saw the class 4 student trying to leave the building, the principal grabbed him and began to shout at him. The student broke from the grasp of the principal and ran through the halls, where he was eventually caught by the superintendent, who shook and slapped him three or four times. Eventually the principal and superintendent physically pushed the student out of the school.

In the cases described above, the school officials were able to identify the social-class origins of their students through their personal contact within the local community. In larger educational systems social-class identification is often made through the dress of the student, the ethnic or racial background, the location of the home within the community, and informal discussions. For instance, a student might be referred to as coming from a particular section of town, which when mentioned is understood to be an area inhabited, say, by blue-collar workers in a local factory or by executives in major industries. Ethnic names in large metropolitan areas can also cause a response related to the social-class nature of the family or attitudes toward learning.

A more recent example of the relationship between social class and tracking in schools has been given by Jeanne Ballantine in her book, *The Sociology of Education*. Ballantine's example, taken from a study of two mid-western school systems, compares the number of students from differing social-class backgrounds who were in the top academic track with the actual number of students qualified for admission to that track. For students from upper-class backgrounds it was found that 80 percent of those qualified to be in the top academic track were in that track. On the other hand, it was found that only 47 percent of those students from lower-class backgrounds who qualified for the top academic track were actually in that track. In other words, 53 percent of the lower-class students who were qualified for the top academic track were not being given the full benefits of an academic educa-tion. For middle-class students, 65 percent of those qualified for the top academic track were in that track.

Jeanne Ballantine also provides evidence that race is a factor in the separation of students into academic tracks, with the differences in tracking between whites and African Americans increasing over time. In the evidence presented, 44 percent of the white student body of a seventh-grade class was in the academic track, whereas 33 percent of the African-American student body of the same seventh-grade class was in that track. The percentages changed dramatically as the same group of students moved through the eighth and ninth grades. In the eighth grade the percentage of the white student population in the academic track increased to 47 percent, whereas the percentage of the African-American population in that track decreased to 20 percent. In the ninth grade the percentage for whites decreased to 30 percent whereas the percentage for African Americans decreased to 10 percent.

A contributing factor to social-class and racial bias in schools is *teacher expectations*. Sometimes, teachers and other school officials expect certain students to act in certain ways. In its simplest form, this stereotyping results in the expectation that students from middle- and upper-class families will do well in school, whereas children from lower-class backgrounds are expected to do poorly. Research findings suggest that one problem with such stereo-typing is that students live up to expectations about them. If students are expected to do poorly, they do poorly; if expected to do well, they do well. This is referred to as the *self-fulfilling prophecy*.

The most famous study of the tendency to live up to expectations is Robert Rosenthal and Lenore Jacobson's *Pygmalion in the Classroom*. In the first part of the study, a group of experimenters was given a random selection of rats and told that certain rats came from highly intelligent stock. The rats labeled as coming from highly intelligent stock tended to perform better than the other rats, even though they were randomly grouped. The two psychologists tested their results in a school to see if teacher expectations would affect student performance. After giving students a standardized intelligence test, they gave teachers the names of students whom they called "late bloomers" and told teachers to expect a sudden spurt of learning from them. In fact, the names of these students were selected at random from the class. A year later the intelligence tests were administered again. The scores of the supposed "late bloomers" were compared with those of other children who received scores on the original test similar to the supposed "late bloomers." It was found that those students who were identified to teachers as "late bloomers" made considerable gains in their intelligence-test scores when compared with students not designated as "late bloomers."

The principal inference of this study is that teacher expectations can play an important role in determining the educational achievement of the child. This might be a serious problem in the education of children of poor and minority groups, where teachers develop expectations that these children will either fail or have a difficult time learning. Some educators, such as teacher and educational writer Miriam Wasserman, argue that teacher expectations are one of the major barriers to educational success for the poor and for certain minority groups.

Wasserman, in her case study of the New York school system, *The School Fix: NYC, USA*, relates the issue of teacher expectations to what she calls the "guidance approach to teaching." The guidance approach means that when planning instructional units, the teacher tried to take into account the students family background, social life, and problems outside school. On the surface this sounds like good educational practice in relating teaching methods and materials to the background and needs of the student. In practice, Wasserman discovered the tendency to label all students from poverty areas as having learning problems, as not being interested in school, and as probably not succeeding in school. Teachers tended to provide material that was not very challenging to students so labeled, or explained their own failure to teach the student in terms of the student's background.

In further investigation of this problem, Wasserman interviewed students from poverty backgrounds who had been successful in school. She found that these students believed the major element in their successful educational career was having a teacher who was primarily interested in the student's learning and who emphasized and demanded high-quality work. These teachers had high expectations for their students, expectations that were not influenced by the social-class backgrounds of the students.

The combination of the classification of students according to abilities and curriculum plus the expectations of teachers and other school officials all seem to contribute to the social-class divisions of the surrounding society being reflected in the placement and treatment of students in the school. In addition, it has been found that in terms of educational achievement the differences between children from different social classes become progressively greater from the first grade through high school.

SHOULD TRACKING AND ABILITY GROUPING BE ABOLISHED?

In 1992, with the backing of Governor William Weld and the Commissioner of Education Robert Antonucci, the Massachusetts Department of Education began an active campaign to eliminate grouping by academic ability in local schools. Since the 1920s, the separation of students by academic ability has been criticized because the result is often separation by socioeconomic class and race. In 1985, these practices again became an important issue with the publication of Jeannie Oakes' *Keeping Track: How Schools Structure Inequality*. As the name of the book suggests, Oakes documented the use of grouping by academic ability as a means of fostering social inequality. By 1993, the debate over grouping by academic ability had reached a point that, in the words of educational researcher Robert Slavin, "Whenever anybody holds a meeting on this topic, it is packed to the rafters." And, as I discussed in Chapter 3, the National Education Association adopted a resolution in 1992 condemning the use of academic tracking as a means of segregation by social class, race, and gender.

Participants in the debate refer to two forms of grouping by academic ability. One form is tracking, where students are divided into separate classes according to their academic ability. The other form is ability grouping, where students within a single classroom are separated according to academic abilities. Opponents of tracking and ability grouping argue that these practices primarily promote inequality without benefiting the fast or slow learner. An analysis of the National Education Longitudinal Study concluded that a group of eighth graders separated by academic ability and studied for two years showed few benefits from the practice. In this analysis, separation by ability worsened the educational achievement of low achievers and did nothing for high achievers.

While criticizing academic ability grouping that results in discrimination by social class, race, and gender, supporters argue that the practice makes it easier for teachers and it allows high achievers to progress at a more rapid rate. Teachers of gifted and talented classes are particularly upset at the idea of ending academic ability grouping. A defender of ability grouping, Peter D. Rosenstein, the executive director of the National Association of Gifted Children, worries that it has become "politically correct to deny that there are different potentials among children."

While supporters might be correct that there are different academic potentials among children, the reality is that tracking and ability grouping are frequently used as a means of discrimination. As I discuss in Chapter 5, many educators charge that tracking and ability grouping results in second generation segeregation. While tracking and ability grouping are one source of inequality in education, school finance is another major source.

SAVAGE INEQUALITIES

One of the major causes of the unequal distribution of educational opportunities between social classes and racial groups is *unequal school expenditures.* The measure of unequal school expenditures is the amount of money spent per student. The majority of school districts in the United States receive approximately 50 percent of their financial support from local taxes. This means that children attending schools in districts with a great deal of taxable wealth will have more money spent on their education than children attending schools with little taxable wealth. These differences in spending affect the quality of education which, in turn, affects the ability of graduates to compete for jobs.

The differences that can exist between the amount of money spent by individual school districts on a student's education is illustrated in Table 4.3.

As indicated in Table 4.3, there is a major difference between the $17,435 per student spent in the Long Island community of Shoreham-Wading River and the $7,299 spent per student in New York City. The differences illustrated in Table 4.3 can be found across the United States. Highland Park, Texas, a wealthy suburb of Dallas, spends twice as much per pupil as two other area school systems. Teachers' salaries are 50 percent higher at New Trier High School in Illinois as compared to the Du Sable, Illinois, school system. The average teacher in the Belmont, Massachusetts, school system earns $36,100, while those in Chelsea, Massachusetts, earn $26,200.

Differences in expenditures per student do affect the quality of education, as amply demonstrated by Jonathan Kozol in his disturbing book, *Savage Inequalities: Children in America's Schools.* Kozol opens his indictment of the

TABLE 4.3 Differences in Spending per Student in New York Metropolitan Area, 1991

District	
Shoreham-Wading River	$17,435
Great Neck	15,594
Greenburgh	15,128
Manhasset	15,084
William Floyd	7,614
Sachem	7,309
Miller Place	7,305
New York City	7,299

Source: This table was adapted from "Poorer New York School Districts Seek More Aid," *New York Times* (6 May 1991): A1, B4.

financial and educational disparities between school districts with a description of the economically depressed East St. Louis school system. Taken on a tour of the local high school, Kozol meets frustrated vocational education teachers who are unable to prepare their students for the world of work because of antiquated and broken shop equipment. The high school science teacher shows Kozol a physics lab where the lab stations have empty holes that once contained pipes. Balance scales and other lab equipment are either broken or outdated. The biology lab has no laboratory tables. The lack of tables didn't seem to matter since the school district could not afford to buy dissecting kits. The chemistry lab, Kozol is informed, is not used because it is considered unsafe. The school has no VCRs and, therefore, is unable to use any of the latest visual aid material.

A major problem contributing to the low quality of education in financially strapped school districts is the lack of a regular teaching force. Because of low salaries and poor working conditions, many urban school districts are unable to retain good teachers and must rely on substitute teachers. Consequently, many students spend idle time in classrooms as they face a steady stream of substitute teachers. In Chicago, more than a quarter of the teachers are low-paid substitutes. In addition, there is even a shortage of substitute teachers. On an average morning in the Chicago schools, 190 classrooms are without teachers. One high school student complained to Kozol that he had been in a class for an entire semester and there still wasn't a regular teacher. A student in an auto mechanics class said that he hadn't even learned to change a tire because the substitute teacher only wanted them to sit quietly.

One way the teacher shortage is handled is to increase the number of required study halls. Therefore, many students find themselves sitting idly in classes managed by substitute teachers who do not know the subject matter of the course and then spend more idle time attending two or three study halls. No wonder many of these students do not feel that it is worthwhile going to school.

In Camden, New Jersey, Kozol found student learning hindered by both poor health conditions and poor school facilities. It is difficult for children to learn if they come to school sick. Often, poorer school districts have a flood of students with medical and dental problems that their parents cannot afford to correct. The Camden school nurse complained to Kozol about children coming to school with rotting teeth and chronic and untreated illnesses. They sit in class in a state of discomfort unable to really pay attention to the class work. And, even if they could pay attention, they would be receiving an inadequate education. A typing teacher showed Kozol a typing room full of 10-year-old manual typewriters. The training in this class, she reflected, was completely out of touch with the world of word processing and computers. Buying computers is out of the question when the Camden school district can barely pay its teachers.

Kozol found savage inequalities even within the same school district. In New York City, he uncovered disconcerting differences between public schools in the poorer sections of the Bronx and a public school in the wealthy

Riverdale section of the Bronx. At one school in the Bronx, he found classes being conducted in a former roller-skating rink lacking any windows. While the school's capacity is 900, more than 1,300 children attend. A shortage of textbooks requires students to share social studies books. Because of a lack of classroom space, two first-grade classes share the same classroom with a blackboard being used as a divider. In some parts of the school, Kozol found four classes taking place within the same undivided space. On the top floor of the school, Kozol encountered fifty-nine students and four adults of a bilingual class and a regular sixth-grade class sharing a classroom which in a suburban school would be assigned to twenty students.

In contrast to the conditions in this school, an elementary school in the Riverdale section of the Bronx allows gifted students to have access to a school planetarium. At this school class sizes are kept to around twenty-two. Each classroom has a computer. Classes have in-class research centers stocked with up-to-date sources. The school does not depend on substitute teachers and, therefore, classwork follows in an ordered fashion. Whereas in other section-schools in the Bronx students find themselves being forced to sit idly, students at the Riverdale school are engaged in constant learning activities that emphasize the use of reason and critical thinking.

Besides certain privileged urban schools, savage inequalities become most apparent when comparing schools with low per student expenditures to schools in wealthy suburban districts and elite private schools. In contrast to Chicago schools, where students must worry about having a regular teacher and textbooks, New Trier High School, which serves wealthy Chicago suburban communities, provides four-year courses in six foreign languages and elective courses ranging from the literature of Nobel winners to computer languages. The school even operates its own licensed television station. The average class size is twenty-four. Each freshman is assigned an adviser who remains the student's counselor through graduation. Each counselor has only 24 students to advise as compared to Chicago schools, where counselors advise an average of 420 students. In contrast to the problems facing students in the Camden school district, the nearby wealthy Cherry Hill suburban school district offers fourteen different courses in its physical science department and eighteen biology electives. In the Princeton, New Jersey, schools, students are provided with "music suites" and computer equipped subject-related study halls. Besides having up-to-date equipment, a large variety of courses, and a dedicated teaching staff, elite private schools such as Exeter maintain class sizes of about thirteen.

The obvious cause of these savage inequalities is differences in community wealth. The New Trier district has approximately $340,000 of taxable property for each child while the Chicago schools have approximately $70,000 per student. As I will discuss in Chapter 11, there have been many court cases and legislative attempts to equalize school expenditures, but at this point in time, little has been accomplished. The savage inequalities continue.

The consequence of these savage inequalities is the perpetuation of social class differences. A child attending an impoverished school district is receiving less of an opportunity to gain an education than students in elite suburban and private schools. Without the availability of computers, a broad range of electives in humanities and science, regular teachers, and advisers with small student loads, children in impoverished school districts are not being prepared for college or to enter high paying jobs. Even if they go to college, the graduates of the East St. Louis, Chicago, and Camden schools will have difficulty competing with their better prepared counterparts from Exeter, New Trier, and Princeton.

THE NEW JOB MARKET

The savage inequalities between school districts creates inequality of opportunity in competition for jobs. President Bill Clinton's secretary of labor, economist Robert Reich, outlined this relationship in his book, *The Work of Nations: Preparing Ourselves for 21st-Century Capitalism*. As indicated in Table 4.4, Reich defines three new broad categories of employment which he calls *routine production services, inperson services,* and *symbolic-analytic services.* It is important to note that within his job classification scheme, the majority of occupations do not require a high level of education.

As Reich points out, two of these new job classifications, routine production services and inperson services, do not require a high level of education. Reich includes in *routine production services* traditional assembly-line factory work, repetitive office work, and the low- and mid-level managers of these repetitive tasks. While high technology originally promised freedom from the drudgery of routine work, Reich argues, the reality is an army of workers doing repetitive work to support the new age of computers. Nothing is more tedious and boring, Reich states, than working on an assembly line putting circuit boards in computers or doing routine coding for software programs. What Reich calls the "foot soldiers" of the new information age are the hordes of data processors tediously putting information into computers.

Inperson services, Reich argues, are also boring and require only a low level of education. The major difference between inperson servers and routine producers is that inperson services are provided person-to-person. Reich puts

TABLE 4.4 Distribution of Occupations

Job Classification	Percentage of Labor Market
Routine production services	25%
Inperson services	30
Symbolic-analytic services	20
Farmers, miners	5
Government workers (including teachers and defense)	20

Source: Table 4.4 was adapted from Robert Reich, *The Work of Nations: Preparing Ourselves for 21st-Century Capitalism* (New York: Alfred Knopf, 1991), pp. 171–82.

into this job classification such occupations as retail sales workers, waiters and waitresses, hotel workers, janitors, hospital attendants, nursing aides, house cleaners, auto mechanics, flight attendants, and other personal service workers.

The best paid jobs requiring the highest levels of education are, according to Reich, in *symbolic-analytic services.* As the name implies, these are the occupations that involve the analysis and manipulation of information. Included in this job classification are scientists, engineers, investment bankers, advertising executives, art directors, architects, film makers, publishers, writers and editors, journalists, musicians, television and film producers, and university professors. Also included are a whole range of consultants for management, finance, taxes, energy, agriculture, armaments, information management, organization development, planning, and systems analysis.

Many of the farmers and miners require only a minimum of education. On the other hand, some government workers require a high level of education. Reich includes under *government workers* civil service workers, public school teachers, employees working for utilities, engineers working in the defense industry, and physicians supported by Medicaid and Medicare. Many civil service workers perform tasks similar to those performed in routine production services and inperson services.

In Reich's analysis of the future labor market, he believes that the highest wages will be given for symbolic-analytic services, while the lowest wages will be paid to routine production services and inperson services. This means that there is a direct relationship between the level of educational requirements and the level of income. According to Reich's job classifications, more than 60 percent of the jobs require only a high school diploma or less. This minimum education is required for routine production services, inperson services, some farmers and miners, and government workers performing tasks that are similar to routine production services and inperson services. The highest levels of education are required for symbolic-analytic services and some government workers.

SAVAGE INEQUALITIES, THE JOB MARKET, AND THE GLOBAL ECONOMY

Reich's discussion of the educational requirements of the labor market includes an analysis of the savage inequalities between school districts that is similar to Kozol's. But, unlike Kozol, Reich explains these savage inequalities in the context of a global economy. From Reich's perspective, the United States educates the finest symbolic-analysts. The education of these symbolic-analysts takes place in the elite public and private schools identified by Kozol. In the advanced tracks of the best primary and secondary schools, Reich argues, students learn the critical thinking skills and methods of dealing with information that are necessary to succeed as symbolic-analysts. On the other hand, the majority of students in the United States receive either a traditional education or, in the poorest school districts, no education at all. This traditional education prepares students for the tedious and routine occupations in production and inperson services.

Reich believes that the savage inequalities in education are a product of two factors. One factor is that parents who are symbolic-analysts want to pass their privileged positions and income on to their children. They can accomplish this goal by living in protected suburban enclaves with elite public schools or by sending their children to elite private schools. From the perspective of these parents, it doesn't matter what the quality of education is in most urban schools or in communities such as East St. Louis and Camden. In fact, these poorer school districts become the source of inexpensive labor for the inperson services provided to privileged symbolic-analysts and for the production services in the companies that they manage and plan.

The second factor is the growth of a global economy and the development of an internationalized labor force. Under current conditions, Reich argues, corporations move from state to state or country to country in search of the cheapest labor. In addition, corporations can demand of local, state, and national governments tax breaks and privileges with the threat that they will locate in another geographical area. The consequence is that large corporations are reducing their financial support of public school systems. This reduction in support enhances savage inequalities.

This withdrawal of financial support, Reich argues, is reflected in the financial problems faced by states and local school systems in the 1980s and 1990s as taxes were reduced on corporations and the wealthy. This reduction in financial support occurred at the same time that corporations were demanding better schools. In *The Work of Nations,* Reich writes, as an example of the duplicity of corporations regarding education policy, that the "executives of General Motors...who have been among the loudest to proclaim the need for better schools, have been the most relentless pursuers of local tax abatements." For instance, in Tarrytown, New York, General Motors was able to reduce its contribution to local tax revenues by $2.81 million. The result, according to Reich, was the laying off of scores of local teachers. Reich claims that after changes in federal, state, and local taxes in the 1980s, the income tax on the wealthiest citizens in the United States was the lowest in the world.

From this perspective, the general financial decline of many American schools does not matter to corporate leaders and other symbolic-analysts as long as their children have access to privileged public and private schools. The vast majority of American workers do not require a high level of education. While many workers in routine production services will need minimum technical skills for assembly-line work and computer processing, the major educational concern is the development of a work ethic that prepares workers to accept tedious and routine occupations.

Considered from the framework of social inequalities, this analysis of the job market and inequalities in educational opportunities suggests the perpetuation of social-class differences in the United States. If the highest paid jobs will be in symbolic-analytic services, then it seems very unlikely that many children living in poverty will be able to escape their social conditions. Their parents cannot afford to live in elite school districts or send their children to elite private schools. The schools that these children must attend do not have the curriculum, teachers, computers, and other scientific and technical equipment needed to prepare them for higher paying jobs. While symbolic-analysts attempt to pass on their economic privileges to their children, low-income parents are forced to pass on their economic conditions to their children. From this perspective, the savage inequalities in education are resulting in the continuation and possible increase in social-class differences.

SOCIAL REPRODUCTION

The discussion so far in this chapter would suggest that schools play a role in maintaining differences between social classes. This argument is called *social reproduction*. Simply defined, social reproduction means that the schools reproduce the social-class structure of society. Economists Samuel Bowles and Herbert Gintis are the major proponents of the concept of social reproduction. They contend that the school causes occupational immobility. This argument completely reverses the idea that the school creates occupational mobility to the idea that the school hinders mobility. Bowles and Gintis, in constructing this thesis, accept the findings that mobility rates are consistent throughout Western industrialized countries and that family background is one of the major factors in determining economic and social advancement. What they argue is that the school is a medium through which family background is translated into occupational and income opportunities.

This translation occurs with regard to personality traits relevant to the work task; modes of self-presentation such as manner of speech and dress; ascriptive characteristics such as race, sex, and age; and the level and prestige of the individual's education. Bowles and Gintis insist that the four factors—personality traits, self-presentation, ascriptive characteristics, and level of educational attainment—are all significantly related to occupational success. They also are all related to the social class of the family. For instance, family background is directly related to the level of educational attainment and the prestige of that attainment. In this particular case the economic level of the family determines educational attainment. Children from low-income families do not attain as high a level of education as children from rich families. From this standpoint the school reinforces social stratification and contributes to intergenerational immobility. In terms of ascriptive characteristics such as race, the social advantages or disadvantages of a particular racial group are again related to levels of educational attainment.

Personality traits and self-presentation are, according to Bowles and Gintis, important ingredients in occupational success. These characteristics are a direct product of child-rearing practices and reflect the social class of the family. Also, the economists assert, child-rearing patterns are directly related to the occupation of the head of the family. This argument is based on the work of Melvin Kohn, whose study of *Class and Conformity: A Study of Values,* found that middle-class parents are more likely to emphasize children's self-direction and working-class parents to emphasize conformity to external authority.

In other words, working-class families tended to be more authoritarian and violent toward their children than upper-class families. Children are more often punished with beatings in lower-class families than upper-class families. On the other hand, children in upper-class families are often given more freedom to pursue their own interests than children in lower-class families. Working-class parents value obedience, neatness, and honesty; higher-status parents emphasize curiosity, self-control, and happiness. Even when racial and religious divisions are considered, Kohn found that social class still stands out as the more important determinant in child-rearing values. Kohn argues that the most important thing that determines how children are treated in a family is the type of job held by the head of the household. If the head of the household works in a factory or other workplace where they primarily take orders, they will give orders to their children. On the other hand, if the head of the household has a job with a great deal of freedom to make independent decisions, then the children in their family will be granted the same freedom.

The more self-direction experienced on the job by the head of the family,the more likely it is that child-rearing patterns will emphsize self-direction. Self-direction on the job is directly related to the social class of the family. Higher-status and higher-income jobs usually involve self-direction; lower-status and lower-income jobs tend to be more routine and require more conformity to imposed rules.

In *Schooling in Capitalist America,* Bowles and Gintis support Kohn's conclusions. Child rearing, they declare, is important in developing personality traits related to entrance into the work force. Personalities evidencing a great deal of self-direction tend to have greater success in high-status occupations. The differences in child-rearing patterns, the authors state, are reflected in the schools attended by different social classes. Schools with populations from lower-income families tend to be more authoritarian and to require more conformity than schools attended by children from higher-income families. This is often reflected in the differences between educationally innovative schools in high-income suburbs and the more traditional schools in low-income, inner-city neighborhoods. In some cases, parents place pressure on local schools either to be more authoritarian or to allow more self-direction. The nature of this pressure tends to be related to the social class of the parents.

In this manner, Bowles and Gintis argue, the child-rearing patterns of the family are reflected in the way schools treat children. Authoritarian schools prepare children to work at jobs that require little independent thinking. Children from authoritarian families are prepared by authoritarian schools to work at low-paying jobs that do not require independent thinking and decision making. And the reverse is true for children coming from upper-income families and schools. They are socialized to high-paying jobs that require independent thinking. In this manner, education reproduces social classes.

EFFECTIVE SCHOOLS

Reproduction theory paints a dim picture of what schools can do to overcome problems caused by differences in the social-class backgrounds of students. Schools are portrayed as being unable to improve the achievement of students, and as inevitably reproducing the family background of students. Other studies suggest a more complex and hopeful picture of the role of the school. The more-effective-schools movement is premised on the idea that certain improvements in schools will lead to improvements in the academic achievement of children from lower socioeconomic backgrounds. Other studies argue that the school does not simply reproduce social-class backgrounds, but that a mediation occurs between the culture of the school and the culture of the student's family. This mediation has its own consequences for the academic and social development of students.

The book that provided the first insights into how schools might be reformed to improve the academic achievement of students from lower-class backgrounds is Michael Rutter's *Fifteen Thousand Hours.* The title refers to the number of hours a child spends in British schools from the age of 5 to the age when leaving school. The study focused on twelve schools in the inner city of London.

The general purpose of the study was to find the relationship between educational inputs and outcomes—to find the things a school can do that will make a difference in the education of children. The study was conducted at a time when a great deal of research was saying that the school makes very little difference and that the primary cause of educational outcome is family background. Previous research found that the amount of money spent, the types of buildings and libraries, and other educational inputs were not as important as family background.

Fifteen Thousand Hours concluded that certain variations that exist between schools in the social and academic outcomes of students could *not* be explained by family background, size of school, age of buildings, space available, or administrative organization. The study found that some schools had better attendance, better student behavior, less delinquency, and better examination scores because of the characteristics of the school as a social institution. The characteristics found to be related to better behavior, less delinquency, and better examination scores were degree of academic emphasis, how teachers acted during lessons, system of rewards and punishments, degree of responsibility assumed by students, and social conditions of the pupils in school.

More specifically, the study found better behavior in the classroom when the teacher prepared a lesson in advance, arrived on time, and taught the class as a whole. It found classroom conditions to be better when the teacher provided ample praise; frequent disciplinary actions by the teacher were linked to disruptive behavior. Like other experts, the researchers for *Fifteen Thousand Hours* found better student behavior and performance linked to expectations and standards. Students had higher academic success when there was a frequent assignment of homework and when teachers expressed high academic expectations to the students. In more commonsense terms, when teachers prepare their lessons and expect their students to learn, there is a greater chance for academic success.

The study also found that if teachers act as if they care about their students, and if good care is taken of school buildings, then students receive the message that schooling and student activities are valued. In addition, attendance was better and delinquency less frequent in schools where the entire staff planned the curriculum and the methods for handling discipline. Positive results were also found when there were shared activities between students and staff, and when students were given positions of responsibility in the school.

Fifteen Thousand Hours found a relationship between all the above factors and educational outcomes. No single factor could be identified in isolation from other factors as causing better behavior, higher attendance, and higher examination scores. All the factors combined to create a social ethos that affected educational outcomes. The study also found relationships among behavior, exam success, and attendance. Schools with high rates of exam success had good attendance and few behavior problems. The social ethos of a school creates a general pattern of social behavior among students.

The findings of *Fifteen Thousand Hours* suggest that it is meaningful to talk about equality of educational opportunity in terms of educational outcomes. In the context of the study it would mean that some schools are better than others for children from the same family background. Children from lower-class backgrounds *can* attend schools that will make a difference, and that difference is primarily determined by the factors making up the social ethos of the school. Equal educational opportunity can be improved if teachers prepare lessons and have high expectations of their students, if there is an ample system of reward, if the staff and administration work cooperatively, and if students assume responsibility. The major limitation of *Fifteen Thousand Hours* is that it focused on schools attended by a particular social group.

The findings reported in *Fifteen Thousand Hours* had a strong impact on what has been referred to as the "more-effective-schools" movement in the United States. It reinforced many of the findings of researchers working in the early 1980s in elementary schools located in low-income areas of inner cities. These researchers were finding that schools with characteristics similar to those found by Rutter in successful schools in England were having a positive effect on achievement-test scores. These characteristics have been identified as the following:

1. A principal with strong leadership in instruction
2. Teachers with high levels of expectations for student learning
3. School climate

4. Increased time on instructional tasks
5. Regular and systematic student evaluations
6. Community support and adequate resources

The reader should understand that the more-effective-schools movement has a very distinct definition of a successful school. It is a definition that makes the results of achievement-test scores the major criteria of educational success. The most common definition of educational success in the more-effective-schools movement is bringing an equal percentage of a school's upper and lower social classes to minimum mastery of basic skills. By describing success in these terms it has been hoped that an equal emphasis will be given to the teaching of students from both upper and lower social-class backgrounds.

As effective-school projects were instituted in many cities, there was some variation in what were considered the characteristics of a successful school. For instance, Daniel U. Levine and Robert J. Havighurst report in their book, *Society and Education*, that the Connecticut School Effectiveness Project defined the characteristics of effective schools as follows:

1. A safe environment that is conducive to learning
2. Clear school goals
3. Instructional leadership from the principal
4. A climate of high expectations
5. A high percentage of time on task
6. Frequent evaluation of student performance
7. Community support

Levine and Havighurst also report the findings of a survey conducted by Phi Delta Kappa on the characteristics of effective inner-city elementary schools, in which the only additions to the above lists would be low adult-child ratios in the schools and greater parental involvement.

In *Schools in the Central Cities*, Kathryn Borman and Joel Spring report that in Milwaukee the effective-schools project named RISE (Rising to Individual Scholastic Excellence) adopted the following three assumptions: (1) Virtually all students, regardless of their family background, can acquire basic skills; (2) inappropriate school expectations and practices are the major cause of low achievement by low-income and minority students; and (3) the literature on effective schools has identified expectations, norms, practices, and policies associated with high achievement.

Many of the characteristics identified with effective schools appear on the surface to be common sense. Certainly, a school should have a leader who is interested in instruction. The problem is that many school principals are overwhelmed with the noninstructional aspects of their jobs. Many principals spend endless hours worrying about paperwork, maintenance of school buildings, the school cafeteria, community relations, and discipline problems. Very often principals are not adequately trained to be instructional leaders.

Placed in this context, the expectation that principals should be instructional leaders represents a major revolution in the activities of many school leaders. In a similar manner, one would expect teachers to have expectations that their students will learn. But, as was described earlier in this chapter, teachers tend to have low levels of expectations for children from minority backgrounds and lower social classes. Many teachers in inner-city schools view their jobs as primarily baby-sitting and have reduced their levels of instructional expectations. This is why the more-effective-schools movement has placed a great deal of emphasis upon teachers expecting and demanding high-quality academic work from all children.

One would also assume that the majority of time in a school and in a classroom would be spent on instructional tasks. In many cases this has not been so, because of all the noninstructional tasks that are given to schools and the amount of time spent in the classroom by teachers on noninstructional activities. For instance, a great deal of school time can be devoted to assemblies, playground activities, collecting money for various activities, the filing of reports, attendance monitoring, and other noninstructional activities. Placing emphasis upon time on task in instruction is simply stating that the primary goal of the school should be instruction in subject matter.

School climate and community resources are two related aspects of the more-effective-schools movement. School climate refers to the general atmosphere of the school. In many ways it cannot be clearly defined to a person who has not visited a variety of inner-city schools. Some schools look dirty, are poorly maintained, and have students drifting through the halls, and the noise from the classrooms suggests more chaos than engagement in instructional activities. Other inner-city schools project just the opposite impression, with chaos giving way to reasonably happy students interested in school activities. Obviously, school climate depends to a great extent on the leadership of the principal. But it also depends on community resources and support. Without that support it is difficult to maintain the physical plant of the school, provide teachers with adequate instructional materials, and maintain reasonable class sizes. Under poor conditions, teacher and student morale begins to decline and the general atmosphere of the school is no longer conducive to learning.

The emphasis in the more-effective-schools movement on constant monitoring of student progress has two important aspects. On one hand, it is reasonable to assume that good teaching requires knowing how your students are progressing. This could mean testing them at regular intervals to determine how well they are advancing through their lessons. On the other hand, testing does take time away from instructional tasks and does increase the work of the teacher. This is particularly true if the school system requires that the teacher report test scores to some central office.

Also, testing has become increasingly political as teachers, principals, and superintendents are evaluated on the basis of students' test scores. For instance, merit pay for teachers could be based on the test scores of their students; principals in many school districts are being evaluated on this basis. In the same manner, superintendents are often evaluated on the basis of the test scores for the entire district. For these reasons, high test scores are important for job security and advancement in school systems. As a result there is an increasing tendency to teach to the test. In other words, the primary objective of school administrators and teachers under these circumstances can become teaching for improvement on specific test items. In these cases, the test determines the content of instruction.

Although some criticism can be directed at the more-effective-schools movement's overreliance on testing, a very positive aspect of the movement is the emphasis it places on the ability of lower-income students to learn. This emphasis is a major change from the despair of the 1960s and 1970s when many people began to abandon any hope of improving schools. Rather than seeing educational outcomes as inevitably linked to family background, the more-effective-schools movement holds out some hope that schools can make a difference.

On the other hand, like most of the theories discussed in this chapter, the more-effective-schools movement treats students as passive recipients of knowledge. The language and images of the movement convey a sense of students being manipulated to do schoolwork and then responding by doing well on standardized tests. It is assumed that if schools follow a prescribed procedure then students will conform by learning set lessons. But, as the next section on resistance suggests, students are not passive objects that are easily manipulated by school authorities.

RESISTANCE

As educational philosopher Henry Giroux argues, most educational studies assume that students are nonresistant recipients of instruction and that they can be easily managed by the school. Certainly, arguments that schools simply reproduce the social-class structure create an image of submissive students being molded for their place in society. Even the more-effective-schools movement assumes that students can be easily managed to achieve higher test scores. But any teacher will tell you that students are not that easily controlled and manipulated. Many students balk at following instructions, and they go out of their way to make life difficult for teachers. Students have an agenda regarding life that might have little to do with the goals of the school.

Giroux contends that students often resist the plans made by teachers and school administrators. In this case, *resistance* means the culture developed among students to oppose the goals of teachers and the schools. The pioneer study of this phenomenon is Paul Willis' *Learning to Labour*. Willis studied a group of students from working-class backgrounds who attended an all-male comprehensive high school in an industrial area of England. These students learned to manipulate the environment of the school in order to make sure that they would have a good time. They created a peer culture that was antischool. Their culture differed sharply from what they called the "ear-'oles." The "ear-'oles"—students who appeared to do nothing but sit and listen in school—represent the student who conforms to the authority and the expectations of the school.

The working-class students resented both the "ear-'oles" and the authority of the school. They felt that the school was out of touch with real life and had little relationship with the male working-class world that they came from and expected to enter as adults. They took every opportunity to play pranks on school officials, teachers, and "ear-'oles." Their culture was a rejection of hopes for upward mobility through schooling and the values of schooling and learning.

Ironically, Willis portrays this antischool culture as preparation for the generalized labor force the students will be entering. The pranks they play in school are similar to the pranks they will later play on the shop floor. The peer culture they develop is similar to the culture of their fathers at work and the culture they will experience when they enter the work force. This interpretation provides a more complex picture of the interaction between family background and the school. The students create an antischool culture that plays a determining role in assuring the perpetuation of their working-class status.

In Willis' account, the school is not the villain that takes account of family background to reproduce existing social classes. Rather, the culture of the school comes into conflict with the culture of the students. The result is the creation of a student culture that rejects the values of the school and is preparation for continued working-class status.

The antischool culture that developed among these students was not in their best interests. The school did hold out the opportunity for them to gain an education and improve their status in life. In addition, the student culture described in Willis' study is sexist and racist. Given these facts, the notion of an antischool culture should not be romanticized as something to protect.

On the other hand, students do resist school programs that they know are not working in their interests. Some students develop an antischool culture when they note that the real benefits of schooling seem to go to students in the upper-curriculum tracks and ability groups. Often, this resistance is exhibited as a general defiance of school authority. In addition, many students develop a sense of rage as they witness their life's chances slipping away. Rage turns to anger and anger sometimes results in physical violence.

Within this framework, the key to improving the schools for the children of the poor is to understand that school learning is really a function of the interaction between student culture and the school's intentions. Students at many times have reasons for feeling oppressed. Consequently, educational change should be a product of a dialogue between students and school authorities. This dialogue might result in the school adjusting to the culture of students and students adjusting to the culture of the school. One might argue that this is the method for ensuring that the school provides equality of opportunity.

In *Theory of Resistance: A Pedagogy for the Opposition* and his many other writings, Henry Giroux argues that student resistance can be the vehicle for developing an educational method that will empower students and teachers to transform society. I do not have room in this book to cover Giroux's arguments in any depth, but at the end of Chapter 10 there is a brief discussion of critical theory that forms the framework for Giroux's argument. Critical theory suggests that by itself education can never provide equality of opportunity. Not only may the pursuit of equality of opportunity through schooling be a false hope, but it may also distract people from the real issues. In could be that equality of opportunity depends on concrete economic changes in society.

In the next chapter, I will explore the question of equality of education versus social transformation in the context of issues related to gender, ethnicity, and race. Related to this question and set of issues is the problem of equal educational opportunity.

EXERCISES

1. A major issue discussed in this chapter is the relationship between social class and inequality of educational opportunity. Was this a factor in your education? Can you remember if social class was related to ability grouping or different curriculum tracks?
2. Select a high school in your community and determine whether social class is related to the curriculum in which the students are placed. Are students at this school who are from particular social groups the major participants in extracurricular activities?
3. Make a chart tracing the major occupational changes in the last several generations of your family. Try to determine the major factors that caused social mobility in your family.
4. In a group discussion or essay discuss whether you think the school should be used as an institution to foster equality of opportunity.
5. Investigate differences in expenditures per student in your community. Do these differences reflect the racial and social-class backgrounds of the students? Do inequality of expenditures result in unequal educational opportunities?
6. Ask your local Chamber of Commerce or appropriate local government office for their determination of the distribution of jobs in your community. Match this job distribution to Robert Reich's job categories of routine production services, inperson services, symbolic-analytic services, farmers and miners, and government workers. Based on these job classifications, make a rough estimate of the educational requirements of your local job market.
7. Based on exercises 5 and 6, determine whether or not inequalities in educational expenditures per student in your community will result in some students being trapped in lower paying jobs.

SUGGESTED READINGS AND WORKS CITED IN CHAPTER

Ballantine, Jeanne. *The Sociology of Education*. Englewood Cliffs, N. J.: Prentice-Hall, 1983. Chapter 3 of this study of the sociology of education contains information on the relationship between education and social stratification.

Borman, Kathryn, and Joel Spring. *Schools in Central Cities*. New York: Longman, 1984. Chapter 7 of this study of central-city schools provides an analysis of the more-effective-schools movement.

Bowles, Samuel, and Herbert Gintis. *Schooling in Capitalist America*. New York: Basic Books, 1976. This book by two neo-Marxist economists argues that schooling in the United States maintains the existing social-class structure for the benefit of an economic elite.

Freeman, Richard B. *The Overeducated American*. New York: Academic Press, 1976. Freeman provides a summary of research on education and income and a study of the effects of supply and demand on that relationship.

Giroux, Henry. *Theory of Resistance: A Pedagogy for the Opposition*. South Hadley, Mass.: Bergin and Garvey, 1983. In this book Giroux criticizes reproduction theorists and presents his theories of resistance.

Hollingshead, A. B. *Elmtown's Youth*. New York: John Wiley, 1949. The classic study of the effect of social class on adolescent life in a small town.

Jencks, Christopher. *Inequality*. New York: Harper and Row, 1972. A major study of the effects of family and schooling on inequality.

Kohn, Melvin. *Class and Conformity: A Study of Values*. Homewood, Ill.: Dorsey, 1969. A study of the relationship between child-rearing practices and social class.

Kozol, Jonathan. *Savage Inequalities: Children in America's Schools*. New York: Crown Publishers, Inc., 1991. Kozol details the inequalities in spending per student between school districts and the resulting inequalities in the quality of education.

Levine, Daniel U., and Robert J. Havighurst. *Society and Education*. 6th ed. Boston: Allyn and Bacon, 1984. Chapters 3, 4, and 5 of this study of the sociology of education are devoted to the issue of education and opportunity.

Oakes, Jeannie. *Keeping Track: How Schools Structure Inequality*. New Haven: Yale University Press, 1985. This book explores the issue of tracking as a source of inequality.

Persell, Caroline. *Education and Inequality*. New York: Free Press, 1979. The best available summary of research on the causes and consequences of inequality of educational opportunity.

"Poorer New York School Districts Seek More Aid." *New York Times* (6 May 1991): A1, B4. This article provides statistics on differences in school expenditures in the New York City metropolitan area.

Reich, Robert. *The Work of Nations: Preparing Ourselves for 21st-Century Capitalism*. New York: Alfred Knopf, 1991. This study by President Bill Clinton's secretary of labor outlines the educational requirements for jobs in a global economy.

Rosenthal, Robert, and Lenore Jacobson. *Pygmalion in the Classroom: Teacher Expectation and Pupils' Intellectual Development*. New York: Irvington, 1988. The classic study of the effects of teacher expectations.

Rutter, Michael, et al. *Fifteen Thousand Hours*. Cambridge, Mass.: Harvard University Press, 1979. A study of the differences among twelve inner-city schools in London and how those differences are related to behavior and academic achievement.

Schmidt, Peter. "Debate Over Ability Grouping Gains High Profile." *Education Week* (13 January 1992): 23. This article covers the different arguments for the support or nonsupport of grouping by academic ability.

_____ . "Mass. Leads Mounting Charge Against Ability Grouping." *Education Week*(13 January 1992): 1, 22. This article discusses the attempt by the Massachusetts Department of Education to end ability grouping in local school districts.

Sexton, Patricia. *Education and Income*. New York: Viking, 1961. A study of the relationship between family income and ability grouping, tracking, and achievement in a large city.

Wasserman, Miriam. *The School Fix: NYC, USA*. New York: Outerbridge and Dienstfrey, 1970. First section of the book has case studies of students who did and did not make it successfully through the New York schools.

Willis, Paul. *Learning to Labour*. Lexington, Mass.: D. C. Heath, 1979. A study of the development of an antischool peer culture among working-class students in England.

CHAPTER 5

Equality of Educational Opportunity

At the heart of education-related discussions about gender, race, and ethnicity is the issue of *equality of educational opportunity*. Simply defined, equality of educational opportunity means that everyone has an equal chance to receive an education. In the United States, as I will discuss later, women and racial and ethnic minorities have been deprived of this opportunity and continue to struggle for an equal chance to receive an education. This sorry chapter in the history of the American school illustrates how education can be a source of freedom or a tool of oppression.

Throughout the world, educational systems that are designed to enslave women and racial and ethnic minorities can be found. This is done by either denying these groups access to an education or providing an education that teaches them that they are inferior. But there are also educational systems that serve as a means for ensuring equality of opportunity and for cultivating pride in being a woman or a member of a racial or ethnic minority.

When defined as an equal chance to attend publicly supported schools, equal educational opportunity is primarily a legal issue. In this context, the provision of equal educational opportunity can be defined solely on the grounds of justice: If government provides a service like education, all classes of citizens should have equal access to that service.

But legal equality of opportunity to attend public schools does not guarantee that education will be a source of freedom. As mentioned earlier, public schools can be structured to deny equal educational opportunity. This is illustrated by events in Selma, Alabama, in the early 1990s. During the 1950s and 1960s, Selma was a center of violent civil rights protests to demand equal voting rights and integrated education. As a result, by the time of the school protests of 1990, legislation guaranteed African-American children equal educational opportunity to attend publicly supported schools. But this right of attendance was undermined by a system of tracking students into different curricula. The dispute in 1990 centered on the racial distribution in advanced placement and college preparatory courses offered in Selma's public high school.

Selma, like many other communities in the South, separates races within the public schools by placing them in different curriculum tracks, such as college preparatory and advanced placement. The racial bias underlying the placement of students in such tracks is clearly evident in Selma's high school. In Selma 90 percent of *all* white students were placed in college preparatory and advanced-placement tracks, while only 3 percent of *all* African-American students were placed in those tracks. According to Phyllis McClure, an education specialist with the Legal Defense and Education Fund of the National Association for the Advancement of Colored People (NAACP), this form of racial segregation through tracking is common throughout southern states.

When Dr. Norward Roussell, Selma's first African-American schools superintendent, tried to correct this racial imbalance by increasing the percentage of African-American students in college preparatory and advanced-placement tracks to 10 percent, he was notified by the white-dominated school board that he was being dismissed. Dr. Roussell stated that the school system was violating students' rights by tracking them primarily on the basis of teachers' recommendations. "And of course, as you might imagine, the majority of students in the bottom levels were black," he said in an interview in the February 21, 1990, issue of *Education Week*, "despite the fact that many had standardized-test scores as high or higher than those in the upper level." It required a school boycott by African-American students before he was reinstated. White parents reacted with threats to remove their children from the public schools and send them to private institutions.

Therefore, equality of educational opportunity requires more than just an equal chance to attend a publicly supported school. It also requires equal treatment within schools. Inequality of treatment in school can be a result of other factors as well. For many years handicapped students were denied equal access to an education because of the lack of provisions to accommodate their special needs. Entry into buildings and movement between floors was difficult for many handicapped students because they could not negotiate stairs, and neither ramps for wheelchairs nor elevators were provided. Equal educational opportunity for handicapped people has meant making physical changes in buildings.

In addition to providing equal treatment in placement in curricular tracks and physical access to buildings, equality of educational opportunity requires positive recognition of the gender, race, and ethnic background of the student. Equality of educational opportunity has little meaning if students gain equal access to an education and then are taught they are inferior.

Inequality of treatment can occur in very subtle ways. This is particularly evident in the history of discrimination against women in education. For instance, while doing research on the history of education during World War II, Felecia Briscoe encountered a reproduction of a poster of which the National Education Association had distributed 50,000 copies in 1944 as part of its "teacher-recruiting and morale-building campaign." Titled "The Teacher," the poster depicts a female teacher and an elementary school-age boy and girl standing around a world globe. The little girl is wearing a neat dress and her hair is perfectly groomed. She is staring passively at the globe with a blank expression on her face, and her empty arms dangle beside her. The teacher is seated between the two children. Her head is turned away from the girl and she gazes with approval at the boy. The boy clutches a book in one hand and points to a place on the globe with the other. Unlike the girl, his hair is rumpled and his face is animated. The poster clearly conveys an impression that males are active learners and intellectually superior to females, whereas girls are passive and intellectually dull.

Equality of educational opportunity can be denied also to children from homes where English is not the spoken language, when no special provision for this language problem is made by the schools. Courts have ruled that children who do not fully comprehend the language of the school are being denied equal access to instruction. Equality of educational opportunity in this situation means that the schools must provide special help for children with non-English-speaking backgrounds.

In summary, the concept of equal educational opportunity covers a broad spectrum of educational issues including equal opportunity to attend public supported schools, educational practices within schools, the content of curriculum and textbooks, and recognition of the cultural and language background of the student.

EQUALITY OF EDUCATIONAL OPPORTUNITY AND EQUALITY OF OPPORTUNITY

There is an important distinction between equality of opportunity and equality of educational opportunity. As defined in Chapter 4, equality of opportunity means that everyone has the same chance to compete for positions in society. Equality of educational opportunity means that everyone has the same chance to receive an education. Equal educational opportunity does not guarantee equal opportunity in the labor market. It can be argued that equality of educational opportunity is essential for equality of opportunity in society. But this argument can be maintained only if there is proof that education does in fact provide equality of opportunity, and, as shown in the previous chapter, the ability of education to provide equality of opportunity is still debatable.

One important role education can play in aiding equal opportunity for women and racial and ethnic minorities is the eradication of prejudices and stereotypes. Prejudices and stereotypes often hinder the advancement of these groups in the economic system. From this standpoint, educating students to tolerate diverse groups can be one of the most important contributions of schools to equal opportunity. This opinion was expressed with regard to Native Americans by Joseph Abeyta, superintendent of the Santa Fe Indian School, at a 1990 conference on Native-American education. As reported in the February 21, 1990, issue of *Education Week,* Abeyta declared that the greatest educational challenge is to "help change the attitudes of this country regarding Native-American students."

Highlighting the importance of eliminating prejudices and stereotypes to ensure equal opportunity are recent findings on promotion opportunities for women working in corporations. Despite greater educational opportunities for women and corporate programs designed to keep women in the work force, such as on-site day care and parental leave, women continue to have difficulty moving up the corporate ladder. In 1990, Cindy Skrzycki, a *Washington Post* staff writer, reported that in interviews conducted with fifty professional and managerial women who left major American corporations after five or more years of employment, their primary reason for leaving was a feeling of being "dead-ended" in their jobs. She found that corporate chief executives admitted the existence of a "glass ceiling" that prevented women from reaching top corporate positions. Interviews with two hundred top corporate leaders revealed that the major stumbling blocks to the advancement of women are stereotyping and preconceptions about female abilities.

These findings suggest that an important role for education in providing equality of opportunity is the elimination of prejudices and stereotypes. As will be discussed in the next section, the historic struggle for civil rights includes the fight against prejudice and a struggle for both equality of opportunity and equality of educational opportunity.

THE STRUGGLE FOR CIVIL RIGHTS

American history is the story of the steady struggle for increased civil participation in society. Usually the term *civil rights* means the right to an equal opportunity to gain economic and social advantages, and equal treatment by the law. Since the founding of the republic, groups have struggled to remove barriers that deny equal access to economic opportunities, institutions, and political power. It is important to understand that an increase in civil rights occurred only because of active participation and struggle by citizens. The reason improving civil rights requires struggle is that it usually results in reducing the advantages held by one class of citizens over another class of citizens.

The two most important struggles for equal civil rights have been by women and by racial minority groups. For both groups the struggle was for equal political power, equal access to economic opportunities, equal treatment and access to social institutions, and equality of educational opportunity. One important struggle for women in the United States was for the right to vote. Although the suffrage movement was international, in the United States its final resolution was the adoption in 1920 of the Nineteenth Amendment to the Constitution.

Another important struggle for women is gaining equal access to economic opportunities. Historically, women were relegated to certain sectors of the labor market. In the nineteenth century, the primary sources of employment for women outside the home were as domestic help, teachers, factory work-ers, and in other service occupations. These employment opportunities were usually occasions for economic exploitation. For instance, women and chil-dren comprised a large sector of industrial employment in the nineteenth century because they were a cheap form of labor. As pointed out in Chapter 2, women were allowed to enter the ranks of teaching primarily because they were viewed as a cheap and steady work force. In the latter part of the nineteenth and early part of the twentieth centuries, women came to domi-nate the professions of nursing and social work, which are often referred to as the helping professions. Again, the wage scales of these professions were considerably below those in professions dominated by men.

With the growth of white-collar occupations in the twentieth century, women became the major source of workers for office positions such as secretaries, typists, and clerks. In the twentieth century, schools played an important role in assuring the perpetuation of women in these occupations. One of the most successful vocational education programs has been in busi-ness and secretarial skillls. These programs tend to enroll women primarily. This means that a sex-segregated curriculum contributes to the maintenance of a sex-segregated sector of the labor market.

Educational institutions are central to the struggle by women for equal access to occupations. First, although women have composed a majority of the teaching force since the nineteenth century, they do not hold an equiva-lent number of administrative positions in public schools, nor have they held an equivalent number of positions on university faculties. Second, education-al training is the primary means of entering many professions, such as law and medicine. Gaining equal access to these educational programs is an important part of women's struggle for equality of opportunity.

One important gain for women was the passage by the federal govern-ment of the Higher Education Act of 1972. Title IX of this legislation provided both for sexual equality in employment in educational institutions and for sexual equality in educational programs. The legislation applied to all educa-tional institutions, including preschool, elementary and secondary schools, vocational and professional schools, and public and private undergraduate and graduate institutions. A 1983 U.S. Supreme Court decision, *Grove City College* v. *Bell,* restricted Title IX in its application to specific educational programs within institutions. In the 1987 Civil Rights Restoration Act, Con-gress overturned the Court's decision and amended Title IX to include all activities of an educational institution receiving federal aid. This decision will be discussed in more detail in Chapter 9.

Like oppressed women, minority groups have struggled for equal civil rights. For African Americans, the major problem has been struggling against the legacy of slavery. After the Civil War, two amendments to the Constitu-tion promised to give African Americans equal political status. The Four-teenth Amendment to the Constitution, ratified in 1868, guaranteed equality before the law. This amendment is extremely important in arguments for equality of educational opportunity. It will be discussed and mentioned throughout this chapter and other chapters in the book. The Fifteenth Amendment to the Constitution, ratified in 1870, guaranteed that the right to vote would not be denied on account of race, color, or previous condition of servitude.

The promise of equality before the law was denied to African Americans in southern states in the latter part of the nineteenth century with the passage of "Jim Crow" laws. These laws made it extremely difficult for African Americans to vote, and mandated segregation in public schools and other public institutions. The abolition of these restrictive laws was a major focus of the African-American community's civil rights struggle, beginning in the late nineteenth century and continuing through the 1960s, when Congress passed legislation protecting civil rights and the right to vote for African Americans.

The African-American community in the United States believed ending racial segregation in schools was a means of improving equality of opportunity, because desegregation would help to remove the stigma of racial inferiority and would provide greater opportunities for upward occupational mobility. This is why educational aspirations are high in the African-American community. Historically, much of the hope of the African-American community centered on gaining equality of educational opportunity.

Like women, minority groups found themselves relegated to low-wage sectors of the labor force. In fact, there is a direct relationship between segregation in education and economic exploitation. One clear example is found in the state of California, which at different periods in history segregated Chinese, Japanese, Chicanos, Indians, and African Americans. Segregation of these groups coincided with their exploitation as workers. For instance, Chinese were segregated in California during the period when they were brought into the country as inexpensive labor to work on the railroads; Japanese were segregated at the time they were being brought in as agricultural workers. In the South, African Americans were segregated during a period when their labor was considered necessary for the building of the new industrial South.

Problems of employment discrimination continue in the 1990s. For instance, according to a 1990 study by the National Science Foundation, African Americans accounted for 2.5 percent and women accounted for 15 percent of all employed scientists and engineers. While African Americans showed gains from a 1.6 percent figure in 1976, the numbers still did not reflect the fact that African Americans represented 10 percent of the work force. The percentage of women scientists and engineers was also up from 9 percent from 1976. For Hispanic Americans, only 2 percent were scientists and engineers while they constituted 7 percent of all workers. The National Science Foundation was particularly disturbed by these figures because within the next thirty years about 70 percent of those entering the work force will be women, immigrants, and those now considered minority members.

As discussed earlier in the chapter, segregation carries with it the stigma of racial inferiority. The belief in the racial inferiority of one group allows other groups to rationalize its place at the bottom of the labor market. In other words, one can justify placing racial groups in positions of economic exploitation by claiming that they are inferior and unsuitable for other positions. Historically, segregated education in the United States and other countries was a means of perpetuating myths of racial superiority and inferiority.

Institutional racial discrimination occurs in the same form in which social-class discrimination occurs. There is a tendency for white school teachers and principals to have lower expectations for African-American students than for white students. This is not necessarily an example of overt racism but is primarily a result of the cultural isolation of the white community from the African-American community and the lack of awareness by the white community of the high educational aspirations of African-American parents and students. In addition to the problem of teachers' low expectations, there is a tendency in large school systems for younger and less experienced teachers to be placed in schools that are predominantly nonwhite.

The greatest impact of civil rights struggles on schools is the process of desegregation. Desegregation helped to fulfill the promise of equal educational opportunity and changed the organizational structure of education by fostering the development of magnet schools. This chapter will next explore the process of desegregation, the problems of institutional segregation and racism, and the effects of the struggle of women for equal rights.

DESEGREGATION OF AMERICAN SCHOOLS

The historic 1954 Supreme Court school desgregation case, *Brown* v. *Board of Education of Topeka*, gave legal meaning to the idea that segregated education means unequal education. Until 1954, segregated schools in the United States operated under a ruling given by the Supreme Court in 1895, *Plessy* v. *Ferguson*, that segregation did not create a badge of inferiority if segregated facilities were equal and the law was reasonable. The decision in both cases centered around the meaning of the Fourteenth Amendment to the Constitution. This amendment was ratified in 1868, shortly after the close of the Civil War. One of its purposes was to extend the basic guarantees of the Bill of Rights into the areas of state and local government. The most important and controversial section of the Fourteenth Amendment states: "No State shall make or enforce any law which shall abridge the privileges or immunities of citizens . . . nor . . . deprive any person of life, liberty, or property, without due process of law; nor deny to any person within its jurisdiction the equal protection of the laws."

The 1895 decision, *Plessy* v. *Ferguson*, involved Homer Plessy, who was one-eighth African American and seven-eighths white. He was arrested for refusing to ride in the colored coach of a train, as required by Louisiana state law. The Supreme Court's decision in this case, that segregated facilities could exist if they were equal, became known as the "separate but equal" doctrine.

The 1954 desegregation decision, *Brown* v. *Board of Education of Topeka*, overturned the "separate but equal" doctrine by arguing, on the basis of the findings of social science, that segregated education was inherently unequal. This meant that even if school facilities, teachers, equipment, and all other physical conditions were equal between two racially segregated schools, the two schools would still be unequal because of the fact of racial segregation.

In 1964 Congress took a significant step toward speeding up school desegregation by passing the important Civil Rights Act. In terms of school desegregation, Title VI of the 1964 Civil Rights Act was most important because it provided a means for the federal government to force school desegregation. In its final form, Title VI required the mandatory withholding of federal funds from institutions that practiced racial discrimination. Title VI states that no person, because of race, color or national origin, could be excluded from or denied the benefits of any program receiving federal financial assistance. It required all federal agencies to establish guidelines to implement this policy. Refusal by institutions or projects to follow these guidelines was to result in the "termination of or refusal to grant or to continue assistance under such program or activity."

Title VI of the 1964 Civil Rights Act was important for two reasons. First, it established a major precedent for federal control of American public schools, by making explicit that the control of money would be one method used by the federal government to shape local school policies. (This aspect of the law will be discussed in more detail in Chapter 9.) Second, it turned the federal Office of Education into a policing agency with the responsibility of determining whether or not school systems were segregated, and if they were, of doing something about the segregated conditions.

One result of Title VI was to speed up the process of school desegregation in the South, particularly after the passage of federal legislation in 1965 that increased the amount of money available to local schools from the federal government. In the late 1960s southern school districts rapidly began to submit school desegregation plans to the Office of Education.

In the North prosecution of inequality in educational opportunity as it related to school segregation required a different approach from that used in the South. In the South, school segregation existed by legislative acts that required separation of the races. In the North there were no specific laws requiring separation of the races. But even without specific laws, racial segregation existed. Therefore, it was necessary for individuals bringing complaints against northern school districts to prove that the existing patterns of racial segregation were the result of purposeful action on the part of the school district. It had to be proved that school officials intended racial segregation to be a result of their educational policies.

The conditions required to prove segregation were explicitly outlined in 1974, in the Sixth Circuit Court of Appeals case *Oliver* v. *Michigan State Board of Education*. The court stated, "A presumption of segregative purpose arises when plaintiffs establish that the natural, probable and foreseeable result of public officials' action or inaction was an increase or perpetuation of public school segregation." This did not mean that individual motives or prejudices were to be investigated, but that the overall pattern of school actions had to be shown to increase racial segregation. In the language of the court: "the question whether a purposeful pattern of segregation has manifested itself over time, despite the fact that individual official actions, considered alone, may not have been taken for segregative purposes. . . ."

The most politically explosive and controversial aspect of both court actions and actions under Title VI are desegregation plans. The issue of busing as a means of desegregation hit the national scene with full force in 1971, when the Supreme Court in *Swann* v. *Charlotte-Mecklenburg Board of Education* supported busing as a legitimate tool for bringing about the desegregation of school districts. The Court warned that "schools all or predominantly of one race in a district of mixed population will require close scrutiny to determine that school assignments are not part of state-enforced segregation."

NATIVE AMERICANS

While African Americans were at the forefront of the struggle for equal educational opportunity, Native Americans and Mexican Americans joined the civil rights movement with complaints that government schools were destroying their cultures and languages, and that they were subject to segregation. In particular, Native Americans wanted to gain control of the education of their children and restore their cultural heritage and languages to the curriculum. The demand for self-determination by Native Americans received consideration in government decisions after the election of John F. Kennedy in 1960. The Kennedy administration advocated Indian participation in decisions regarding federal policies. Kennedy's secretary of interior, Stewart Udall, appointed a Task Force on Indian Affairs which, in its 1961 report, recommended that Native Americans be given full citizenship and self-sufficiency.

One of the results of the drive for self-determination was the creation of the Rough Rock Demonstration School in 1966. Established on a Navajo reservation in Arizona, the school was a joint effort of the Office of Economic Opportunity and the Bureau of Indian Affairs. One of the major goals of the demonstration school was for Navajo parents to control the education of their children and to participate in all aspects of their schooling.

Besides tribal control, one of the important features of the Rough Rock Demonstration School was the attempt to preserve the Navajo language and culture. In contrast to the attempts to destroy Native cultures and languages that took place in the nineteenth and early twentieth centuries, the goal of learning both Navajo and English was presented as a means of preparing children to live in both cultures.

The struggle for self-determination was aided by the development of a pan-Indian movement in the United States. The pan-Indian movement was based on the assumption that Native-American tribes shared a common set of values and interests. Similar to the role played by CORE and SCLC among African Americans, pan-Indian organizations, such as the American Indian Movement (AIM) and the Indians of All Tribes, led demonstrations demanding self-determination. In 1969, members of the Indians of All Tribes seized Alcatraz Island in San Francisco Bay as a means of calling attention to the plight of Native Americans and demanding that the island, which Indians had originally sold to the federal government for $24 worth of beads, be made an Indian cultural and education center. In 1972, AIM organized a march on Washington, D.C., called the Trail of Broken Treaties. Members of the march seized the Bureau of Indian Affairs and hung a large sign at its entrance declaring it the American Indian Embassy.

It was in this climate of civil rights activism and political support for Indian self-determination that the U.S. Senate Committee on Labor and Public Welfare issued in 1969 the report, *Indian Education: A National Tragedy— A National Challenge*. The report opened with a statement condemning previous educational policies of the federal government: "A careful review of the historical literature reveals that the dominant policy of the Federal Government toward the American Indian has been one of forced assimilation . . . [because of] a desire to divest the Indian of his land."

After a lengthy review of the failure of past educational policies, the report's first recommendation was for "maximum participation and control by Indians in establishing Indian education programs." In its second recommendation, the report called for maximum Indian participation in the development of educational programs in federal schools and local public schools. These educational programs were to include early childhood education, vocational education, work-study, and adult literacy education.

The Congressional debates resulting from the report eventually culminated in the passage of the Indian Education Act in 1972. The declared policy of the legislation was to provide financial assistance to local schools to develop programs to meet the "special" educational needs of Native-American students. In addition, the legislation created a federal "Office of Indian Education."

In 1974, the Bureau of Indian Affairs issued a set of procedures for protecting student rights and due process. In contrast to the brutal and dictatorial treatment of Indian students in the boarding schools of the late nineteenth and early twentieth centuries, each Indian student was extended the right "to make his or her own decisions where applicable." And, in striking contrast to earlier deculturalization policies, Indian students were granted "the right to freedom of religion and culture."

The most important piece of legislation supporting self-determination was the 1975 Indian Self-Determination and Education Assistance Act which gave tribes the power to contract with the federal government to run their own education and health programs. The legislation opened with the declaration that it was "an Act to provide maximum Indian participation in the Government and education of Indian people; to provide for the full participation of Indian tribes in programs and services conducted by the federal government. . . ."

The Indian Self-Determination and Education Assistance Act strengthened Indian participation in the control of education programs. The legislation provided that a local school district receiving funds for the education of Indian students which *did not* have a school board composed of a majority of Indians had to establish a separate local committee composed of parents of Indian students in the school. This committee was given the authority over any Indian education programs contracted with the federal government.

The principles embodied in the Indian Self-Determination and Education Assistance Act of 1975 were expanded upon in 1988 with the passage of the Tribally Controlled Schools Act. In addition to the right to operate schools under federal contract as provided in the 1975 legislation, the Tribally Controlled Schools Act provided for outright grants to tribes to support the operation of their own schools.

MEXICAN AMERICANS

Similar to African Americans, Mexican Americans experienced many years of segregation in schools throughout the Southwest and attempted to redress their grievances through the courts. In Ontario, California, in 1945, Mexican-American parents demanded that the school board grant all requests for transfer out of segregated Mexican schools. When the board refused this request Gonzalo Mendez and William Guzman brought suit for violation of the Fourteenth Amendment to the Constitution. The school board responded to this suit by claiming that segregation was not based on race or national origins but on the necessity of providing special instruction. In other words, the school district justified segregation on the basis that Mexican-American children required special instruction because they came from homes where Spanish was the spoken language.

In 1946 a U.S. District Court ruled in *Mendez et al.* v. *Westminster School District of Orange County* that the only possible argument for segregation was the special educational needs of Mexican-American children. These needs centered around the issue of learning English. Completely reversing the educational justification for segregation, the judge argued that "evidence clearly shows that Spanish-speaking children are retarded in learning English by lack of exposure to its use by segregation. . . ." Therefore, the court ruled segregation was illegal because it was *not* required by state law and because there was no valid educational justification for segregation.

Heartened by the *Mendez* decision, the League of United Latin American Citizens (LULAC), the Mexican-American equivalent of the NAACP, forged ahead in its legal attack on segregation in Texas. With support from LULAC, a group of parents in 1948 brought suit against the Bastrop Independent School District charging that local school authorities had no legal right to segregate children of Mexican descent and that segregation was solely because the children were of Mexican descent. In *Delgado* v. *Bastrop Independent School District*, the court ruled that segregating Mexican-American children was illegal and discriminatory. The ruling required that the local school district end all segregation. The court did give local school districts the right to separate some children in the first grade, only if scientific tests showed that they needed special instruction in English and the separation took place on the same campus.

In general, LULAC was pleased with the decision. The one point they were dissatisfied with was the provision for the separation of children in the first grade. This allowed local schools to practice what was referred to in the latter part of the twentieth century as second generation segregation. Second generation segregation refers to the practice of using educational justifications for segregating children within a single school building. In fact, many local Texas school districts did use the proviso for that purpose.

While the *Mendez* and *Delgado* decisions did hold out the promise of ending segregation of Mexican Americans, local school districts used many tactics to avoid integration, including manipulation of school district lines, choice plans, and different forms of second generation segregation. For instance, the California State Department of Education reported in 1966 that 57 percent of the children with Spanish surnames were still attending schools that were predominantly Mexican American. In 1973 a civil rights activist, John Caughey, estimated that two-thirds of the Mexican-American children in Los Angeles attended segregated schools. In *All Deliberate Speed: Segregation and Exclusion in California Schools, 1855–1975,* Charles Wollenberg estimates that in California by 1973 more Mexican and Mexican-American children attended segregated schools than in 1947.

In 1970, Mexican Americans were officially recognized by the federal courts as an identifiable dominated group in the public schools in a MALDEF case, *Cisernos* v. *Corpus Christi Independent School District.* A central issue in the case was whether or not the 1954 school desegregation decision could be applied to Mexican Americans. The original Brown decision dealt specifically with African Americans who were segregated by state and local laws. In his final decision, Judge Owen Cox ruled that blacks and Mexican Americans were segregated in the Corpus Christi school system and that Mexican Americans were an identifiable dominated group because of their language, culture, religion, and Spanish surnames.

THE RESULTS OF DESEGREGATION

While the civil rights struggle held out the hope for greater equality of educational opportunity for many groups that were traditionally oppressed in American society, its actual results regarding desegregation have been rather dismal. On the positive side, there no longer exist state laws requiring school segregation. On the negative side, segregated schools continue to exist around the country. In 1992, the following figures (see Table 5.1) were re-

TABLE 5.1 Segregation of African Americans and Hispanics by State
(Percentage attending schools with 50 to 100 percent minority population)

AFRICAN AMERICANS	
Illinois	88.8%
New York	85.7
Michigan	84.6
New Jersey	79.6
California	78.7
Maryland	76.1
Wisconsin	75.3
Texas	67.9
Pennsylvania	67.5
Connecticut	65.9
HISPANICS	
New York	86.1
Illinois	85.0
Texas	84.3
New Jersey	84.1
California	79.1
Rhode Island	77.8
New Mexico	74.4
Connecticut	72.4
Pennsylvania	66.9
Arizona	56.9

Source: This table was adapted from Karen DeWitt, "The Nation's Schools Learn a 4th R: Resegregation," *New York Times* (19 January 1992): E5.

ported regarding the percentage of African Americans and Hispanics attending segregated schools. As Table 5.1 indicates, Illinois, New York, Michigan, New Jersey, California, and Texas now lead the nation in the extent of segregation.

MAGNET SCHOOLS AND CHOICE

As school desegregation proceeded across the country it caused a fundamental change in the organization of school curricula, with the introduction of magnet or alternative schools. Magnet or alternative schools are designed to provide an attractive program that will have wide appeal throughout a school district. Theoretically, magnet schools will attract enough students from all racial backgrounds to achieve integrated schools. For instance, a school district might establish a school for creative and performing arts that would attract students of all races from all areas of the district. If one criterion in selecting students is the maintenance of racial balance, then that school becomes a means of achieving integration.

The great attraction of magnet schools, and a major reason why they are widely supported, is that they provide a means of voluntary desegregation. Also, they are supported because it is believed they will reduce the flight of middle-class and white families from school districts undergoing desegregation. It is hoped that by providing unique and attractive programs, school districts will stabilize their populations as voluntary desegregation takes place.

The concept of magnet schools also received support from the federal government, which aided in their rapid adoption by school districts. The 1976 amendments to the Emergency School Aid Act (ESAA) provided financial support specifically for magnet school programs. In addition, President Ronald Reagan's administration in 1984 used magnet-school plans as its method of achieving out-of-court settlements of desegregation cases. This will be discussed in more detail in Chapter 9.

Some school districts developed elaborate plans for magnet schools. In Houston, Texas, magnet schools were established ranging from Petro-Chemical Careers Institute to a High School for Law Enforcement and Criminal Justice. In most school districts, magnet schools are introduced by first offering a program in creative and performing arts. For example, both Philadelphia and Cincinnati established a School of Creative and Performing Arts as their early magnet-school offering. In Philadelphia, school-desegregation plans resulted in schools offering programs that range from the study of foreign affairs to community-based education. In many cases, special programs already in existence, particularly for academic excellence and vocational training, were classified as magnet schools.

In evaluating the desegregation aspect of magnet schools, a distinction must be made between mandatory and voluntary desegregation plans. According to Mark Smylie in a 1983 article for *Urban Education*, "Districts implementing mandatory plans achieved over three times the racial balance among schools achieved by districts implementing voluntary plans." In some situations, magnet-school programs established as a part of involuntary desegregation plans are viewed as a means of reducing the potential hostility of parents. In these situations, the choice is not between a segregated neighborhood school and a desegregated magnet school, but a choice among (1) forced reassignment to a desegregated school, (2) leaving the school system, or (3) selecting a desegregated magnet school. Christine Rossell in a 1979 article in *Urban Education* reported that in Boston, where magnet schools were part of a court-ordered desegregation plan, they "reportedly have long waiting lists . . . and were perhaps the only 'successful' aspect of the plan despite greater busing distance and numbers bused."

By the 1990s, the magnet school movement was incorporated into the concept of "choice" in education. Conservative and Republican political leaders in the 1980s argued that public schools would improve if they were forced to compete for students. A free marketplace idea of quality through competition was introduced into education. If schools were unable to attract students in a school district, they would either have to improve or close their doors.

During the 1992 presidential campaign, both George Bush and Bill Clinton supported the idea of choice. The difference between their positions was that Bush supported choice between private and public schools, while Clinton wanted choice between public schools. By 1992, eight states had passed laws allowing students to choose any public school in the state. These states were Arkansas, Idaho, Iowa, Minnesota, Nebraska, Ohio, Utah, and Washington.

By the early 1990s, in a reversal of previous thinking on the issue, choice was being attacked as a cause of segregation, as reflected in the title of an article by Isabel Wilkerson in the *New York Times*, "Des Moines Acts to Halt White Flight after State Allows Choice of Schools." In the case of Des Moines, the Iowa state legislature passed a choice law with the assumption that poor and minority students would choose to go to suburban schools to receive a better education. But just the opposite happened. Rather than poor or minority students taking advantage of the law, white parents began to send their children to suburban schools. The result was a decline in the number of white students and, as a further result, an increase in segregation.

SECOND GENERATION SEGREGATION

Second generation segregation refers to forms of racial segregation that are a result of school practices such as tracking, ability grouping, and the misplacement of students in special education classes. Unlike segregation that existed by state laws in the South prior to the 1954 Brown decision, second generation forms of segregation can occur in schools with balanced racial populations. In schools with balanced racial populations, students can be segregated by, for instance, placing all white students in one academic track and all African-American or Hispanic students in another track.

In some cases, second generation segregation is not accidental, but the result of conscious school policies. The situation in Selma, Alabama, in 1990 is a perfect example of consciously planned second generation segregation.

As I discussed in the first part of this chapter, the boycott of Selma schools was prompted by the school board's attempt to fire the African-American superintendent who tried to increase the percentage of African-American students in the upper-ability tracks of the high school from 3 to 10 percent. The obvious purpose of the tracking system was to segregate white from African-American students. This segregation paralleled the economic segregation existing in the community.

The continuing economic segregation in Selma is highlighted in an interview with Professor William Bernard of the University of Alabama, conducted by Ronald Smothers for the *New York Times*. Bernard describes what he considers to be the "dual view of great change and no change." In this case, "the great change" is the appearance of African Americans on the city councils and school boards of the South and the "little change" is the continuation of a segregated social order and white domination of economic power. Professor Bernard provides the following description of the economic order of the South:

> Like Sinclair Lewis's "Main Street," there is a group of real estate, banking and other professional people who are the power in town, and much of the

way people live is more affected by the decision of the banker than of the City Council. You don't have black bankers, but neither do you have white bankers from the wrong side of the tracks.

In reporter Smothers' interviews, African Americans refer to the "white elite" and whites to the "blue bloods" who controlled the town's economy and political system. Aspiring African-American business people spoke of their inability to get loans to start new businesses because of the economic elite working behind the scenes. Obviously, new African-American businesses would compete with existing white businesses. This white power elite controls Selma's city council which includes four African Americans among nine members. In Selma, the school board is appointed by the city council and includes five African Americans among eleven members. Thus, the city council and school board reflect Professor Bernard's statement about the "dual view of great change and no change." The great change is the presence of African Americans on the city council and school board, and the little change is the continuing economic power of a white elite.

Also, tracking in the Selma high school reflects the "dual view of great change and no change." The "great change" is the integration of the school building and the 3 percent of African Americans placed in the high-ability tracks with 90 percent of the white students. The "no change" is the racial segregation that continues with the tracking system. The segregation resulting from the tracking systems reflects the economic differences in the community. Tracking is a method of closing the door to equal economic opportunity for African Americans in Selma.

Nationally, a number of studies examine the process of great change and no change as integration of schools results in segregation within schools. One collection of studies can be found in Ray Rist's *Desegregated Schools: Appraisals of an American Experiment.* The studies describe the subtle forms of segregation that began to occur as white and African-American students were placed in integrated schools for the first time. For instance, in one recently integrated school, African-American students were suspended for committing the same offenses for which white students received only a reprimand. A teacher in the school complained that, unlike African-American students, when white students were sent to the principal's office, they were immediately sent back to class. In this school, equal opportunity to attend the school did not result in equal treatment within the school.

Unequal treatment of different races within the same school is one problem in integrated schools; the establishment of racial boundaries among students creates another. One study in the Rist book describes how racial boundaries were established in a high school in Memphis, Tennessee, after the students of an all-African-American school were integrated with the students of an all-white school. Here, white students maintained control over most student activities. Activities in which African-American students began to participate after integration were athletics and cheerleading. When this occurred, the status of these activities was denigrated by white students. On the other hand, whites were able to maintain control of the student government, ROTC, school clubs, and the staff of the yearbook.

This division of control among student activities reflected the rigid social boundaries that existed in the high school between the two groups. Individuals who crossed these social boundaries had to adapt to the social customs of those on the other side. For instance, African-American students changed their style of dress and social conduct in order to be accepted by white students. African-American students who crossed racial lines by making such changes found themselves accused by other African-American students of "acting white" and were subsequently rejected by "unchanged" African-American students. The same was true of white students who crossed racial boundaries.

The racial boundaries that continue to exist in high schools after integration reflect the racial barriers that continue in the larger society. The social life of a school often reflects the social world outside the school. Integration of a school system can help assure equality of educational opportunity, but it cannot break down society's racial barriers. Although schools attempt to deal with this problem, its solution requires a general transformation of racial relationships in the larger society.

The following story of "Black Suburbia" exemplifies the different forms racism can take in a school district. The story also shows the complicated set of factors that put a school system on the path of discrimination and the tragedy that often strikes minorities in their quest for equal educational opportunity.

BLACK SUBURBIA

One particular suburban community of about 40,000 people is on the border of a major midwestern industrial city. Prior to the 1960s, the majority of the populations was white; family incomes were primarily in the lower-middle and middle range. During the mid-1960s, the population of the community began to shift rapidly from a majority of white residents to a majority of African-American residents. This was dramatically reflected in the school enrollments. In 1965, the percentage of African-American students enrolled in the school system was 10 percent. By 1970, the percentage of African-American students was 87 percent, and in 1974 it was 97 percent. By the middle of the 1970s the few remaining white children were in one elementary school in the more affluent section of the suburb.

The African-American population that moved into Black Suburbia was primarily in the middle-income range and very concerned about the quality of the educational system. When income figures from the 1960 and 1970 censuses for this suburban area are compared and 1960 dollars are adjusted to 1970 dollars, it is revealed that the African-American population moving into Black Suburbia in the 1960s had slightly higher incomes than the whites moving out of the community. The bulk of the African-American population moving into the area during this period was in the middle-income range and could be viewed as a group interested in upward mobility.

A study of the community in the late 1960s showed the mobility concerns and educational aspirations of the new African-American population. The study provided profiles of nine different social groups, including old and new white residents at different income and age levels and new African-American residents at different income and age levels. The study found that both middle-aged and young middle-class African-American residents had high expectations of upward mobility and believed that quality schools were a major element in a quality community. The population group labeled "new, middle-aged, black middle-class residents" were earning more than $10,000 a year and were employed as managers, proprietors, and professionals. This group was found to have an "extraordinarily high degree" of expectations for continuing upward mobility and a concern about the quality of schools. The same expectations and concerns were held by the "new, young, black middle class," who were earning between $6,000 and $9,000 per year and also were employed as managers, proprietors, and professionals. (It should be remembered that the incomes quoted are in 1960 dollars, which were worth considerably more than current dollars.)

The middle-aged and young African-American working class described in the study evidenced varying degrees of concern about the quality of schooling. For the middle-aged, African-American working-class family, schools were not an important reason for moving to Black Suburbia. This group comprised unskilled workers earning between $6,000 and $7,000 per year. On the other hand, the quality of schools was important to the young African-American working-class residents, who were earning between $5,000 and $9,000 per year and were employed primarily in skilled and semiskilled jobs.

During the early 1970s the high mobility and the educational aspirations of African-American residents who arrived in Black Suburbia in the 1960s were threatened by the rapid influx of a poor African-American population. The introduction of a large group of low-income African-American families was reflected in the percentage of children from welfare families in the school system. Between 1965 and 1970 the percentage of children from welfare families in Black Suburbia increased from 6 to 16 percent as the racial composition of the population changed. Between 1970 and 1973 the percentage of children from welfare families increased dramatically, from 16 to 51 percent. The migration of upwardly mobile middle-class African Americans was followed by the rapid migration of African-American welfare families.

The educational aspirations of those in the early African-American migration were frustrated both by the response of the local school system to these new residents, and by the later migration of poor African Americans. One of the first things to happen was that the educational expectations of the mainly white teachers and administrators in the school systsem began to fall. This seemed to be caused by the assumption of the white school staff that the African Americans moving into the community were not interested in education and would create major problems in the school system. This assumption is most clearly shown when the educational expectations of elementary school principals are compared with the educational expectations of the African-American community.

In the early 1970s, a local government survey of Black Suburbia included a question dealing with the level of educational aspirations. The survey asked parents how far they would like their sons or daughters to progress in school. Seventy-three percent of the parents wanted their sons to complete college, and 71 percent had that goal for their daughters. More important, when asked how far they believed their sons or daughters would actually go in school, 60 percent believed their sons would complete college, and 62 percent believed their daughters would do the same.

The contrast between the educational aspirations of the parents and the expectations of the elementary school principals illustrates the problems and frustrations encountered by African-American residents. When I asked elementary school principals what percentage of the students in their schools they felt would go to college, the responses from three of the principals were 3 percent, 12 percent, and 10 percent. Two elementary school principals evaded the question and claimed it had nothing to do with their work in the elementary school, and one elementary school principal gave a figure of 50 percent.

One of the important things about these responses is that the 50-percent figure was given by a new African-American elementary principal, who clearly was closer to understanding the values of the local community. All the other principals were white, and were principals in the school system before the racial change occurred. The educational expectation levels of these principals not only were considerably below those of the community, but were also below those of the teachers. A survey of elementary school teachers found that they thought that 29 percent of their students would graduate from college. Although this figure was still lower than the figure for the community, it was at least closer to community expectations than were the principals' estimates. One of the reasons for this might be that the teaching staff changed more than the elementary administrative staff and there was a recent effort by the school district to recruit African-American teachers.

Several examples can be used to show how the lower expectations of school staff translated into practice. When I interviewed the head of the local community library, he informed me that in the years prior to the racial change, scholarly and professional journals were heavily used by high school students. This was not because the students read these journals for pleasure, but because teachers gave homework assignments in the journals. After the racial change, teachers stopped giving homework assignments in these advanced journals. The African Americans who moved to the community because of its relatively high educational standards suddenly found those standards being lowered as their children entered the system.

The director of the local YMCA stated that a person who really wanted to know what was going on in the local school system should park his car outside the high school at closing time and count the number of students carrying books home from school. The director claimed that only a few students carried books, and this was another indication that teachers were no longer giving homework assignments and had given up trying to teach.

Complaints about teachers not teaching were echoed by students in the tenth and twelfth grades of the high school. I interviewed a random sample of the tenth graders and asked about their future plans and if they had any complaints about the school system. Fifty-eight percent of the tenth-grade students who were interviewed had expectations of attending and graduating from college. The major complaint of the students was the quality of the teaching staff.

Twelfth-grade students were chosen to be interviewed from a list of those students designated by the school administration as the "best." Sixty percent of these students expressed concern and even bitterness about the teaching staff. Their major complaint was that certain teachers made no effort to teach and wasted most class periods. One student stated that he had teachers who probably accomplished one day's worth of teaching out of every five days in the classroom. Another student stated that many teachers did not seem to care whether or not students did the work or learned. No attempt was made to make students want to come to class. One student argued that the reason teachers did not care was because they were so upset at trying to control "rowdy" students.

The issue of rowdy students entered almost every discussion about the quality of education in the local high school. There seemed to be an underlying assumption in any conversation with a community member that the rowdy students came from low-income African-American families. This reflected a tension between the middle-class African Americans who moved into the community in the 1960s and the low-income African Americans who moved into the community in the 1970s. Low-income families represented a threat to the aspirations and status of the middle-class residents of Black Suburbia.

One example of this was an African-American member of the local school board who pounded the table and exclaimed that all he wanted was to live a middle-class existence and provide a home and future for his family. This, he stated, was why he moved to the community. Now he felt his dreams were not being realized, as crime increased in the community, and he feared that his children were not receiving an adequate education at the local school. He complained that every time his children left the house, he worried that they would get involved with the rowdy youths of the community. Currently he was sending his daughter to a private school, but his son went to the local high school. He worried constantly that his son would get in with the "wrong" group in the school.

This particular school board member led a group in the community that demanded a strict dress code. The reason for this was that those students identified as rowdy very often wore large hats and high-heeled shoes. The community members demanding the dress code saw it as a means of controlling and disciplining rowdy students. One result of this campaign were signs throughout the high school restricting the wearing of hats.

That the community related rowdiness with low-income background was evident from discussions with other community members. One leader of a community welfare organization claimed that rowdy juveniles were organized into natural street groupings, with one street in rivalry with another street. These street groupings, he argued, were primarily based on economic differences; kids from better streets put down kids from poorer streets. The community social-welfare worker saw rowdy juveniles as a product of poverty who were characterized by their lack of a sense of direction, which easily led them to drift into a life of stealing, drugs, and gambling. Another social-welfare worker, who dealt directly with cases of juvenile delinquency, described middle-class youth in the community as walking a thin line where, at any time, pressures from this delinquent subculture could persuade the student to join the rowdy culture. This was very much the fear expressed by the school board member.

Students at the high school tended to see the issue of rowdy students as one of the problems with the teaching staff. Teachers generalized from the misbehavior of a few students to all students. One of the common complaints of tenth graders was the way teachers handled discipline problems. The majority of students felt that teachers were unable to control students in a just and fair manner. The problem was compounded, students believed, because teachers did not know how to control rowdy students and, consequently, acted "mean" toward all students.

The process of generalizing from a few students to all students might be one of the factors contributing to the failure of teachers in the school system to understand or attempt to respond to the educational aspirations of the middle-class African-American community. Perhaps the delinquent subculture reinforced existing stereotypes held by white teachers and administrators about the way African-American students acted and learned. This would influence the levels of teacher expectations, as reflected in not assigning homework or not expecting students to use the community library.

For middle-class African Americans who entered the community in the 1960s with high aspirations for upward mobility and quality education for their children, the school system became a source of frustration and disillusionment. Teachers did not provide the instruction parents hoped for and, in addition, they came to fear that their children might enter a delinquent subculture. For the more affluent African-American residents, the solution was a rejection of the public school and the transfer of their children into private schools.

African-American families and students who were not interested in college but hoped that the school could provide some form of immediate job training also were frustrated in attaining their goals, as a direct result of racial discrimination. In the early 1970s the school system in Black Suburbia built a new vocational high school directly connected to the traditional high school. The vocational school was the product of a state master plan for vocational education, which mandated the establishment of joint vocational-school districts or individual vocational schools within each district. The problems of the vocational school in Black Suburbia were directly related to the discriminatory policies of the surrounding white suburban communities.

The story of Black Suburbia's vocational school came from the local superintendent and his staff, as well as a superintendent in the district next to Black Suburbia. After the resolution of the vocational-school issue, these superintendents were no longer on speaking terms. The problem began when a meeting of all the superintendents in one suburban area of this metropolitan area was called to discuss the formation of a joint vocational-school district as a method of complying with state requirements. The suburbs in this area were mostly white, except for three integrated suburban communities and Black Suburbia. Before the actual meeting, the superintendents of the predominantly white suburbs agreed by telephone to form their own vocational district, which would exclude the three integrated school districts and Black Suburbia. When the four school superintendents representing the suburbs having sizable African-American populations arrived at the meeting, they found that all decisions had been made and that they would be forced to work together in establishing a separate vocational district.

There is no agreement on what happened after this meeting. The superintendent of Black Suburbia claimed that the three integrated suburbs were hesitant about working with his school district, because those three communities had a higher-income population. Consequently, the superintendent of Black Suburbia was forced to build a vocational high school next to the one regular high school in the community. The superintendent of the adjoining integrated community claims the whole situation was a misunderstanding and that his community was willing to work on a joint vocational-school district.

The establishment of a separate vocational school in Black Suburbia had the effect of increasing the degree of segregation between white and African-American suburban schools. A joint vocational school covering the entire eastern area would have made a major contribution to school integration. The segregation of Black Suburbia's vocational school assured that its training programs would be inferior to the joint vocational school's programs, because an all-American school faced major problems in establishing links with unions, which traditionally excluded African Americans, and with white businesses. Because it was difficult for an all-African-American school to establish these contacts, it was very hard to place students graduating from the vocational program.

This problem was highlighted in a conversation with the head of the vocational high school. In his vocational training programs he could claim the placement of only three welders in the last three years. The superintendent admitted conducting his own telephone survey to determine the problems in placement of the graduates in cosmetology. He found that only a few African-American graduates were able to get jobs in beauty parlors, and those jobs were at very low wages. Even those who got jobs found they lasted only a short time, because beauty parlors depend on a high turnover of personnel.

Another problem now faced by the Black Suburbia school system was that it had a vocational building that had to be filled and a teaching staff that needed to protect their jobs by attracting students. The size of the vocational school required that almost half the students in the eleventh and twelfth grades enroll in its programs. In the tenth grade the students were shown through the school and given a choice between entering the vocational program the following year or continuing in an academic program. From the perspective of the staff of the vocational school, it was important to persuade students to enter their programs.

When the guidance counselor in the vocational school was asked what methods were used to persuade students to enter programs that could not promise jobs, his response was that they lied to the students. He justified this in terms of needing students to build good programs in the future, and said that even though jobs would be difficult to find for the students, the training they would be receiving in the vocational program would be more useful than that received in the traditional academic program. From his perspective, very few of the students in the secondary school were capable of going on to college.

A different interpretation was given by the African-American director of the local YWCA. She felt that the vocational school was keeping students from going to college. When she was asked what percentage of local high school students she felt would go on to college, she stated that before the vocational high school was established, about 70 percent of the girls attending the YWCA planned on attending college. After the establishment of the vocational school, the number dropped to 30 or 40 percent. She argued quite strongly that if the community were all white, the vocational school never would have been built. It was, she felt, a racist institution designed primarily to give African-American students an inferior education. Another observer referred to the vocational program as "education for welfare."

The story of Black Suburbia highlights some fundamental problems encountered by minority groups in the United States. The fact that the expectations of teachers and school administrative staffs can be far below the aspirations of the minority group can cause a major decrease in the quality of education. In addition, the school staff can generalize from the behavioral problems of children from low-income families to all members of the minority group. In this case study, students directly felt this process of generalization. The tension in Black Suburbia between middle-class and lower-class African Americans highlights the importance of social class as a factor in discussions of segregation.

While Black Suburbia highlights some of the major problems encountered by minority groups in American schools, recent studies suggest that some of the worst practices of second generation segregation can be reduced by the exercise of effective political power. As the next section suggests, there is evidence of a relationship between decreasing second generation segregation, the election of Hispanics and African Americans to school boards, and the hiring of Hispanics and African Americans as teachers and school administrators.

SECOND GENERATION SEGREGATION AND POLITICAL POWER

Two important books—Kenneth Meier, Joseph Stewart, Jr., and Robert England, *Race, Class, and Education: The Politics of Second-Generation Discrimination*, and Kenneth Meier and Joseph Stewart, Jr., *The Politics of Hispanic Education*— focus on the relationship between political involvement and second generation segregation. The two books are concerned with political organizations that promote segregative practices in schools and deny certain groups equality of educational opportunity. In addition, they link segregative practices with student achievement. They consider student achievement to be dependent on equal access to educational opportunities.

The main conclusion of their studies is that segregative practices in schools are reduced by the presence on boards of education and in educational bureaucracies of representatives from affected groups such as Hispanics and African Americans. Therefore, their suggested reforms focus on ways to increase representation from dominated groups.

In their research, they found that schools still practice segregation through academic grouping, such as placement in special education classes, ability grouping, curriculum tracking, and segregated bilingual education. In addition, they found that discipline is applied in different ways to different ethnic and racial groups. For instance, Hispanic and African-American students might be suspended or expelled from school at different rates than white students. And finally, they concluded that all of these segregative practices have a negative effect on high school graduation rates.

With regard to Hispanic Americans, they conclude that the larger the number of Hispanic representatives in an educational system the less chance of second generation segregation. In their study, representation includes boards of education, educational bureaucracies, and teachers. In other words, there will be less second generation segregation if there are more Hispanics on boards of education, and working as school administrators and teachers.

In addition, Meier and Stewart found an interrelationship between representation on boards of education, and representation in the bureaucracy and teaching ranks. The higher the level of representation of Hispanics on boards of education, then the higher the level of representation of Hispanics in the school administration. In other words, Hispanic representation on boards of education creates a greater than normal possibility that the board will choose Hispanic administrators. In turn, they found, the higher representation of Hispanics in the bureaucracy, then the higher the number of Hispanic teachers.

These findings suggest a chain reaction. Hispanics are elected to the board of education and they select more Hispanic administrators, who in turn select more Hispanic teachers, which results in a decline in second generation segregation and greater equality of educational opportunity. Specifically, they found that greater Hispanic representation is associated with proportionately fewer Hispanic students in special education classes and larger numbers of Hispanic students in gifted programs. Also, higher rates of Hispanic representation are related to less disparity in discipline. And finally, a higher representation of Hispanics is related to a higher proportion of Hispanics graduating from high school.

Policy recommendations follow logically from these conclusions. Of course, Meier and Stewart recommend greater representation of minority populations on school boards. They recommend greater federal scrutiny of second generation forms of discrimination and that school districts hire more Hispanic administrators and teachers. They recommend the elimination of most academic grouping.

In the final analysis, the most important message in their research is that political power is the key to having a school system serve a group's educational interests. And in the case of Hispanics, African Americans, and Native Americans, this political power is essential to ending forms of inequality of educational opportunity. Just as African Americans in the South had to organize to stop segregation, other groups must exercise political muscle to stop second generation forms of segregation.

RACIAL OR SOCIAL-CLASS DIFFERENCES?

School people must remain sensitive to the possibility of racial differences being translated into socioeconomic differences. Sparking this debate is sociologist William J. Wilson's book, *The Declining Significance of Race: Blacks and Changing American Institutions.* Wilson argues that as a result of the civil rights movement racial differences are less important in explaining social differences between African Americans and whites; socioeconomic differences are now more important than differences of race.

To support his argument, Wilson cites statistics on the changing pattern of the occupational structure in the African-American community and the increasing gap in social conditions between middle- and lower-class African Americans. Wilson notes a dramatic change in African-American social mobility during the 1950s and 1960s. In 1950, 16.4 percent of African-American males were employed in middle-class occupations. In 1960, this percentage reached 24 percent, and in 1970, it rose to 35.3 percent. These changes reflect the dramatic increase in civil rights for minority groups during these two decades.

But during the 1970s, Wilson argues, the gap between middle-class and poor African Americans began to increase, thus making it more difficult for African-Americans born into a state of poverty to experience social mobility.

He notes the steady decrease in the number of African Americans below the poverty line, from 48.1 percent in 1959 to 29.4 percent in 1968; in the 1970s, however, this percentage did *not* undergo any significant change, with the percentage of African Americans below the poverty line persisting at 27 to 28 percent.

Not only has the percentage of African Americans below the poverty line remained about the same since the 1960s, but the gap in income between middle-class and lower-class African Americans has been increasing. The unemployment rate for young African Americans from poor families also has been increasing, and many have given up looking for work. In addition, there has been a steady increase in single-parent families among poor African Americans, which has a direct effect on family income. What all this adds up to, according to Wilson, is deteriorating social and economic conditions for poor African Americans.

Wilson's findings were supported in a 1989 report of the National Research Council titled *A Common Destiny: Blacks and American Society*. A primary concern of the report was that the economic status of African Americans relative to whites deteriorated from 1970 to the 1980s. Particularly worrisome was the growing gap between middle-income and low-income African Americans. The report stated that between 1970 and 1980 the proportion of African-American families with incomes above $35,000 increased from 18 to 22 percent, while the proportion of incomes below $10,000 also increased from 26 to 30 percent. In addition, in 1985 the number of African-American families headed by single females was 50 percent and these families received only 25 percent of total African-American family income.

The deteriorating conditions for many African Americans were reflected in the findings of a study conducted by Deborah Carter and Reginald Wilson for the American Council of Education on the decline in college enrollments among middle and low-income minorities. Based on census figures, they found that there was a drop in the number of African-American high school graduates attending college between 1976 and 1988 from 30.8 percent to 30.3 percent. In addition, during this time the number of African Americans receiving college degrees declined by 4.3 percent. For Hispanic Americans the drop was even more dramatic from 50.4 percent to 35.2 percent during the same period. On the other hand, the percentage of low-income white high school graduates attending college rose slightly during the same period from 36.9 percent to 38.8 percent. For all races and incomes, college enrollment increased to 57.5 percent in 1988 from 53.4 percent in 1976.

The authors of the report conclude that the main reason for the decline in minority college attendance is the decline in student financial aid. Without economic resources and with the continuing increase in college costs, low income minority students are finding it difficult to attend college. The report states, "comprehensive and sustained efforts are needed at the institutional level to recruit, retain, and graduate larger numbers of minority students."

Thus, teachers and administrators must not only be aware of racial barriers but also socioeconomic barriers. It would be relatively easy for school people to integrate student activities and classrooms with middle-class African Americans, without giving consideration to social-class differences within the African-American community. Integration of middle-class students could only give teachers or administrators a false sense of having solved racial problems when, in fact, they might be contributing to the development of a permanent underclass.

A major problem that could result from the accomplishment of equal educational opportunity among races is increased inequality in educational opportunity among social classes. For instance, magnet schools might bring about racial balance but also might result in a social-class stratification in particular schools. It is not beyond the realm of possibility that white and African-American children of working-class parents both might receive counseling that sends them to vocational schools, while upper- and middle-class children are counseled to select academic programs. Although the high aspirations of middle-class African-American parents might be satisfied, there would be a danger of increased segregation between social classes.

This is particularly important when we consider the relationship between education and social mobility, as discussed in the previous chapter. The high educational aspirations held by the African-American community are related to a belief that schooling is a means of social mobility. It is also true that segregated education has been a means of maintaining a stratified society by keeping African-American people separated from the career routes available to the majority of the population. Integrated education will be a means of moving the African-American population into the mainstream of occupational mobility in the United States. This could be one of the important consequences of integration.

On the other hand, as discussed in Chapter 4, receiving equal education does not guarantee social mobility, which is not directly related to the school but to the job market. In addition, there is some evidence that the school's role includes a combination of facilitating the movement of people into new occupations as they occur and maintaining stratification between social classes. It is certainly good that poor African-American people receive equal education, but the frustrations now felt by poor whites in using the school as a means of social mobility might well be shared by poor African Americans as the middle-class African-American population reaps the rewards of integration.

SEXISM AND EDUCATION

While racial differences are one source of inequality of educational opportunity, gender differences are another source. Historically, equality of educational opportunity was to provide equal access to occupations. Women tend to dominate certain professions while finding it difficult to enter other professions. For instance, Daniel Levine and Robert Havighurst report in their book, *Society and Education*, that in 1980 the nursing profession was 96 percent female and the teaching profession was 71 percent female. On the other hand, only 4 percent of engineers and only 13 percent of lawyers and judges were females. It should be immediately noted in these examples that the professions in which women are the majority are the lower-paying occupations. Probably the most revealing contrast is between nurses and physicians. In 1980, 14 percent of physicians and osteopaths were women. In this case men, as physicians, are in authority over women, as nurses.

In addition, women sought equality of opportunity in order to gain access to occupations within the field of education. For instance, Patricia O'Reilly and Kathryn Borman report in their essay, "Sexism in Education: Documented Biases, Destructive Practices and Some Hope for the Future," that in 1980, "99 percent of school superintendents and 97 percent of high school principals [were] male." When contrasted with the fact that 71 percent of teachers are female, the disparity becomes obvious. O'Reilly and Borman describe this situation as "men rule women and women rule children."

There are also actual gender differences in teacher salaries. A 1989 nationwide study of high school teachers found women earned an average of $2,300 to $3,300 less than male high school teachers. Years of experience and education do not explain the difference. Valerie Lee, who conducted the study, hypothesized that the differences were the result of the fact that many female teachers move from district to district as their husbands are transferred or seek other employment. School districts do not give full credit for years of experience when determining salaries. Therefore, because many female teachers follow their husband's career they never receive full credit for all their years of experience.

To solve the problems represented by the preceding occupational statistics, equal treatment is required for women as students and as employees of educational institutions. This means that sexual discrimination needs to be eliminated in curricula in which men are the majority. Second, women need to be encouraged to enter curricula such as engineering and law. In order to accomplish this, socialization patterns need to be changed in families and in schools. Within educational institutions, affirmative action needs to be taken to assure equal access to administrative positions.

An important issue related to encouraging women to enter occupations where men are presently in a majority is sex-role stereotyping. During childhood certain activities become associated with one sex as opposed to the other. For instance, active and aggressive behavior is associated with boys, whereas passive and nurturing behavior is associated with girls. This type of socialization can contribute to boys and girls selecting occupations that reflect learned patterns of behavior. An obvious example is that of boys selecting work as policepersons or firepersons, and girls selecting work as nurses and teachers.

Avoiding sex-role stereotyping in educational institutions is very important in assuring equal opportunity for women and men. It is important to remember that sex-role stereotyping also places limits on male actions. Of course, sex-role stereotyping provides economic benefits primarily to men.

One issue in sex-role stereotyping is the content of materials used in the classroom. For instance, elementary-school readers might picture only women working in the kitchen while men work outdoors. History textbooks might contain very little about the role of women in history. Of particular importance is the history of women's struggle for civil rights. Jeanne Ballantine reports in *The Sociology of Education* that recent studies still find girls and women being placed in stereotypic roles. She writes, "For instance, math problems involving girls often show them jumping rope, buying clothes, sewing, cooking, or calculating the grocery bill. This can limit what girls see as viable options and uses for their studies." In other words, girls learning arithmetic from these types of texts are not being prepared to see themselves using mathematics in engineering or science. Many of the discriminatory features of textbooks were corrected, but it is important that all educational material be closely checked to assure that it does not contain any sex-role bias.

Sex-role bias also exists in the way many teachers treat students. O'Reilly and Borman report in their previously cited study that "from nursery school on most teachers talk more to boys than they do to girls and interact more with boys, whether 'asking questions, criticizing, accepting or rejecting ideas, giving approval and disapproval.'" It has been found that teachers tend to do tasks for girls, whereas they give boys instructions on how to accomplish tasks by themselves. Obviously, this provides boys with more training for independent action than is received by girls. In addition, teachers tend to react to boys no matter where they are in the classroom, whereas they respond mainly to girls who are phyically near. This supports independent activity by boys and clinging, dependent behavior by girls.

These differences in treatment were found to be related to occupational choice. Ballantine found this most obvious in the fact that women enter college less inclined than men to select majors in math, science, and engineering. The avoidance of these majors is related to the tendency for women to underrate their abilities in these areas. Using the research of Donna Kaminski, Ballantine writes that the social, cultural, psychological, and educational factors influencing women not to enter math-related areas are the "perceived incompatibility with raising children; stereotypes of appropriate gender behavior; few role models for women; less preparation from high school courses; early socialization experiences; and parental values and attitudes which are unsupportive." Ballantine argues that the middle-school years are the most crucial for determining the choices women will make about their future areas of study.

Sex-role bias also appears in other areas of the curriculum. It is often difficult to determine if this is the result of socialization or pressures on women from the educational institution to select particular areas of the curriculum. In either case sexual discrimination is involved. As in math and science, there are clear patterns of sexual discrimination in vocational-education programs. Levine and Havighurst report that according to enrollment figures for vocational-education programs in 1979, men are in the majority in fields of study such as agriculture, technical, and trade and industrial. In agriculture, the enrollments are 83 percent male and 17 percent female; technical education is 80 percent male and 20 percent female; trade and industrial education is 82 percent male and 18 percent female. On the other hand, office education is 72 percent female and 28 percent male, and health education is 75 percent female and 25 percent male.

Correcting the sex bias of the curriculum not only involves changes in patterns of socialization and in the content of textbooks, but also legal action. The most important legislation to deal with these problems is Title IX of the Higher Education Act of 1972. As mentioned earlier in the chapter, Title IX guarantees equal educational opportunity for women, as employees in educational institutions and as students. This means that educational institutions must take positive action to assure that women have equal access to all curricula.

In addition, the federal courts found gender bias in standardized testing. In 1989, a federal judge ruled that the awarding of New York State scholarships using the Scholastic Aptitude Test (SAT) discriminated against female students. The case was brought to court by the Girls Club of America and the National Organization for Women. The court argued that the scholarships were to be awarded on the basis of academic achievement in high school and that the SAT was not constructed to test achievement but to determine college performance. The court's decision states, "The evidence is clear that females score significantly below males on the SAT while they perform equally or slightly better in high schools."

Levine and Havighurst report that the National Advisory Council on Women's Educational Programs reviewed changes since the passage of Title IX and concluded that there has been significant progress in extending equality of educational opportunity to women. The council found improvements: Student services such as counseling, health, and financial aid were being operated on a more equal basis between men and women, and more equal support was being given to extracurricular activities, particularly athletics. But the council also expressed disappointment that women were not gaining significant improvements in employment by educational institutions as principals, school superintendents, and full professors.

There is a certain tragedy in the fact that women are not more equally represented in the administration of American shools. Studies show that women tend to make superior educational administrators. The previously mentioned study by O'Reilly and Borman argues that women principals are likely to be more interested than are their male counterparts in instructional supervision, democratic leadership styles, and involvement with students and with the community. These are generally considered to be the traits most associated with the principals of effective schools. The tragedy is in the previously cited figure that 97 percent of high school principals are male. In fact, according to O'Reilly and Borman, in recent years the total percentage of women holding positions as both assistant principals and principals fell from 15.2 percent in 1970–1971 to 12.9 percent in 1976.

During the period of decline in the percentage of women in educational administration, there was an actual increase in the number of women receiving master's and doctorate degrees in educational administration. Most states require a certain number of courses in educational administration before they will grant a certificate to hold a position as assistant principal, principal, or superintendent. According to O'Reilly and Borman, in 1970 women earned only 2 percent of the master's degrees and 6 percent of the doctorate degrees in educational administration. By 1976, these percentages had increased: Twenty-nine percent of the master's degrees and 20 percent of the doctoral degrees in educational administration were earned by women.

The decline in the percentage of women in school administrative roles during the same period in which there was an increase in the number of women earning degrees in educational administration suggests that the core of the problem is discriminatory hiring practices in the schools. This is also suggested by statistics dealing with regional patterns of employment of women. O'Reilly and Borman report, in one survey, that 35 percent of all female principals were employed in the highly urbanized mid-Atlantic states, and only 14 percent of female high school principals held positions in cities with a population of less than 149,999.

What these figures suggest is that there is more discrimination against women in rural and suburban school districts than in urban school districts. O'Reilly and Borman quote one researcher who stated, "Those in rural regions and those with less education express more prejudiced attitudes even when respondent age and acquaintance with a female administrator are taken into account." One way of interpreting this finding is to say that the attitudes held by current school administrators and school boards are primarily responsible for the denial to women of equal access to jobs in educational administration. Although many improvements were made in the elimination of sexual bias from the curricula of educational institutions, there remains the important issue of allowing women to have equal employment opportunities. This primarily is an issue of power. Positions in educational administration are positions of power within the educational system.

Feminists take a different perspective on the causes of inequality of opportunity. For instance, the question of why there are few women school-administrators can be explained by attributing the characteristics of gender to the organization of schools. O'Reilly and Borman use this approach when they argue, "prevailing school organization mythology is based upon a 'masculine ethic' emphasizing the leadership strength of a (white, male) rational planner." In this argument, women are excluded from positions of school administration because the organization of schools is based on an authoritarian and rational model imposed by men. The administrative structure of school requires the use of behavioral traits that are not normally exercised by women. Within the framework of this feminist argument, equality of opportunity for women in public school administration requires transforming the organizational structure of schools to reflect feminine traits.

The feminist argument that institutions and social practices reflect male or female traits was born in the early part of the twentieth century in the struggle for women's rights. In *The Grounding of Modern Feminism*, Nancy Cott argues that there were three characteristics to the feminist movement as it developed between 1910 and 1920. The first characteristic was a general opposition to claims that one sex was superior to another. The second was an argument that the women's condition was socially constructed. This argument rejected the idea that a divine being or nature predestined women to work in kitchens and be subservient to males. This also meant that society could be changed to allow for greater rights and freedom for women. And lastly, Cott argues, early feminists believed that women perceived themselves as a social grouping and shared a common consciousness.

The combination of these three characteristics as they developed in modern feminist thought resulted in several important questions. How are women to achieve equality and retain the special characteristics of being a woman? And, are the special characteristics of women the result of biological differences from men or differences in social experiences? In addition, there is the question of how educational practices and institutions should change.

In Carol Gilligan's *In a Different Voice: Psychological Theory and Women's Development* and Mary Belenky et al.'s *Women's Ways of Knowing: The Development of Self, Voice, and Mind,* answers are proposed for these questions. Gilligan begins by criticizing traditional psychological and developmental theorists for using male models as defining normal behavior. Judged against these male models, Gilligan argues, women are pictured as abnormal. For many years it was just assumed that these models of male behavior could be applied to women. But, she writes, "At a time when efforts are being made to eradicate discrimination between the sexes in the search for social equality and justice, the differences between the sexes are being rediscovered in the social sciences."

Gilligan states that the qualities most often associated with adulthood are primarily male characteristics. These include independent and autonomous thinking, clear decision making, and a belief that the exercise of law maintains social order. In contrast to these characteristics. Gilligan finds that women primarily see themselves as part of a web of relationships; they are concerned about care and mercy, and believe that resolving conflicts in relationships is the best method of maintaining social order.

For Gilligan, the important distinction between males and females is their attitudes about relationships. She uses the image of the hierarchy and the web. For men, relationships are perceived as a hierarchy composed of autonomous individuals. Men tend to connect violence with intimacy in relationships. On the other hand, women see relationships as a web of connections and they desire intimacy. Therefore, men and women have different concepts of how laws and rules should be applied in a society. Gilligan contends, "While women thus try to change rules in order to preserve relationships, men, in abiding by these rules, depict relationships as easily replaced."

Gilligan outlines stages in the moral development of women. Each of these stages leads to a greater sense of caring about other individuals and a desire to increase and maintain relationships. This is the image of the web. In the first stage, women focus on themselves to ensure personal survival. Engulfed by feelings of selfishness, women progress through a transitional stage were good is associated with caring for other people. Fully developed, this feeling of caring for others leads to a universal condemnation of all exploitation and hurting of others.

At this stage of caring, women are caught in a dilemma of considering any concern for themselves as an act of selfishness. This leads to a tension between care and independence. At this stage, women fear that their personal freedom might cause them to abandon their responsibilities for other people. For some women, this could lead to an opposition to equal rights for women. This interpretation of women's development can be used to explain why some women opposed the suffrage and currently oppose the movement for women's rights. Within the framework of this interpretation, it can be argued that some women feel that equal rights will result in an abandonment of concerns about caring; particularly, they fear that it will result in women neglecting a caring and nurturing role in the family.

At the final stage of development, Gilligan asserts, women are able to combine a desire for caring with a need to act responsibly toward themselves. They are able to connect the need to care for others with a desire to protect their own rights. In this manner, the women can champion both equal rights and the end to oppresssion in the world. "When the concern with care extends from an injunction not to hurt others," Gilligan concludes, "to an ideal of responsibility in social relationships, women begin to see their understanding of relationships as a source of moral strength."

Therefore, Gilligan sees the distinctive qualities of women to be concern about relationships with other people and a desire to care for others. The primary obstacle for women's development is the fear of being judged selfish. These are very appealing traits. It is difficult to resist the idea of a world order based upon care and loving tenderness. Implicit in her argument is that these traits would produce a better world than has the concern of men with obeying rules and with autonomous and rational thinking. As a backdrop for feminist action, the argument suggests that institutions should be changed to foster traits of caring about relationships. Rather than being concerned about maintaining order through obedience to rules, institutions should be organized to reward those who care about others and to operate according to a web of human relationships. In the classroom, Gilligan's argument implies replacing competition with cooperation among students and the creation of an atmosphere where all students want to help each other to learn.

While Gilligan's work focuses on moral development, *Women's Ways of Knowing* is concerned with the stages in which women learn. These stages are

1. Silence
2. Received knowledge
3. Subjective knowledge
4. Procedural knowledge
5. Constructed knowledge

Each of these stages is related to family life and the way women are treated in our society.

Family violence traps women in the stage of silence. Women at this stage feel they are mindless and voiceless. Sitting in stony silence in classrooms, they feel themselves incapable of learning, and they fear being asked to participate in any school activities. Their parents utter words with force and violence, and they yell to gain influence over others. Women in the stage of silence experience males as authoritarian and aggressive. They are passive and dependent. For the authors, the silent woman should be helped to gain confidence in the ability of her own mind to interpret experience. She needs confidence in herself and an understanding that she can act independently of an outside authority.

Women in the stage of received knowledge grew up in families where talk was one way. Parents told the women everything. The parents in these families, the authors state, "assumed that their daughters should and would listen to them, that they would understand them, and that they would obey." In class, these women listen but do not talk. They accept authority about learning but do not act independently. They rely on authority for knowledge and fear having to arrive at their own opinions. These women enter traditional marriages where the husband will do most of the talking and the wife will follow his authority. This stage is characterized by men talking and women listening.

The transition from the received stage of knowledge to the subjective stage often involves a rebellion against doctrinaire and authoritarian parents. It involves a discovery that they can turn from the parents' commands and rely upon their own inner feelings about what is good, right, and important. In the classroom, women at this stage begin to rely on their own ability to think independently and make judgments. At the received stage of knowledge, they begin to develop procedures and methods for learning and analyzing experience. This provides the means fo achieving procedural and constructed knowledge.

Family life for women who do not have to go through the transitions from silence to received to subjective knowledge is often typified by equality of relationships and equality of conversations. In these families, parents do not talk at children but they talk with children as equals. In the classroom, women acting in the category of procedural knowledge are capable of independent thought but only when asked by external authority. They can act independently but they rely on established methodologies and procedures. They are oriented toward external rules and they do not make a connection between their inner self and the outside world. "Women who rely on procedural knowledge" the authors state, "are systematic thinkers in more than one sense of the term. . . . They can criticize a system, but only in the system's terms, only according to the system's standards."

In the category of constructed knowledge, women are able to make the connection between themselves and external knowledge. They accept responsibility for evaluating knowledge and participating in the creation of new knowledge. Unlike women who rely on established procedures and methodologies, these women demand to participate in the process of learning and to relate knowledge to their own experience. In describing women in the category of constructed knowledge, the authors write, "Each was ambitious and fighting to find her own voice—her own way of expressing what she knew and cared about. Each wanted her voice and actions to make a difference to other people and in the world."

The conclusion of Gilligan and Belenky et al. that women have unique ways of knowing raises a major issue in education. The basic issue is should men and women receive different forms of education based on their psychological needs? When this issue is extended to multicultural education, the question becomes: Should African Americans, Hispanics, and Native Americans receive unique forms of education based on their cultural differences? The problem is that trying to provide different forms of education based on supposed psychological differences might lead to a new form of segregation and denial of equal educational opportunity. As I will discuss in Chapter 6, the same possibilities exist for schools based on cultural differences.

The adaptation of education to supposed psychological differences could possibly lead to the end of coeducation. Girls and boys would be educated in separate schools according to their supposed psychological differences. If this were to occur, it is possible that overt forms of discrimination might reappear. For instance, girls' schools might receive less funding than boys' schools. There might be more prestige for teachers to work in boys' schools. Recruitment for jobs might be different in boys' and girls' schools. These possibilities highlight the difficulty of providing equal educational opportunity while at the same time considering real differences that might exist between social groups.

STUDENTS WITH SPECIAL NEEDS

By the 1960s, the civil rights movement encompassed students with special needs, including students with physical handicaps; special mental, emotional, and behavioral needs; and hearing and visual impairments. Within the concept of equality of educational opportunity, students with special needs could only participate equally in schools with other students if they received some form of special help. Since the nineteenth century, many of the needs of these students were neglected by local and state school authorities because of the expense of special facilities and teachers.

The political movement for federal legislation to aid students with special needs followed a path similar to the rest of the civil rights movement. First, finding themselves unable to change educational institutions by pressuring local and state governments, organized groups interested in improving educational opportunities for students with special needs turned to the courts. This was the path taken in the late 1960s by the Pennsylvania Association for Retarded Children (PARC).

PARC was one of many associations organized in the 1950s to aid citizens with special needs. These organizations were concerend with state laws that excluded children with special needs from educational institutions because they were considered ineducable and untrainable. State organizations like PARC and the National Association for Retarded Children campaigned to eliminate these laws and to demonstrate the educability of all children. But, as the civil rights movement discovered throughout the century, local and state officials were resistant to change and relief had to be sought from the judicial system.

In *Pennsylvania Association for Retarded Children (PARC)* v. *Commonwealth of Pennsylvania*, a case that was as important for the rights of children with special needs as the *Brown* decision was for African Americans, PARC objected to conditions in the Pennhurst State School and Hospital. In framing the case, lawyers for PARC focused on the legal right to an education for children with special needs. PARC, working with the major federal lobbyist for children with special needs, the Council for Exceptional Children (CEC), overwhelmed the court with evidence on the educability of children with special needs. The state withdrew its case, and the court enjoined the state from excluding children with special needs from a public education and required that every child be allowed access to an education. Publicity about the PARC case prompted other lobbying groups to file thirty-six cases against different state governments. The CEC prepared model legislation and lobbied for its passage at the state and federal levels.

In 1975, Congress passed Public Law 94-142 (Education for All Handicapped Children Act) which guaranteed equal educational opportunity for all children with special needs. One of the issues confronting Congress during the debates over the legislation was that of increased federal control over local school systems. One way that Congress decided to resolve this issue was to require that an *individual education plan (IEP)* be written for each student with special needs. This avoided direct federal control by requiring that each student's IEP be developed at the local level.

IEP's are now a standard part of education programs for children with special needs. Public Law 94-142 requires that an IEP be developed for each child jointly by the local educational agency and the child's parents or guardians. This gives the child or the parents the right to negotiate with the local school system about the type of services to be delivered.

Another concern regarding the education of children with special needs is their isolation from other students and lack of access to the educational opportunities of a regular classroom. Federal legislation called for placing students in the "least restrictive environment." The result was the practice of *mainstreaming*. The basic idea of mainstreaming is that students with special needs will spend part of their day in a special education classroom and part of the day in regular classrooms. Obviously, this arrangement requires the classroom teacher to have some knowledge of the requirements of students with special needs. Working together, special education teachers and regular classroom teachers plan the mainstreaming of students with special needs into regular classrooms.

Many parents of students with special needs and many special education professionals felt that mainstreaming did not go far enough in providing a "least restrictive environment." They demanded *full inclusion*. Full inclusion is different from mainstreaming because students with special needs spend all their time in a regular classroom. The basic argument for full inclusion is that even with mainstreaming, students with special needs spend a majority of their time segregated from regular students. Similar to any form of segregation, the isolation of children with special needs often deprives them of contact with other students and denies them access to equipment found in regular classrooms, such as scientific equipment, audiovisual aids, classroom libraries, and computers. Full inclusion, it is believed, will improve the educational achievement and social development of children with special needs.

In 1990, advocates of full inclusion received federal support with the passage of the Americans with Disabilities Act. This historic legislation bans all forms of discrimination against the disabled. The Americans with Disabilities Act played an important role in the 1992 court decision, *Oberti* v. *Board of Education of the Borough of Clementon School District*, which involved an 8-year-old classified as educable mentally-retarded: Rafael Oberti. U.S. District Court Judge John F. Gerry argued that the Americans with Disabilities Act requires that people with disabilities be given equal access to services provided by any agency receiving federal money, including public schools. Judge Gerry decided that Rafael Oberti could manage in a regular classroom with special aides and a special curriculum. In his decision, Judge Gerry writes, "Inclusion is a right, not a privilege for a select few."

In 1992, the National Association of State Boards of Education gave its support to the idea of full inclusion with the issuance of its report, "Winners All: A Call for Inclusive Schools." The report calls for a fundamental shift in the provision of services for students with special needs. As the report envisions the full inclusion process, rather than teaching in a separate classroom, special education teachers would provide their services in regular classrooms by team-teaching with the regular teacher or providing other support.

The Education for All Handicapped Children Act, IEP, mainstreaming, the Americans with Disabilities Act, and full inclusion highlight the extent to which the civil rights movement reached out to include concerns for equal educational opportunity for all children, including children with special needs. It is a matter of justice that if all citizens are taxed to support schools, then all citizens should have an equal opportunity to attend school and benefit from an education.

CONCLUSION

Unequal educational opportunities continue to plague American schools. Even though the civil rights movement was able to overturn laws requiring school segregation, racial segregation between schools and second generation segregation in schools continue to be problems. And, as I discussed in Chapter 4, the differences between school districts in expenditures per student tend to increase the effects of segregation. Many Hispanic, African-

American, and Native-American students attend schools where per student expenditures are considerably below those of elite suburban and private school. These reduced expenditures contribute to unequal educational opportunity which, in turn, affects a student's ability to compete in the labor market.

It is possible, according to the discussion of the labor market in Chapter 4, that unequal school expenditures, segregation, and second generation segregation will result in the vast majority of Hispanics, African Americans, and Native Americans being confined to boring and tedious jobs in routine production services and inperson services. Of course, large numbers of low-income whites will also fill the ranks of these occupations. If education remains the key to advancement to high paying and interesting work, and if present inequalities and forms of segregation continue, then it is possible that the children of routine production and inperson workers will be trapped in the occupations of their parents. If the promise of America is that hard work will lead to social mobility, then these conditions might foretell the end of the American Dream.

EXERCISES

1. Have students write a short paper on their own experiences with segregated schools. For instance, students should consider whether or not they attended schools that were primarily one race schools. Often, white students will say to me that they never experienced segregation because they lived in a community that was all white. I immediately ask if this isn't a form of segregation. On the other hand, African-American, Native-American, and Hispanic students identify their attendance at schools composed of mainly one race as segregation. The reason for the difference, as I perceive it, is that white students benefit from segregation and therefore never spend much time thinking about segregation, while African Americans, Native Americans, and Hispanics do not benefit from segregation and therefore are more aware of its existence.

   Therefore, in writing this paper, students should explore the reasons for segregation or the lack of segregation in the schools they attended. Also, students should consider whether or not their education was improved or harmed by attendance at an integrated or segregated school. In addition, students should consider whether or not students attending schools in surrounding districts were harmed by segregation or integration.

2. Students should write a paper on their experiences with second generation segregation. Similar to the previous exercise, I frequently encounter white students who never experienced second generation segregation because they attended a school that was all white. If a student attended a one race school, then he or she should be asked to interview a student who attended an integrated school and report that student's experience with generation segregation.

3. Divide students into small groups. Have each group write a lesson plan for teaching sixth-grade students about discrimination against girls in the classroom. Have each group present this lesson to the class.
4. Divide students into small groups. Have each group write a short skit on the development of an individual education plan (IEP). Have these skits presented in class. This exercise will require students to do research on the educational needs of children with special needs and the concerns of parents of children with special needs.

SUGGESTED READINGS AND WORKS CITED IN CHAPTER

Ballantine, Jeanne. *The Sociology of Education.* Englewood Cliffs, N.J.: Prentice-Hall, 1983. Chapter 4 is devoted to a discussion of sexism in education.

Borman, Kathryn M., and Joel Spring. *Schools in Central Cities.* White Plains: Longman, 1984. Chapter 6 analyzes the impact of desegregation on the curriculum..

Committee on Labor and Public Welfare, U.S. Senate 91st Congress, 1st Session. *Indian Education: A National Tragedy—A National Challenge.* This is the report that set the stage for recent efforts in Indian education.

DeWitt, Karen. "The Nation's Schools Learn a 4th R: Resegregation." *New York Times* (19 January 1992): E5. This article provides statistics on the degree of segregation in the United States.

Kluger, Richard. *Simple Justice.* New York: Random House, 1975. A good history of *Brown v. Board of Education* and the struggle for equality.

Krsycke, Cindy. "Efforts Fail to Advance Women's Jobs: 'Glass Ceiling' Intact Despite New Benefits." *Compuserve Executive News Service, Washington Post* (20 February 1990). This article summarizes studies of difficulties encountered by women in trying to climb the corporate ladder.

Levine, Daniel, and Robert Havighurst. *Society and Education.* 6th ed. Boston: Allyn and Bacon, 1984. Chapter 18 is devoted to women in education.

Meier, Kenneth, and Joseph Stewart, Jr. *The Politics of Hispanic Education.* Albany: State University of New York Press, 1991. This is an important study of the relationship between second generation segregation and Hispanic political power.

Meier, Kenneth, Joseph Stewart, Jr., and Robert England. *Race, Class, and Education: The Politics of Second-Generation Discrimination.* Madison: University of Wisconsin Press, 1989. This book studies the politics of second generation segregation.

"Mid- and Low-Income Minorities in Decline on College Rolls." *New York Times* (15 January 1990): A13. This article reports on a study by the American Council of Education on the decline in minority college attendance.

Neal, David, and David Kirp. "The Allure of Legalization Reconsidered: The Case of Special Education." In David Kirp and Donald Jensen, eds., *School Days, Rule Days: The Legalization and Regulation of Education.* Philadelphia: Falmer Press, 1986. This is an important study of the evolution of court cases and laws affecting students with special needs.

O'Reilly, Patricia, and Kathryn Borman. "Sexism in Education: Documented Biases, Destructive Practices and Some Hope for the Future." *Theory into Practice* 23, no. 2 (Spring 1984). A good summary of information on institutional sexism in education.

Orfield, Gary. *The Reconstruction of Southern Education: The Schools and the 1964 Civil Rights Act.* New York: Wiley-Interscience, 1969. A study of the desegregation of southern schools following the passage of the 1964 Civil Rights Act.

Prucha, Francis Paul. *Documents of United States Indian Policy.* Lincoln: University of Nebraska Press, 1990. This volume contains reprints of all the important laws, court cases, and reports affecting Indian education.

Reyhner, Jon, and Jeanne Eder. *A History of Indian Education.* Billings: Eastern Montana College, 1989. This book provides a history of Indian education to present times. It discusses recent Native-American civil rights actions and recent legislation.

Rist, Ray. *Desegregated Schools: Appraisals of an American Experiment.* New York: Academic Press, 1979. This book provides many examples of second generation segregation.

Rossell, Christine. "Magnet Schools as a Desegregation Tool." *Urban Education* 14, no. 3 (October 1979). A study of the role of magnet schools in desegregation plans.

San Miguel, Jr., Guadalupe. *"Let All of Them Take Heed": Mexican Americans and the Campaign for Educational Equality in Texas, 1910–1981.* Austin: University of Texas Press, 1987. This is a good history of the events and court cases surrounding efforts by Mexican Americans to end segregation.

Schmidt, Peter. "Outlook Is Bleak for Many Blacks Study Concludes." *Education Week* (2 August 1989): 1, 29. Summary of report by the National Research Council titled, *A Common Destiny: Blacks and American Society.*

Sims, Calvin. "The Overlooked." *New York Times* (18 February 1990). Article reports on studies of the decline in minority college attendance.

Smothers, Ronald. "In Pupil 'Tracks,' Many See a Means of Resegregation." *New York Times* (18 February 1990): E5. A report on how the use of tracking as a means of second generation segregation caused a school boycott in Selma, Alabama.

——. "In School Conflict, Selma Discovers Old Racial Tensions Are Unresolved." *New York Times* (20 February 1990): A12. A report of student boycotts caused by second generation segregation.

Smylie, Mark. "Reducing Racial Isolation in Large School Districts: The Comparative Effectiveness of Mandatory and Voluntary Strategies." *Urban Education* 17, no. 4 (January 1983). A good analysis of the different types of school desegregation plans.

Snider, William. "Schools Are Reopened in Selma amid Continuing Racial Tension." *Education Week* (21 February 1990): 1, 14. A report of the school boycott and second generation segregation in Selma, Alabama.

Viadero, Debra. "'Full Inclusion' of Disabled in Regular Classes Favored." *Education Week* (30 September 1992): 11. This is a report on the court case, *Oberti* v. *Board of Education of the Borough of Clementon School District,* involving full inclusion.

——. "NASBE Endorses 'Full Inclusion' of Disabled Students." *Education Week* (4 November 1992): 1, 30. This article discusses the report supporting full inclusion of students with special needs. The report, "Winners All: A Call for Inclusive Schools," was issued by the National Association for State Boards of Education.

——. "Va. Hamlet at Forefront of 'Full Inclusion' Movement for Disabled." *Education Week* (18 November 1992): 1, 14. This article describes the implementation of a full inclusion plan in a community in Virginia.

Walsh, Mark. "Judge Finds Bias in Scholarships." *Education Week* (15 February 1989): 1, 20. This article describes the court ruling that found the awarding of scholarships using test scores to be biased against female students.

West, Peter. "Interior Dept. Sets 4 Objectives for Indian Education: Tribal Leaders Asked to Help Shape Goals." *Education Week* (21 February 1990): 1, 22. A report on some of the new plans for the education of Native Americans.

Wilkerson, Isabel. "Des Moines Acts to Halt White Flight After State Allows Choice of Schools." *New York Times* (16 December 1992): B9. This article briefly describes choice plans instituted by states and focuses on the issue of choice plans resulting in white flight from urban areas.

Wilson, William J. *The Declining Significance of Race: Blacks and Changing American Institutions.* Chicago: University of Chicago Press, 1979. This book argues that social class is a more important factor than race in determining equality of opportunity among African Americans.

Wollenberg, Charles. *All Deliberate Speed: Segregation and Exclusion in California Schools, 1855–1975.* Berkeley: University of California Press, 1976. This is a good history of segregation in California. It includes a discussion of the important school decision regarding Mexican Americans, *Mendez et al.* v. *Westminster School District of Orange County.*

CHAPTER 6

Multicultural Education

There are two major sources for the development of multicultural, bicultural, and bilingual forms of education. The first source is the concern with integrating into society the large numbers of immigrants that entered the United States after the 1970s. The second source is the civil rights movement. Some members of the civil rights movement argue that equal education opportunity cannot be achieved for African Americans, Native Americans, Mexican Americans, and Puerto Ricans unless the schools incorporate the culture of these groups into their curriculum. As I will discuss later in this chapter, there is also an argument that educational achievement can be increased if children are exposed to a curriculum that reflects their particular culture.

In considering the issues involved in multicultural education, there are certain terms and concepts that need to be clarified. First, the *dominant* culture of the United States is European American. This is the culture brought to the colonies and the United States by immigrants from Europe, and modified by the social and political conditions in America. Traditionally, the curriculum of public schools has been based on European-American traditions. In this sense, European-American culture is the dominant culture of public schools.

Second, there is a distinction between immigrants who freely come to the United States and groups that have been forcefully incorporated into the United States. The cultures that have been forcefully incorporated into the United States are referred to as *dominated* cultures. In this case, dominated culture refers to domination by European-American culture. For instance, Africans were forcefully brought to the United States as slaves, and their African cultures were changed by the domination of European-American culture to produce an African-American culture. Native-American tribes were conquered by the United States government, which instituted educational programs in boarding schools designed to replace Native-American cultures with European-American culture. Currently, in the aftermath of these attempts to destroy native cultures, Native Americans are in the process of restoring their cultural traditions.

Mexicans living in the Southwest were forcefully made part of the United States with the signing in 1848 of the Treaty of Guadalupe Hidalgo. The treaty, which concluded the Mexican-American War, annexed to the United States the northern parts of Mexico, including California, Nevada, Arizona, and New Mexico. In addition, the war resulted in the annexation of the Republic of Texas. The public schools in these states attempted to replace Mexican culture and the Spanish language with European-American culture and English. Today, many Mexican Americans are interested in the maintenance of their cultural traditions and the Spanish language against the domination by European-American culture.

The Spanish-American War of 1898 resulted in the forceful annexation of Puerto Rico to the United States. Puerto Ricans are another dominated culture which the United States government tried to change through educational policies designed to replace Puerto Rican culture and Spanish with European-American culture and English. Currently, Puerto Ricans and Mexican Americans are working together to ensure the preservation of the use of Spanish.

And last, the term *deculturalization* refers to the conscious attempt to destroy a culture for the purpose of replacing it with another culture. At one time, many Christian-European Americans considered the cultures and religions of Africans and native Americans a threat to civilization as they conceived of it. Conscious policies were instituted to deculturalize these groups. For instance, it was not until 1978 that a Congressional Resolution on American Indian Religious Freedom granted Native Americans the right to the free exercise of their religions. And deculturalization policies were instituted against Mexican Americans and Puerto Ricans. Since language is an important part of culture, a central focus of these deculturalization policies was the replacement of Spanish with English.

The following section of this chapter will discuss recent patterns of immigration into the United States and their effect on public schools. The next section will deal with the educational problems of dominated groups—African Americans, Native Americans, Mexican Americans, and Puerto Ricans. After the discussions of immigrant and dominated cultures, the chapter will examine some of the educational policies designed to deal with these cultural issues, including bilingual education, bicultural education, ethnocentric education, and multicultural education.

THE NEW IMMIGRANTS

The resistance of established populations to immigrant groups is a persistent problem in the United States and other countries. Those already living in an area frequently feel economically threatened because of the possibility that immigrants might be willing to accept lower wages and, consequently, cause a general reduction in wages. In fact, immigration often occurs because of the promise of a higher standard of living in the host country. Also, immigrants are perceived as a threat to existing political and social relations. The combination of these economic and political fears can magnify differences in customs and religious practices, causing the development of prejudices and discriminatory practices.

The problems associated with immigrant populations fall heavily on public schools. The schools must develop techniques for teaching children that come from homes with different languages and customs. The choice of techniques is a politically charged issue. Since the 1970s, large numbers of new immigrants to the United States made the education of differing ethnic and language groups a major issue. In Los Angeles, New York City, and towns scattered across the country, neighborhoods identified with emigrants from particular South American, Caribbean, Asian, and Central-American countries sprang up in the 1970s. In New York City, a traditional home for new immigrants, a Spanish Yellow Pages telephone directory was issued in the 1980s, and most advertising on the subway system is now in Spanish. Throughout New York, emigrants from South Korea took over greengrocer businesses and opened manicure salons, while other emigrant groups took over newspaper stands and restaurants. In the Brighton Beach section of Brooklyn, the presence of Jewish emigrants from the Soviet Union can be seen in the ethnic goods in stores and the foreign titles in bookstores.

The new wave of immigration into the United States since the 1970s was made possible by the Immigration Act of 1965. Prior to 1965, immigration was determined by the ethnic quota section of the 1924 Immigration Act. Under the 1924 act, passed during a period of extreme racism, the annual quota of a national group allowed to immigrate to the United States was determined by the percentage that national group comprised of the total U.S. population in 1920. The openly stated purpose of the 1924 immigration legislation was to limit immigration of nonwhite populations.

As a consequence of the 1924 Immigration Act, the depression of the 1930s, and World War II, immigration to the United States declined from the late 1920s through the early 1950s. Immigration began to increase again in the 1950s and underwent a dramatic change after passage of the 1965 Immigration Act. Before 1965, the proportion of emigrants from Europe remained approximately constant relative to those from Asia and the rest of the Americas. But after 1965, the proportion of emigrants from Europe dramatically declined and the proportion from Asia and the Americas dramatically increased.

Between the late 1960s and the 1990s, the largest number of emigrants each year came from Mexico. In recent years, more and more emigrants have arrived from Asian sources, although Mexico continues to provide more than any other single country. In 1969, the order of immigrant sources to the United States was Mexico, Italy, the Philippines, Canada, and Greece. By 1973, Canada and Greece dropped off the list, which read Mexico, the Philippines, Cuba, Korea, and Italy. Two years later Italy was replaced by China-Taiwan. Through the rest of the 1970s, the proportion of emigrants from Asia and the Pacific steadily increased. In 1980, the top five sources of immigrants were Mexico, Vietnam, the Philippines, Korea, and China-Taiwan.

During the 1980s, the Asian population of the United States grew by 70 percent from 3.8 million in 1980 to 6.5 million in 1988. One-third of the Asian population settled in California. Asian immigrants represented a wide variety of nationalities and language groups. At least 80 percent of the Asian immigrants in the 1980s came from China, Taiwan, Hong Kong, Vietnam, Cambodia, Laos, the Philippines, Japan, South Korea, and Micronesia. Most of the Asian immigrants have higher professional and educational training than earlier groups. Table 6.1 indicates the total numbers and percentages of the general population of Asian Americans, Hispanics, and African Americans given in a special U.S. Census Bureau report for 1988. The report was limited to these populations.

The primary reasons for immigration since the 1970s are economic, political, and familial. The 1965 Immigration Act established a preference system that favored family ties. In the distribution of immigration visas, preference is given to spouses, children, and siblings of U.S. citizens. Also, preference is given to professionals and persons of exceptional ability who will benefit the U.S. economy and to skilled workers who are needed in the economy. Finally, preference is given to political refugees.

This preference system resulted in immigrants with differing economic and educational backgrounds. For instance, large numbers of Mexicans have legally entered the United States because of family ties with Mexican Americans. Many of these Mexicans, along with those entering the country illegally, were poorly educated and were escaping the harsh economic conditions in Mexico.

On the other hand, the large Cuban and Vietnamese immigration of the 1970s fell under the political refugee preference category of the 1965 legislation. Many of these refugees were from the professional and business classes of their countries.

The preference given to professionals provided the means for large numbers of medical doctors and other educated workers to immigrate. Most often, the foreign professional immigrates because of higher salaries in the United States. For instance, by the mid-1970s more than half of the interns in municipal hospitals in New York City were immigrant Asian doctors. By 1976, about 40 percent of all Filipino doctors practiced in the United States. The most dramatic case was in 1972 when almost the entire graduating class of a new medical school in Thailand chartered a plane and flew to the United States.

TABLE 6.1 Special U.S. Census Report for 1988

	Total Number (in Millions)	Percentage of Total Population
Total Population	247.6	100.0
Asian-American	6.5	2.6
Hispanic	20.0	8.0
African-American	30.5	12.3

In *Still the Golden Door: The Third World Comes to America*, David Reimers describes a typical pattern for Asian immigration, which begins with an Asian student coming as a nonimmigrant to complete his or her education. Near the end of the student's studies, the student finds a job and is given immigrant status. After a few years, the immigrant becomes a citizen and is able to sponsor, under the preference system, brothers and sisters as immigrants. In turn, the brothers and sisters can use the preference system to sponsor their spouses and children. This is why, according to Reimers, the 1965 legislation is often called the "brothers and sisters act."

The educational response to the new immigrant is quite different and more complicated than the primarily assimilationist approach of the early twentieth century. In an essay in a book he edited titled *Clamor at the Gates: The New American Immigration,* sociologist Nathan Glazer points out that immigrant education programs of the 1920s emphasized the teaching of English and the American way of life. Often, these assimilationist programs included saluting and pledging allegiance to the flag, teaching an American diet, and convincing the student of the decadence of most foreign governments when compared to the United States.

The educational response to the new immigration, however, is complicated by court decisions and political divisions. The most important U.S. Supreme Court decision affecting new immigrants is *Lau et al.* v. *Nichols* (discussed in detail in Chapter 11). This 1974 decision required schools to provide special aid to students from families in which English was not the spoken language.

The language issue is one of the major problems confronting public education. As I will explain in a later section of this chapter, schools have implemented a variety of programs to deal with this increasing diversity of languages. Using statistics from the 1991–1992 New York City school year, Table 6.2 provides a vivid example of the language problems that must now be dealt with by the public schools. During the 1991–1992 school year, there were 120 different languages spoken in the New York City public schools by students who were not proficient in English. As Table 6.2 indicates, Spanish and Chinese were the languages most often spoken by non-English-speaking students.

Besides the problem of the language and culture of the public schools, there is the continuing problem of educational discrimination against immigrant groups. Current discrimination against Asian Americans can be compared to the plight of the Jews in the 1920s who were discriminated against in higher education by a quota system on enrollments. In 1987, *Time* magazine called Asian Americans the "new whiz kids." *Time* reported that Asian Americans comprised 25 percent of the entering class at the University of California at Berkeley, 21 percent at the California Institute of Technology, 20 percent at the Massachusetts Institute of Technology, and 14 percent at Harvard. *Time* magazine, in 1987, reported that as a result of quota systems many qualified Asian Americans were being refused admission to major

TABLE 6.2 Number of Students Who
Were Not Proficient in English Who
Are Native Speakers of Each Language
in the New York City Schools During
the 1991–1992 School Year

Language	Number of Students
Spanish	88,894
Chinese	12,921
Haitian Creole	7,166
Russian	5,332
Korean	3,467
Arabic	1,883
Urdu	1,421
Bengali	1,184
Vietnamese	986
French	928
Polish	862
Italian	732
Hindi	683
Albanian	595
Farsi	509

Source: This table was adapted from Joseph Berger,
"School Programs Assailed As Bilingual Bureaucracy,"
New York Times (4 January 1993): 1, B4.

universities. The largest number of complaints centered on the admission policies of the University of California at Berkeley. *Time* quotes the co-chairperson of the Asian American Task Force on University Admissions, Alameda County Superior Court Judge Ken Kawaichi, that university administrators envision a campus that "is mostly white, mostly upper class with limited numbers of African Americans, Hispanics and Asians. One day they looked around and said, 'My goodness, look at this campus. What are all these Asian people doing here?' Then they started tinkering with the system."

The issues of discrimination and Americanization probably will be resolved for most immigrant groups through the use of political power in the educational system. Those groups that are able to organize sufficient political power will have the schools serve their needs. Those who are unable to exercise political power will have to accept whatever programs are developed within the schools. In this context, achieving equality of educational opportunity is primarily a political issue.

DOMINATED CULTURES

Anthropologist John Ogbu makes an important distinction between the educational experience of immigrant children and children from dominated cultures such as African Americans, Native Americans, Mexican Americans, and Puerto Ricans. In investigating these differences, Ogbu was interested in why many children of immigrant parents are more successful in school than children from dominated cultures. In addition, he wondered why many children from dominated cultures develop attitudes that are antischool.

One of his important conclusions is that the historical experience of dominated groups has resulted in the development of a basic distrust of the major institutions in American society. For instance, a history of forced subjugation and slavery, segregation, discrimination, and harassment by police and government officials has left many members of the African-American community with the feeling that the government works primarily to benefit European Americans. This general distrust of institutions includes public schools. Segregation and second generation segregation have left many African Americans feeling that public schooling is organized to keep African Americans at the bottom rungs of America's social and economic system.

Many Native Americans feel a strong hostility toward schools because of the deculturalization programs they experienced in government-operated boarding schools. For instance, Mick Fedullo, in his wonderful book on Indian education, *Light of the Feather: Pathways Through Contemporary Indian America,* recounts a discussion with an Apache bilingual education teacher, Elenore Cassadore, about Apache attitudes toward schools. As she tells Fedullo, many Apache parents were sent to Bureau of Indian Affairs' boarding schools were they "came to believe that their teachers were the evil ones, and so anything that had to do with 'education' was also evil—like books." Now, she explains, they only send their children to school because of compulsory education laws. "But they tell their kids not to take school seriously. So, to them, printed stuff is white-man stuff."

Mexican Americans and Puerto Ricans not only encountered the hostility embodied in segregation and second generation segregation, but also policies hostile to their native language. In many schools throughout the Southwest, students were punished for speaking Spanish on school grounds. Similar policies existed in Puerto Rico during the early part of the twentieth century. Similar to African Americans and Native Americans, Mexican Americans and Puerto Ricans have been subjected to harassment and intimidation by the police and other government officials.

According to Ogbu, these historical conditions created a *cultural frame of reference* among dominated groups that is quite different from that of many immigrants and European Americans. *Cultural frame of reference* refers to the manner in which people interpret their perceptions of the world. A person's cultural frame of reference is formed, in part, by his or her family's historical experience. For instance, an African-American child might not have witnessed a lynching of a black person by a white mob, but knowledge of these incidents might be passed on to the child through the recounting of family history and experience in the United States. A Mexican-American child might not have experienced discrimination in employment, but he or she might frequently hear about it through family conversations. The history told by families and a person's experiences play a major role in shaping one's cultural frame of reference.

Differences in cultural frames of reference can result in differing interpretations of the same event. For instance, a European American might interpret his or her perception of a school as viewing an institution that is benign and helpful. In contrast, a member of a dominated group might perceive a school as an institution not to be trusted. The actions of a disgruntled waiter in a restaurant might be interpreted through the cultural frame of reference of a European American as resulting from the waiter not feeling good about his job. On the other hand, the cultural frame of reference of African Americans, Native Americans, Mexican Americans, and Puerto Ricans might lead members of these groups to interpret the waiter's actions as hostile and prejudicial.

Also, differences in cultural frames of reference can result in differences in action in particular situations. For instance in the above example, a European American might give little attention to the actions of a disgruntled waiter. On the other hand, members of a dominated group might act in a hostile manner to what they perceive to be the prejudicial actions of the waiter.

Ogbu argues that the negative cultural frame of reference regarding school held by some students from dominated cultures can cause low academic achievement. Ogbu identifies three ways this can occur. First, for some members of dominated groups, as exemplified by the above quote from the Apache teacher, doing well in school requires "acting white." Peer pressure against acting white can result in students actually avoiding academic achievement. From this standpoint, doing well in school symbolizes a rejection of one's culture for a European-American culture.

Second, the cultural frame of reference held by students from dominated cultures can cause conflicts with European-American administrators, teachers, and students. Of course, these conflicts might be in response to real feelings and actions demonstrated by school officials and other students. These conflicts contribute to a distrust of the institution of schooling and a rejection of school rules. The open rejection of school rules leads to suspension, expulsion, and other forms of school punishment. These attitudes about school rules and the resulting punishment also contribute to low academic achievement.

And third, the cultural frame of reference of many students from dominated cultures can cause them to begin school disillusioned about their ability to achieve. This can result in little effort being put into academic work.

These three effects of a dominated group's cultural frame of reference can result in what Ogbu calls the *low academic effort syndome* and *counter academic attitudes and behavior. Low academic effort syndrome* refers to lack of effort in doing school work, which results from peer pressure, conflict, and disillusionment. *Counter academic attitudes and behavior* refers to actions that are hostile toward the school and its rules.

Obviously, there are large numbers of students from dominated groups that succeed in school and who do not display a low academic effort syndrome or adopt counter academic attitudes and behavior. Despite their success in school, many of these students still interpret their educational experience through a cultural frame of reference that is quick to note prejudice and unfair treatment. This type of cultural frame of reference can be found in Jake Lamar's autobiography *Bourgeois Blues: An American Memoir.* Despite the fact that his father was a successful businessman who could afford to live in wealthy neighborhoods in New York City and send his children to elite private schools, Jake discovered that racism was still a major factor in his life. In his autobiography, *Hunger of Memory: The Education of Richard Rodriguez*, Richard Rodriguez interprets his academic success through the cultural frame of reference of a Mexican American. Of particular importance in understanding the problems of students from dominated cultures is the pain Rodriguez felt as his academic success widened the gap between him and his family culture.

For students from dominated cultures whose low academic achievement is a result of low academic effort syndrome and counter academic attitudes and behaviors, one possible solution is the creation of educational programs that are taught from their cultural frame of reference. For instance, as I will discuss in the next section, there has recently developed educational programs based on the cultural perspective of African Americans, Native Americans, and Mexican Americans. These *ethnocentric* programs are designed to overcome the problems of a low academic effort syndrome and counter academic attitudes and behaviors.

ETHNOCENTRIC EDUCATION

In *ethnocentric education*, subjects are taught from the perspective of a particular culture. Obviously, this is what public schools have been doing in the United States since their beginnings. But, of course, the curriculum of public schools is organized around the cultural frame of reference of European Americans, while the curriculum of new ethnocentric schools is organized around the cultural frames of reference of African Americans, Native Americans, and Hispanics.

The purpose of these new ethnocentric schools is twofold. First, these schools want to overcome among some children of dominated cultures the resistance to schooling that results in low academic effort and counter academic attitudes and behaviors. Second, these schools want to preserve the cultural traditions of each dominated group.

The preservation of culture is considered important because of what is believed to be some of the shortcomings of European-American culture. For instance, many Native Americans feel that European Americans show little respect for nature and that they are primarily concerned with the control of nature. The result of these attitudes is massive environmental destruction. What Native-American culture can contribute is an understanding of how to live with nature and an attitude that shows respect for nature and desires its preservation.

The concern with student resistance to schooling and with preservation of culture resulted in the establishment of Afrocentric schools. In 1990, a proposal for the establishment of an Afrocentric school for black males in Milwaukee was quickly followed by similar proposals in Detroit, Minneapolis, and New York. In February, 1991, a Hispanic-centered school was proposed for the Denver public school system.

The proposal for a Hispanic school was advanced by the advocacy group Latin American Research and Service Agency. As reported in an Associated Press article, "Hispanic Schools," the executive director of the organization, Audrey Alvardo, argues, "What our children need is a school that works, and they need it now." In Denver, Hispanic students are the fastest-growing part of the school population, with nearly 40 percent of the students being Hispanic. Hispanic students have the highest dropout rate of any ethnic student and are among the lowest scoring students on college entrance examinations. Alvardo states, "Not only do Hispanic youths enter school slightly behind their white counterparts, but they continue to fall further and further behind as they go through school."

The proposals for Hispanic and Afrocentric schools are designed to redirect resistance cultures and build student self-esteem. A major source of inspiration for ethnocentric schools comes from the work of Jawanza Kunjufu, president of the Chicago-based African American Images. African American Images serves as a publishing house for Kunjufu's books and other books and videos focused on the teaching of African-American culture. One of the things offered by African American Images is a model curriculum called *SETCLAE: Self-Esteem Through Culture Leads to Academic Excellence.* The stated goals of the curriculum are to improve academic achievement, discipline, and school climate, while transmitting racial pride and enhancing students' knowledge of culture and history and its significance to contemporary living.

Kunjufu's discussion of the experience of African-American students is similar to that of John Ogbu. Kunjufu argues that for most African-American students, being successful in school means acting white. Kunjufu exemplifies this situation by a dialogue between a group of African-American students about two other academically successful African-American students in his book *To Be Popular or Smart: The Black Peer Group*:

> "Girl, she thinks she's something, making the honor roll."
> "I know, she's beginning to act like Darryl. They both think they're white, joining the National Honor Society."

One of the effects of American slavery, Kunjufu argues, is the public characterization of Africans as intellectually inferior. The expectation of intellectual inferiority eroded the confidence in academic success among black youth. In addition, having been stripped of their cultural heritage, slaves internalized white ideals about beauty and culture. Consequently, later black resistance to domination involved the creation of a culture that opposed certain white ideals. Kunjufu found that when black teenagers are asked, "How do you act black?" they respond in terms of cultural issues. From their perspective, being black is speaking Black English, listening to rap and rhythm and blues, and attending parties. On the other hand, being white is considered by black students as speaking standard English, listening to rock and classical music, and going to museums.

Kunjufu found the same pattern among black college students. Recalling his own years in college in his book *To Be Popular or Smart: The Black Peer Group,* Kunjufu states he was almost ostracized by his fellow black students when he joined the college debating society. What saved him from cultural exclusion was being an athlete, liking to dance, and "talk the talk." On the other hand, white students made comments such as "You're different and you're not like the rest of them." Out of the 1,000 African Americans in his entering class only 254 graduated. In Kunjufu's words, "Many of them flunked out while pledging, roller skating, partying, talking in the cafeteria or dormitories, playing ball or records, and getting high."

In the context of this concern about the development of a self-destructive resistance culture among African-American students, Kunjufu advocates the teaching of an Afrocentric curriculum as a means of breaking cultural stereotypes. He wants African-American students to know that Africans have a long history of learning and creativity. He wants them to understand that within African cultural traditions it is alright to be black and to be an intellectual. He wants them to realize that studying hard and learning is not being "white," but follows the best traditions of African culture.

In addition, he wants black students to understand that there is an Afrocentric way of viewing the world that is different from that of a Eurocentric view. Molefi Kete Asante, chairperson of the Department of African-American Studies at Temple University and one of the proponents of an Afrocentric curriculum, argues that Afrocentricity is a transforming power involving five levels of awareness. On the first four levels of this transforming experience, individuals come to understand that their personality, interests, and concerns are shared by African people around the world. Afrocentricity is achieved on the fifth level when people struggle against foreign cultures that dominate their minds. At this stage, Asante argues in his book *Afrocentricity,* "An imperative of will powerful, incessant alive, and vital, moves to eradicate every trace to powerlessness. Afrocentricity is like rhythms; it dictates the beat of your life."

By purging images given by white culture of African Americans as stupid and powerless, African-American students can, according to the arguments of those advocating Afrocentricity, gain a new image of themselves as a people of ability and power. In this sense, Afrocentricity is considered a curriculum of empowerment. In addition, the students lose the lenses that filter the world through a white Eurocentric perspective and replace them with a set of Afrocentric lenses.

Therefore, ethnocentric curriculum in the United States creates a cultural battle at two levels. At one level, ethnocentric curriculum is an attempt to give equal value to different cultural traditions. At the second level, it means purging a Eurocentric view of the world from Native-American, Hispanic, and African-American children's minds and replacing it with a different cultural frame of reference. The purpose of this cultural battle is to empower Native-American, Hispanic, and African-American children so that they believe they can succeed in the world and so that they are not self-destructive. From this perspective, getting ahead in the economic and social system is not a matter of being white, but learning to believe in oneself and one's cultural traditions.

Ethnocentric education is one method for helping children from dominated groups succeed in school. Another method is bilingual education. Bilingual education, as I will discuss in the next section, is particularly important for Native Americans, Mexican Americans, and Puerto Ricans because of the conscious attempt by public schools in the past to destroy their languages.

ISSUES OF LANGUAGE

The struggle for bilingual education in public schools was led by organizations representing Mexican Americans, Native Americans, and Puerto Ricans. In general, *bilingual education* refers to teaching a person to be proficient in the use of two languages. For instance, Native-American students can be taught to be proficient in the use of their own native languages and English, while a Mexican-American or Puerto Rican child can be taught to be proficient in Spanish and English.

In addition, there are several specific types of bilingual education, including *maintenance bilingual, transitional bilingual,* and *two-way bilingual.* As the term suggests, *maintenance bilingual* programs are designed to maintain the ability to speak, read, and write in the student's language, while at the same time learning English. For instance, a student might enter school speaking only Spanish with little or no knowledge of English. The ability to speak Spanish does not necessarily mean that the child knows how to read and write in Spanish. Similarly, most English-speaking students entering school do not know how to read and write in English. During the early years, maintenance bilingual education programs conduct classes in the language of the student, while also teaching English. Therefore, during the period that students are learning English, they are also learning the content of the curriculum, including how to read and write in their native tongue. This avoids the problem of learning being delayed until students know English. After learning English, students continue to receive lessons in both their native languages and in English.

One of the strongest arguments for maintenance bilingual education is that students are better able to learn English if they know how to read and write in their native language. In *Affirming Diversity: The Sociopolitical Context of Multicultural Education*, Sonia Nieto argues that children who know how to read and write in their native language will be more successful in school than children whose language is neglected by the school and who do not become literate in their native tongue.

In contrast, *transitional bilingual* does not have the goal of making the student literate in two languages. The student's native tongue is used in class until the student learns English. After the student learns English, classes are taught only in English. *Two-way bilingual* programs include both English-speaking and non-English-speaking students. By conducting class in two languages, English-speaking students are able to learn the language of the non-English speakers, while the non-English speakers learn English. For instance, a class might be composed of both Spanish- and English-speaking students with the subject matter being presented in both languages. The goal is for all students to become bilingual in English and another language.

Of course, language is linked to culture. Many Mexican Americans, Puerto Ricans, and Native Americans believe that maintenance bilingual education programs are essential for the retention of their cultures. As I discussed earlier in this chapter, many of the deculturalization programs were directed at stamping out the use of Spanish and Native-American languages. In addition, a person's cultural frame of reference is directly related to attitudes regarding the use in the United States of languages other than English. The issue of cultural perspective is highlighted in Humberto Garza's comment regarding a requirement that Los Altos, California, city employees speak only English on the job. Garza is quoted by Rosalie Pedalino Porter in her book, *Forked Tongue: The Politics of Bilingual Education*: "Those council people from Los Altos should be made to understand that they are advocating their law in occupied Mexico [referring to the U.S. conquest of Mexican territory, including California]. . . . They should move back to England or learn how to speak the language of Native Americans."

Garza's remarks reflect the political explosiveness of bilingual education issues. In fact, the bilingual education movement was born during the civil rights upheavals of the 1960s. During the 1960s, Mexican Americans demonstrated for the use of Spanish in schools and the teaching of Mexican-American history and culture. In 1968, Mexican-American students boycotted four East Los Angeles high schools, demanding bilingual programs, courses in Mexican-American history and culture, and the serving of Mexican food in school cafeterias. In addition, students demanded the hiring of more Spanish-speaking teachers and the firing of teachers who appeared to be anti-Mexican American.

The school boycotts in Los Angeles attracted the attention of the newly formed La Raza Unida. La Raza Unida was formed in 1967, when a group of Mexican Americans boycotted federal hearings on the conditions of Mexican Americans and started their own conference. At the conference, La Raza Unida took a militant stand on the protection of the rights of Mexican Americans and the preservation of their culture and language. As quoted by Guadalupe San Miguel, Jr., in his book *"Let All of Them Take Heed": Mexican Americans and the Campaign for Educational Equality in Texas 1910–1981*, the statement drafted at the first conference proclaimed: "the time of subjugation, exploitation, and abuse of human rights of La Raza in the United States is hereby ended forever. . . ." La Raza Unida's statement on the preservation of culture and language reflected the growing mood in the Mexican-American community that public schools needed to pay more attention to dominated cultures and languages. The statement drafted at the first conference affirmed "the greatness of our heritage, our history, our language, our traditions, our contributions to humanity and our culture. . . ."

Politicians responded to Mexican-American and Puerto Rican demands for the preservation of Spanish in the schools. Senator Ralph Yarborough of Texas, believing that he would lose the 1970 election to a wealthy and conservative Democrat, decided that Hispanic support was crucial for his coalition of blacks, Mexican Americans, and poor whites. In an effort to win Hispanic support, Yarborough, after being appointed to a special subcommittee on bilingual education of the Senate Committee on Labor and Public Welfare, launched a series of hearings in major Hispanic communities.

The testimony at these hearings came primarily from representatives of the Mexican-American and Puerto Rican communities, and not educational experts or linguistic theorists. The hearings concluded in East Harlem, with Senator Edward Kennedy and the Bronx Borough President Herman Badillo decrying the fact that there were no Puerto Rican principals and only a few Puerto Rican teachers in the New York City school system.

Yarborough supported bilingual legislation that focused on students whose "mother tongue is Spanish." The legislation included programs to impart knowledge and pride about Hispanic culture and language, and to bring descendants of Mexicans and Puerto Ricans into the teaching profession. The legislation was clearly designed to win political support from the Hispanic community in Texas. Yarborough's efforts resulted in the passage of the previously mentioned Bilingual Education Act of 1968.

As I discussed earlier in this chapter, Native Americans along with Mexican Americans and Puerto Ricans welcomed the idea of bilingual education. On the other hand, some members of the Republican party joined a movement opposing bilingual education and supporting the adoption of English as the official language of the United States. The movement for making English the official language was led by an organization, U.S. English, founded in 1983 by S. I. Hayakawa, a former Republican Senator.

In 1986, in reaction to the Reagan administration, the National Association of Bilingual Education increased its political activities and intensified its public relations efforts. In reference to S. I. Hayakawa and U.S. English, Gene T. Chavez, the president of the association, warned that those advocating only the use of English were motivated more by political than by educational concerns. At the same meeting, the incoming president of the organization, Chicago school administrator Jose Gonzalez, attacked the Reagan administration and the Department of Education for entering an "unholy alliance" with right-wing groups opposing bilingual education, groups such as U.S. English, Save Our Schools, and the Heritage Foundation.

While bilingual education remains a controversial issue, large numbers of non-English-speaking students are served primarily by *English as a Second Language (ESL)* programs. While the teachers of these programs might speak the language of the students, the primary purpose of ESL classes is to teach students English so that they can learn the content of instruction in English. Unlike bilingual education programs, no attempt is made to teach reading and writing in the native language of the students.

The differences between bilingual and ESL education programs highlight the *bicultural* aspects of bilingualism. The general goal of ESL is the learning of English and, as a result, the gaining of knowledge about European-American culture. On the other hand, Mexican Americans, Native Americans, and Puerto Ricans advocate bilingualism as a method of retaining both the student's native language and culture, while learning English and European-American culture. As I will explain in the next section, bicultural education is supposed to teach a student how to function in two different cultures.

BICULTURAL EDUCATION

Bicultural education provides another method of dealing with the resistance to schooling exhibited by students from dominated cultures. *Biculturalism* means being able to function in another culture without losing ties to one's original culture. Currently, biculturalism is an important part of Native-American education. Until the 1960s and 1970s, federal Indian education policies were premised on the idea the deculturalization had to take place before the Native American could function in the world of the European American. In contrast to these policies, biculturalism is designed to help Native-American youth function in the world of the dominant culture without having to sacrifice traditional Indian cultures.

One of the important advocates of biculturalism for Native Americans is educator and poet Mick Fedullo. The central feature of Fedullo's approach to biculturalism is easing Indian children into the use of English by having them do creative writing on themes relevant to Indian culture. In this manner, learning English does not serve as a tool of deculturalization but it serves as a means of expressing cultural pride. Indian children can cross over into the use of English without feeling they are betraying their cultural heritage. Through student publications and the creation of calendars using student poetry, Fedullo makes students proud of their culture and their ability to write in English.

In addition, Fedullo helps Indian students to understand the cultural differences between Native Americans and European Americans. One of his most striking lessons was given to Apache students on the subject of prejudice against Indians. The lesson opened with a brief discussion of the meaning of the word *prejudice* and quickly moved on to the question of the types of prejudice encountered by the Apache students. The first issue raised by the students was being stared at by whites in the local town. In the cultural world of these Apache students, being stared at is a sign of hostility and prejudice. As Fedullo led the students through the discussion, the students began to realize that being stared at is not necessarily a result of hostility and prejudice. Some whites might be staring because of curiosity and interest, while others might truly be hostile. The lesson left the students with less apprehension and greater understanding about crossing the border into white culture. In this lesson, Fedullo did not ask the Apache students to abandon their cultural rules that staring is impolite and aggressive, but he helped them understand that white society functions under different cultural rules.

As Fedullo introduces Indian students to the dominant culture, he constantly reminds them that there is nothing wrong with their cultural traditions and that these traditions do not have to be abandoned in order to function in the world of the dominant culture. For instance, Fedullo accompanied a group of Apache students from the Apache reservation in Arizona to Spokane, Washington. It was the first time many of these students had visited a city, and they were in awe of such things as parking meters and escalators. One of the major events on the trip was eating in an expensive restaurant. Prior to going to the restaurant, Fedullo prefaced his instructions on table etiquette by explaining that there were many ways of conducting oneself at a meal. For instance, reservation manners require that at Indian feasts children, and other adults do not approach the food until after the elders are served. Also, Fedullo explained to the children that the manners they were teaching the children were appropriate for restaurants but not for all situations.

The destructive consequences of European Americans failing to learn to be bicultural are well illustrated in Fedullo's story about the anger Navajo students felt toward a new counselor who, in the context of Navajo culture, was too probing and aggressive in his questioning. By unknowingly breaking the rules of Navajo culture, the counselor gained nothing but the hatred and scorn of the students.

The consequences of not receiving a bicultural education are also well illustrated in the previously mentioned autobiography by Richard Rodriguez. The autobiography describes Rodriguez's education from elementary school to his eventual graduate work in one of the temples of European culture—the British Museum. Throughout the autobiography, he describes his increasing alienation from the Mexican-American culture of his family as he absorbed the dominant European-American culture. He is never taught how to move between the two cultural worlds and to appreciate the long history of Mexican culture. His education involves the subtraction of one culture and its replacement by another. Bicultural education would have made European culture an addition to his existing cultural framework rather than requiring a subtraction of his Mexican-American heritage.

While many dominated cultures advocate ethnocentric, bilingual, and bicultural programs, recent immigration has resulted in calls for *multicultural education.* As I will describe in the next section, multicultural education programs attempt to teach students to view the world from different cultural frames of reference.

MULTICULTURAL EDUCATION

Multicultural education programs have four important goals. The first goal is to build tolerance of other cultures. The second goal is to eliminate racism. The third goal is to teach the content of different cultures. And the fourth goal is to teach students to view the world from differing cultural frames of reference.

Advocates of multicultural education believe that it will greatly reduce racial and ethnic tensions in the United States. Sonia Nieto, one of the leading proponents of multicultural education, argues that multicultural education should pervade every aspect of the curriculum, including mathematics and science. For instance, history can be taught from a variety of cultural frames of reference. A teacher can help a student understand how a Mayan's view of events in the ninth century A.D. would be different from that of a European or Asian. Literature courses can be expanded to include examples from a variety of the world's cultures. Concepts of government can be viewed from a variety of cultural perspectives. For instance, a student can be helped to understand why a fundamentalist Moslem might prefer a theocratic state as opposed to the Western model of a secular state. A history of different cultural contributions to the development of math and science can be taught in appropriate math and science courses. Differing cultural views of math and science can be taught. For example, as I mentioned earlier in this chapter, there is a striking difference between Native-American and European-American concepts of nature.

Besides pervading the curriculum, Nieto argues that multicultural education must be considered part of the basics of education. Not only must people learn reading, writing, arithmetic, and basic computer functions to survive in modern society, Nieto argues, but they must also become tolerant of other cultures in a world with global corporations and an internationalized labor force. Today, in any small city around the United States there is a culturally mixed labor force reflecting the population changes of the new immigration.

Also, Nieto includes education for social justice as part of multicultural education. This aspect of multicultural education reflects the reform impulse in the movement. The goal of building cultural tolerance also includes the goal of cultural justice. This means eliminating all social and economic barriers that keep a particular racial or ethnic group from having equal opportunity. In other words, multicultural education should create a spirit of tolerance and activism in students. An understanding of other cultures and of differing cultural frames of reference will, it is assumed, spark students to actively work for social justice.

Multicultural education, therefore, is distinctly different from ethnocentric and bicultural education. Ethnocentric education is designed to teach students from a particular cultural frame of reference as opposed to multiple frames of reference. For instance, many Native-American educators are more concerned with restoring Indian traditions and helping students understand an Indian perspective of the world than they are with teaching children the cultural frames of reference of Asians and Europeans. Also, bicultural education is primarily focused on preparing a student to exist in two different cultures as opposed to all the world's cultures.

The opposition to multicultural education is similar to the opposition to bilingual education. While opponents of bilingual education want to maintain English as the dominant language, the opponents of multicultural education want to maintain European traditions as the center of American culture. Critics of multicultural education, such as educational historian Diane Ravitch, historian Arthur Schlesinger, Jr., and former Secretary of Education William Bennett, want the schools to teach about other cultures but, at the same time, to unite students around European culture. They argue that European traditions should remain at the center of American culture because the United States' system of government and its major institutions are a product of these traditions.

Opponents of multicultural, bicultural, and ethnocentric education also worry that these forms of education will lead to greater social friction rather than greater tolerance. They believe that the promotion of cultural pluralism will lead to cultural rivalry. The way to avoid cultural friction, they argue, is for all students to be united around a particular cultural framework. From this point of view, for instance, students might be taught about Native-American culture, but the basic values stressed during instruction would be those of European Americans.

In the New York Task Force on Minorities' report, *A Curriculum of Inclusion*, these two views of cultural education were highlighted by comparing a traditional family dinner table (European traditions as the center of the curriculum) to King Arthur's Round Table (multicultural education as the focus of the curriculum). With regard to maintaining European traditions, the report states, "European culture is likened to the master of a house ruling over a dinner table, himself firmly established at the head of the table and all other cultures being guests some distance down the table from the master, who has invited the others through his beneficence. . . ."

In contrast, the report describes multicultural education: "The new model is likened to the fabled Round Table of King Arthur, with all cultures offering something to the collective good, each knowing and respecting others, and each gaining from the contribution of others; no culture is master of the new table."

CONCLUSION

The struggle over issues of language and culture will continue into the future as dominated groups struggle for equality of opportunity and as new immigrant groups adjust to American society. On a global scale, issues of multicultural, ethnocentric, bicultural, and bilingual education will become increasingly important with the development of a global economy and the internalization of the labor force. The United States is not the only country confronting these issues. Many European countries have instituted multicultural education programs as a result of the influx of foreign workers. Germany is suffering from the rise of hate groups that have physically assaulted foreign workers and refugees.

In the United States, a central conflict will continue to be between those who want to maintain the supremacy of English and European traditions, and dominated cultures whose members want to protect and maintain their cultural traditions. Many Native Americans, African Americans, and Hispanics reject the image of European culture at the head of a dinner table ruling over other cultures. In addition, many immigrant groups might not be willing to give up their cultural traditions to a European model. But whatever the conclusion of this conflict, American public schools will never be the same after the impact of the cultural and language demands of dominated groups, and the adjustment of educational programs to meet the needs of the new immigrants.

EXERCISES

1. I use the following exercise to introduce students to the concept of cultural frame of reference and the dynamics of racism. If students are of European-American descent, I ask them to write one page on how African Americans might view them. If they are African American, Native American, Asian, or Hispanic, I ask them to write one page on how European Americans might view them.
2. One of the things frequently stated by students is that immigrants should become Americans. Of course, this leads to the issue of what is an American. To deal with the problems associated with defining Americanism and the new immigration, I divide the class into small groups and assign them the task of determining what it means to become an American based on the immigrant experience presented in the novel *Jasmine* by Bharati Mukerjee. The novel traces the life of an immigrant woman from a small village in India to her marriage to a paraplegic banker in Iowa and adoption of a Vietnamese refugee.
3. I found the best fictional introduction to the concept of dominated cultures to be Mehdi Charef's *Tea in the Harem*. One value of this book for American students is that it presents this concept in a different cultural framework. The book is about the delinquency among Algerian youth living in Paris. The novel includes all of the factors that have a negative impact on dominated groups, including the school system.
4. To help students understand ethnocentric education, I divide the class into small groups and I have them read Jawanza Kunjufu's *Countering the Conspiracy to Destroy Black Boys*. Based on Kunjufu's book and library research, I ask the groups to write a lesson plan for an Afrocentric class.

5. To help students understand the concept of biculturalism, I assign the contemporary autobiography of Native-American Mary Crow Dog, *Lakota Woman*. The class is divided into small groups and each group is asked, based on what they learned about contemporary Native-American culture and problems from *Lakota Woman*, to write a lesson plan designed to teach biculturalism to Native-American students.

6. Using Sonia Nieto's *Affirming Diversity: The Sociopolitical Context of Multicultural Education*, I ask small groups of students to write a multicultural lesson plan for a classroom composed of students from dominated cultures, immigrant families, and European-American backgrounds.

SUGGESTED READINGS AND WORKS CITED IN CHAPTER

Asante, Molefi Kete. *Afrocentricity.* Trenton, N.J.: Africa World Press, Inc., 1988. This is an important discussion of the philosophy of Afrocentricity.

Barringer, Felicity. "Asian Population in U.S. Grew by 70% in the 80s." *New York Times* (2 March 1990): A4. This article provides immigration statistics for the 1980s.

Berger, Joseph. "School Programs Assailed as Bilingual Bureaucracy." *New York Times* (4 January 1993): 1, B4. This article provides statistics on the languages spoken by students in the New York City schools and the problems involved in bilingual education programs.

Brand, David. "The New Whiz Kids." *Time* (31 August 1987). A report of the education aspirations and problems of Asian-American students.

Charef, Mehdi. *Tea in the Harem.* London: Serpent's Tail, 1989. This novel is about the delinquency among Algerian youth living in Paris. The novel includes all of the factors that have a negative impact on dominated groups, including the school system.

Crow Dog, Mary. *Lakota Woman.* New York: HarperCollins, 1990. A wonderful autobiography of a Native-American woman who is very involved in the contemporary Native-American movement.

Fedullo, Mick. *Light of the Feather: Pathways Through Contemporary Indian America.* New York: William Morrow and Company, Inc., 1992. Fedullo provides a beautiful description of the development of bicultural education among Native Americans.

Glazer, Nathan. "Immigrants and Education." In Nathan Glazer, ed., *Clamor at the Gates: The New American Immigration.* San Francisco: Institute for Contemporary Affairs, 1985, 213–41. This article provides an analysis of education policies regarding the new immigrants.

"Hispanic School." *Compuserve Executive News Service*, no. 1442 (8 February 1991). This article contains arguments by Audrey Alvardo on the reasons for the establishment of a school reflecting Hispanic cultures.

Kunjufu, Jawanza. *Countering the Conspiracy to Destroy Black Boys.* Chicago: African American Images, 1985. This book provides a strong argument for the necessity of an Afrocentric curriculum.

———. *To Be Popular or Smart: The Black Peer Group.* Chicago: African American Images, 1988. This is a discussion of the attitudes of African-American youth regarding education.

Lamar, Jake. *Bourgeois Blues: An American Memoir.* New York: Penguin, 1992. A powerful contemporary autobiography detailing the racism encountered by an upper-middle class African American.

Mukerjee, Bharati. *Jasmine*. New York: Fawcett Crest, 1989. This novel traces the life of an immigrant woman from a small village in India to her marriage to a paraplegic banker in Iowa and adoption of a Vietnamese refugee.

Nieto, Sonia. *Affirming Diversity: The Sociopolitical Context of Multicultural Education*. White Plains: Longman, Inc., 1992. A good introduction to issues in multicultural education.

Ogbu, John. "Class Stratification, Racial Stratification, and Schooling." in Lois Weis, ed., *Class, Race, & Gender in American Education*. Albany: State University of New York Press, 1988, 163–183. In this article, Ogbu outlines his basic theory for the development of resistance to schooling among dominated cultures in the United States.

Porter, Rosalie Pedalino. *Forked Tongue: The Politics of Bilingual Education*. New York: Basic Books, 1990. Porter attacks maintenance bilingual education programs. The book is a good introduction to the controversy surrounding bilingual education.

Reimers, David. *Still the Golden Door: The Third World Comes to America*. New York: Columbia University Press, 1985. This book provides a history and portraits of recent immigrants.

Rodriguez, Richard. *Hunger of Memory: The Education of Richard Rodriguez*. New York: Bantam Books, 1982. An important autobiography of the emotional and social struggles of a successful Mexican-American student.

San Miguel, Jr., Guadalupe. *"Let All of Them Take Heed": Mexican Americans and the Campaign for Educational Equality in Texas, 1910–1981*. Austin: University of Texas Press, 1987. This is a good history of the school experience of Mexican-American children.

SETCLAE: Self-Esteem Through Culture Leads to Academic Excellence. Chicago: African American Images, 1991. This is a model Afrocentric curriculum.

Task Force on Minorities. *A Curriculum of Inclusion*. Albany, New York: State Education Department, 1989. This is an important report on multicultural education.

PART TWO

Power and Control
in American Education

CHAPTER 7

Power and Control in the Local School District

WHO SHOULD CONTROL KNOWLEDGE IN A DEMOCRATIC SOCIETY?

The public school is a central institution for the distribution of knowledge in modern society. The method of controlling public schools has profound implications for both individual and social development. For instance, who should decide what subjects will be taught in public schools? Parents? Students? Government officials? Teachers? School Administrators? As I discussed in Chapter 1, there are often important differences between what subjects parents and government officials think should be taught. Should more history be taught and less science? The answer can vary from group to group. Also, decisions must be made about content. Textbooks are not magically created and whimsically selected by schools. As I will discuss in Chapter 10, political decisions are made about the content of textbooks. These decisions are not value free. There are different ways of interpreting the American Revolution and decisions are made about how to present issues such as those pertaining to the environment. Many groups have a stake in what is taught in public schools, and they try to exert their influence on public schools.

Another way of thinking about this problem is to imagine yourself sitting in what I will call an "Educational Chair." Imagine that at a flick of a lever this chair has the power to shape your morality, to control your behavior, and to teach you any subject. This Educational Chair can be considered a public school that works. After all, the goals of public schooling include moral instruction, shaping behavior, and transmitting knowledge.

Now the question is who should control this Educational Chair? In other words, who should decide your morality, behavior, and knowledge? You? Your parents? Your professor of education? Elected officials? How you answer this question will reflect the political values you have regarding the control of public schools.

In the 1990s, the debate over who should control education ranges from the business community to religious organizations to minority parents. Many groups have a stake in the outcomes of public schooling. The business community wants graduates with knowledge and behaviors that conform to its needs. Some religious organizations want schools to teach their versions of morality. In fact, a major controversy in recent years has involved fundamentalist Protestant churches accusing the public schools of teaching a morality that is destructive to their religious principles. Minority parents complain that public schools are damaging to their children because they teach the culture and values of the white elite.

Understanding the concept of representation is important for answering the question of who should control American education. The United States is primarily composed of representative forms of government. That is, people elect government officials to represent them on school boards, in state legislatures, and in Congress. In only a few situations, such as voting on local property taxes, are decisions made by the direct vote.

REPRESENTATION AND THE RESTRUCTURING OF AMERICAN EDUCATION

In debates over the control of American schools, the most frequently mentioned types of representation are—trustee, delegate, and professional. The concepts of representation will be considered in the context of local school politics. In most American communities some form of appointed or elected board of education is responsible for representing public opinion in school matters. Whether or not the board is appointed or elected and how it is appointed or elected varies from community to community. In general, boards of education formulate educational policy, which is then administered by the school staff. In the local school district the superintendent of schools is responsible for administering educational policy and advising the board on the needs of the local school system.

The central office staff is usually composed of an administrative staff, which deals with the overall organization of the school system's curriculum, financial matters, personnel policies, and all programs that affect any of the schools within a district. In terms of the control of local education, the central office staff is very important because it often controls the lines of communication between the building principals and teachers, and the superindendent. Building principals have the responsibility of administering school policy within their particular elementary or secondary school.

Within the context of this general pattern for controlling schools at the local level, a *trustee* form of representation acts to achieve a general common good or public interest. For instance, a school board member acting as a trustee would make decisions based on what he or she believes is good for the general public. These types of decisions might often be contrary to what the public actually wants. The public interest or general good as defined by the board member might not represent the true wishes of the public. Support of trustee forms of representation is premised on the idea that decisions, particularly about social institutions such as schools, should be removed from the immediate control of the general population. The reason one wants an elite board membership that is well educated and successful is to assure that decision making conforms to what the elite believes is the public good.

Delegate forms of representation are an attempt to conform to the desires of the population. Decision making is based on what the representative believes is wanted by the public. This form of representation is preferred by those who believe that social institutions should function according to what people want and not on the basis of some individual's personal interpretation of the public good. It is argued that those who try to make decisions based on a set of beliefs about what constitutes the public good cannot separate their own beliefs from the decision-making process. The issue of trustee versus delegate representation has become an important issue in the controversy over representation of minority groups on boards of education. To understand this issue one must consider the relationship between the type of representation used and the particular organization of school board elections that results from it.

Most school board elections in the United States are organized around the concept of trustee representation, in order to limit public participation in direct control of school board affairs. This is accomplished through at-large and nonpartisan elections. In at-large elections a person running for the school board must be elected by the entire voting population of a school district. This means a person must have enough money and organizational support to campaign throughout the entire school system. In contrast, during the nineteenth century the voting districts for many school board elections were confined to limited geographical areas within a school district. In such situations a person does not need a great deal of financial backing to campaign within a small area and could win elections based on neighborhood contacts. This method of election made in easier for the average person to win elections to the school board. It can be argued that at-large elections tend to favor trustee forms of representation, while the other type of election favors delegate forms of representation because there is more direct contact between the elector and the elected.

Nonpartisan elections also tend to favor the election of elites to school boards. In one of the most complete studies of the issue, *Nonpartisan Elections and the Case for Party Politics*, Willis Hawley argues that nonpartisan elections create a partisan bias in favor of Republicans. In this argument he is associating "Republican" with community elites. Nonpartisan means that regular political parties cannot nominate and campaign for a particular candidate. When this is the case, Hawley argues, informal networks begin to operate to select and provide support for candidates. These informal networks are generally composed of civic-business clubs such as the Chamber of Commerce, Kiwanis Club, Rotary, and other luncheon-service clubs.

A traditional criticism of boards of education in the twentieth century is that their membership constitutes an elite. What is meant by *elite* is that the membership primarily is drawn from the professional and business groups in the local community. This is not as true in rural communities, where there is often heavy representation from the farm community. Most boards of education in the United States tend to be composed of white male professional or business persons. The representation from this group on boards of education tends to be out of proportion to their actual numbers in comparison with the rest of the population. The membership of boards of education in the United States does not tend to reflect the social composition of the local community.

This general picture of the composition of school boards is reflected in national statistics. Nationally, a disproportionate number of board members are male, have college educations, are in upper-income groups, and have high-status occupations. A survey of school board members reported in 1991 by the *American School Board Journal* found that the typical school board member was male, between 41 to 50 years old, married, held a graduate degree, worked as a professional, earned between $40,000 to $49,000 a year, and owned a home.

Some educators view the elite nature of the social composition of school boards as a positive asset to the local school district. Joseph M. Cronin in his history, *The Control of Urban Schools,* found that educators during the early part of the twentieth century believed it was important to have successful and well-educated men on the school board because this social group was more knowledgeable and more interested in education than the rest of the population. In fact, the whole trend in the early part of the twentieth century toward centralization and reduction in size of urban school boards was premised on the idea of limiting public participation in school affairs to the social leaders of the community. Opposition to this trend came from organized labor, which felt that board membership drawn from only one sector of the community would result in the domination of school policy by certain political and economic views.

As mentioned previously, at-large and nonpartisan elections have created a problem for those seeking representation of minority groups on boards of education. Members of minority groups do not often have access to the informal networks described earlier. In addition, it is often difficult for a member of a minority group to win an election in an at-large campaign because of lack of support from white voters. On the other hand, it would be much easier for minority groups to win representation on school boards if board members were elected from a small geographical area that primarily included members of that minority group.

An example of this is the change that took place in the Dallas, Texas, school district that, in 1974, ended its method of electing a nine-member board of education by at-large elections. The new method of election, which was mandated by the Texas legislature in 1973, divided the school system into nine districts of approximately 89,500 each. The change to election by district did have a significant effect on the social composition of the board of education, because it allowed representation of minority members. Before 1974 the board of education was composed primarily of whites. After 1974 the board was composed of six Anglos, two blacks, and one Mexican American.

Professional representation involves issues different from those associated with trustee and delegate. In this concept of representation, it is assumed that the expert or professional can best represent the needs of the client. It can be argued that the control of schools should be given to professional teachers and administrators because they are primarily concerned about the welfare of children. Unlike elected members of boards of education, teachers and administrators do not have debts to special interest groups. Free of this type of political control, they can concentrate on helping students.

Certainly, teachers' unions are strong advocates of professional representation. As I discussed in Chapter 3, teachers' unions are interested in extending their power over many areas of educational policy. This fact highlights some of the limitations of professional representation. Teachers and administrators are not disinterested parties working for the welfare of students. They are concerned about salaries and working conditions. There could be a situation where concerns about salaries and working conditions would work against the interests of students. Teachers might gain higher salaries at the expense of providing educational materials for students. Teachers might, out of self-interest, negotiate a reduction in the length of the school day, which could reduce educational opportunities for students. Professional representation is an issue in the current trend of developing site-based management of schools.

SITE-BASED MANAGEMENT OF SCHOOLS

In current experiments in restructuring education through site-based management of schools, professional representation is present while in others delegate representation holds sway. The idea of restructuring includes new methods for controlling schools and reorganization of the learning environment. The concept of site-based management involves the establishment of a council at a school that has the power to control the school's budget and educational activities. This council can be a combination of teachers and administrators at the school, and representatives from the community. If the power is primarily given to administrators and teachers, then the school operates under a professional form of representation. In other situations, delegate representation can happen when the majority of power is given to parents and community members.

In some situations, site-based management can create conflict between principals and teachers. In the 1980s, Superintendent Joseph Fernandez introduced site-based management in the Dade County, Florida, school system. Under this plan, schools were to be managed by a committee composed of the principal, teachers, and parent. In some situations, teachers were allowed to overrule principals. When Fernandez was hired as Chancellor of the New York school system in the fall of 1989, the New York Council of Supervisors and Administrators immediately announced their intention to resist any attempts to introduce school councils. In a letter, the Council, which is a union, told Mr. Fernandez that while they could accept some aspects of site-based management, "the final authority must rest with the principal." In situations of this type, professional representation degenerates into struggles over power.

An exciting experiment in maximizing delegate representation was launched in Chicago at the beginning of the 1989–1990 school year. In an effort to improve Chicago schools, the Illinois state legislature passed a bill that gave power over local schools to councils dominated by elected parents. The Chicago Board of Education retains control of broad policy issues and the appointment of the superintendent. The school councils have the power to hire and dismiss principals, approve budgets, and make recommendations on the curriculum and textbooks.

The organization and election of the Chicago school councils optimizes the opportunity for delegate representation. Each council has six parents, two teachers, and two community representatives. The majority of power is in the hands of the elected parent. Since the elections are for each school, this increases the opportunity for all parents to participate. In the first election in the fall of 1989, 5,400 officials were elected to the school councils in what the October 11, 1989, issue of the *New York Times* described as a process "galvanizing many poor, minority communities . . . [with a] new sense of power."

From the standpoint of delegate representation, for the first time in the twentieth century a political means was available to the average Chicago citizen for influencing local schools. Previously, it was almost impossible for mosts citizens to influence Chicago's school board. The populist quality of the Chicago election was captured by the *New York Times* description of Veronica Kyle, a school council candidate, standing outside her son's elementary school urging parents to vote for her. Like the other 9,733 parents who participated in the election, Kyle canvassed neighborhoods, knocked on doors, distributed leaflets, and answered questions at community forums. On a typical Saturday during the election, Kyle described how she and a few friends "wolfed down a grilled turkey sandwich, ran off some fliers at the church, put on our Reeboks and jogging suits, and hit the neighborhood in twos."

The rise of delegate authority in Chicago meant a decline of professional authority. The most controversial part of the Chicago plan was giving parent-controlled school councils the power to hire and fire principals. In the past, Chicago school principals had tenure and could not be dislodged from their schools except under extreme circumstances. The reasoning behind the new law is that the principal is the key to school improvement and that parents are the best judges of a quality principal.

In early March, 1990, angry parents packed a meeting of the Chicago Board of Education to protest the firing of some principals. The claim was that the dismissals were based on race or ethnicity. Students pulled fire alarms and teachers joined picket lines. At Morgan Park High School, two police officers and six students were injured, and ten students were arrested during protests over the firing of a white principal. White principals at three predominantly Hispanic schools claimed they were being forced out by the school councils because they were not Hispanic. On the other side, Hispanic dominated councils claimed that their efforts at school reform were being stopped by white principals and teachers. Some claimed that members of the white school staff used ethnic slurs when talking to council members. Ben Natske, a white principal of twelve years at the predominantly Hispanic Spry Elementary school said, "To this day, I haven't been told why I was voted out. It's as if they're saying, 'If you're not Hispanic, then get out.' "

Of course, this is the type of turmoil one would expect in a system moving from trustee to delegate representation. Over the years, the Hispanic community in Chicago has had little influence on school policy. Given power, the Hispanic community would obviously be concerned that the schools served their interests. Ellis Levin, a Democratic State Representative who heads the House committee that oversees the plan, said, "What looks like a chaotic situation—that's democracy. School reform is not guaranteed to work 100 percent in every school, but it can't be any worse than it was before."

Site-based management is one aspect of the attempt to restructure American education. As I will discuss in the next section, charter schools are another step in the attempt to shift power from local and state educational bureaucracies to individual schools.

CHARTER SCHOOLS

"I view charter schools as an incentive to enhance public education," proclaimed Minnesota State Senator Ember D. Reichgott, a cosponsor of the first state law providing for the establishment of charter schools. The basic idea of a charter school is that a group of teachers or parents can petition a local school board or state agency to establish a public school or create a special program in an existing public school. Once the charter school is approved it operates in a semiautonomous fashion and receives public funds for its support. The basic idea is to create public schools that can act with a certain degree of independence from local and state educational bureaucracies. Freed from bureaucratic control, it is hoped that charter schools will develop and maintain unique and innovative alternatives to traditional public schools.

For instance, the 1991 Minnesota law specifies that only licensed teachers can apply to local school boards to establish charter schools. In addition, proposals for charter schools must be approved by the state department of education. To maximize their autonomy, the only power given to local school boards is to assure that a charter school fulfills the outcome of its original charter. Otherwise, school board members and administrators are not allowed to interfere in the operation of the charter school. Under this law, the first charter school to be approved is the Bluffview Montessori School which operated for three years as a private school before deciding to seek public support.

In 1992, California became the second state to adopt a charter school law. Under the California legislation, charter schools would not be required to follow most state regulations for traditional schools. They would be required to specify their educational programs, what outcomes they expect from their students, and how they intend to measure student progress. The new law requires that charter schools be free, nonsectarian, and nondiscriminatory. Establishing a charter school requires the signatures of at least 10 percent of teachers in a school district, or 50 percent of teachers in a school building. The signatures and plan for the charter school are given to the local school board. After a public hearing, the school board can reject or accept the charter school plan. Once approved, the charter school, funded by the state and local school district, would be allowed to operate for five years before seeking renewal of its charter.

Acting on their own initiative, several local boards of education around the country have established plans for charter schools. In Philadelphia, charter schools are used to break down the anonymity within traditional high schools. These chartered schools exist as independent schools within the walls of a traditional high school. As of the 1992–1993 school year, there were ninety-seven charter schools in local high schools with each charter school serving 200 to 400 students and run by a staff of ten to twelve teachers. To insure innovation and independence, teachers in the charter schools develop their own curriculum and methods of instruction. The charter schools also try to involve parents in the planning process.

In Detroit, twenty charter schools are operating. Under the school board plan, a petition for opening a charter school requires the approval of its principal, 75 percent of its teachers, and its parents council. In a major controversy in 1991, the Detroit Board of Education chartered three all-male academies for African-American boys. After a brief struggle in the courts, the three academies were required to admit girls along with boys.

The strongest objections to charter schools have come from teachers' unions. As I discussed in Chapter 3, the Detroit School Board's proposal that charter schools would not have to conform to the requirements of the contract between the board and the local teachers' union resulted in a strike. In an interview in the November 25, 1992, issue of *Education Week,* the president of the Minnesota Federation of Teachers, Sandra Peterson, said that her members viewed the charter school law as a step toward the privatization of public education and they were particularly upset because charter schools would not have to conform to local union contracts. She claimed, "We would probably have less resistance to the whole charter schools notion if the collective-bargaining process were intact."

The charter school idea promises greater flexibility and innovation in public schools. It is part of a broader trend to find ways of breaking the standard mold of public school education. As I will discuss in the next section, choice plans are another attempt to achieve this end.

CHOICE

During the 1992 presidential campaign, the Republican contender George Bush supported choice between public and private schools, while his opponent Bill Clinton supported choice only within the public school system. The choice issue had been present in the previous three presidential campaigns. The basic idea of choice is to present parents and students with the opportunity to choose whatever school they want to attend. Under public-private choice plans, some form of government financing would allow the choice of a private or public school. Under choice plans that are limited to public schools, the parents would be allowed to send their child to any public school within their district, or in the case of some states, to any public school within the state. Traditionally, parents do not choose a particular public school for their children but must send them to the one assigned by the local school district.

The concept of choice dates back to the 1950s, when economist Milton Friedman advocated giving parents vouchers that could be used to purchase an education for their children at any school. As a free market economist, Friedman blamed the poor quality of public schools on the lack of competition. Also, he argued that impoverished parents are often trapped in poor school systems because they cannot afford to move to the school districts with better schools. With vouchers, parents would not have to move to choose better schools.

An important source of support for the public-private model of choice came from Protestant fundamentalists who complained that the moral values taught in public schools are destructive of the values of Christianity. Consequently, there has been a rapid growth of privately operated fundamentalist schools across the country. These groups advocate choice between public and private schools through vouchers or tuition tax credits. Under a voucher plan, a set amount of money would be allotted to each family to choose between public and private schools. With tuition tax credits, a plan backed by the Reagan and Bush administrations, parents would receive a credit toward their taxes for money spent for private or public schooling.

In 1990, the choice idea received support from the work of two political scientists, John Chubb and Terry Moe. In their book, *Politics, Markets & America's Schools,* they argue that a major hindrance to student achievement is the existence of large bureaucracies which impose their will on local schools. They maintain that bureaucracies work against the basic requirements of effective school organizations by imposing goals, structures, and requirements. Bureaucracies do not allow, according to Chubb and Moe, principals and teachers to exercise their professional expertise and judgment, and deny to them the flexibility needed to work effectively together to assure student achievement. Chubb and Moe argue that schools controlled by competition in a free market have less bureaucracy and, consequently, promote student achievement.

While Chubb and Moe support the idea of choice, Ernest Boyer's 1992 report for the Carnegie Foundation for the Advancement of Teaching, "School Choice," found little parental support for the choice idea. In his survey, Boyer found that 70 percent of parents with children currently enrolled in a public school indicated that if given the opportunity, they would not want to send their children to another private or public school. In states that adopted choice plans, only 2 percent of the parents were participating. Only 15 percent of the parents interviewed believed that the competition generated by choice plans would improve public schools. On the other hand, 82 percent responded that the best way to improve public education was to provide greater resources to neighborhood schools. In addition, public school parents opposed private school choice plans by a 2 to 1 margin.

Boyer's findings were supported by the results of the Minnesota law providing for parental choice of any school in the state. As I discussed in Chapter 5, Minnesota was one of eight states in 1992 allowing choice between public schools. The other states were Arkansas, Idaho, Iowa, Nebraska, Ohio, Utah, and Washington. In Minnesota, only one-half of one percent of the parents of public school children took advantage of the law. Of those who did change their children's school, the major reason given was academic.

Besides statewide choice plans, individual cities have adopted choice systems. In 1990, the Wisconsin state legislature passed a bill allowing 970 students in the Milwaukee public schools to attend private, nonsectarian schools. Wisconsin Governor Tommy Thompson, in describing the reasons for the plan in the March 28, 1990, issue of the *New York Times*, said, "Choice gives poor students the ability to select the best school that they possibly can. The plan allows for choice and competition, and I believe competition will make both the public and private schools that much stronger." In response to the governor's remarks, Robert Peterkin, superintendent of Milwaukee schools, warned that the bill "threatened public education by leaving the city schools with the hardest-to-educate students and with fewer resources."

Under the Wisconsin plan, a student whose parents' income is less than 75 percent of the poverty level established by the federal government would be allowed to transfer to a nonsectarian, private school. The schools receiving these students would receive $2,500 per student in state aid. It is important to recognize that the legislation was initiated because of a belief that private schools in Milwaukee are doing a better job of educating low-income students for less money than public schools. The sponsor of the bill, state representative Annette Williams, is quoted in the March 28, 1990, issue of *Education Week*, "We're now going to show that our children can be educated successfully for less than half the money that the Milwaukee schools use to miseducate our students."

Choice is a form of political power that is exercised by the acceptance or rejection of a school. For state representative Annette Williams, the Wisconsin choice plan gives political power to the poor by allowing them to choose not to attend public schools. In her words, "The state is directly helping families who have drive, who have high expectations, but who don't have money, to vote with their feet."

In the fall of 1992, the New York City Board of Education, one of the largest school systems in the country, unanimously adopted a plan that would allow parents to choose any public school in the system. While school officials applauded the announcement of the plan, they believed that few parents will take advantage of the plan because of overcrowding in schools, the lack of money to pay for transportation, and because parents would prefer to send their children to neighborhood schools. Under the plan, parents would be given priority in enrolling their children in their neighborhood school. If space is available after this initial enrollment, the school must accept any transfers from other schools.

The comments by New York school officials that few parents will probably participate highlights a major problem in choice plans. The experience in Minnesota and the findings of Ernest Boyer suggest that most parents would prefer to send their children to neighborhood schools. They do not want choice, but they do want better neighborhood schools. In addition, as I discussed in Chapter 5, it was discovered that the Iowa choice law was resulting in white flight from the Des Moines school district. Using the choice law, many white parents were sending their children to suburban schools, while most poor parents did not take advantage of the law. Milton Friedman assumed that choice would provide the opportunity for the poor urban child to escape city school systems. It appears that just the opposite is happening. On the other hand, the supporters of choice still contend that competition will improve public schools and break the supposed hold of the educational bureaucracy. Along with charter schools, choice will continue to be part of the debate about restructuring American public education.

COMMUNITY POWER AND SCHOOL BOARD POLITICS

Restructuring the control of schools often involves a challenge to existing structures of community power. In the twentieth century, most school boards operate under a trustee form of representation. In many cases, this involves an informal power structure influencing the decisions of boards of education. This informal power structure usually includes community leaders in business, finance, and media. While members of this informal power structure are not on school boards, they influence the decisions of elected school board members.

The importance of the informal power structure is highlighted in struggles over school desegregation. David Kirby et al., in their study of *Political Strategies in Northern School Desegregation*, found that school desegregation is a political decision made by elites and not by the masses. Their study surveyed ninety-one cities ranging in size from 50,000 to large cities over 250,000. The primary goal of the study was to look at the major political actors in relationship to the characteristics of the cities and the political structure of their educational systems. The study looked specifically at the civil rights movement, the school board, the superintendent, civic leaders, and white protest against desegregation plans.

To support their conclusion that elites make the most important decisions regarding school desegregation, they provided a statistical overview of elite membership on school boards. In their sample drawn from ninety-one cities, over 50 percent of the membership of civic elites were bankers, industrialists, and heads of local businesses. The others included lawyers, heads of local utilities, newspaper people, civic association executives, clergy, university administrators, and professionals. Only 5 percent of this civic leadership were identified as liberals representing labor and civil rights organizations.

The nature of the informal power structure varies from community to community. In *Politics, Power, Polls, and School Elections,* Michael Y. Nunnery and Ralph B. Kimbrough define several different power structures that can exist within local schools. They argue that understanding the nature of the local power structure is important for understanding the politics of the board of education, the community support structure, and the methods used to gain support for educational policies.

Nunnery and Kimbrough argue that there are four basic types of local power structures, ranging from monopolistic systems to those characterized by democratic pluralism. A community with a monopolistic power structure is controlled by a single group of businessmen, professionals, and politicians. Sometimes this occurs in one-industry towns or in rural areas governed by groups of large landowners. Within a monopolistic system, a few top influential people make the major decisions for the community. In these systems there is characteristically very little conflict and confrontation.

A second, somewhat closed system is the multigroup and noncompetitive power structure. In this power structure, although rival groups exist within the structure seeking their own economic advantage, there is still general agreement about the basic policies to be followed within the local community. For instance, leaders of the different groups within this power structure might compete for such things as contracts for building schools and who will provide the schools with insurance, but still agree upon general educational policy.

The third type of power structure is characterized by competition between elite groups. This often occurs when a community is undergoing social change, such as a rural community rapidly changing into a suburban community. In this case, major competition is seen between the established and the newer elite groups over questions such as zoning, planning, industrialism, and education. There are frequent differences of opinion between competing elite groups about basic school policy. For instance, a traditional rural-community elite might place less emphasis on preparation for college than a new elite associated with suburban development. Although strong conflict exists in this structure between competing elite groups, there is still little general citizen participation in the power structure.

The fourth type of power structure is characterized by democratic pluralism, where the system is continually open to new persons and groups gaining positions of power. Very often, the people who are influential in the community decision-making process change, depending upon the issue being considered. For instance, people who are influential in the educational decision-making process might be different from those involved in other community affairs. Within this structure there is a great deal of citizen participation.

Nunnery and Kimbrough believe that for a school administrator to work effectively, it is essential that he or she understand the power structure within the local community. It is equally true that in order to understand the politics of the local school board and its policies, one must understand the power structure that is responsible for election or appointment to the board. One of the difficulties in doing this is being able to generalize from one community to another. No two communities are necessarily alike in terms of their power structures and the informal networks that lead to board membership. Each community must be studied to determine its particular power structure.

Nunnery and Kimbrough suggest some methods that school administrators can use to determine the nature of the local power structure. These methods are also valuable to the student and local citizen in coming to understand the political and social forces behind the school board. Nunnery and Kimbrough recommend the following procedure. First, a person should become acquainted with the variety of literature on community power structures as a basis for interpreting any data gathered. Second, a person should become acquainted with the leaders in different areas of the community. Nunnery and Kimbrough recommend beginning with the heads of the local chamber of commerce, women's clubs, unions, churches, political parties, newspapers, and radio and television stations. In addition, prominent attorneys, physicians, and bankers should be contacted.

In discussions with these persons, questions should be asked about important issues, problems, and decisions; notes should be taken with regard to the names most frequently mentioned. Also, discussion should be encouraged about whom the community leaders think are the most influential people in the community. From these conversations a person can begin piecing together an outline of the relationships among those people considered the most influential in the community. Next, one should check the membership lists of local boards of directors of financial institutions, community groups, and the chamber of commerce. With this information a person should be able to outline the informal power structure of the community. After this is done, the results can be tested through participation in community activities in order to observe the degree of citizen participation and the importance of the power structure in the decision-making process.

The same methods recommended by Nunnery and Kimbrough can be directly applied to a study of the membership of the local board of education. Interviews with current and former board members can reveal why they got involved in board activities and their relationship to the general community power structure. Of extreme importance in this regard are informal contacts. Through membership lists of organizations and direct questions it can be determined whether a great deal of informal contact takes place among board members or among themselves and other members of the local power structure. Very often decisions about school issues and school board participation are made at informal social gatherings and parties in homes and in social clubs. This is true for both economic elite groups, such as businessmen and professionals, and social-interest groups, such as racial and ethnic organizations.

Although the linkage between the school board and the community power structure is important for understanding the actions of board members, it is also important for understanding the linkages between the board and the school administration. It is essential in terms of being effective and for job protection for the superintendent of schools to have a cooperative and friendly board of education. For this reason, school administrators tend to favor school board members who have successful business or professional backgrounds.

In *The School Managers: Power and Conflict in American Public Education,* Donald McCarty and Charles Ramsey provide a classification of the relationships between community power structures, school boards, and administrative styles. They assume that the type of community power structure determines the nature of the school board and the administrative style of the superintendent. They divide community power structures into the following:

1. Dominated
2. Factional
3. Pluralistic
4. Inert

In dominated communities majority power is exercised by a few persons or one person. In most cases, these people are part of the community's economic elite, though in some cases they could be leaders of ethnic, religious, or political groups. Factional communities are usually characterized by two factions competing for power. Very often these factions differ in values, particularly religious values. Pluralistic communities have a great deal of competition between a variety of community-interest groups with no single group dominating school policies. And in inert communities, there is no visible power structure and there is little display of public interest in the schools.

McCarty and Ramsey argue that the following relations exist among these power structures and types of school boards and superintendent styles:

Community Power Structures	Types of School Boards	Superintendent Styles
1. Dominated	1. Dominated	1. Functionary
2. Factional	2. Factional	2. Political
3. Pluralistic	3. Pluralistic	3. Adviser
4. Inert	4. Sanctioning	4. Decision making

In a *dominated* community, the local elite control access to membership on the school board and, consequently, control school board policies. In order to retain his or her position, the superintendent must follow the wishes of the community elite. McCarty and Ramsey studied one dominated community where a superintendent protested his firing by a school board acting against the wishes of the local power elite. In response to the situation, the community elite met in the offices of a local bank and decided, in order to avoid community conflict, to let the superintendent be fired. At the same time, they decided the school board had gotten out of control. The most respected member of the elite group was made chairman of the school board's nomination committee and its membership was selected to assure elite control. Traditionally, those recommended by the nomination committee were elected to the school board without opposition. And finally, the leading members of the community kept a close watch on the nominating committee for several years to assure the selection of candidates they approved.

In a *factional* community, the survival of a superintendent depends on his or her ability to function as a political strategist balancing the concerns of each community faction. In a factional community studied by McCarty and Ramsey, the major competing groups were a permissive Jewish and a conservative Catholic population. The two groups represented almost equal populations in the school district, and the control of the school board shifted from group to group in each highly contested election. The campaigns were very emotional, with each group accusing the other of undermining the quality of education. When McCarty and Ramsey arrived in the community, liberals on the school board had lost their majority to conservatives who immediately fired the superintendent. The fired superintendent, according to McCarty and Ramsey, failed as a political strategist because he appeared to favor the previous liberal majority.

The competition among a variety of groups in a *pluralistic* community results in constantly shifting coalitions on the school board. In the community studied by McCarty and Ramsey, a dispute over a bond issue created a coalition of Catholics, the Chamber of Commerce, and a labor union in opposition, and Protestant churches and the PTA in support. The superintendent in this community played the role of the professional adviser. On the bond issue, his support was given in professional statements about the need for additional classrooms and more teachers. In performing the role of professional adviser to a pluralistic board, the superintendent should move cautiously to avoid adverse community reaction to proposals for change.

And finally, *inert* communities give the majority of power over school issues to the superintendent. McCarty and Ramsey describe inert communities as being ideologically homogeneous and without a sense of purpose. In most situations, the composition of the board is indirectly controlled by the superintendent. Board members turn to the superintendent for leadership and decision making. In some cases, McCarty and Ramsey report, the superintendent claimed that board members accepted 99 percent of his or her proposals. Very seldom in inert communities does the board turn to leaders outside of the school system for advice on educational matters.

In all four of these categories, superintendents prefer school board members who have successful business or professional backgrounds. In *Governing American Schools*, Zeigler and Jennings found that board members from lower socioeconomic groups tend to be more involved in administrative detail than those from higher social economic groups. From the standpoint of the superintendent, board-member involvement in administrative details can restrict the actions of the administrative staff. In most cases, superintendents prefer board members to restrict their activities to general educational policies.

This finding supports the argument given in the early part of the twentieth century that board membership should be restricted to the successful and educated because of their greater interest in educational policy. But this does not mean that lower-status board members are not interested in educational policy. What it does mean is that they have a greater interest in the actual control of the educational system. In fact, higher-status board members gave more importance than did lower-status board members to the opinion of the superintendent; consequently, there was less conflict between higher-status board members and the superintendent than between lower-status board members and the superintendent. This might be because the superintendent and the higher-status board members tend to share the same social world. They often attend the same social gatherings and belong to the same civic-service clubs and other social organizations. This situation may result in the superintendent and the board members sharing the same point of view about the components of a good educational program and other social and economic policies.

The major objection to the elitist composition of American school boards is that they do not reflect the interests and opinions of all members of the community. Basic disagreements can occur between social groups in our society over educational policy. For instance, higher-status groups in a community may give strong support to a vocational program for lower-status children, whereas lower-status groups may disapprove of this type of program because they want a college-preparatory program for their children as a means of providing upward mobility. Which group is right in this case is not important in terms of this discussion. What is important is that fundamental differences between social groups can exist over educational policy. Because of the social composition of school boards and their linkage to the informal power structures of local communities, however, these differences are not reflected in debates among school board members.

School board members and community leaders often complain that the real power over local schools is in the hands of the school administration. Whether this is true or not is difficult to measure. But certainly the complaints about the power of the educational bureaucracy, particularly in large cities, warrants some discussion. Any meaningful attempts to change the political structure of American schools will have to consider the politics of the superintendent and central administration.

THE EDUCATIONAL BUREAUCRACY

Arguments supporting site-based management, charter schools, choice, and other forms of restructuring usually attack the power of the educational bureaucracy. The goals of all of these plans are to give individual schools more autonomy by breaking the hold of the bureaucratic structure. When proponents of these plans refer to the educational bureaucracy they mean at the local level the superintendent and his or her administrative staff. The responsibilities of this staff, which is generally located in the central offices of a school district, include the supervision of instruction, planning of curriculum, building maintenance, finance, teacher personnel matters, student personnel, and transportation.

This section of the chapter will examine the workings of this local educational bureaucracy, beginning with the superintendent of schools. To understand the political strategies of superintendents, one must first consider their major career objectives. Ernest House, in *The Politics of Educational Innovation*, describes two aspirations that are characteristic of superintendents. One superintendent aspires to remain within the community as long as possible and eventually plans to retire from the position. House calls this type of superintendent "place bound." The other superintendent views his or her current position as one step to another, better superintendent's position. House calls this type of superintendent "career bound" and characterizes his or her actions as primarily directed toward gaining recognition outside the local community, as a means of attracting other job offers.

These two types of superintendents have different types of relationships with the local power structure. Both depend on its support for initial appointment to the position. But after acquiring the job, the place bound superintendent is concerned about acquiring a loyal following among members of the community and establishing support from the local power structure, whereas the career bound superintendent is more interested in winning recognition at either the state or national level. The career bound superintendent tends to show less loyalty to the desires of the local power structure and spends less energy on building a following within the local community.

Whether place or career bound, superintendents develop strategies for trying to control their school boards. Zeigler and Jennings in their study, *Governing American Schools*, measured the methods superintendents use to control and influence school boards. They argue that there are specific ways in which this can be done. One way is through gatekeeping, or control of information received by the board. According to this argument, the superintendent is ideally situated to select the information that he or she wants the board to hear. In addition, superintendents can convince boards that most issues require technical expertise and should be decided on the basis of advice from the school staff.

Zeigler and Jennings measure the degree of gatekeeping in superintendent and board relationships in the United States by determining the degree of control exercised by superintendents over agenda setting at board meetings. Agenda setting is a very important political function at board of education meetings because it determines what will be discussed and in what order. In some situations a member of the board or a board committee may have responsibility for determining the agenda. In other cases it may be the superintendent, or the superintendent and a board member. If the superintendent determines the agenda, it means that he or she has a great deal of power as a gatekeeper to decide what issues will appear before the board.

Zeigler and Jennings found in their national survey that in 70 percent of the school districts in the United States the superintendent had the primary responsibility for setting the agenda, and in two-thirds of the districts superintendents were solely responsible for agenda setting. Zeigler and Jennings felt these findings indicated that superintendents did occupy powerful gatekeeping positions and had the potential power to strongly influence board members.

The other measurement made by Zeigler and Jennings was to ask board members to name their four most important sources of educational information of a technical or professional nature. The purpose was to determine how much control superintendents had over the information received by the board. The study found that in over half the districts, the proportion of information received from the superintendent was over 30 percent. Even though this indicated that a sizable amount of information passed through the hands of the superintendent to board member, it was not enough to support the argument for the gatekeeping function of superintendents with regard to educational information. Determination of the agenda was a more important function.

Control of information is also an important political strategy of the central office staff. In "The Politics of Education: A View from the Perspective of the Central Office Staff" Joseph McGivney and James Haught argue that one of the inherent goals of the administrative staff is to maintain control over the educational system. Techniques used by the staff to maintain its power include controlling communication among groups attempting to place pressure on the school system. In addition, the members of the central office staff play a key role as gatekeepers of information flow among a building principal and school staff, the superintendent, and the board of education. Members of the central office staff hold meetings with principals, teachers, and students. They also hold meeetings with the superintendent and school board committees, in which they convey information and concerns from the rest of the school system. This gatekeeping function can be very important in influencing educational policy.

McGivney and Haught find that through the control of information the central office staff has a major effect on the decision-making process of the board of education. Boards of education seldom reject proposals that come from the central office. Proposals from outside groups that are contrary to the desires of the central office staff are often intercepted by the staff before they reach the board. One technique the central office staff can use against outside groups is to question their information base and their sincerity.

House argues in *The Politics of Educational Innovation* that the gatekeeping functions of the central office staff are pivotal to any attempts to change or introduce new programs into a local school system. The staff controls the flow of information to teachers about the program and the flow of information from the system to outside sources. House found in one case that the central office staff tended to manipulate information. In a special-education program for gifted children, the central staff of a local district did not tell one-third of the teachers that they had been listed in a proposal to the state as teachers of the gifted. Teachers also received this information from the state office only when the central office staff had informally approved the information.

House describes the central office staff as a type of elite governing group that can be found within any organization. There is some debate about whether the superintendent or the central office staff is more influential. In terms of introducing change into the educational system, it was found that the values of the inner-circle elite were more important in predicting innovation than those of the director and staff. The attitudes of the central office staff tend to be more important than the attitudes of the superintendent or teachers influencing educational policy within a school system.

The central office staff cannot, of course, function independently of the superintendent. A new superintendent will attempt to organize a staff that will reflect his or her policies. But total staff change when a new superintendent begins usually is not possible, and there are usually many members of the central office staff who maintain their positions through a successive number of superintendents. These long-term staff members very often exercise a great deal of power within a school district.

The combined power of the central office staff and the superintendent has led writers (such as James Koerner in *Who Controls American Education?*) to argue that the real control of the school is in the hands of the professional educators who occupy those positions. Most decisions in a school district are turned over to the expertise of these professional groups. The role of the school board in most cases is to place its stamp of approval on decisions recommended by the superintendent and the central office staff. When this is the case, it can be argued that local public control of education has been replaced by local professional control of education.

CONCLUSION

After considering the concepts of representation, site-based management, charter schools, choice, the power and politics of local school boards, and the educational bureaucracy, you should again imagine that you are sitting in the

Educational Chair. Who should control the switch? Should it be controlled by a team of teachers, administrators, and community members engaged in site-based management? Should the options for throwing the switch be determined by petitioners for charter schools? Should it be controlled by parental choice? Should an elected school board control the switch? Should it be controlled by the educational bureaucracy? Should it be controlled by a combination of the above possibilities?

Whatever your choice, the important thing is for you to understand that the political structure of education determines the content of education which in turn directly affects what a student learns. Often, students go through school without questioning the reasons for being subjected to a particular curriculum or textbook. The content of learning in public schools is determined by a political process. But local politics of education is only one part of the process. As I will discuss in the next two chapters, state and federal governments also play a role in controlling the Educational Chair.

EXERCISES

1. Determine the occupations of members of a local board of education and compare them with the distribution of the local population in different occupational categories in the U.S. census. Is the school board representative of the population of the community?
2. Using the methods of Nunnery and Kimbrough described in this chapter, determine the power structure of your local community. For practical reasons, you may want to limit interviews to a few leading members of the community.
3. Interview local board members to determine how one can get elected to the board. Remember, it is important to find out about the local informal power structure and if the backing of certain groups is required for actual election.
4. Interview a local school superintendent about the amount of power this person feels he or she has in relationship to the central office staff, the school board, the state, and the federal government.
5. Interview a group of parents about their feelings regarding charter schools and school choice.
6. Working in small groups, you should try to reach a consensus on who should control the Educational Chair. In your discussions, you should consider the options of site-based management, charter schools, and choice.

SUGGESTED READINGS AND WORKS
CITED IN CHAPTER

Barbanel, Josh. "Board of Education Votes a School-Choice Program." *New York Times* (14 January 1993): B3. This article describes the New York Board of Education choice plan.

Borman, Kathryn, and Joel Spring. *School in Central Cities.* New York: Longman, 1984. Chapters 2 and 3 of this book provide an analysis of school board and administrative politics in central-city schools.

Bradley, Ann. "Crusaders in Detroit Fight to Keep Board Seats." *Education Week* (21 October 1992): 1, 10. This article discusses the development of chartered schools in Detroit and the political battles surrounding their development.

————. "Reforming Philadelphia High Schools from Within." *Education Week* (18 January 1992): 1, 17. Part of series on "New Arrangements: The Changing Definition of Public Schools in America." This article discusses the development of charter schools in Philadelphia.

Chubb, John E., and Terry Moe. *Politics, Markets & America's Schools.* Washington, D.C.: The Brookings Institution, 1990. An important study of the relationship between political control and student achievement. The book supports choice as a means of improving student achievement.

Cronin, Joseph N. *The Control of Urban Schools.* New York: Free Press, 1973. This is a history of the control of American schools and an exploration of the major issues surrounding the relationships between the public, school board members, and professional staff.

Davis, Lee. "The School Board's Struggle to Survive." *Educational Leadership* (November 1976): 95–96. This issue of *Educational Leadership* is devoted to the politics of education.

Education Week. This excellent weekly newspaper contains news about local, state, and federal politics of education.

Fiske, Edward B. "Finding a Way to Define the New Buzzword of American Education: How about Perestroika?" *New York Times* (14 February 1990): B6. As education reporter for the *Times,* Fiske briefly reviews the different aspects of the restructuring of American schools.

Gans, Herbert J. *Levittowners.* New York: Random House, 1969. This study of a community provides a good description of school board politics in a new suburban community.

Hansen, Lee H. "Political Reformation in Local Districts." *Educational Leadership* (November 1976): 90–94. An associate superintendent's view of shifts in power in a local school district.

Hawley, Willis D. *Nonpartisan Elections and the Case for Party Politics.* New York: John Wiley and Sons, 1973. This is a study of the effects of nonpartisan elections.

House, Ernest. *The Politics of Educational Innovation.* Berkeley, Calif.: McCutchan, 1974. The first four chapters of this book are excellent studies of the internal politics of local school systems.

Iannaccone, Lawrence, and Frank Lutz. *Politics, Power and Policy: The Governing of Local School Districts.* Columbus, Ohio: Charles E. Merrill, 1970. This study focuses on school board politics in a small community.

Kirby, David, et al. *Political Strategies in Northern School Desegregation.* Lexington, Mass.: Lexington Books, 1973. A major study of the politics of school desegregation in northern cities.

Koerner, James. *Who Controls American Education?* Boston: Beacon, 1968. Koerner argues that professional educators control American education.

Lewis, Neil. "Union Warns Fernandez on Proposals." *New York Times* (29 September 1989): B3. A report on the resistance of New York's principals to site-based management.

McCarty, Donald, and Charles Ramsey. *The School Managers: Power and Conflict in American Public Education.* Westport, Conn.: Greenwood, 1971. A study of the different types of community power structures and the resulting style of boards of education and school superintendents.

McGivney, Joseph, and James Haught. "The Politics of Education: A View from the Perspective of the Central Office Staff." *Educational Administration Quarterly* (Autumn 1972): 18–38. Another good study of the internal politics within a local school system.

Nunnery, Michael Y., and Ralph B. Kimbrough. *Politics, Power, Polls, and School Elections.* Berkeley, Calif.: McCutchan, 1971. A guide to studying local politics of education and community power structures.

Olsen, Lynn. "A Matter of Choice: Minn. Puts 'Charter Schools' Idea to Test." *Education Week* (25 November 1992): 1, 10. This is one of a series of articles called "New Arrangements: The Changing Definition of Public Schooling in America." This particular article focuses on the Minnesota law for charter schools.

_____. "Calif. Is Second State to Allow Charter Schools." *Education Week* (30 September 1992): 1, 23. This article discusses the California law providing for the establishment of charter schools.

_____. "Claims for Choice Exceed Evidence, Carnegie Reports." *Education Week* (28 October 1992): 1, 12. Summary of Carnegie Foundation for the Advancement of Teaching's report, "School Choice."

_____. "Open-Enrollment Survey Finds Modest Effects in Minn." *Education Week* (4 November 1992): 5. Report on the percentage of parents taking advantage of the Minnesota choice plan.

Snider, William. "Voucher System for 1,000 Pupils Adopted in Wis." *Education Week* (28 March 1990): 1, 14. A description of voucher plan for students from poor families adopted by the Wisconsin legislature.

"Vital Statistics." *The American School Board Journal,* 178, no. 1 (January 1991): 35. This is a report of survey on the typical characteristics of a school board member in the United States.

Wells, Amy. "Milwaukee Parents Get More Choice on Schools." *New York Times* (28 March 1990): B9. A report on the choice plan for students from poor families passed by the Wisconsin legislature.

Wilkerson, Isabel. "Chicago on Brink of New School System." *New York Times* (11 October 1989): 10. A description of the law passed by the Illinois state legislature establishing parent-controlled councils at each public school in Chicago.

_____. "Fate of Principals Splits Some Chicago Schools." *New York Times* (2 March 1990): A10. A description of the hostilities that erupted after newly elected school councils in Chicago exercised their power to fire school principals.

Zeigler, L. Harmon, and M. Kent Jennings. *Governing American Schools: Political Interaction in Local School Districts.* North Scituate, Mass.: Duxbury, 1974. A major national study of local boards of education.

CHAPTER 8

Power and Control
at the State Level

President Bill Clinton's choice for secretary of education, the former governor of South Carolina Richard Riley, exemplifies the importance of education in state politics. Similar to his predecessor as secretary of education, former governor of Tennesee, Lamar Alexander, Riley built his political career around state educational reform. As governor, Riley is credited with proposing and assuring the passage of a legislative package that resulted in increasing student achievement and raising teachers' salaries. His Education Improvement Act raised teachers' wages to the Southeast average and mandated testing for basic skills. Riley worked with Bill Clinton, who also focused on educational issues while governor of Arkansas, on educational issues in the National Governors' Association.

While Riley exemplifies the importance of education in gubernatorial politics, Paul Hubbert's announcement in 1990 that he was running for the governorship of Alabama reflects the importance of teachers' unions in state politics. As the executive secretary of the Alabama Education Association, Hubbert decided to take union concerns directly to the governor's mansion. As I discuss later in this chapter, in most states the major struggle to influence state educational legislation is between the teachers' unions and the business community. Reflecting this animosity, a survey of business leaders in the Alabama Alliance of Business and Industry found that 90 percent believed the teachers' union had a negative effect on the state's business climate and 96 percent said the union had too much political influence. Hubbert tried to overcome these differences by going directly to the Alabama business community. In the March 21, 1990, issue of *Education Week*, Mr. Barnard, a University of Alabama historian, describes the success of Hubbert's campaign: "Then business people, who have viewed him as the devil incarnate, come out scratching their heads and saying, 'Gee, I've heard bad things about this fellow but he doesn't seem so bad.' " In the 1980s according to Barnard, the business community mobilized forces to stop an " 'unholy triad' of educators, blacks, and trial lawyers."

Paul Hubbert's career in the teachers' union and state politics exemplifies the new style of state educational politics. Born to a family of poor farmers, Hubbert recalls, "my mother coming to the end of a cotton row, pushing her bonnet back and saying, 'Son, when you grow up I want you to get an education so you don't have to be a clodhopper like your Daddy and me.' " He claims that during his first years of teaching, an announcement by the county school board that teachers might not be paid caused him to be concerned about teachers gaining power.

In 1969, he took charge of the Alabama Education Association and transformed it into a powerful union. The transformation of the union paralleled what was happening in other states. This national trend is characterized by Alabama State Senator MacParsons in his description of Hubbert's work. MacParsons describes the union prior to Hubbert's ascendancy as a "ladies' tea-drinking society." In MacParsons's words, "Paul [Hubbert] took an organization that met once a year in Birmingham and did a lot of shopping in town and ended up with a plastic bag full of trinkets and a yardstick, and turned it into a political organization that has become a player in state government."

Hubbert's candidacy, current teachers' strikes, the work of the National Governors' Association, and lobbying by the business community all characterize the current condition of state educational politics. In elaborating on these themes, I will first describe the general organization of state education systems and then I will examine the role of business and teachers' unions in state politics. Following these sections, I will summarize the legislative trends over the last decade. The chapter will conclude with the fundamental issue of whether or not state governments should regulate public and private schools.

THE ORGANIZATION OF STATE SYSTEMS OF EDUCATION

The Constitution of the United States does not mention education; consequently, education is a power reserved to the states. As I will show in Chapter 9, the federal government does have other means of exercising control over state education systems. Most state constitutions give legal responsibility for local education to the state. These two conditions, in theory at least, give state governments greater authority over education than is exercised by any other government unit in the United States. A school district, in most cases, is legally an agent of the state. Local school boards have and can exercise only those powers that are granted explicity by the state legislature.

In the early nineteenth century, state governments exercised very little control over local education. In the 1830s Horace Mann worked in Massachusetts for increased state involvement in education through the establishment of teacher-training institutions and by promoting good schools in local communities. Throughout the century, state departments of education remained relatively small and confined their activities to collecting statistics related to education and promoting good schools and teacher training. In the late nineteenth and early twentieth centuries, states expanded their role in education with the passage of compulsory education laws and laws requiring specific curriculum content in the schools. Compulsory education laws required expanded staffs to ensure their enforcement. Early state curriculum requirements were often the result of state lobbying by "patriotic organizations" and groups concerned about the Americanization of immigrants. Over the years these curriculum requirements expanded in many states to cover a great deal of the course content offered in local school districts. Teacher-certification requirements also increased and became more complex. As a result of the enforcement requirements of these laws, state educational bureaucracies grew steadily in the twentieth century.

The increased involvement of the federal government in education in the 1960s further extended the importance of state departments of education. Federal money was provided for the expansion of state educational bureaucracies, as a means of strengthening their role in funneling federal money and programs to local school districts. This widening of state power over education carried with it seeds of controversy. For some, an expanded state-controlled education enterprise signaled the collapse of local control of education. For others, state control of education appeared to be lost as federal money increasingly determined the functions of state education bureaucracies.

This situation changed in the early 1980s with the election of President Ronald Reagan. President Reagan advocated the return of control and power to local governments through a block grant program, a program that helped to strengthen state departments of education in relationship to the federal government and local systems of education.

Today, most states exercise the following functions with regard to education. Most states set minimum standards for curriculum, pupil promotion and graduation, and for specific education programs such as kindergarten, vocational education, and high school. Some states have detailed courses of study for specific subjects such as social studies and math, and adopt textbooks that are distributed to local schools. Most states have detailed regulations regarding the physical features of school buildings and the size of school libraries. States define the length of the school day and year. State regulations are very detailed with respect to requirements for the certification of teachers.

States increasingly are playing a major role in financing local schools. In some states, tax limits are set for local districts and requirements are made for certain local budget breakdowns. States will assume greater shares of education expenses as state courts rule that existing systems of financial support provide unequal educational opportunities. Court cases dealing with this issue are discussed in more detail in Chapter 11, when we will examine the involvement of the courts in education.

The importance of school finance in the overall spending by state governments is reflected in the following figures. In 1991, education accounted for the largest percentage of state government expenditures. During that year, state governments spent 35.4 percent on education, 22.4 percent on public welfare, 8.5 percent on highways, 8.3 percent on health and hospitals, 4.2

percent on interest on general debt, 3.5 percent on correction, and 17.7 percent on other items. Since education is the largest expenditure for state governments, taxpayers' organizations and business groups interested in lower taxes keep a sharp eye on any proposals to increase state educational spending and constantly search for ways to cut spending on education.

The broad authority that states have over education is usually exercised through a governmental system that includes the governor's office, the state legislature, a state superintendent of education, a state department of education, and a state board of education. The actual arrangement and relationship of these groups varies from state to state. The selection of the state superintendent or chief state school officer also varies from state to state. In some states the superintendent is elected; in other states the person is appointed by the governor or state board of education.

The state department of education is the administrative staff of the chief state school officer or superintendent and the state board of education. The staff of the state department of education is mainly composed of professional educators, who do most of the administration and regulation of state education laws and programs. Some of the major activities of state departments of education include the actual operation of state schools for the handicapped, and involvement in the operation of vocational programs and teachers' colleges. The regulatory activities of state departments of education can extend into areas such as curriculum and teaching standards, school construction, school buses, civil defense and fire drills, and other items specified in the state code or constitution.

Most state legislatures have a specific legislative committee that is responsible for proposing legislation pertaining to education, conducting hearings on proposed legislation, and recommending to the legislature the passage or defeat of specific laws affecting education. Sometimes legislation concerning education is initiated by the governor's office and is reviewed and placed before public hearings by the education committee of the state legislature. Legislation is often proposed by the state department of education and by outside lobbying groups representing professional educators. In fact, the major role of these two groups in proposing and campaigning for specific legislation often leads to the charge that professional educators dominate state educational politics. However, as I will discuss in the next section, the business community also exercises a major influence over state educational politics.

BUSINESS AND TEACHERS' UNIONS
IN STATE POLITICS

Increasingly, the primary influences over state politicians in education matters are the teachers' unions and the business community. Sometimes the business community and the unions form alliances, and at other times they are at war.

The increasing influence of these two groups occurred as state education-al policy-making became concentrated at the state level and governors made education a central focus of political campaigns. As politicians, governors try to please both the teachers' organizations and the business community. To the business community, governors promise to improve the economic system through better schooling. To teachers, they promise improved salaries and a restructured profession. Sometimes governors are forced to choose one group over another. Most often the choice is the business community.

While there is a trend toward centralization and increased influence of teachers' organizations and business, there are still differences in patterns of influence between states. These differences were studied by Catherine Marshall, Douglas Mitchell, and Frederick Wirt. These researchers synthesized previous studies of influence in state politics and identified by order of influence the major political actors in Arizona, West Virginia, California, Wisconsin, Pennsylvania, and Illinois.

Within government, the researchers rank-ordered the following in regard to influence over state education policies:

1. The state legislature
2. The chief state school officer and senior members of the state department of education
3. The governor and executive staff
4. The legislative staff
5. The state board of education

Obviously, as the lawmaking body of state government, the legislature would have the most power. Within the legislature, certain legislators special-ize in educational issues and guide the votes of others. In general, chief state school officers function as long-term bureaucrats who work patiently to establish educational policies. As Marshall, Mitchell, and Wirt note, gover-nors increased their involvement in educational policy in the early 1980s. Members of legislative staffs gain their influence by being links between interest groups and members of the state legislature. At the bottom of the list are state boards of education.

With regard to the influence on educational policy-makers in government by groups outside of government, Marshall, Mitchell, and Wirt listed the following groups by order of importance:

1. Education associations
2. Noneducation groups (business leaders, taxpayers' groups)
3. Lay groups (PTAs, school advisory groups)
4. Educational research organizations
5. Producers of educational materials

In the six states studied by the researchers, education associations have the greatest influence on government officials. Teachers' associations are the most influential, with a coalition of educational associations running a close second. School board associations are slightly more influential than organizations representing school administrators. The combined figures for all six states give education groups more influence than noneducation groups except Arizona, where the "Phoenix 40," a group of prestigious business people that meets informally once a month, exercises strong influence over state education policy.

Other state lobbying groups from time to time exert considerable influence on particular features of state educational policy. Patriotic organizations such as the American Legion campaign for increased emphasis on patriotism in the schools. Farm groups work hard for greater support of agricultural education programs. Labor organizations are interested in ridding the schools of antiunion bias and making sure that vocational education is not used to undermine union apprenticeship programs. One could construct an almost endless list of people and organizations who would like certain subjects and ideas made mandatory in the schools by state legislative action.

One of the things contributing to increased educational lobbying is the expanded role of state governments in regulating local schools. During the 1980s and 1990s, as I discuss in the next section, state legislatures passed many laws involving course requirements, teacher training, testing of both students and teachers, graduation requirements, choice, charter schools, and school finance. Many of these measures increased state regulation of local schools. In addition, some form of state monitoring is required by choice and charter school laws. As a result, state governments are a focal point for lobbying groups wanting to influence educational policy.

STATE EDUCATION REFORM

The school reform efforts of the 1980s and 1990s are creating a revolution in state responsibilities in education. The rhetoric of state school reform focuses on economic development. Many governors and state legislators believe that school reform will contribute to the economic development of their states. According to the Center for Policy Research in Education's report, "State Education Reform in the 1980s," "More state activity aimed at improving public education took place in the 1980s than ever before. State legislators introduced an unsurpassed number of education-related bills, increased state aid, and examined the findings of hundreds of state-level task forces and commissions."

The record of this activity provides a guide to current state involvement in local schools. The center's report finds the greatest amount of state activity in mandating academic courses for local schools, and making changes in teacher certification and compensation. This activity is not surprising considering the power of business and teachers' unions in state politics. The emphasis on increasing academic requirements is linked to concerns with improving state economies and the ability of the United States to compete in world trade. Increased academic requirements are supposed to produce better-educated workers. The center found that forty-five states increased requirements for graduation or specified them for the first time. In addition, many states instituted statewide testing of students. Probably the most extreme example of attempts to control local schools is the effort by California to coordinate curriculum requirements, student testing, and textbook selection.

The power of teachers' unions in state politics is reflected in the increase in teachers' salaries of 22 percent in real terms between 1980 and 1988. Also, because of complaints that the quality of teachers was reducing the quality of schools and causing the country to lag behind Japan and West Germany, certification standards were increased. Twenty-seven states adopted minimum grade point averages for beginning teachers.

The report of the center finds that state legislatures tended to reject reforms that were expensive, that redistributed money from the rich to the poor, and that were complex. This is why increasing academic requirements was the most popular reform. Except for the hiring of specialized teachers to cover increased enrollments in required courses, there were no direct costs for increasing academic requirements.

Educational reform without increasing expenditures for education is a hallmark of school reform in the 1980s and 1990s. It reflects the tension between the desire of the business community to improve education and, at the same time, maintain low taxes by keeping down educational expenditures. Certainly, increasing academic standards meets these requirements.

A search for inexpensive methods of control continues to be the pattern of state involvement in schools. This primarily means increasing requirements and introducing more tests without raising taxes. The center's report gives as an example of this pattern Florida's recent tightening of teacher certification requirements and Pennsylvania's development of a statewide test for high school students.

During the 1990s, state school reform has shifted to issues of restructuring. Restructuring refers to finding new methods of school management and control. As I discussed in Chapter 7, Chicago's experiment in parents' councils is a result of legislative action by the Illinois government, and choice and charter schools are being promoted by state governments. It is believed that these efforts at restructuring will improve student achievement by making local schools more responsive to parental wishes.

On the surface, state testing and tighter control of the curriculum and graduation requirements would seem to contradict efforts to make schools more responsive to parents. But a closer look at these state laws suggests that they are not contradictory. State mandated academic requirements and student testing define what subjects students will study and the content of those subjects. In other words, these reforms are designed to control the knowledge taught to the student. On the other hand, restructuring reforms are designed to assure that schools efficiently teach the knowledge mandated by the state. Parents' councils, site-based management, choice, and charter schools are promoted as a means of improving student achievement where achievement is measured by a state mandated test.

Another way of understanding the apparently contradictory movement to increase state control of what students learn and to increase parent and teacher management of schools is the "Educational Chair" described in Chapter 7. Under current trends in state education reform, state governments will control the knowledge and behaviors given to the student sitting in the chair. Parents and teachers are given increased power to manage the operation of the chair so that they can assure that it effectively passes on the knowledge and behaviors specified by the state government.

THE POLITICS OF STATE EDUCATION

With increased centralization of the control of local schools at the state level, lobbying groups have expanded statewide activities. During the early 1990s, teachers' unions developed new techniques to influence state legislatures, particularly in the areas of school finance. These new techniques involved extensive public relations campaigns. In Florida, both teachers' unions in 1992 joined forces to conduct a massive television ad campaign to restructure the state's tax system to provide more money for education. The focus of the ads was on the disparity between the state taxes paid by average citizens and those paid by business. The ads showed a family paying out money on taxes, while business people held on to their money. One ad proclaimed, "That's not fair: Everyone should help fund Florida's future." Another ad presented pictures of state senators and how to reach them by telephone.

The New York State United Teachers used a similar method in 1992, spending $1 million on a media blitz involving television, newspaper, and billboard advertisements. The ads warned citizens that if proposed state cuts in educational funding occurred, their children's futures would be seriously jeopardized. The ads included a toll free telephone number that provided citizens with information on how to contact state legislators. In an interview in the October 7, 1992, *Education Week*, Linda Rosenblatt, the chief spokesperson for the United Teachers, said, "We were able to get the funding [because] of the people who live in the districts where the lawmakers live who vote on these issues. . . . They sent a message, loud and clear."

Some public relations methods involved demonstrations. In Mississippi and Iowa, teachers' unions in 1992 organized marches on the state capitals with demands for more money for schools. This technique proved effective in Iowa where an extra $85 million was appropriated by the legislature. The Pennsylvania State Education Association takes their demands directly to members of the state legislature during six lobbying days. During these six days, the union brings 200 teachers from around the state to the capital. During the first day, union leaders instruct the teachers on the unions' legislative agenda. After this training session, teachers head to their respective legislators' offices to plead the union case.

The California Teachers Union used a negative campaign to stop a school voucher proposal from getting on the 1992 fall ballot. The reader is reminded that teachers' unions object to vouchers because they provide support for the choice of a private school. Unions want public funding to go to public schools. To stop the initiative from getting on the ballot, union members were stationed in shopping malls and other public spaces where voucher advocates were trying to collect signatures. To hinder these efforts, union members shouted arguments against the voucher plan.

In New Mexico, teachers' unions in 1992 focused their efforts on meeting with legislative members from their home districts. Similar to efforts in Florida, the two teachers' unions in New Mexico are combining forces to increase state spending on schools. In addition, the two unions in New Mexico are putting extra effort into attempts to rally teachers around the unions' legislative proposals.

An example of other groups' lobbying methods can be found in an excellent study by Tim Mazzoni and Betty Malen on tuition tax credit legislation in Minnesota between 1971 and 1981. They analyzed the lobbying techniques of the Minnesota Catholic Conference (MCC), representing six Catholic dioceses, and the Citizens for Educational Freedom (CEF), an organization composed of supporters of private schools.

These two organizations formed an alliance in the late 1960s to campaign for state transportation aid for private schools. Following this campaign, the alliance sought state tax concessions for non-public-school pupils. As a single-issue lobbying group, the alliance constantly hounded state legislators regarding their attitudes toward financial aid to private schools. Their persistent efforts forced many legislators to bow to the pressure in order to avoid harrassment or being labeled as opponents. According to Mazzoni and Malen, legislators placed the issue in the same category as gun control or abortion, where nonsupport of that single issue, no matter what other issues a politician stood for, would be considered sufficient reason by the voter not to support the politician.

In other words, a single-issue interest group will force a politician to support its position by making all other issues secondary. One unidentified member of the Minnesota legislature stated, "Their people [the MCC-CEF alliance] spoke out: 'We'll beat you if you vote against our bill.' And it didn't matter if you had done 5,000 things right. . . . That gave me and a lot of other people real concern . . . and it was, I think, a statewide effort."

The alliance campaigned with phone calls, orchestrated mailings, and persistent contact with state legislators. During the 1971 legislative debate on tuition tax credits, the alliance sent busloads of supporters to the state capital to make direct contact with their representatives. Legislators reported that constituents would look them in the eye and say, "You aren't going to let us down now are you?" Mazzoni and Malen quote legislators who pleaded for passage of the bill just to get alliance supporters off their backs. In addition, the alliance brought private-school supporters to legislative hearings to remind lawmakers of their promises. There were complaints that during the hearings on non-public-school aid, parents and kids flooded the hallways and legislative chambers.

The unanimous opinion of Minnesota legislators is that the successful passage of tax concessions for private schools in 1971, 1978, and 1981 was primarily due to the power of the MCC-CEF alliance. The key tactics of the alliance were identified as: "(1) keep the issue continuously on the legislative agenda; (2) energize sympathetic lawmakers to carry its bills, attract supporters to these bills, and maneuver them through the legislative process; and, most important, (3) mobilize grassroots constituency pressure to sway votes in the Legislature." And, from the standpoint of Mazzoni and Malen, the constant face-to-face contact between lobbyists and lawmakers was the most effective lobbying technique.

Another contributing factor to the success of the alliance was the lack of a well-organized opposition. Traditionally, the two teachers' unions have led strong national opposition to any form of tax concession to private schools. But, according to Mazzoni and Malen, the Minnesota Education Association and the Minnesota Federation of Teachers did not concentrate any effort on the issue raised by the MCC-CEF alliance. Unlike the alliance, the two unions did not try to impose a political price on legislators who supported tax concession legislation. With no strong opposition from such a major influence in state educational politics, the alliance was able to achieve an easy victory.

These examples of lobbying methods provide insight into the political methods that can be used to influence state legislatures. Many business groups, as I discussed in Chapter 4, use threats of relocating their companies to other states as a means of reducing their state taxes. In addition, they provide sponsorship for educational reform groups that advocate school reforms designed to educate better workers for their companies. And, as I discussed earlier in this chapter, many governors link school reform with economic reform in order to persuade industries not to relocate to another state or country, and to attract new industries to the state. But, as the previously discussed media campaign by Florida teachers' unions suggests, there is a basic conflict between business's desire to reduce taxes and teachers' unions' desires to increase state spending on schools.

THE NATIONALIZATION OF STATE POLICIES

In recent years, several nongovernment organizations have been contributing to the nationalization of state educational policies. In this context, *nationalization* means creating uniformity in policies between states. Three of these organizations, the National Governors' Association, the Council of Chief State School Officers, and the Education Commission of the States, serve as forums for the discussion of educational policies and for the coordination of state educational efforts.

In a larger sense, the efforts of these organizations represent a centralization of state educational policy beyond just centralization within a state. In addition, these organizations tend to coordinate their efforts. In the 1980s and 1990s such coordination is directly related to the increased involvement of governors in educational issues and the resulting strengthening of ties between governors through the Education Commission of the States.

A good example of this interrelationship of activities is the report of the Task Force on Education for Economic Growth of the Education Commission of the States. The Education Commission of the States was founded in 1966 as a nonprofit, nationwide interstate compact to help state governments develop education policies. The organization strongly depends on outside funding from foundations and private corporations to support its coordinating activities. For instance, the Task Force on Education for Economic Growth received support from fifteen leading corporations and foundations, including the Aetna Life & Casualty Insurance Foundation, AT&T, Control Data, Dow Chemical, Xerox, Time Inc., Texas Instruments, RCA, the Ford Motor Company Fund, and IBM.

The membership of the task force, which was almost evenly divided between state politicians and business leaders, exemplifies the coming together of state politicians and the business community in the formulation of educational policy. The chair of the task force was Governor James Hunt of North Carolina, and the cochairs were Frank Cary, chairman of the executive committee of IBM, and Governor Pierre S. DuPont of Delaware. In addition, there were eleven other governors and three members of state legislatures. Of the total of thirteen governors, two made the impact of educational reform on economic development a central focus of their political campaigns. These were the chair, Lamar Alexander of Tennessee, and the cochair, Thomas Kean of New Jersey. The business community was represented by chief executive officers from fourteen of the most powerful corporations in the United States, including RCA, Texas Instruments, Ford Motor, Xerox, Dow Chemical, Control Data, and AT&T.

Interestingly, a comparison of financial supporters of the task force with its membership reveals that the corporations represented on the task force were also its major financial supporters. This created the interesting situation of corporations funding a task force that brought together state leaders and the business community for the purpose of formulating state educational policy.

In addition to the Education Commission of the States, the National Governors' Association has tried to coordinate educational policies among the states. Until the 1980s, the organization paid little attention to broad educational issues. But in 1985, the National Governors' Association established seven task forces to plan state educational improvement to the year 1991. The task force topics included teaching, leadership and management, parent involvement and choice, school readiness, technology, facilities, and college quality.

A logical interest of governors is to enhance their prestige and power by concentrating control of education at the state level. This interest was reflected in a controversial proposal to allow states to declare school districts academically bankrupt. Taken as a last resort, the declaration would allow states to oust local officials and assume state control of a local school district. The major supporter of the idea, Governor Thomas Kean of New Jersey, stated, "As Governor of New Jersey, I couldn't sleep at night if I thought our schools were continuing to turn out unequalified graduates year after year after year, and I wasn't doing anything about it."

The National Governors' Association played a leading role in developing the educational goals for the Bush administration. Bush's reliance on the National Governors' Association meant that the nationalization of state policies would be linked to federal goals. At meetings of the National Governors' Association, then governor of Arkansas, Bill Clinton, worked closely with his future secretary of education, Governor Richard Riley of South Carolina, on educational policy issues.

The Council of Chief State School Officers has shared the same economic concerns as the governors. Many members of the organization, leading state educational politicians, were influenced by the same pressure groups as the governors. For instance, in 1985, the organization studied the relationship between education and economic development. It decided to focus on the decreasing supply of high school graduates available for entry-level employment, the employment needs of small business, the impact of technology, and how education officials could attract new industry to their states.

The combination of activities by the National Governors' Association, the Council of Chief State School Officers, and the Education Commission of the States increases the rate of centralization of state educational policies while increasing the importance of the role of the governor in educational policies. Combined with the increasing involvement of the federal government in education, these nationalizing trends continue to remove control of educational policy from the direct power of the average citizen.

SHOULD STATES HAVE COMPULSORY-EDUCATION LAWS?

The major authority states have for regulating public and private schools is compulsory-education laws. In most states parents can be arrested if they do not send their children to school. The state usually defines a "school" as *an educational institution that conforms to state standards and regulation, including curriculum and teacher-certification requirements.* This means that if an educational institution is not accredited by the state as complying with all state school requirements, its pupils are technically truant and their parents are liable for criminal prosecution. Without compulsory-school laws, parents would be free to send their children to educational institutions that do not conform to state regulations.

Compulsory-school-attendance laws vary from state to state in their actual form and interpretation by state courts. Robert P. Baker, a lawyer, reviewed judicial interpretations of compulsory school laws in an article titled "States Law and Judicial Interpretations" in *The Twelve Year Sentence*, edited by William F. Rickenbacker. Baker divides compulsory-schooling laws into what he calls the "other-guy type" and the "cookie-cutter type." The argument given for the other-guy type of law is that although most people would educate their children without compulsory-schooling laws, there is somebody somewhere who would not educate his or her children. Compulsory-school laws in this case are designed to protect children from parents who are not willing to educate them. Where adopted, the other-guy type of interpretation results in a compulsory-schooling law requiring no more than what most parents would do anyway.

The cookie-cutter type of law is based on the idea that all children should have the same experiences within the same kind of institution. The most extreme example of a cookie-cutter type of law was a 1920 Oregon statute that required all children to attend public schools. One purpose of the law was to close Catholic schools. The U.S. Supreme Court ruled in 1925 that the law was not constitutional. The Court stated: "The fundamental theory of liberty upon which all governments in this Union repose excludes any general power of the state to standardize its children by forcing them to accept instruction from public teachers only." But the ruling also upheld the right of the state to regulate private schools, which continued its right to enforce some form of standardization.

The differences between the other-guy and the cookie-cutter laws are best exemplified in judicial interpretations. For instance, in New Jersey in 1937 a Mr. and Mrs. Bongart were accused of being disorderly persons because they themselves were educating their children in their home. The New Jersey compulsory-schooling law required attendance at school or equivalent instruction. Education in the home was not considered equivalent instruction by the trial judge because, in his words, "I cannot conceive how a child can receive instruction and experiences in group activity and in social outlook in any manner or form comparable to that provided in the public school." This is what Baker would call a "cookie-cutter" interpretation of the law. In a similar case, a young girl in Washington State was considered a delinquent and was made a ward of the court for not attending school. The trial court found that the instruction being given to the girl in her home was at least the academic equivalent of that available in the public schools. Despite this finding, the Washington Supreme Court ruled against the child and her parents, with the argument that no school existed unless instruction was being given by a teacher certified by the state of Washington.

The other-guy type of judicial interpretation can result in a more flexible application of compulsory-schooling law. The most famous case was in Illinois in the 1950s in *People* v. *Levisen*, in which the parents, who were Seventh-Day Adventists, believed that educating their daughter in a public school would create an un-Christian character. The parents argued, "For the first eight or ten years of a child's life, the field or garden is the best schoolroom, the mother the best teacher, and nature the best lesson book." Education in the parents' home was considered adequate: The father was a college graduate and the mother had received training in pedagogy and educational psychology. Unlike the New Jersey and Washington courts, the Illinois courts formulated the other-guy philosophy in their ruling that "the law is not made to punish parents who provide their children with instruction equal or superior to that obtainable in the public schools. It is made for the parent who fails or refuses to properly educate his child."

The interpretation and application of state compulsory-schooling laws and education regulations will vary from state to state between the cookie-cutter and other-guy interpretations. In recent years all states have been limited in their application of the law as interpreted by the U.S. Supreme Court in the 1972 Amish case, *State of Wisconsin, Petitioner* v. *Jonas Yoder et al.* In this case, Amish parents in Wisconsin were arrested in 1968 for refusing to comply with the state's compulsory-education law requiring the parents to enroll their children in high school. The Amish in Ohio, Pennsylvania, Iowa, and Wisconsin fought compulsory-schooling laws for years because they believed that high schools taught values that undermined their religious and communal lifestyle. The Amish eventually won their case against state-imposed compulsory education. The Court ruled that religious freedom was more important than state compulsory-schooling laws and that state law could not abridge the practice of religion (see Chapter 11 for a detailed analysis of their suit). This meant that if parents could prove in court that attending public school would interfere with the practice of their religion, they could not be forced to conform to state compulsory-schooling laws. Thus the Supreme Court recognized that public schools were not in all cases neutral in terms of religion. The social life, curriculum, and educational goals of the public schools could be in conflict with some religious customs and practices.

One of the most thorough criticisms of state regulation of education is made by one of the participants in the Amish case. Professor Donald Erickson provided expert educational testimony defending the right of the Amish to maintain their own educational practices. Erickson summarized some of his views in *Super-Parent: An Analysis of State Educational Controls*, written for the Illinois Advisory Committee on Nonpublic Schools.

In his critique Erickson argues that two major reasons are given for state programmatic control of education. One reason is to ensure that all children have a reasonable chance to pursue happiness as free individuals. Education might be able to provide the individual with some of the intellectual tools required for autonomous behavior. The second major reason given for state control of the schools is the protection of society from unemployment, indigence, crime, juvenile delinquency, mental illness, and political strife. This reason encompasses the social purposes of education discussed in the first chapter of this book.

In response to the first reason, that state-controlled education ensures autonomous individuals, Erickson points out that state-prescribed education is in direct conflict with the autonomy of all parents and does not provide the child with a model of a society of freely acting individuals. Erickson states, "In complex societies all over the world, however, state-controlled education arouses parental resistance. The reason is that child-rearing practices sponsored or required by the state in pluralistic societies are at odds with many parental views of the good life and how to prepare for it."

Erickson argues that what is essential for the development of the autonomous individual in modern society is to learn reading, writing, arithmetic, and the fundamental workings of society's political, legal, and economic institutions. But even if we agree that knowledge of these subjects is essential for autonomous action, it does not, according to Erickson, justify the maintenance of the current system of compulsory school attendance and regulations. Parents and children could be given complete freedom to decide how the specified competencies were to be learned, and the child could be required to demonstrate through a national system of tests that progress is being made. This system would require compulsory education, but not compulsory school attendance.

The distinction between compulsory education and compulsory school attendance is very important for Erickson's argument. Compulsory education without compulsory school attendance would allow for the protection of those children suffering from parental neglect, without burdening all children with attendance at a state-regulated school. If during the course of examinations the state found that a child was not learning the basics, it could prescribe some form of remedial action like required attendance at a state school.

With regard to education beyond elementary school, Erickson argues, there is no agreement among scholars about what knowledge is of most worth and what is essential for autonomous growth. This being the case, he feels that parents and children can make their own determination of what they should know and how they should learn it. Even if state officials can identify indispensable understandings and skills beyond the elementary ones described above, this does not require programmatic state regulation of schools. State intervention could be limited to those cases in which tests show that children are not making satisfactory progress toward the acquisition of required competencies.

Erickson rejects the second major reasaon given for state regulation of schools, which is protection of society from crime, unemployment, political strife, and other social problems. First, Erickson argues that no one knows what attitudes, understandings, and skills are truly necessary for the survival of a society. Second, no one knows how much consensus about social and political beliefs is required before that same consensus actually becomes harmful to a society by limiting the freedom to find new ideas and adapt to new situations. The reader should remember from the first chapter that the argument for the achievement of the social and political purposes of schooling centers on the development of a consensus of political and social beliefs. Erickson rejects state involvement in this process with the argument that "state officials are probably the last group we should trust to decide how much commonality is essential to the general weal. It is in the interest of these officials to discourage the dissension and diversity that may jeopardize their positions, subject them to challenge, and make public institutions more difficult to govern smoothly."

In addition, it has never been proved that a relationship exists between the amount and quality of education available in a society and a decrease in crime, unemployment, and other social, economic, and political problems. In the twentieth century the amount of education received by each person in society has steadily increased. At the same time crime has either remained the same or increased; unemployment has fluctuated with changes in the economy and labor market; indigence continues; and mental illness seems un-affected by the quantity of education. The nineteenth-century dream of schooling as a panacea for social problems does not seem to have been justified by the events of the twentieth century.

While these facts might throw doubt on the reasons for compulsory-education laws, there appears to be little chance of their demise. For instance, it would not be in the interest of teachers' unions to abandon compulsory-education laws because it would threaten student enrollments and teachers' jobs in public schools. In the past, teachers' unions strongly resisted vouchers and tuition tax credits for similar reasons.

Certainly, the combined interests of teachers' unions and the business community will continue to focus state efforts on issues of teacher compensation and the education of good workers. On the other hand, the replacement of the Republican administration in the federal government by a Democratic administration might also signal a change in state involvement in education. I will discuss the power of the federal government over educational policies in the next chapter.

CONCLUSION

Increased involvement of state governments in school finance, curriculum, testing, and teacher certification has made state legislatures a battleground for educational interest groups. The current trend is for more state government control over the content of instruction in schools, teacher training, and school finance. While state governments increase their control over the knowledge disseminated by schools, they are increasing parental and teacher involvement in school management through site-based management plans, charter schools, and choice. As I suggested earlier in the chapter, these trends give governments increasing power over the knowledge placed in the head of the person sitting in the Educational Chair, while having teachers and parents ensure that the Educational Chair is able to carry out its mission. In this situation, the real power over the Educational Chair's switch is in the hands of the state government.

EXERCISES

1. Interview a local representative to the state legislature about the political process as it relates to educational legislation. Inquire about the important lobbying organizations and the role of the state department of education.
2. In a discussion group or in an essay discuss whether there should be complete professional control of education.
3. In a discussion group or in an essay discuss what areas of education you think the state should regulate.

4. Contact your state department of education and find out the extent of regulation of schools in your state.

5. In a discussion group or in an essay discuss whether there should be compulsory-education laws.

SUGGESTED READINGS AND WORKS CITED IN CHAPTER

Carnegie Foundation Task Force on Education for Economic Growth. *Education for Excellence*. Denver: Education Commission of the States, 1983. This report provides an example of the work of the Education Commission of the States.

Diegmuller, Karen. "Teacher Unions Try New Strategies to Lobby for Share of State Funding." *Education Week* (7 October 1992): 1, 24. This article reviews the lobbying techniques used with state governments by teachers' unions.

Education Week. Published by Editorial Projects in Education. This excellent weekly newspaper is a good source of information on state educational politics.

Erickson, Donald. *Super-Parent: An Analysis of State Educational Controls*. Written for the Illinois Advisory Committee on Nonpublic Schools, n.d. An important critique of the concept and practice of state regulation of schools.

Fiske, Edward. "In Kentucky, Teachers, Not Legislators, Will Be Writing the Lesson Plans." *New York Times* (4 April 1990): B6. Report on the changes in Kentucky's educational system.

Fuhrman, Susan. "State-Level Politics and School Financing." In Nelda Cambron-McCabe and Allan Odden, eds., *The Changing Politics of School Finance*. Cambridge, Mass.: Ballinger, 1982. An analysis of the school finance reform movement on the structure of state politics of education.

Iannaccone, Lawrence. *Politics of Education*. New York: Center for Applied Research in Education, 1967. This book classifies the major types of state lobbying groups.

Keim, Albert. *Compulsory Education and the Amish*. Boston: Beacon Press, 1975. This book provides background and discussions of *State of Wisconsin, Petitioner* v. *Jonas Yoder et al.*, the important U.S. Supreme Court decision regarding compulsory education.

Marshall, Catherine, Douglas Mitchell, and Frederick Wirt. "The Context of State Level Policy Formation." Paper given at the American Educational Research Association Meeting in San Francisco, California, April 16–20, 1986. A study of the differing degrees of influence of government officials and lobbying groups over state education policy.

Masters, Nicholas, et al. *State Politics and the Public Schools: An Exploratory Analysis*. New York: Alfred A. Knopf, 1964. An early and important work about state educational politics.

Mazzoni, Tim and Betty Malen. "Mobilizing Constituency Pressure to Influence State Education Policy Making." *Educational Administration Quarterly* 21, no. 2 (Spring 1985): 91–116. This article studies the efforts of lobbying groups to enact the Minnesota law allowing for tax deductions of educational expenditures.

Rickenbacker, William F., ed. *The Twelve Year Sentence*. Chicago: Open Court, 1974. Essays in this book discuss legal, historical, and philosophical arguments against compulsory education.

Sroufe, Gerald. "Recruitment Processes and Composition of State Boards of Educa-
    tion." Paper presented at the American Educational Research Association meet-
    ing in 1969. This paper provides general information about the backgrounds of
    members of state boards of education.
"State Education Reform in the 1980s." *CPRE Policy Briefs*. New Brunswick, N.J.:
    Center for Policy Research in Education, 1990.
"State Education Spending, 1991." *Education Week* (28 October 1992): 3. This article
    provides percentages of state government expenditures spent on different public
    services.
Task Force on Education for Economic Growth. *Action for Excellence*. Denver: Educa-
    tion Commission of the States, 1983. This set of recommendations for educational
    reform was written by a task force composed of governors and leading heads of
    corporations. It has had a major influence on recent state activities in education.
Thompson, John Thomas. *Policymaking in American Public Education*. Englewood Cliffs,
    N.J.: Prentice-Hall, 1976. Chapters 6, 7, and 8 provide summaries of state educa-
    tional politics.
Viadero, Debra. "Head of Alabama Teachers' Union Tests Power in Governor's Race."
    Education Week (21 March 1990): 1, 14.
Wirt, Frederick, and Michael Kirst. *Political and Social Foundations of Education*. Berk-
    eley, Calif.: McCutchan, 1975. Chapter 7 provides a good introduction to state
    educational politics.

CHAPTER 9

Power and Control
at the National Level

Despite control being concentrated in state governments, public schools across the nation are very similar. Even by the late nineteenth century, schools in Maine were similar to those in California. There are a number of factors that have nationalized American public schools. Prior to the 1940s, the National Education Association (NEA) played a major role in nationalizing curricula, school and classroom organization, and methods of instruction. While the NEA was not a government organization, its meetings attracted school leaders from around the country who shared ideas and developed standards for public schools. After the 1940s, the federal government continued the nationalization of public schools.

In addition, uniformity among state school systems is fostered by the cooperation among states in organizations such as the National Governors' Association. As I discussed in Chapter 1, this group, working in cooperation with the federal government, created national educational goals for the year 2000. In addition, private philanthropic foundations have nationalized educational policy and practices through the support of research and policy commissions. For instance, as I said in Chapter 2, it is the Carnegie Corporation that is responsible for the creation of the National Board for Professional Teaching Standards. Agencies that accredit public schools are another factor in nationalizing education. And, of course, as I will discuss in Chapter 10, textbooks disseminate a common body of knowledge through the nation's public schools.

None of these nationalizing forces exist without some element of political controversy. Certainly, the federal government's involvement in education made education a part of national politics. I will examine the nationalizing forces in American education and the resulting political controversies by first discussing the methods of federal control over the schools and the national politics of education. Following these two sections, I will discuss private foundations and accrediting agencies.

METHODS OF FEDERAL CONTROL

The federal government primarily influences state and local educational policy through indirect means. These indirect means are *persuasion, categorical aid, civil rights legislation,* and *research funding. Persuasion* refers to using the office of Secretary of Education, borrowing Secretary of Education William Bennett's term in the 1980s, as a "Bully Pulpit" to convince states and local schools to follow particular policies. The most important of these indirect means of control is the offering of financial aid if a school system adopts certain programs, materials, or curricula. Money granted for specific programs is called *categorical aid.* Whether or not federal support should be in the form of categorical aid has been a major concern of the Republican party.

Another major means of federal control is the threat to withhold federal funds if a local school district is found in violation of the *civil rights* guidelines of the federal government. The major differences between the two political parties over this form of control have focused on the degree of implementation and interpretation of the civil rights statutes. Republicans have tended to seek a narrower enforcement of the statutes, while the Democrats have pursued strong enforcement.

The third major method of control is the *funding of research* and the *development of educational materials.* The funding of research is a means of control because it shapes future knowledge and influences decision making. It is important to understand that the federal government does not support all research, but determines types of research to be supported on the basis of policy objectives. And it is precisely the issue of what types of research should be supported that sometimes divides Democrats and Republicans.

The use of categorical aid to control the actions of local schools began in the 1950s, when educators sought federal aid to relieve two problems caused by the post-World War II baby boom—a severe teacher shortage and a need for more school buildings. At this time, educational groups such as the National Education Association wanted the federal government to provide general aid, to be controlled in local school districts. But there existed a general sentiment against federal involvement in education. It took an international problem to finally push the federal government to action. This occurred when the Soviet Union launched the first space flight and threatened the United States' position as the world's technological leader.

The response to this crisis came in the form of the National Defense Education Act (NDEA), which was proposed and passed under the leadership of Republican President Dwight Eisenhower. The NDEA was not a general-aid package for the schools, but one that contained categorical aid for the specific purpose of improving mathematics, science, and foreign language instruction.

The National Defense Education Act linked federal support for schools with national policy objectives. This dramatically shifted part of the control of educational policy from the local to the federal level. The next major federal educational legislation, the 1965 Elementary and Secondary Education Act

(ESEA), also was tied to national policy objectives and caused dramatic changes in local school systems. The ESEA, like the NDEA, was not designed to provide general aid to solve financial problems of local schools; the assistance was in the form of categorical aid given to schools as part of a broad social policy to end poverty in the United States. Like the National Defense Education Act, the Elementary and Secondary Education Act was part of a social policy in which schools were to be used as instruments to solve major social problems.

The 1965 ESEA, more than any other legislation, made categorical funding a method for shaping local educational actions according to a particular political and social philosophy. This political and social philosophy included ideas about educational and cultural deprivation that were to influence educators around the country. The legislation influenced local schools not only through direct funding of specific programs, but also by spreading a particular philosophy about poverty and the role education could play in eliminating it. The premise of this philosophy was that poverty continued in the United States as the result of a set of causal factors that were mutually interdependent. A poor education restricts employment opportunities, which causes a low standard of living and, consequently, poor medical care, diet, housing, and education for the next generation. This model of poverty suggested that one could begin at any point in the causal relationships and move around the "circle of poverty." Improving medical care for the poor would mean more days of employment and thus more money for better housing, diet, and education. Theoretically, the same chain reaction would occur if you improved any of the interrelated causal factors.

The Elementary and Secondary Education Act was the main component of the attack on poverty through improved education for the children of the poor. The most important section of the legislation was Title I, which received approximately 76 percent of the money initially appropriated for the legislation. The purpose of Title I was to provide improved educational programs for children designated as educationally deprived. Title I specifically stated that "the Congress hereby declares it to be the policy of the United States to provide financial assistance . . . to expand and improve . . . educational programs by various means . . . which contribute particularly to meeting the special educational needs of educationally deprived children."

At the time of its passage, the Elementary and Secondary Education Act was the most important piece of educational legislation ever passed by Congress. It strengthened Title VI of the 1964 Civil Rights Act by making available large sums of money to local schools that complied with desegregation orders. Noncompliance with desegregation orders meant a loss of funds from the Elementary and Secondary Education Act. Desegregation of schools in the South had been progressing at a very slow rate. With the passage of this new legislation, desegregation occurred at a more rapid rate.

Because of the difficult financial situation of most public schools in the United States, there was a rush to get funds, particularly under Title I. This resulted in local schools expanding their administrative staffs to be able to apply for funds and fill out what in later years would seem like endless government forms. While the legislation claimed no federal control over local education, in reality local school administrators and boards gave up part of their local autonomy as they were forced to comply with federal standards in order to receive the funds.

The pattern that emerged from the federal legislation of the 1960s and 1970s was one in which the federal government provided money in areas apparently neglected by local and state educational systems. The role of the federal government was not to support all schooling but only those parts of schooling that appeared not to be receiving support by the local governments. By the 1970s the American public school system was functioning under three levels of financing and control. State governments were providing regulations and requirements to local districts, which in turn were administering these regulations and requirements in terms of local needs. The federal government provided the money and planning for innovative programs such as ESEA programs under Title I and, later, ESEA amendments such as the bilingual education and ethnic heritage legislation.

The major challenge to the pattern of control represented by categorical grants came with the election of President Ronald Reagan in 1980. President Reagan wanted to reduce federal control over local school systems by giving greater administrative control of federal programs to state and local governments. The Reagan administration tried to achieve this objective through a combination of deregulation and decentralization. Deregulation involved revocation of existing rules and regulations, and reduction of enforcement. Within a year of President Reagan's election, his secretary of education, Terrel Bell, revoked thirty sets of rules governing nineteen programs.

The key attack on the power of categorical grants came in the form of advocacy of block grants, which would be administered by state governments. This process of decentralization represented the first major change in federal programs in education since the beginning of categorical grants in the 1950s. It did not represent a complete abandonment of categorical aid but an attempt to give state governments more control.

The block-grant philosophy was embodied in the 1981 administration-sponsored legislation called the Education Consolidation and Improvement Act (ECIA). Title I of the Elementary and Secondary Act of 1965 became Chapter 1 of the new legislation. Under Chapter 1 of the ECIA, requirements were simplified—administrative authority was given to the states and responsibility for program design was given to local school districts. Of major importance was the lack of detailed regulations from the Department of Education to local school districts handling program design under Chapter 1.

President Reagan's administration also attempted to change the degree of control of civil rights legislation over local school systems, by reducing and limiting enforcement efforts. Federal control, through insistence on the protection of civil rights, had its origins in Title VI of the 1964 Civil Rights Act. This legislation provided the federal government with the method and means to regulate education and protect civil rights in the schools.

Title VI established the precedent for using government money as a means of controlling educational policy. It required the mandatory withholding of federal funds from institutions practicing racial, religious, or ethnic discrimination. Title VI stated that no person, because of race, color, or national origin, could be excluded from or denied the benefits of any program receiving federal financial assistance. It required all federal agencies to establish guidelines to implement this policy. Refusal by institutions or projects to follow these guidelines was to result in the "termination or refusal to grant or to continue assistance under such program or activity."

The strength of Title VI resulted from the government extending its activities in many educational institutions around the country. Federal spending had spread to most of the educational institutions in the United States through the activities of the National Science Foundation and the National Defense Education Act. In addition, research money flowed into universities from other government agencies, including the Department of Defense. Many institutions received funds for the Reserve Officers Training Corps. Federal spending in education continued to increase in the 1960s, particularly after the passage in 1965 of the Elementary and Secondary Education Act. Title VI announced that all aid to institutions and school districts that failed to comply with federal guidelines would end. This was certainly a powerful government weapon. The most extreme concern about Title VI was voiced by Senator Sam Ervin of North Carolina, who claimed that "no dictator could ask for more power than Title VI confers on the President."

The justification for using federal money in this manner was given by Senator Hubert Humphrey during the Senate floor debate over the civil rights bill. The major concern at the time was the extent of racial segregation in educational institutions. Humphrey argued that Title VI was not designed to be punitive, but was designed to make sure that funds were not used to support segregated programs. He also claimed that Title VI did not create any new government authority. "Most agencies," he stated, "now have authority to refuse or terminate assistance for failure to comply with a variety of requirements imposed by statute or by administrative action." While Title VI represented an unquestioned power of the federal government to establish the terms under which funds shall be disbursed, Humphrey made the point that "no recipient is required to accept Federal aid."

Title VI completely reversed the relationship existing between the Office of Education and local and state school districts. The Office of Education traditionally defined its constituency as local and state school officials. The doctrine of local control and opposition to federal control resulted in most money being disbursed by the Office of Education with minimum requirements and regulation. The Office of Education was viewed as a public servant of each local and state educational system.

With Title VI, the Office of Education was forced to embark on a path that put it in an adversary position in relation to many school systems. School systems would now be required to show proof of compliance with civil rights guidelines, and the Office of Education would be placed in the position of judging the adequacy of the actions of local school systems. The Office of Education was also given responsibility for drafting guidelines that would be used in enforcing the provisions of Title VI in government educational programs. This meant the Office of Education was placed in the position of being both interpreter and enforcer of the law. An agency that had always avoided any hint of federal control was suddenly handed the problem of protecting the constitutional rights of children around the country.

The precedent for using the threat of withholding federal money as a means of protecting civil rights also provided the basis for government attempts to end sex discrimination in the schools. Title IX of the 1972 amendments to the Higher Education Act stated: "No person in the United States shall, on the basis of sex, be excluded from participation in, be denied the benefits of, or be subjected to discrimination under any education program or activity receiving Federal Assistance." President Reagan's administration tried to restrict the application of this law to programs directly receiving aid, but Congress broadened its scope in the late 1980s.

In 1974, federal protection of civil rights in the schools was again expanded with the passage of what was known as the Buckley Amendment, named after its sponsor, Senator James Buckley of New York. The Buckley Amendment was a rider to the Educational Amendments of 1974; it stated that educational institutions would lose federal funds unless they gave parents the right to examine and challenge school records. Senator Buckley stated in an interview in the January 1975 issue of the *Nation's Schools and Colleges* that the idea for the amendment came from an article he had read in a Sunday supplement in a newspaper. The concern was that teachers and school officials often put damaging statements into student files and never provided an opportunity for children or parents to see these statements. A careless comment by a third-grade teacher calling a student a "born liar" might follow the pupil through school and affect the attitudes of other teachers and the pupil's whole educational career. Moreover, student files remain with the school through college and are sometimes referred to when students seek employment. Senator Buckley stated in the magazine interview: "When you're talking about records that affect the life of an individual, that affect decisions that are being made about him, then he has a right to see them and to determine their accuracy."

The Buckley Amendment gives parents the right to examine school records, to challenge items they feel are inaccurate, and to have misleading records changed. Parents must also give their consent before any records are shown to any individuals or groups outside the school. The same rights of inspection and challenge are given to any student 18 and over who is attending an institution of higher learning. Specifically, parents and older students are allowed to inspect and review at will "official records, files and data, including all material that is incorporated into each student's cumulative record folder." These records include, in the words of the legislation: "identifying data; academic work completed; level achievement (grades, test scores); attendance data; scores on standardized intelligence, aptitude, and psycho-

logical tests; interest inventory results; health data; family background information; teacher or counselor ratings and observations; and verified reports of
serious behavior patterns."

Support of educational research is also affected by changes in the political
climate. The major involvement of the federal government in educational
research came with the passage of the 1965 Elementary and Secondary Education Act, which provided legislative and financial support to the idea of
government-sponsored research and development in education. It is important to understand that the sponsorship of research-and-development activities is considered a method for indirectly controlling the actions of local
school systems. In this particular case, the concern about control was voiced
in terms of educational change; educational research was to be the means of
changing the actions of local school systems.

This argument was specifically stated by a government planning group,
the Gardner Task Force, which was responsible for the research section of the
Elementary and Secondary Education Act. The report of the Gardner Task
Force declared: "We must overhaul American education." The key to this
overhaul was changing educational practices through research funding. The
report stated, "We now know, beyond all doubt, that educationally speaking,
the old ways of doing things will not solve our problems. We are going to
have to shed outworn educational practice, dismantle outmoded educational
facilities, and create new and better learning environments."

Under the Elementary and Secondary Education Act federal government
became the major supporter of educational research. Educational research
was further highlighted in the early 1970s, during the administration of
President Richard Nixon, with the establishment of the National Institute of
Education (NIE). The primary argument for the establishment of the NIE was
that past educational policy and programs had failed because research had
not been conducted before implementation. The purpose of the NIE was to
determine through research the best methods of achieving particular goals of
educational policy.

This is precisely what did happen in the early 1980s. Once he assumed
office, President Reagan appointed to the NIE a series of new directors whose
research agendas were clearly conservative. Of major importance was the
funding of research to investigate vouchers and tuition tax credits. Tuition tax
credits had been the most important part of President Reagan's political
platform for education. The dramatic shift in research emphasis in the NIE
that took place with the election of President Reagan highlights the political
nature and political uses of educational research.

During the term of President Reagan's last secretary of education, William
Bennett, persuasion became a favored means of indirect control. As secretary
of education, Bennett would use his office as a "Bully Pulpit" to harangue
educators to change their educational practices. By the early 1990s, President Bush emphasized the idea of the government establishing national standards for different school subjects, as I will discuss in more detail in Chapter 10, without enforcing those standards on the schools. And, in fact,

when the first national standards in the field of mathematics were announced, forty-one states voluntarily incorporated those standards in their state curriculum.

The key to the use of persuasion by the federal government is the creation of educational models that will appeal to state and local educators. These models are not forced on states and local school systems; they are accepted voluntarily. It is the job of federal officials to convince others to accept these models. President Clinton, similar to his predecessor President Bush, supports the development of national standards in education. These national standards cannot be required of schools, but federal officials can try to persuade schools to adopt them.

A similar method is being used by the National Board for Professional Teaching Standards which, as I discussed in Chapter 2, is developing national certification. The board does not have the power to require states and local schools to accept this certification, but it can try to convince them that its method of certification is the best. In fact, the whole premise of the operation of the National Board for Professional Teaching Standards is that its testing program for teacher certification will be so good that states and local schools will voluntarily recognize its certificates.

In summary, persuasion, categorical aid, civil rights legislation, and research funding are the principal means by which the federal government influences the operation of public schools. Because these methods of indirect control are so powerful, federal influence on educational policy has increased greatly since the 1950s. Since the 1950s the federal government has called on the schools to win the military race with the Soviet Union, end poverty, solve problems of unemployment, and win in the arena of international economic competition. Of course, as I discuss in the next section, one result of tying education to national policies is to make education an important factor in national politics.

THE POLITICS OF EDUCATION
AT THE NATIONAL LEVEL

Federal involvement in education increased the importance of education in national politics. Prior to the 1950s, education played a minor role in national politics. But with increased federal involvement in education and the growing political activity of organized educational interest groups, education became a major political issue by the 1980s. One example is the growing importance of educational issues in the mind of the voter. In a 1983 poll conducted for *Time* magazine by Yankelovich, Skelly, and White, voters were asked how much influence a presidential candidate's stand on a particular issue would have on a decision to support that candidate. Education ranked third, after inflation and unemployment (it was tied for third place with the issue of relationships with the Soviet Union). A poll conducted by the Gallup Organization for *Newsweek* in 1983 asked a similar question and found the issue of "the quality of public education" to be second in importance to the highest-ranking issue of "economic conditions in the country."

Growth of voter concern about education issues parallels the rise of education issues as a national campaign issue. In the 1950s and 1960s education was not a major campaign issue, but the topic grew in importance due to presidential politics. President Eisenhower used his advocacy of federal involvement in education through the National Defense Education Act as a means of answering the political problems created by the Soviet Union's early advances in technology related to space travel. In the same manner, President Johnson, in the 1960s, used education as a political tool in his war against poverty. One result of the actions of both of these presidents was that educational interest groups turned to the federal government for increasing financial support for the public schools and for maintaining existing programs. As the federal government became the focus of these groups, others who were critical of federal involvement and of the public schools also began to organize to influence politics at the national level. The result of the political activity of these groups was that education became a major issue in national politics.

The 1980 presidential election ushered in the new era of national educational politics. The incumbent, President Jimmy Carter, tried to win votes and build a strong campaign by gaining the support of major educational organizations. During the 1976 campaign President Carter promised the National Education Association (NEA), the largest teacher organization, that a separate Department of Education would be established. This proposal was bitterly opposed by a rival teacher organization, the American Federation of Teachers (AFT), out of fear that the NEA would dominate the new department. In the 1980 campaign the NEA supported President Carter; the AFT supported Senator Edward Kennedy during the presidential primaries and only reluctantly supported Carter after Kennedy was unable to gain the Democratic party nomination.

President Carter gave the NEA and the newly apppointed secretary of education, Shirley Hufstedler, a significant place in his 1980 campaign strategy. When Ms. Hufstedler was appointed as secretary, there was considerable concern in the education community about her lack of background in education. Most commentators felt that President Carter planned to make her the first woman to sit on the U.S. Supreme Court.

One thing was certain during the 1980 campaign: Ms. Hufstedler spent more time campaigning for President Carter than she did organizing the new Department of Education. Part of the campaign strategy was for Secretary Hufstedler to speak before local chapters of the NEA, portraying President Carter as the champion of the public school and urging members to hit the campaign trail and get out to vote for the incumbent.

President Carter's opponent, Ronald Reagan, appealed to a constituency different from that of the professional education organizations. Reagan attacked the federal government's role in education and called for the abolition of the Department of Education. His campaign platform included a proposal for tuition tax credits for parents choosing to send their children to private schools. This won the support of private-school interests, particularly parochial schools, and of that section of the public dissatisfied with the public schools. Reagan's proposal for tuition tax credits was vehemently attacked by the NEA and the AFT.

After President Reagan was elected in 1980 he continued to emphasize education as part of his political strategy. His major problem was his inability to get Congress to pass proposals to abolish the Department of Education, and to establish tuition tax credits and school prayer. Therefore, before the impending 1984 election, Reagan found himself being criticized by his original supporters for being ineffective and by the public-school establishment for his apparent lack of support of public education. To counter this situation President Reagan tried to use a report, *A Nation at Risk,* issued by his administration in 1983—one year before the 1984 election—as a politically safe method of trying simultaneously to project an image of himself as a friend of public education without alienating his original educational constituency.

The conservative nature of Reagan's education policies was apparent in his appointment in 1985 of William Bennett as secretary of education. With the appointment of Bennett, the report of the Moral Majority, a conservative religious group, announced in headlines, "Finally a Friend in Education." During the Reagan years the Moral Majority gained strength in the Department of Education. For instance, in 1985, Thomas Tancredo, Department of Education's Region VIII representative in Denver, distributed at government expense a speech written five years previously by the then-executive-director of the Moral Majority, Robert Billings. The speech declared that "godlessness has taken over America." President Reagan appointed Billings to direct the Department of Education's ten regional offices.

During confirmation hearings before the Senate Committee on Labor and Human Resources, Bennett, under oath, admitted he was screened for the position of secretary of education by twelve conservative organizations meeting under the umbrella of the Committee for Survival of a Free Congress. He claimed that pressure from the White House forced him to attend the meeting. Bennett told the Senate committee that he received a call from Ms. Lynn Ross Wood of the Office of Presidential Personnel. "The advice to me," he said, "was to attend the meeting, that they requested that I should attend this meeting."

Again, during the 1988 campaign, the platform of the Republican party called for school prayer and choice in education as a result of pressure from the religious right. And, again, both teachers' unions gave their support to the Democratic Party. Bush's claim that he would be the "education president" made, at least, images of education a central focus of national politics. It would be difficult to determine if Bush's claim aided his election. But balancing the campaign promise of being the education president was the promise not to raise taxes. This meant that any actions as the education president would not involve a significant increase in federal spending for public schools.

Prior to the 1992 campaign, President Bush was criticized for focusing on foreign policy issues instead of domestic issues. Consequently, he appointed Lamar Alexander, former governor of Tennessee, as secretary of education to develop and campaign for Bush's educational agenda. During the 1988 campaign, Bush presented himself as the "education president." But by 1991 there was little in the way of federal legislation and administrative actions that showed that Bush had lived up to the image of education president.

In the spring of 1991, Secretary Alexander launched the education part of the Bush reelection campaign by focusing on four major projects. These projects included the designing of model schools; the creation of national standards; the writing of voluntary national achievement tests; and the promotion of parental choice plans that included both public and private schools. As I discuss in the next chapter, the development of national standards is proceeding at a rapid rate. National achievement tests are being developed in conjunction with the creation of national standards. And during the summer of 1992, grants were given for designing new model schools.

Critics charged that the Bush campaign failed to address several of the goals originally agreed upon by state governors and the administration. Missing from the campaign plans were the goals of improving preschool preparation, lowering the dropout rate, and banishing illegal drugs from schools.

In opposition to the Bush campaign, Bill Clinton relied on the power of the two teachers' unions. As I discussed in Chapter 3, the NEA and the AFT were not welcome in the White House during the twelve years of Republican administrations. Both unions committed money and personnel to the Clinton campaign. They rallied their membership to support Clinton and hit the campaign trail to drum up votes from the general public. While it is difficult to measure the effect of union activities on the outcome of the election, the two unions probably made an important contribution to Clinton's victory.

The major difference on educational issues between Bush and Clinton during the campaign was over the issue of choice. Bush hoped to win votes from conservatives, the religious right, and parents wanting to send their children to private schools by advocating that government funding be used to allow parents to choose between public and private schools. In harmony with teachers' unions' concerns that private school choice would take money away from public schools, the Clinton campaign advocated that choice should be limited to choice between public schools.

In general, educational issues in the Clinton campaign were tied to economic concerns. A major argument of the Democratic campaign was that Bush neglected the economy and that Clinton would make it a focus of his administration. Using this method, Democratic strategists hoped to win over voters concerned about unemployment and the decline in the standard of living among middle- and lower-class families. Consequently, Clinton repeatedly linked educational issues to economic issues. In outlining his educational proposals during the second television debate, Clinton declared, "Those things [his educational proposals] would revolutionize American education and take us to the top economically."

In the second television debate, Clinton listed five major educational policies he intended to implement if elected. The first was to give matching funds to states to provide on-the-job education "to teach everybody with a job to read in the next five years and give everybody with a job a chance to get a high school diploma." The second promise was to provide apprenticeship training to all high school graduates who do not go on to college. This promise reflected the concerns of his best friend and later secretary of labor, Robert Reich, that the skills of the work force needed to be improved. The third promise was to open the doors to a college education for any high school graduate by providing student loans that could be paid off in part by community service. Fourth, he pledged to fully fund Head Start. And fifth, he promised school reform that would increase choices within the public school system. In making this promise, he reiterated his opposition to private school choice: "I favor public schools or these new charter schools . . . I don't think we should spend tax money on private schools but I favor public school choice."

When Clinton spoke of school reform, he was referring to a number of reforms I discussed in Chapter 7. As noted above, he looks favorably on the idea of charter schools. In addition, he supports decentralization and site-based management. In the second television debate he stated, "I favor radical decentralization and giving more power to better-trained principals and teachers, with parent councils to control their schools."

When Clinton won the election, the two teachers' unions clamored for him to appoint an educator as secretary of education. But, in what appeared to be a political payoff, Clinton appointed the former governor of South Carolina, Richard Riley. The appointment appeared to be a political payoff because of the active and important role Riley played in the Clinton campaign. During the campaign, newspapers described Riley as Clinton's "personnel boss." On the other hand, as I discussed in Chapter 1, as governor of South Carolina, Riley placed education reform at the top of his agenda and worked on educational issues with then Governor Clinton on the National Governors' Association. In his acceptance speech, Riley declared:

> The Clinton-Gore education agenda is extraordinarily challenging and important to America's future. It's an agenda of opportunity and of responsibility, one that will give every single child a fair chance . . . one that will offer training to high school students who must compete for jobs in the future, one that will give young people a chance to serve their nation [and] . . . in return . . . help with their higher education.

The Clinton campaign highlights the increased importance of education in national politics. This is in marked contrast to earlier in the century when national educational issues were primarily worked out in professional organizations, such as the National Education Association, and by local and state governments. With the Clinton administration linking educational policy to domestic economic issues, education will continue to be an important fixture in national politics.

PRIVATE FOUNDATIONS

Private foundations are an important means of nationalizing educational policies and practices. Often the activities of foundations result in government action. In *The Politics of Knowledge: The Carnegie Corporation, Philanthropy, and Public Policy*, Ellen Condliffe Lagemann writes, in reference to one of the major foundations to affect educational policy, " . . . the Corporation's [Carnegie] policymakers sometimes assisted government policymakers in realizing a program or plan. . . . [In turn] the federal government often invited the Corporation to participate in policy-making or implemented the recommendations of Carnegie-supported groups."

In the United States, private foundations are established as philanthropic institutions by possessors of great wealth. Some of the largest foundations include the Ford Foundation, the Rockefeller Foundation, the Lilly Endowment, the W. K. Kellogg Foundation, and the Carnegie Corporation of New York. The names of the foundations indicate the sources of the fortunes that went into the establishment of these charitable organizations.

Because of their resources, private foundations are able to provide large sums of money to support studies, research, and organizations. These foundations have had a major impact on social policy in the United States. The broad scope and variety of activities sponsored by the foundations have led to their activities being attacked by both the political left and the political right in the United States. Right-wing groups attack foundations as instruments of large corporate wealth designed to promote a social policy that works against the interests of smaller industrial groups. Right-wing groups see foundations as restricting competition and supporting monopoly control of the marketplace through their funding of particular organizations and policies. In a similar fashion, left-wing political groups have been concerned about foundations exerting control over American social policy.

The real power of foundations lies in their ability to influence or control the areas in which they choose to spend money. Until the recent expansion of the federal government in the funding of research and social-action projects, foundations were the main source of funds for these activities in the United States. In many ways, the decisions of the boards of directors of these foundations about the type of research, social projects, and organizations to be funded have determined the evolution and direction of scientific and social research, as well as social policy in the United States.

A good example of how foundation support of particular projects affected the basic structure of American education can be seen in the rise of segregated, vocational education for African Americans in the South after the Civil

War. As Henry Bullock explains in his prizewinning book, *A History of Negro Education in the South,* money from large foundations made possible the implementation of segregated, vocational education designed to train a labor force for the emerging industrial South in the early part of the twentieth century. Money for the support of segregated education came from the Peabody Fund, the General Education Board of the Rockefeller Foundation, the Slater Fund, and the Rosenwald Fund. One of the concerns of this group of philanthropists was the development of a nonimmigrant and nonunion labor force for the new industrial South. It was believed that freed African-American people, if given adequate vocational education, could provide this labor pool.

Evaluation of the deeds of philanthropy in the South reveals one of the basic dilemmas in the historical role of private foundations in a democratic society. The power of philanthropic aid can be criticized because it supported a segregationist educational structure and reflected the self-interest of the donors in providing a controllable industrial work force. On the hand, there might not have been any large-scale development of schools for African Americans in the South if the money had not been given by these large foundations. The foundations can be credited with providing money that was not available from other sources. In either case, the private foundations had a tremendous influence on the development of segregated education in the South.

Another example of how foundation action resulted in shaping educational policy through particular projects was the Ford Foundation's support of the Mobilization for Youth program in the late 1950s. As Peter Marris and Martin Rein describe it in their *Dilemmas of Social Reform,* the Ford Foundation had previously used two approaches in granting aid to solve urban problems. One of these promoted the establishment of metropolitan governments that would reintegrate the central cities with the suburbs. The other promoted urban renewal, which was designed to attract prosperous residents and business back to the central city. Dissatisfied with both these approaches to reform, the Ford Foundation in the late 1950s backed Mobilization for Youth, which had community action as a central feature. The basic assumptions of community action were the existence of the poverty cycle and the lack of opportunity for the poor. It was believed that existing social-service agencies, such as those for education, medical care, and welfare, were making the poor dependent rather than self-reliant. The goal of community action was to make the poor self-reliant through their participation in the management and policy decisions of these agencies. This idea was incorporated in the Economic Opportunity Act of 1964 in the form of a requirement that all programs sponsored by the legislation have maximum feasible participation. Because the Head Start program for early-childhood education resulted from this legislation, community participation became one of its features.

Community-action programs resulted in a great deal of political controversy. Some people charged that it led to conflict between elected local officials and groups sponsored through community-action programs. Other groups charged the program with sponsoring local radicals who tried to take over special agencies. What it did accomplish in the 1960s was to increase community participation in the schools and establish school advisory committees.

Foundations have also sponsored research projects that have affected American schools. One of the most famous and important studies sponsored by the Carnegie Corporation contributed to the U.S. Supreme Court decision ending school segregation in the South. The subject of the study was African Americans. It began in 1938 under the leadership of Swedish social scientist Gunnar Myrdal. World War II slowed down the work, and the final study, *An American Dilemma: The Negro Problem and American Democracy,* was published in 1944. It was this study, cited in the 1954 Supreme Court case ending school segregation, that was a main component of the social-science evidence demonstrating that segregated schools were inherently unequal.

During the 1950s the Carnegie Corporation sponsored James Conant's influential study, *The American High School Today.* The study was conducted at a time when there was a strong public criticism of the failure of the schools to produce enough scientists and engineers. One of the major recommendations of the Conant study was that high schools should consolidate so that a wider range of programs could be offered to students. It was believed that in small high schools students could not be properly differentiated into programs geared toward their future social roles. The Conant report's recommendations for larger high schools resulted in a national movement to consolidate high schools.

Foundations also have helped to strengthen and establish organizations that had a direct influence on educational policy. Charles Biebel, in his 1976 article in the *History of Education Quarterly,* "Private Foundations and Public Policy: The Case of Secondary Education during the Great Depression," states that during the 1930s John D. Rockefeller's General Education Board reorganized and supported the American Council of Education as a vehicle for instituting the General Education Board's own plans to restructure American secondary education. In addition, the General Education Board established the American Youth Commission and provided money to the National Education Association to establish the Educational Policies Committee. All these groups were extremely influential in the formulation of secondary-school policy.

An extremely important organization that the Carnegie Corporation helped to establish in 1947 was the Educational Testing Service (ETS). Most college students and candidates for professional schools in recent times have taken some test administered by ETS. The two major testing enterprises originally brought together in ETS were the Scholastic Aptitude Test (SAT) and the College Entrance Examination Board (CEEB). Over the years ETS has expanded its testing activities to become one of the major gatekeepers to the professions and to institutions of higher learning. By the 1970s consumer advocate Ralph Nader criticized ETS for its almost monopolistic control of testing and for the high cost of taking ETS examinations.

In recent years, the Carnegie Corporation has been responsible for the establishment of the National Board for Professional Teaching Standards. If national certification of teachers does occur in the United States it will be primarily the result of the work of this foundation. In addition, the Carnegie Corporation provided seed money for the establishment of the National Center on Education and the Economy. This organization is playing a major role in linking public schools to business needs.

Because of the controversial nature of foundation activity in the United States, and the criticism of its activity from every part of the political spectrum, it is difficult to make any single general judgment about the role of foundations in American education. Any person interested in the workings of a particular foundation must ask certain questions.

The most important question is about the social composition and political views of the members of the board of directors of the foundation. This is important because it is usually this group that establishes the guiding philosophy for determining the projects to be funded. It should be remembered that where the money is spent can have a tremendous influence over shaping educational institutions and policy.

The next important question is about the relationship between foundation staff and the community. The informal activities of the staff can result in the solicitation of particular proposals for funding and for certain information being received by the board of directors. Very often the major contact of staff members and boards of directors is with social elites within communities. This might not be true if the foundation were to aggressively pursue broader contacts within the community.

A third important question is whether the past record of foundation activity reflects any particular social or political philosophy. Sometimes the answer to this question can be found in those groups the foundation refused to support. If, for instance, a foundation has provided money to support particular organizations and not others, the question must be asked, why? The same question must be asked of research and projects funded by foundations. Very often a careful reading of statements by foundation officials about what they think is a good education or a good society will give clues to the general social and political philosophy behind foundation activity.

Foundations will continue to have an important impact on American society and education. It is only through regulatory legislation that the general public can directly control the activities of foundations. Local groups can indirectly place pressure on foundations by surveying their activities, writing letters of praise or criticism to local newspapers, and seeking other public forums for discussion of foundation influence over community life. A combination of these approaches should be used by those interested in public control of the influential power of these tremendous foundations of private wealth.

ACCREDITING ASSOCIATIONS

In addition to the federal government and private foundations, accrediting agencies play a role in nationalizing educational policies. A major criticism of the actions of accrediting agencies is that they increase the control of professional educators over educational policies. Accrediting associations are nongovernmental professional organizations that establish standards and criteria for educational institutions. Six major regional agencies accredit institutions of higher education and secondary schools in the United States. The six range in size from the North Central Association of Colleges and Secondary Schools, with 500 institutions of higher education and nearly 4,000 secondary schools on its accredited list, to the Northwest Association of Secondary and Higher Schools, with fewer than 100 institutions on its list.

Accrediting agencies originally focused on the problem of admission of students from high schools into colleges. In the nineteenth century this was a major problem for many high schools because each college and university had its own admission examination and requirements. This sometimes meant that high schools would have to prepare students differently, depending on the particular college they planned to attend. Two kinds of institutions were developed to deal with this problem. One was the testing organization, which developed common tests to be used for admission to a variety of colleges. The College Entrance Examination Board (CEEB) was established for this purpose. The other organization was the accrediting association, whose accrediting activities ensured that students would be admitted to college if they graduated from an accredited high school. This is still true in many states, where graduation from an accredited high school guarantees admission to a state university or college. Most institutions of higher education now use a combination in their admissions requirements of attendance at an accredited institution and test scores.

Accrediting agencies can exert a great deal of influence over secondary education. The standards of judgment established by these agencies touch almost every aspect of school life. They range from administration to relationships with the community to curriculum and extracurricular activities. Periodic inspections by accrediting agencies require schools to compile answers to long lists of questions and to undergo several days of on-site inspection. Visiting accrediting teams usually conclude their visits with an evaluative statement about the school's performance and a list of recommendations for improvements and changes.

A major critic of accrediting is James Koerner, past president of the Council for Basic Education. One of Koerner's complaints is that accrediting groups tend to perpetuate mediocrity in education. Since institutions are not rated in terms of one institution being superior to another, the only real function of accrediting is to deny accreditation to borderline institutions. This means that simply because an institution is accredited does not guarantee that the institution has a high-quality program.

Koerner also criticizes accrediting practices because they destroy a certain amount of local control over education. This is one of Koerner's major concerns in his book, *Who Controls American Education?* Koerner believes that local control of the schools has been replaced by the control of professional educators. From his perspective, accrediting associations are one more group of professional educators imposing outside standards over local schools. As he states in his book: "These agencies can therefore bring irresistible pressure to bear on institutions to force them to conform to what people outside the institutions think are desirable practices in matters of faculty, budget, instruction, facilities, or most other matters of moment in education."

Some of Koerner's major criticism is directed at the National Council for Accreditation of Teacher Education (NCATE), which accredits programs in professional education. NCATE is one of the largest and most powerful of the professional agencies that accredits particular subjects and degrees. One reason for this is that teacher education is one of the larger areas of higher education, in terms of numbers of undergraduates and graduate programs for teachers, school administrators, and future professors of education.

Koerner's concern about NCATE is "its monopolistic power and narrowness of its policies, but mostly because it was an organization of, by and for the professional establishment." This statement from *Who Controls American Education?* articulates the recurring argument that it is the professionals who control education, and that accrediting agencies are merely one part of the network of professional control. In addition, Koerner complains about the failure of NCATE to rate teacher education and provide some means of judging the superiority of one institution over another. Koerner feels that NCATE contributes, in the same way as do the accrediting agencies for secondary schools, to maintaining a level of mediocrity in teacher education around the country.

Koerner does admit that there is a great deal of value in having accrediting associations to assure that some standard of education is maintained in secondary schools and institutions of higher education. There is also value, in his opinion, in providing the general public with information about which institutions attain certain standards. The major issues with regard to accrediting agencies are who should control them and how extensive their rating of institutions should be. Should there be public control rather than professional control of accreditation? Should accrediting institutions inform the public about which high schools are superior to other high schools? Should teacher education be rated? If, in the future, the answer to these questions is yes, it would mean more influence and power for accrediting associations.

CONCLUSION

The nationalization of educational policy and practices raises a number of important questions. The following list of questions should be considered in the context of the Educational Chair. If you were sitting in the Educational

Chair, how would you respond to these questions? What influence might the answers to these questions have on the control of the knowledge disseminated by the Educational Chair?

1. Should the goals of public schools be tied to national policy issues?
2. Should the policies and practices of public schools be enmeshed in national politics?
3. Should private wealth be able to influence schools through the work of philanthropic foundations?
4. Who should control accreditation?

All of the above questions are related to the more general question of how knowledge should be controlled in a democratic society. In the next chapter, I will deal with this question from the perspective of the political determination of the public school curriculum, methods of instruction, and textbooks.

EXERCISES

1. Compose a list of the educational goals and concerns of the president of the United States. What other groups in the United States share these goals and concerns?
2. Contact a local member of Congress and ask what he or she thinks are the most important educational issues for the federal government. Ask if educational issues are important in his or her campaigning for Congress.
3. Investigate what percentage of financial support in local schools is received from the federal government.
4. Contact an official of a local school system and ask him or her the current requirements and guidelines of the federal government for compliance with the demands of federal legislation.
5. If a private foundation operates in your local area, investigate the social composition of its board of directors and the kinds of projects and organizations it sponsors. Try to determine what effect it might have over local social and educational policy.
6. As a way of understanding accreditation, ask to see the NCATE evaluation of your department or college of education.

SUGGESTED READINGS AND WORKS CITED IN CHAPTER

Bailey, Stephen. *Education Interest Groups in the Nation's Capital.* Washington, D.C.: American Council on Education, 1975. A survey of the educational lobbying groups in Washington.
Biebel, Charles. "Private Foundations and Public Policy: The Case of Secondary Education During the Great Depression." *History of Education Quarterly* (Spring

1976). Provides good examples of foundation influence over educational policy and organizations.

Bullock, Henry. *A History of Negro Education in the South*. New York: Praeger, 1970. Chapter 5, "Deeds of Philanthropy," shows the influence of foundations on southern educational policy.

Cardinal Principles of Secondary Education. Washington, D.C.: Bureau of Education, 1918. The major policy statement of the NEA about the goals of the comprehensive high school in the twentieth century. This policy statement had a major impact on shaping the modern high school.

"Clinton-Text." *Compuserve Executive News Service*, no. 0501 (22 December 1992). This article contains the transcript of Secretary of Education Richard Riley's acceptance speech.

Conant, James B. *The American High School Today*. New York: McGraw-Hill, 1959. The Carnegie-funded study of the American high school. This study is discussed in more detail in Chapter 1 of this text.

Cooper, Kenneth J. "National Standards at Core of Proposal: Model Schools Envisioned." *Compuserve Executive News Service Washington Post* (19 April 1991). This article contains the basic educational proposals supported by Bush's secretary of education, Lamar Alexander.

"Education and Politics: A Sample of Public Opinion." *Education Week* (29 February 1984). This "Databank" section of *Education Week* contains polls by *Time*/Yankelovich, Skelly and White, and *Newsweek*/Gallup, ranking public opinion on the subject of the importance of education in decisions made by voters.

Education Week. This weekly newspaper is one of the best sources of information on national educational politics.

Hearing Before the Committee on Labor and Human Resources: William J. Bennett of North Carolina, to Be Secretary, Department of Education. U.S. Senate, 97th Cong., 1st Sess., 28 January 1985. This congressional hearing contains evidence of the conservative influence within the Department of Education during the Reagan administration.

Koerner, James. *Who Controls American Education?* Boston: Beacon, 1968. Koerner argues that professional educators control American education.

Lagemann, Ellen Condliffe. *The Politics of Knowledge: The Carnegie Corporation, Philanthropy, and Public Policy*. Middletown, Conn.: Wesleyan University Press, 1989. A history and analysis of the foundation that has had the greatest impact on educational policy in the United States.

Marris, Peter, and Martin Rein. *Dilemmas of Social Reform*. Chicago: Aldine, 1973. This book gives a good understanding of the influence of foundations over American social policy.

Myrdal, Gunnar. *An American Dilemma: The Negro Problem and Modern Democracy*. New York: Harper and Brothers, 1944. A Carnegie-sponsored study that has had a major infuence on race relations in the United States.

Nielsen, Waldemar. *The Big Foundations*. New York: Columbia University Press, 1972. A survey of the origins and activities of the major foundations in the United States.

Orfield, Gary. *The Reconstruction of Southern Education: The Schools and the 1964 Civil Rights Act*. New York: Wiley-Interscience, 1969. A study of the effects of the 1964 Civil Rights Act on the desegregation of southern schools.

Spring, Joel. *The Sorting Machine: National Educational Policy since 1945.* New York: Longman, 1976. A history and analysis of federal educational policy since World War II.

"Transcript of 2d TV Debate Between Bush, Clinton and Perot." *New York Times* (16 October 1992): 12–14. Transcript includes Clinton's campaign promises regarding education.

White, Eileen. "Reagan, Four Education Officials Meet; N. E. A. Left Out of Talk on Teachers." *Education Week* (15 June 1983): 1. The news story about President Reagan's attempt to capture the support of the AFT.

CHAPTER 10

The Politics of Curriculum, Instruction, and Textbooks

The Japanese schools face a serious problem in teaching about their country's role in World War II. Their problem exemplifies the political nature of knowledge disseminated by public schools. It is the argument of this chapter that the politics of education affects the curriculum, methods of instruction, and textbooks used in public schools. The Japanese example highlights the political quality of knowledge distributed by most government-operated school systems.

In this illustration, Professor Saburo Ienaga, a professor at the Tokyo University of Education, filed a court suit in 1989 against the Japanese Ministry of Education for the censorship of his high school textbooks. At issue was the portrayal of Japanese actions during World War II. Professor Ienaga's battle against censorship began in 1965 when the Ministry of Education insisted the word *invasion* be changed to *advance* to describe Japanese military actions in China. In addition, the government required him to sanitize descriptions of Japanese soldiers killing civilians and raping Chinese women during the 1937 capture of Nanjing. He was also required to remove references of "human body experiments" conducted on thousands of Chinese by the Japanese army. The decision handed down by the Tokyo District Court in 1989 upheld the right of the Ministry of Education to censor Professor Ienaga's textbooks. After the decision, Professor Ienaga said that if Japanese youth are not told the truth about the war, there is risk of history repeating itself.

The court decision had international repercussions. In Korea, which was colonized by Japan from 1911 to the end of World War II, a spokesperson for the ruling Democratic Justice Party criticized the decision as being an effort by Japanese leaders to justify the past. A South Korean newspaper insisted that Japan "stop glossing over its history of atrocities and brutalities."

Textbook censorship in Japan illustrates the political quality of knowledge taught in public schools. For instance, most state governments prescribe a basic curriculum for local schools. As I discussed in Chapter 8, the arena of state politics includes elected officials and lobbying groups such as the business community and teachers' unions. It is the political interaction between these groups that produces state curriculum requirements. For example, in public schools, the increased time recently spent on mathematics and science is a direct result of political decisions that are based on a concern for maintaining the United States' position in world trade. In addition, as I discussed in Chapters 7 and 9, local and national politics affect the curriculum and content of instruction.

Within the school, methods of instruction, or how the curriculum is taught, are primarily determined by the goals of education and the organization of the school. In *How Teachers Taught: Constancy and Change in American Classrooms, 1890-1980,* Larry Cuban argues that despite constant attempts in the twentieth century to change methods of instruction in the schools, actual classroom practices remain the same. Constancy exists in classroom teaching, he concludes, because of the effect of school organization and educational goals on teachers working in classrooms. As I discussed in Chapter 1, the goals of education are politically determined.

Therefore, what is taught and how it is taught in public schools is determined by a complex political network. In this chapter, I will provide a brief history of the curriculum in public schools as an illustration of the political determination of the curriculum and the establishment of national curriculum standards. The second section of the chapter will deal with methods of instruction. In the concluding section, I will discuss the politics of textbook publishing in the United States.

CURRICULUM

The curriculum is a battleground in American education. Business groups, radical reformers, religious organizations, welfare associations, left-wing and right-wing politicians, and many other groups want the public schools to teach subjects that will serve their interests. During the twentieth century, the curriculum has varied with changes in the political, economic, and social climate.

In *The Struggle for the American Curriculum 1893-1958,* Herbert M. Kliebard identifies four types of curricula that have vied for dominance in American public schools. Each of these curricula receive support from issues generated by particular social, economic, and political factors. The curricular struggle Kliebard portrays continues into the 1990s. Kliebard's four curriculum categories are

1. Social efficiency
2. Humanism
3. Social meliorism
4. Developmentalism

The *social-efficiency* curriculum has the greatest influence in American schools. Backed by those who want the schools to primarily serve the needs of the economy, it is designed to prepare students for the work force. Often, social-efficiency curricula emphasize vocational subjects and are associated with the educational goals of human capital as discussed in Chapter 1.

In sharp contrast to the advocate of social efficiency, the *humanist* wants the curriculum to introduce students to the cultural traditions of society. A humanist spurns the idea of a vocational curriculum and favors the development of general intellectual skills. Often the humanist wants the curriculum to be organized around standard academic subjects like literature, history, foreign languages, the arts, and science.

The *social meliorist* wants the curriculum to bring about social improvement and change. Social meliorism reflects the reform element in American education. At the most extreme, the social meliorist will ask for courses to solve each new social problem. Sometimes this means the education of students to bring about general political and economic changes. But more often it means the advocacy of courses to solve problems such as alcoholism, drug abuse, AIDS, and traffic accidents.

In many ways, *developmentalism* is the most radical of the four curriculum types. The developmentalist wants the curriculum organized around the psychological development of the child. This means a curriculum focused on the needs of the individual child as opposed to the focus of social-efficiency educators, humanists, and social meliorists, respectively, on economic needs, the passing on of culture, and social reform. Of the four curriculum types, developmentalism has had the least influence on the public school curriculum. The child-centered curriculum of the developmentalist is often rejected by supporters of the other types of curricula for being anti-intellectual and failing to provide the student with the necessary skills to function in society and the world of work.

Historically, one type of curriculum achieves prominence over another in the public schools as a result of changing political and economic conditions. For instance, in the 1990s humanism receives support because of the perception that a lack of intellectual skills among public school graduates is responsible for America's declining position in world trade. Humanists in the 1990s advocate that all students be required to take a core curriculum emphasizing traditional academic subjects. In the 1970s, however, concerns with unemployment and student unrest resulted in an emphasis on a social-efficiency curriculum which evaluated the worth of each course according to its contribution to a person's future career. Vocational education and career education were the central focus of the social-efficiency education of the 1970s.

The tension between humanists and advocates of social efficiency can be traced to the early part of the twentieth century. Humanists fought against the onslaught of social efficiency by trying to preserve the teaching of Greek and Latin in the schools. They argued, in the tradition of the liberal arts, that the purpose of education should be the training of the mind and, as a result of that training, the development of character. For humanists, the study of classical languages, literature, and history would give students the mental tools and character to be moral and successful.

Social-efficiency educators in the early twentieth century, however, argued that the school should provide individualized training based on a person's future destination in the labor force. The worth of all public school courses, they argued, should be judged by their contribution to a person's social worth in the world of work. Therefore, social-efficiency educators called for abandoning the long-standing tradition of teaching Latin and Greek for more vocational courses.

In their enthusiasm for the practical, social-efficiency educators went so far as to advocate that particular courses be geared to a student's future work. For example, they asked why a prospective mechanic or bricklayer should be taught Shakespeare, when the intended occupation required only minimal language skills. Instead, they proposed that occupations should be analyzed to determine their specific academic requirements, and courses could then be organized around those requirements. Future bricklayers, then, would be taught only the English, arithmetic, and science actually needed for that occupation.

By the 1920s, the battle lines were clearly drawn between the humanists and social-efficiency advocates. Neither side could claim victory, but the social-efficiency philosophy did replace many of the traditional humanist components of the curriculum. In the 1930s, a new group of humanists working under the label of *essentialist* reacted against the overly specialized curriculum of the social-efficiency advocates and declared the need for a common core-curriculum. While essentialists did not base their proposals for a core curriculum on a traditional classical education, they emphasized the importance of teaching a common cultural tradition. Unlike earlier humanists who looked to the past, essentialists examined the cultural requirements of the present.

While the humanist argument for a core curriculum was being modified by the practical outlook of the essentialist of the 1930s, social meliorists were calling for major transformations in the public-school curriculum. Since the early days of the common-school movement of the 1830s and 1840s, public schools had been viewed as a source of social change and improvement. The depression of the 1930s sparked widespread concern with social and economic conditions. Many Americans began to believe that the only hope lay in basic changes in the economic organization of the society.

Influenced by these arguments, a group of educators calling themselves *social reconstructionists* called for the teaching of subjects that would prepare the individual to be an active participant in the economic transformation of society. Often this meant a stress on social studies courses designed to give students the skills to analyze political and economic conditions. In contrast to the social meliorist who accepted the basic structure of society and wanted to reform the individual, the social reconstructionist envisioned social improvement as a product of individual empowerment. For political radicals, social reconstructionism offered the hope that public schools could be used to make fundamental changes in society.

The postwar period of the late 1940s shifted the concern of American educators from the economic problems of the depression to the international problems of the cold war between the United States and the Soviet Union. The rhetoric of the cold war tended to dominate curriculum discussions from the 1940s into the 1960s. The result was a strange amalgam of humanist and social-efficiency ideas. Social-efficiency ideas were present in the call for more courses in mathematics and science to train students to be engineers, scientists, and mathematicians in order to win the military race with the Soviet Union. In addition, there was a call for the teaching of more and a greater variety of foreign languages so that the United States could compete with the Soviet Union for influence in other countries. The common rhetoric of the period was that American schools needed to meet humanpower needs or the United States would succumb to the power of the communist threat.

Humanists joined the chorus of those arguing that the schools needed to meet the humanpower needs of the cold war by stressing the importance of academic rigor and the teaching of intellectual skills. Within the concerns of the cold war, the humanist stress on intellectual skills was complemented by the social-efficiency demand to produce highly trained workers for the war machine. Humanists declared American public schools anti-intellectual and called on academic scholars to gain control of the public-school curriculum.

By the 1960s, the cold war concerns of educators gave way to the pressures of the civil rights movement and fears of increasing poverty. Again, social meliorists were prominent in calls for changes in the curriculum that would prepare minorities and poor people for more equal participation in the economy. For social meliorists of the 1960s, a major goal of education became the elimination of poverty and racism. Discussions of new science and math courses gave way to proposals for compensatory education and Head Start courses. These changes in the curriculum were designed to provide the children of the poor with equal access to education by improving their basic skills. Combined with desegregation, these curriculum changes were to end poverty and racism.

In the late 1960s, the social unrest sparked by the Vietnam War dimmed the hopes of social meliorists. Campus protests and disruptions alarmed conservatives and created demands for the restoration of law and order. Republicans attacked the curriculum changes of the social meliorist as unproven social experimentation. War protestors, however, linked antiwar activities with greater demands for cultural freedom. Included in these demands was greater educational freedom for students to pursue their own interests. In addition, the financial cost of the war and energy problems in the 1970s caused unemployment and economic stagnation.

Thus in the late 1960s and early 1970s, a confused period of curriculum change occurred with conservatives demanding more discipline in the schools, cultural and antiwar protestors demanding more freedom in the schools, and social-efficiency advocates demanding that the curriculum change to solve the problems of unemployment and economic stagnation. The final result in the 1970s was that conservatives and social-efficiency advocates joined forces to emphasize, as a solution to both discipline and economic problems, career-education courses, expanded vocational offerings, and closer linkages between the curriculum and the needs of the labor market. By and large, those seeking greater educational freedom established private alternative schools outside the organization of the public schools. While a number of reasons might be given for the short life of these schools, certainly financial problems made it difficult for them to compete with public schools.

It is important to understand that the private alternative schools established in the 1960s and 1970s were part of a long tradition of efforts to organize a curriculum based on student choice and interest. In most cases this tradition flourished in private schools. A major difficulty in organizing a student-centered curriculum in a public school is that the public school exists to serve the interests of society in general. This means, as we have discussed, that the public school curriculum is primarily determined by constantly shifting social, economic, and political goals.

The attempt to create a child-centered curriculum is part of the developmentalist tradition of adjusting the curriculum to the child's nature. The assumption is that the source of motivation, interest, and learning is within the nature of the child. Education, therefore, involves providing the opportunity for children to learn as their interests and desires unfold. Some educators in this tradition argue that a child passes through different stages of development and that the curriculum should be adjusted for each developmental stage.

The private alternative schools of the late 1960s and early 1970s were often called *free schools* because children were given freedom to learn according to their own needs and interests. They were identified with the English school, Summerhill, established in the 1920s by A. S. Neill. Neill believed that aggression was primarily a product of the repression of a child's free development. Authority and discipline, according to Neill, rather than making a child socially responsible, often created a personality that was destructive and aggressive. At Summerhill children were given complete freedom to determine what they studied and how they lived. The only restriction was that they not interfere with the freedom of others. Neill believed that a free school educated individuals who would strive for a free and peaceful world.

Summerhill was one of many alternative schools in the 1920s. In the United States a variety of schools appeared in the early part of the twentieth century devoted to freedom of learning and natural development. The Modern School opened in New Jersey before World War I and lasted into the 1950s. It was dedicated to a nonauthoritarian education where the children determined their own learning. The Walden School was opened in the 1920s by Margaret Naumberg, who believed that the individuality of the child developed through the study and practice of art. The politically radical Manumit School opened during the same period based on the idea that children should manage their education in the same manner as workers organized in unions. Labor-management contracts defined the relationship between students and teachers.

The educational philosopher most often associated with the development of curricula based on student self-interests is John Dewey. It is difficult to measure the impact of Dewey on American education. Certainly his ideas on learning and curriculum have been widely discussed since the beginning of the century. However, there is little evidence that his ideas caused significant changes in the public schools.

Dewey evaluated the impact of the child-centered education movement on the public schools in a *Time* magazine article in 1952. On the positive side, he said the movement made teachers more aware of the growing human being and personal relations and that the "older gross manifestations . . . of education by fear and repression . . . have, generally speaking, been eliminated. . . ." On the negative side, while these grosser forms disappeared, Dewey argues, the "fundamental authoritarianism of the old education persists in various modified forms." Indeed, he found little cooperative and democratic learning in American schools.

A problem in discussing Dewey's impact is the complexity of his thinking and the varying interpretations that can be made of his writings. Consequently, Dewey's ideas have been attacked as anti-intellectual and catering too much to the whims of children, as politically radical, and as promoting group conformity.

Probably the two most controversial aspects of Dewey's thinking, and the source of his ideas on curriculum organization, are the beliefs that all knowledge has a social origin and that the interests of the child are the primary sources of learning. Of course, the conviction that all knowledge has a social origin is rejected by religious groups who believe that God is the source of knowledge. This is one reason many religious groups have attacked Dewey's ideas. Dewey argues that all knowledge and ideas, including ideas about social organizations and morality, are relative to the social situations that produced them. Principles of morality and the organization of society, according to Dewey, must constantly change to adapt to new problems and social situations.

Therefore, the curriculum should be organized, Dewey argues, so that the child learns that knowledge has a social origin and is socially useful. Rather than the teacher acting as if knowledge fell out of the sky, the teacher is to guide the student to an understanding of the historical and social conditions that produced particular knowledge. For instance, arithmetic can be taught as an abstract set of rules or it can be taught in situations where students learn its social usefulness such as counting other children or objects for a particular purpose.

In keeping with the belief that standards of social conduct and of institutions must constantly adapt to changing situations, Dewey believes schools must adapt to the needs of the modern world. One of the primary problems in the modern industrial and urban world, he states, is the need for a sense of cooperation. He argues that in the modern world the stress on individual economic competition needs to be replaced with economic cooperation. Since modern industry and urban life are not fostering cooperation, Dewey maintains, the school needs to change and become the center for teaching cooperation. For instance, Dewey replaced individual classroom desks with group tables on the belief that individual desks promoted individual economic competition while working at tables promoted cooperation.

Dewey rejects the idea that children are primarily motivated to learn by rewards and punishments. He argues that the source of individual action is not stimulation from an outside reward or punishment, but orginates in individual interests and desires.

Dewey's beliefs result in a curriculum based on student interests and designed to teach the social origins of knowledge and cooperation. In this curriculum, teachers guide student interests to sources of knowledge. In addition, knowledge is taught as a whole and not in isolated fragments. Cooperative group activity is the method of learning. Thus, a student or students might express an interest in milk. The teacher would guide the students to sources about the production, chemistry, and distribution of milk. Groups of students might visit the local dairy and develop a group project on milk for the classroom. In the process of this group study of milk, students might learn chemistry, economics, arithmetic, social history, and cooperation. While Dewey did not agree with many of the experiments in child-centered curricula, his name is most often associated with the movement.

Financial pressures, the decline of a protest culture, and attacks by conservatives contributed to the demise of most private alternative schools by the middle of the 1970s. Within the public schools, social-efficiency advocates dominated and the curriculum was increasingly oriented toward educating for specific careers. Vocational offerings expanded and students were encouraged to choose, based on their future goals, from a wide variety of courses.

In the 1980s, international trade problems caused a sharp reaction to the social-efficiency curriculum of the 1970s. In what seemed like a replay of the 1950s, critics argued that the curriculum did not develop the intellectual skills needed to compete in the development of new technology. Humanists, such as Mortimer Adler and Secretary of Education William Bennett, advocated a core curriculum where all students develop intellectual skills through the study of important historical documents and literature. In general, critics argued that the vocational orientation of the 1970s needed to be replaced with an academic orientation.

The constant changes in the American public school curriculum are primarily the result of constantly changing political and economic needs. As long as the public school serves public purposes, its curriculum will constantly change. The shifting patterns of the public school curriculum primarily involve humanists concerned with maintaining cultural traditions and intellectual skills; social-efficiency advocates wanting the schools to serve the economic needs of society; and social meliorists wanting the curriculum organized to promote social reform. Often, the public-school curriculum is a blend of all three curricular patterns with one or more dominating as a result of the particular political and economic conditions of the time.

NATIONAL STANDARDS

The one point of agreement on educational policy between George Bush and Bill Clinton during the 1992 presidential campaign was the creation of national standards. As currently discussed, national standards could become a national curriculum. The basic idea of national standards is creating a set of guidelines on what a student should know in a particular subject by a particular grade. The reasoning behind this effort is that student achievement in U.S. schools should be compared to world-class standards. By making this comparison, it is hoped, the achievement levels of students will rise and, consequently, the schools will educate a better work force which will improve the ability of the United States to compete in the global economy.

One of the basic problems in creating national standards is determining what knowledge is of most worth to teach. And basic to answering this question is the other question of who should determine what knowledge is of most worth.

The decision about who should determine what knowledge is of most worth is being made by the National Council of Education Standards working in conjunction with the federal Department of Education. Under the direction of the National Council of Education Standards, several organizations are being funded by the federal government to establish standards. For instance, the Department of Education awarded a $500,000 grant to the National Academy of Sciences to develop preliminary standards for science. Some of the other organizations receiving federal funding for developing standards for their respective disciplines include the National Council for Geographic Education, the National Council for History Standards, and the National Council of Teachers of Mathematics.

In 1989, the first national standards to be announced were for mathematics. While there was no political power requiring these standards to be adopted by local schools, their influence was felt throughout the country. In fact, forty-one states adopted the standards as part of their curriculum guidelines for local schools. In addition, the standards were incorporated into new textbooks. In effect, the standards did come to represent a national curriculum in the field of mathematics.

As I discussed in Chapter 9, the Department of Education is not politically neutral. Most often, the views of its members reflect the general philosophical perspective of the administration that is in power at that time. In addition, knowledge is not politically neutral or agreed upon by all scholars. In any discipline there is wide disagreement over what is truth. Walk down the halls of the university and you will encounter many different theories competing for dominance in a particular discipline. For instance, in psychology there is a variety of competing theories of human behavior and research methods. In areas such as history and political science, what is considered truth is often relative to the political beliefs of a particular professor. Since it is impossible to teach all things to all elementary and secondary students, some selection of content must be made. Among all the competing theories in a discipline, some decision must be made about what knowledge is of most worth to teach.

Even in a supposedly politically neutral field such as science there are important decisions to be made about what knowledge is most worth teaching to elementary and secondary students. For instance, consider the list of issues developed by the National Academy of Sciences in 1992 in its preparation for development of national standards. These issues included the following:

1. Should science standards be differentiated by the ability of the students?
2. What should be the boundaries of school science? Should science instruction include topics in engineering, technology, and the social sciences?
3. Should science instruction reflect the tradition and culture of mainstream science?

As I discussed in Chapter 4, the first of these questions, Should science standards be differentiated by the ability of the students?, reflects the debate about tracking. The danger of a differentiated approach is that it might support inequality of educational opportunity and inequality of opportunity. Since an understanding of science is important for access to many high paying jobs as symbolic-analysts, those students taught a science program for low-ability groups would be at a disadvantage compared to those learning a science program designed for high achievers. On the other hand, it could be argued that low achievers cannot understand science as well as high achievers. Whatever position a person takes on this issue has important implications for issues involving equality of opportunity.

Question 2, What should be the boundaries of school science?, reflects the lack of a standardized body of scientific thought. The fact that science spills over into many areas of human living and many other intellectual fields makes it difficult to establish boundaries. Again, a trip down the hall of a science department at a university would probably elicit as many answers to this question as there are professors. Therefore, an equally important question in answer to this question is who should decide the boundaries of school science?

The third question, Should science instruction reflect the tradition and culture of mainstream science?, is the most politically explosive. At a 1992 meeting of the American Association for the Advancement of Science, one member objected to the routine exclusion of Afrocentric approaches to science teaching. As I discussed in Chapter 6, Afrocentric educators try to teach their students to see the world through the cultural frame of reference of African Americans and not Europeans. Given the important political debate in education about ethnocentric education, the neglect of an Afrocentric approach to science in the national science standards would be a political decision.

Of course, Native Americans could raise similar objections to national standards in science based on a European approach to the teaching of science. From the perspective of Native Americans, European science has resulted in death and destruction by the weapons developed for modern warfare, and the destruction of the environment. Native Americans might argue that science should be focused on living with nature and not upon trying to exploit nature.

The debate over cultural approaches to science highlights some of the explosive issues in trying to establish national standards. Probably the most contentious area is social studies, in which groups are preparing national standards for civics, history, and geography. Given the political content of these areas, the possibility of bias becomes a real problem. For instance, consider the development of national standards for history by the National Council for History Standards under the direction of Charlotte Crabtree. One issue is Charlotte Crabtree. Politically, she is an outspoken neoconservative and close associate of historian Paul Gagnon, one of the leading opponents of ethnocentric education. As director of the National Center for History in the Schools, she selected Gagnon as the center's scholar-in-residence.

Whether or not one agrees with Crabtree's neoconservative views is not important. What is important is understanding how these political views or any political views would influence answers to the following questions. For the purposes of this discussion, I have made these questions similar to the ones asked by the National Academy of Sciences.

1. What should be the boundaries of school history? Should history taught in schools include political history, economic history, social history, and intellectual history?
2. Should U.S. history be taught from the perspective of European Americans?

Defining the boundaries of history often reflects political values. Conservatives tend to believe that school history should focus on political history as a means of helping the student understand the operation of the U.S. government and for the purpose of building patriotism. On the other hand, liberals tend to believe that social history is important so that students understand the sources of social inequality and learn how to be political activists. Again, I want to remind the reader that neither the conservative nor liberal position represents "truth." What is important to understand is that the determination of the boundaries of school history does involve political values.

This is also true with respect to the perspective to be used in the teaching of history. There are many opponents of ethnocentric education, including Charlotte Crabtree and Paul Gagnon. As I discussed in Chapter 6, one opposition to ethnocentric education involves a belief that it is best to learn history from the viewpoint of European Americans because they are responsible for the creation of the basic institutions in U.S. society. Indeed, teaching history from the viewpoint of Native Americans and African Americans does not cast U.S. institutions in a very positive light. For instance, it would be very difficult to use history as a means of building patriotism if students were required to read Dee Brown's *Bury My Heart at Wounded Knee: An Indian History of the American West.* Told from the perspective of Native Americans, this history presents the U.S. government as a treacherous institution not to be trusted and the U.S. military as a band of savages involved in massacres and mutilations.

Again, the issue is not which view of history is correct, but the fact that there are different perspectives. With national standards, decisions about the boundaries and interpretations of history would be decided by political forces. It is the same situation as I described at the opening of this chapter with the Japanese government making decisions about how the Japanese role in World War II should be presented in textbooks. Obviously, the Japanese government is not interested in promoting negative feelings by presenting descriptions of Japanese atrocities in its textbooks. Would the same thing be true in discussions about national standards in the United States? Would the national standards recommend teaching about the Colorado militia killing 105 Cheyenne women and children at Sand Creek, Colorado, in 1864, and cutting out the genitalia of the women and stretching them over their saddlebows and wearing them on their hats during parades?

While the goal in establishing national standards is improving student achievement, the process does involve the federal government in curriculum development. It does open the door for the possibility of national standards constantly changing to meet new national objectives determined by politicians. These possibilities highlight three basic questions in curriculum development.

1. Who should decide what knowledge is of most worth?
2. What knowledge is of most worth?
3. What should be the goals of learning?

INSTRUCTION

While the curriculum of the public schools shifts with changing political and economic goals, the actual methods of instruction, despite attempts at reform, remain relatively constant. One reason is that to achieve social and economic goals, the schools must manage student behavior and learning. Certainly, allowing students freedom in learning would not ensure the achievement of the goals of most public school curricula. Even social reconstructionists want to manage students to achieve politically radical ends.

In *How Teachers Taught: Constancy and Change in American Classrooms 1890–1980,* Larry Cuban details the factors that made public-school instruction primarily teacher-centered as opposed to student-centered. Cuban, for the purposes of his history of instruction, defines *teacher-centered instruction* as occurring when teacher talk dominates the classroom, instruction is primarily given to the whole class as opposed to small groups or individuals, the teacher determines the use of classroom time, and the classroom is arranged in rows of desks facing the front of the room. On the other hand, Cuban describes the opposing *student-centered* tradition as occurring when student discussion of learning tasks is equal to or greater than teacher talk, instruction is individual or in small groups, students participate in determining the rules of the classroom, and instructional materials are available for students to use individually or in groups.

Cuban portrays the history of instruction as attempts by advocates of student-centered instruction to change, with modest success, the entrenched patterns of teacher-centered instruction. At the beginning of the century, the physical conditions of schools influenced patterns of instruction. Urban classrooms were constructed for forty and sixty students with bolted-down desks in rows facing the front of the room. The classroom organization was standardized between the 1890s and the 1920s by the architect for the New York Board of Education, C. B. J. Snyder, who according to Larry Cuban designed the standardized classroom based on a prescribed number of permanent desks ranging from forty and forty-eight for each school grade. In addition, teachers were poorly trained and often had to cover ten different subjects daily using textbooks and curricula prescribed by the central administration. The effect on teachers of large classes, arranged classrooms, prescribed textbooks and curricula, and many preparations for teaching, Cuban argues, was the continued reliance on teacher-centered instruction and textbooks as sources of knowledge. In addition to the physical and working conditions of teaching, social-efficiency ideas reinforced patterns of teacher-centered instruction. During the early part of the twentieth century, school administrators developed a mania for bureaucratic efficiency. Viewing the schools as factories, they stressed standardization and uniformity of instruction. Efficiency administrators compared themselves to factory managers, where power flowed from the top of the organization to the bottom. This meant that just as they believed administrators should control and dominate teachers, teachers should dominate and control students.

While working conditions and ideas of social efficiency reinforced patterns of teacher-centered instruction in the early twentieth century, advocates of student-centered instruction, led by John Dewey, began to press their reforms on the public schools. But, by and large, most of these instructional reforms were unable to penetrate the organizational structure of the public schools and received their greatest acceptance in private schools.

Cuban describes a number of attempts before 1940 to introduce student-centered instruction in public schools with the results being only minor and affecting only a few teachers. For instance, the New York City school system began in 1934 to experiment with what was called an *activity program*, which stressed teachers and students working together to select subject matter and learning activities, and a focus on the needs and interests of the students. In addition, classroom schedules were to be flexible with the standard teacher-dominated recitation being replaced by excursions, research, dramatization, and sharing. Controlled discipline was to be replaced by self-control. In 1942, after eight years of attempted instructional reform, it was estimated that only

25 percent of all city elementary schools incorporated activity methods in some classrooms. In a survey of New York teachers in the same year, 93 percent said they preferred conventional forms of instruction.

Between 1920 and 1940, Denver public schools were widely hailed as leaders of student-centered instructional reform. Under the leadership of four superintendents dedicated to the implementation of student-centered instruction, the school district emphasized teacher-constructed curricula, an activity program like that of the New York schools, and the project method. The *project method* involves students learning through the development of individual or group projects. In evaluating the effects of these reforms on high school teaching, Cuban found that only 20 percent of the classrooms during this period had extensive student-centered instruction.

In general, Cuban concludes, reforms based on student-centered instruction between 1920 and 1940 did not significantly change the instructional methods of American teachers because of the structure and organization of the schools. The primary method of instruction remained that of the teacher standing in front of the room, talking to the whole class, and questioning students who mainly listened to the teacher talk. Teachers retained control of the subject matter and manner of instruction.

While these standard practices remained, student-centered reforms, according to Cuban, did loosen up the atmosphere of the classroom. More student movement in the classroom was permitted, desks became movable, and there was less formal recitation characterized by students rising and speaking by their desks.

Following World War II, student-centered instruction came under attack as causing a deterioration of the academic standards considered necessary for winning the cold war with the Soviet Union. Advocates of student-centered instruction, including John Dewey, were accused by the extreme political right of being communists trying to undermine the country by destroying discipline and academic standards in the classroom. Even more-moderate observers claimed that the schools were made anti-intellectual by student-centered instructional methods. Consequently, advocates of student-centered instructional reforms made a hasty retreat and did not appear on the scene again until the late 1960s.

As described in the last section on curriculum, the late 1960s witnessed the growth of alternative schools based on differing forms of student-centered instruction. In the public schools, the major attempt to introduce student-centered instruction came in the form of the open classroom. Originally developed in England, the *open classroom* captured the imagination of many American educators in the 1960s and early 1970s. A flood of newspaper and journal articles and experiments in public school systems seemed to indicate that this instructional method would become a standard part of public-school systems. Indeed, many schools built during this period incorporated the principles of the open classroom into their design.

Like other forms of student-centered instruction, the open classroom emphasized active as opposed to passive learning, and student-directed learning as opposed to teacher-determined instruction. Classrooms were to be large open spaces divided into interest areas or learning centers. Each learning center was to contain a variety of learning materials. Students were to plan their own learning and move from interest station to interest station.

The open classroom movement quickly ended by the middle of the 1970s with demands for student discipline and an emphasis on basic subjects. Competency-based instruction replaced the open classroom movement. In the framework of *competency-based instruction*, teachers develop specific instructional objectives, develop methods to achieve those objectives, and measure the achievement of those objectives. Students learn discrete skills in incremental steps using preplanned instructional packages. The emphasis on measurement contributed to the rise in the importance of standardized testing. Often, this meant the standardized test had a controlling influence over the actions of the teacher and students.

Larry Cuban cites a number of examples of the organizational difficulties encountered in the introduction of student-centered learning in the 1960s and 1970s. For instance, consider the 1968 staff bulletin from the central administration of the New York public school system, which told teachers that students must raise their hands during recitation, they must ask permission to go to the bathroom, and they must regularly clean their desks under the supervision of a teacher. According to Cuban, one New York teacher during this period stated that students were whipped into shape by sitting at their desks for long hours and by using textbooks and notebooks to study formally organized lessons. Silence and good behavior were the standards of classroom conduct.

Cuban identifies three major reasons for the lack of significant change in instructional methods in American public-school classrooms in the twentieth century. The first is that public schools exist to serve larger social purposes to instill behaviors required by the prevailing economic system. This produces teaching practices that emphasize uniformity, authority, and other traits required by bureaucratic organizations. Student-centered instruction, on the other hand, develops traits of individual choice and expression that run counter to the demands of society on the public schools.

The second reason for the persistence of teacher-centered practices, according to Cuban, is the organizational structure of the public school. In most situations, teachers are expected to maintain control, use a textbook, and teach from a prescribed curriculum. Class size and structure inhibit the use of student-centered activities. Teachers find it convenient under these circumstances to have students seated according to a seating chart, to have students raise their hands and wait their turn before speaking, and to allow student movement only with the permission of the teacher. It is also most convenient for the teacher to instruct with lectures, seatwork, and homework using textbooks. Student-centered instruction, on the other hand, does not fit the organizational and structural requirements of the public school, is inconvenient for the teacher, and creates more work.

The third reason for the lack of change in instructional practices is the culture of teaching. According to Cuban, teachers are socialized to be conservative and resistant to change. In many cases their teaching is modeled on that of the teachers they had in school and on the teachers who supervised their student teaching. This modeling tends to perpetuate standard methods of instruction.

In addition, Cuban argues that teacher beliefs and administrative inept-ness contribute to a failure to change. Those teachers who believed in stu-dent-centered instruction did change their classroom practices, but large groups of teachers continued to believe in traditional methods. When at-tempts to implement student-centered instruction did occur, school adminis-trators, Cuban argues, failed to adequately carry through their plans.

For all these reasons, classroom instruction has changed little in the twentieth century. Classroom practices did soften with the introduction of movable chairs, the decline of the requirement that students stand by their desks when speaking, and the growth of informality between teachers and students. But, by and large, teachers continue to instruct from textbooks using planned lessons, and students remain passive learners.

CRITICAL PEDAGOGY

During the 1970s there developed new instructional methods based on the work of Brazilian educational philosopher Paul Freire. Compared in impor-tance to John Dewey and hailed as the leading educational philosopher of his time, Freire's book *Pedagogy of the Oppressed* provided a methodology for educating the world's oppressed peoples. In the framework of Kliebard's curriculum categories, Freire would be classified as a social reconstructionist interested in reforming the world. Freire's concerns go beyond the usual educational issues involved in providing equality of opportunity and equality of educational opportunity. He argues that most educational systems attempt to integrate oppressed people into the very social system that caused their oppression. Obviously, from Freire's perspective, this approach does not provide a permanent solution. His goal is to provide an educational meth-odology that will teach people to understand the economic and political forces determining the structure of society and will prepare them to work for social change.

The central focus of Freire's methods is to help people understand the world in which they live. For instance, one might display to a group of learners a picture of a common scene from their daily lives. Through a process of discussion, people take apart the elements of the scene. Out of this discussion there is developed a critical awareness of the social and political forces in society. In addition, words used by the participants to describe the scene become the basis for the development of reading material. Freire be-lieves that the learning of language can result in enslavement or freedom. When learning to read for freedom, reading is a means for understanding one's world.

An important role for the teacher is that of problem-posing. *Problem-posing* is directly related to the lives of students. Teachers pose problems about aspects of their students' lives. Students and teachers then engage in a dialogue about these problems and from this dialogue there emerge words that are frequently used by the students to describe their lives. These words become the basis for the teaching of reading. In this manner, there is a direct connection between learning how to read and learning how to think about one's world.

To begin this educational process, teachers must investigate the lives of their students. During Freire's early work in adult literacy, teachers would first explain their purpose and then spend time observing the lives of their students. The purpose of this observation is to discover themes in students' lives that can be used in a problem-posing dialogue. For instance, teachers in a small village or urban barrio, Freire states, should take notes on the way people talk, their behavior at church and work, and the general social life of the community. In the initial stages of this process, the teachers frequently gather to compare their observations. It is assumed that their initial observations are distorted by their own personal beliefs and knowledge.

The dialogue between the teachers helps to raise their consciousness about the social conditions being investigated and about the way in which they perceive the world. As in all Freirian-type dialogues, learning takes place at several levels. At one level, the teachers learn about their surrounding world. At another level, they learn how they think about the world. And, finally, they learn why they think about the world the way they do. Freire refers to this last process as reflection.

Reflection involves thinking about the consequences of one's actions and the causes for one's thinking. For instance, a person can make a choice to act in a certain manner. That action will have an effect on the world. In turn, the person can reflect on the impact of that choice and why he or she made the choice in the first place. This process then affects future choices which, in turn, become objects of reflection.

As teachers go through this process of reflection on their observations, they identify contradictions in the lives of their students that can be used in dialogues. These contradictions are then developed into what Freire calls codifications, such as sketches, photographs, dramatizations, and tape recordings. These codifications must reflect the real lives of the participants so that they can recognize the situations depicted within them. Also, they should not be overly explicit or be too obscure. Ideally, the codification will spark a dialogue that will lead to other themes in the lives of the students.

The purpose of the codification is to present students with a representation of their lives for the purpose of dialogue. For instance, a codification presented to tenement residents living in Santiago depicted a drunk staggering down the street and men conversing on the corner. In this situation, many of the tenement dwellers live in a culture of silence. Living in a culture of silence, people do not make their lives an object of reflection. They just act without reflecting on the reasons for their actions. In Freire's language, they are dehumanized. They are objects of history as opposed to being subjects of history. They do not make history; history makes them.

Many people living in a culture of silence, according to Freire, have never considered their lives as an object to be discussed. In presenting these codifications, Freire warns, teachers must not assume that they know reality. For instance, in the codification depicting the drunk, an educator might assume that the person is drunk because of unemployment or lack of virtue. In the actual dialogue, the investigator, who had selected the codification because he had identified alcoholism as a problem in the community, learned that the drunk was considered by the tenement dwellers to be a productive worker who turned to drink because of worries about low wages and supporting his family.

Freire argues that presentation of codifications causes participants to make explicit their consciousness of the world. The participants see how they act while analyzing a situation that they have experienced. For instance, the tenement dwellers in Santiago see how they act when they are drunk and at the same time they analyze the reasons for getting drunk. The process of analysis forces the participants to change their perception of their actions while drinking. This creates new perceptions and the development of new knowledge in the participants.

For example, originally, the participants might have gotten drunk without any thought given to the reasons and consequences. After the process of engaging in a dialogue about the codification of their behavior, the participants might now perceive their actions to be a result of their economic conditions. This perception would fundamentally alter their consciousness with regard to their own actions and the causes of alcoholism. The participants might then engage in reflection on their past perceptions and knowledge. Freire describes this process as "perception of the previous perception" and "knowledge of the previous knowledge." In other words, the participants reflect on why they originally gave little thought to the causes of their own drinking.

Out of the process of codification and dialogue emerge generative words to be used in teaching reading. These generative words must have pragmatic value in helping participants to break with their culture of silence. The generative words are words that participants use in describing their own reality. Of course, some consideration must be given to phonetic difficulty in selection of the initial generative words. Ideally, each new word added to vocabulary would be of increasing phonetic difficulty and would reflect an increasing level of consciousness. In the dialogue about the drunk walking up the street, the teachers might choose for reading instruction words such as *drunk, street, walk, work, wages,* and *family.* As the dialogue progresses, the participants might be introduced to words such as *alcoholism, exploitation, economics, tenement, employment,* and *unemployment.*

The process of learning these words also aids in heightening the consciousness of the students. These words stand as objects of a person's actions. To read or write about one's actions is a process of objectification. In this process of objectification, a person reflects on the action embodied in the word. This process of reflection can transform a person's future actions. For instance, if a person learns the words *drunk, low wages,* and *family* and the person is engaged in a dialogue about the reasons for drinking, then in the future he or she might consciously think of his or her desire for alcohol as resulting from low wages and poor living conditions. With these thoughts affecting their future actions, people might—at least Freire hopes—decide to engage in political actions that will eliminate the social causes of alcoholism. In other words, they will consciously engage in the reconstruction of the world.

One goal of reflection is expulsion of the oppressor from the consciousness of the participants. This reflective process begins with the question: Why did I think the way I did? In the case of the tenement dwellers the question might be: Why did I just accept a life of low wages and seek escape from my misery through alcohol? In reflecting on this question, participants would have to seek the reasons for their previous lack of awareness of how economic and social conditions caused drinking and why they never acted to change their conditions.

In summary, Freire identifies five stages in a dialogue about a codification. In the first stage, the participants simply describe what they see in the theme. In stage two, the teacher poses problems regarding the codified presentation. In the above example, the teacher might ask why the person is drunk and why other men linger on street corners. The problem-posing stage helps participants see their way of life as an object that can be discussed and as something that can be changed. In the third stage, the participants reflect on their previous state of silence regarding their culture. For instance, the participants might wonder why they had never questioned the heavy drinking by so many in their community, and why they never linked low wages and family problems as a cause of drinking. In the fourth stage, participants go through increasing levels of critical awareness as they come to understand how their lives and thinking were shaped by political and economic circumstances. And in the fifth stage, they eject the controlling influence of the oppressor from their minds.

THE TEXTBOOK

In February 1990, New York State Education Commissioner Thomas Sobol announced that he had joined forces with other states, including California, to create a curriculum that would guide textbook publishers. Of major concern was the presentation of African Americans, Hispanics, and Asian Americans in New York State's American history curriculum and in the nation's textbooks. Commissioner Sobol said, "I'm not talking about rewriting facts. Nobody wants to do that. But we ought to look at them from different perspectives."

New York, California, and Texas are large markets for textbooks and, therefore, strongly influence publishers' decisions. As private companies, textbook publishers are primarily interested in profit. It is cheaper to publish one edition of a textbook for the entire nation as opposed to many editions designed for individual school districts or states. Some states, such as California and Texas, have some form of statewide adoption of texts. As I will explain, this means that publishers must pay attention to changes in the political winds in these states.

In contrast to earlier in the century, African Americans, Hispanics, and Asian Americans are now important political groups in New York state politics. In previous times, New York state officials would have given little time to worrying about how these groups were treated in the state curriculum or in the nation's textbooks. But times change and political alignments change. Now the treatment of these groups is an important political issue.

Consequently, Commissioner Sobol appointed a panel of scholars and a watchdog advisory board to remove bias from the state's curriculum and to include greater recognition of African Americans, Hispanics, and Asian Americans. As possible changes, members of the New York Board of Regents suggested recognition in textbooks that George Washington's colonial militia included large numbers of African Americans and that in the nineteenth century Chinese railroad workers labored under slave conditions.

In addition to state governments, a number of national organizations try to influence textbook publishers. A group specifically organized for this purpose is People for the American Way. Contrary to the impression conveyed by its name, this is a politically liberal group claiming a membership of 277,000, which was created to combat the influence of the religious right on textbooks. An example of its tactics is a national mailing in 1989 asking recipients to send three enclosed postcards to leading publishers indicating support of inclusion of the theory of evolution in science textbooks. The letter warns, "The Far Right's objective is to force publishers to censor the theory of evolution and replace it with the biblical story of creation as scientific fact." The postscript to the letter pleads, "HELP ME STOP THE FAR RIGHT FROM CONTROLLING WHAT CHILDREN IN OUR PUBLIC SCHOOLS ARE TAUGHT."

As veterans of many textbook wars, leaders of People for the American Way know where to apply political pressure. In fact, as their letter states, they see themselves competing with the religious right for influence on two key state selection processes—California's and Texas's. "The censors [religious right] know," the letter advises, "that if they change textbooks in Texas and California—the two largest textbook buyers which account for more than 20% of the total national market—publishers will print those texts as *national editions*." The letter warns that officials in California are preparing to tell publishers what to include in textbooks and that the Texas State Textbook Committee will be meeting to select biology and science textbooks.

Members of People for the American Way know that textbook publishers try to avoid any controversy that might hurt sales. The reality is that very few administrators are willing to select for their schools textbooks that could cause controversy in the community. As I discussed in Chapter 7, often a local school superintendent walks a thin political line. Certainly, the desire to protect their jobs would cause administrators to avoid controversial situations. Recognizing this situation, publishers know that they will have a difficult time selling controversial books to local schools. In the words of the president of People for the American Way, Arthur Kropp, "To avoid controversy, publishers may downplay or eliminate ideas criticized by the censorship groups. They've caved in to Far Right pressure in the past."

Historically, writers and publishers know the role of controversy in destroying successful textbook series. For example, in the 1930s historian Howard Beale recorded these feelings of an author of American history texts: "In trying to guard against criticism and opposition, authors are driven to sins of omission and commission." After describing how he adds material of little importance to his history texts and deletes other material because of pressure from political forces, the textbook author told Beale, "And, if any author tells you he is not influenced by such pressure, that he tells 'the truth, the whole truth and nothing but the truth' as far as he knows it, don't you believe him. He is a conscious or unconscious liar."

Beale's study focused on the effect of state legislation and outside interest groups on textbook publishing in the 1920s and 1930s. As part of the study, he interviewed authors and publishers. One head of a publishing firm described the publisher's dilemma as, "He wants to tell the truth, and have his authors do the same. Yet he must sell books." Beale followed this quote with the summary statement, "Therefore even the most honest publishers must modify books to remove 'objectionable' features that will hurt sales, yet at the same time save their own and the author's consciences, and withal rationalize their business reasons into scholarly ones and never admit to the public that they change texts for the sake of sales."

Historically, one of the most important textbook controversies occurred in the early 1940s over Harold Rugg's social studies textbooks. The attacks on the Rugg books caused a dramatic decline in sales and sent a warning to the textbook industry. At the peak of their popularity in 1938 annual sales were 289,000. Six years later the annual sales plummeted to 21,000 copies. The series was based on the idea that children should be educated to assume intelligent control of their institutions and environment. The books did not advocate communism or socialism, but they did argue that intelligence should be applied to planning the economy and operating public institutions.

The first major attacks against the Rugg textbooks came from the Hearst newspapers and B. C. Forbes, financial writer and founder of *Forbes Magazine*. Forbes conducted his campaign against the books at both the national and local level. As a member of the school board of Englewood, New Jersey, Forbes unsuccessfully tried to have the books removed from the community's schools. At the national level, Forbes conducted his attack through articles in *Forbes Magazine* and in columns for the Hearst newspapers. His opening salvo in *Forbes Magazine* came in August of 1939 with an article that called Rugg's books, "viciously un-American . . . he [Rugg] distorts facts to convince the oncoming generation that America's private-enterprise system is wholly inferior and nefarious." In words that must have made the textbook industry tremble, Forbes wrote, "I plan to insist that this anti-American educator's textbooks be cast out . . . I would not want my own children contaminated by conversion to Communism." In his column for the Hearst newspaper chain in 1940, Forbes asked the question every week: "Are too many educators poisoning the minds of the young generation with prejudiced, distorted, unfair teachings regarding the American system of economy and dazzling them with overly-rosy pictures of conditions in totalitarian countries?"

The Advertising Federation of America joined the battle in early 1940 with a pamphlet titled "Facts you Should Know about Anti-Advertising Propaganda in School Textbooks." The pamphlet was specifically directed at the Rugg books, which contained lessons about why consumers should look out for false advertising claims. As an example of what the federation believed was an attempt to turn students against advertising, the pamphlet cited the opening section of a chapter on advertising in one of Rugg's books, which begins,

> Two men were discussing the merits of a nationally advertised brand of oil. "I know it must be good," said one. "A million dollars' worth of it is sold each year. You see advertisements of that oil everywhere."
>
> The other shook his head. "I don't care how much of it is sold," he said. "I left a drop of it on a copper plate overnight and the drop turned green. It is corrosive and I don't dare to use it on my machine."

The pamphlet issued by the Advertising Federation objected to this anecdote because it was hypothetical and bred distrust among students of widely advertised products.

In April of 1940, the president of the Advertising Federation issued a letter to large advertisers that opened: "Advertised products are untrustworthy! That is the lesson taught to the children in 4,200 school systems by a social science textbook of Professor Harold Rugg of Teachers College, Columbia University."

The combined attack of Hearst newspapers, *Forbes Magazine*, the Advertising Federation, and patriotic organizations resulted in dramatic actions by school boards. In September 1940, *Time* magazine reported that the members of the Binghamton, New York, school board called for a public burning of Rugg's textbooks. Also, *Time* reported, "But last fortnight Rugg book burnings began to blaze afresh in the small-town, American Legion belt. In rapid succession the school boards of Mountain Lakes and Wayne Township, N.J., banished Rugg texts that had been used by their pupils nearly ten years. Explained Wayne Township's board member Ronald Gall: 'In my opinion, the books are un-American but not anti-American. . . .'"

Particularly dramatic were the events in Bradner, Ohio, where the community divided over the issue of teaching communism in the schools. According to a Cleveland newspaper account of the events, "The rural Red hunt . . . has resulted in: explosion of a dynamite charge and the burning of a fiery cross in front of the home of . . .[the] school board president." The explosions and cross burning were accompanied by the spectacle of school board members shoving books into the school furnace.

The anticommunist hysteria typified by the crusade against Rugg's books continued into the post–World War II period. Not only textbooks, but school administrators and teachers were targeted by the religious and political right. The censorship of textbooks and books in school libraries remained a favorite method for assuring that a particular ideology would be disseminated by the schools. By the 1980s, the religious and political right listed environmentalist and profeminist statements as forbidden items in public school textbooks.

The role of the religious and political right in textbook censorship, and the important and subtle issues that are raised about textbooks is exemplified in the testimony of Mel Gabler at the 1986 meeting of the Texas State Textbook Committee. Having spent many years criticizing textbooks in all parts of the country, Gabler and his wife are always vigilant for any sign of anti-Americanism, attacks on free-enterprise economics, and suggestions that federal controls might be needed to protect the environment.

Gabler complained to the committee about the treatment of the American revolution in school texts. From his perspective, the War was not a revolution but an instance of colonial obedience to British law. As Gabler argued before the committee, "In other words, the colonists were obeying the laws. Actually, it was Parliament that was breaking the law. Parliament was passing laws contrary to the British rights, the British Constitution."

The way in which U.S. history is interpreted in the public schools profoundly affects the way in which American students view their country. An interpretation that presents the colonial break with Britain as revolutionary creates the image of the United States as the first modern revolutionary power and as a leader of democratic revolutions in the rest of the world. Gabler's interpretation creates an image of a nation of law-abiding citizens whose primary concern is with protection of rights under a system of laws. These two views of history have striking implications for the conduct of foreign policy, the shaping of American attitudes toward other nations, and the development of political culture.

Gabler also complained about a text that "treats agricultural problems, on a number of pages, as something to be solved by government, rather than as problems that government helped to create by interfering with the free market." He appealed to Texas state law which requires that texts for grades seven through twelve advocate the free-enterprise system. This law opens the door to debates over whether an item in a textbook is for or against the free-enterprise system.

This kind of debate is generated by other state textbook laws. Consider the Texas law stating that "Textbooks shall not contain material which serves to undermine authority." On the basis of this law, Lee Gaynier, a nurse, raised objections at the 1986 meeting of the Texas Textbook Committee to a health book's definition of euthanasia because it made the act seem palatable. Gaynier reasoned, "Taking someone's life intentionally is murder. Murder is illegal. The book is teaching that murder is acceptable under certain circumstances, which is in violation of the General Content Requirement and Limitations [on undermining authority]."

Therefore, the selction of textbooks by some states, state legislation, and the activities of both liberal and conservative pressure groups result in highly politicized textbooks. Of course, textbooks do not have that appearance. In most cases, textbooks appear to be bland and boring compendiums of facts containing no political messages. In part, this appearance is caused by the wish of textbook publishers to avoid controversy. On the other hand, imbedded in the blandness are facts and ideas that are the product of a whole host of political debates and decisions.

There are common threads in the history of attacks on public school textbooks in the twentieth century. Throughout the century, the religious right fought the presentation of the theory of evolution in science textbooks. In recent years, the religious right lobbied to place the doctrine of creationism alongside theories of evolution. The removal of any hints of political and economic radicalism from school books topped the list of efforts of so-called patriotic organizations. Of course, special interest groups, such as the Advertising Federation in the 1940s, attempt to have favorable messages included in school textbooks. In addition, other organizations attempt to counteract the activities of the religious and political right, such as People for the American Way. For many years the American Civil Liberties Union fought efforts to censor textbooks.

In conclusion, the question of who should control knowledge in a democratic society can be asked specifically about curriculum, instruction, and textbooks. The battles that transpire, particularly over the curriculum and the content of textbooks, are often unnoticed by the general public. In fact, I encounter very few public school students who are aware that the contents of their textbooks are determined by political decisions.

The question of who should control can be considered in the context of the "Educational Chair" described in Chapter 7. The reader will recall that the imaginary Educational Chair has the ability to implant knowledge in the mind of the person sitting in it. If you were seated in it, who would you want to exercise control over the chair? Who would you want to determine the curriculum you study, the method of instruction by which you learn, and the knowledge to which you are exposed?

EXERCISES

1. Working alone or in small groups, plan a curriculum for an elementary or high school class in U.S. history. In planning this curriculum answer the following questions:
   a. What are the goals of the curriculum? Do these goals fit into any of the categories created by Kliebard?
   b. What are the boundaries of the history curriculum? Does your history curriculum include social, political, economic, and intellectual history?
   c. What cultural perspective wil be used in the curriculum?
2. Working alone or in small groups and using Freire's methodology,

develop a codification to be used to make students in your class aware of the political determination of knowledge in school textbooks.

3. Working in small groups, do a comparison of each group member's memories of the methods of instruction each of them encountered as a student. Each group should rate each method according to its effectivenss.

4. Working in small groups or alone, compare the interpretation of education given in this textbook to other textbooks used for introductory courses in education.

SUGGESTED READINGS AND WORKS CITED IN CHAPTER

Beale, Howard. *Are American Teachers Free?* New York: Scribner, 1936. This is a study of the political pressures placed on teachers and textbook publishers in the 1920s and 1930s.

"Book Burnings: Rugg Texts." *Time* (9 September 1940): 64–65. This is a news report of the burning of Rugg's texts by school districts.

Brown, Dee. *Bury My Heart at Wounded Knee: An Indian History of the American West.* New York: Henry Holt and Company, 1970. This is an excellent example of a U.S. history book written from the perspective of a non-European American.

Cornbleth, Catherine. "Controlling Curriculum Knowledge: Multicultural Education and Policy in New York State." This paper was prepared for the symposium, "Multicultural Education: History, Politics, and the Management of Knowledge," presented at the annual meeting of the American Educational Research Association, San Francisco, April 1992. This paper contains organizational affiliations linking the head of the project to develop national standards in history, Charlotte Crabtree, to the neoconservative movement in education.

Cuban, Larry. *How Teachers Taught: Constancy and Change in American Classrooms, 1890–1980.* White Plains, N.Y.: Longman, 1984. A study of how teachers actually taught in classrooms in American public schools.

Dworkin, Martin, ed. *Dewey on Education.* New York: Teachers College University Press, 1959. A collection of Dewey's writings including Dewey's 1952 statement on the effect of progressive education on the public schools as quoted in this chapter.

Fitzgerald, Frances. *America Revised: History Schoolbooks in the Twentieth Century.* Boston: Little, Brown, 1979. This is a history of history textbooks that depicts the major debates and changes in content in these public school texts.

Freire, Paulo. *Pedagogy of the Oppressed.* New York: Continuum, 1970. This is the basic text in critical pedagogy.

Kliebard, Herbert M. *The Struggle for the American Curriculum 1893–1958.* Boston: Routledge and Kegan Paul, 1986. Kliebard's history of curriculum in the twentieth century stresses the conflict among social-efficiency advocates, humanists, social meliorists, and developmentalists.

Sack, Kevin. "Regents Vote to Revise Teaching of History." *New York Times* (17 February 1990): 129. Article discusses New York State's Education Commissioner's plan to revise American history curriculum and textbooks.

Spring, Joel. *Conflict of Interests: The Politics of American Education.* White Plains, N.Y.: Longman, 1988. Chapter 6 of this book, "The Knowledge Industry," discusses the politics of publishing and testing. Quotes from the 1986 Texas Textbook Committee are taken from this chapter.

Viadero, Debra. "First National Standards Bring Anxiety to Social-Studies Educators." *Education Week* (2 December 1992): 5. A discussion of the initial reaction of educators to national standards in history, geography, and civics.

―――. "Standards Setters Search for Balance Between Excellence, Equity." *Education Week* (23 September 1992): 21. Article discusses some of the issues in establishing national standards.

―――. "U.S. Awards Grants to Help Set Standards in Civics, Geography." *Education Week* (5 August 1992): 36. This article discusses the initial grants for creating national standards in civics and geography.

Weisman, Steven. "Japan and the War: Debate on Censors Is Renewed." *New York Times* (8 October 1989): 8. This article discusses the debate in Japan over the teaching of World War II.

West, Peter. "Academy Unveils 'Principles' for Science Standards." *Education Week* (4 November 1992): 10. This article outlines the important questions regarding national standards, including differential standards, boundaries of a discipline, and cultural perspective.

CHAPTER 11

The Courts and the Schools

Court decisions affect every aspect of schooling. Constitutional issues are involved in school activities ranging from student publications to the selection of books for the school library. One result is the involvement of the courts in the control and regulation of public schools.

Only a limited number of constitutional issues involving the school are discussed here. Court decisions are being made every day, and legal issues are daily becoming more complex. Anyone planning a career in teaching should make a full investigation of the rights and responsibilities of both teachers and students. Education law is at present a whole field of study, and many lawyers are becoming specialists in education issues as school systems spend increasing amounts of time in the courts.

Many court cases involve the First and Fourteenth Amendments to the U.S. Constitution. As mentioned in Chapter 9 on the federal control of education, there is nothing in the federal Constitution dealing specifically with education. But the Fourteenth Amendment does say that states cannot take away any rights granted to an individual as a citizen of the United States. This means that although states have the right to provide schools, they cannot in their provision of schools violate citizen rights granted by the Constitution. The wording of Section 1 of the Fourteenth Amendment is extremely important in a variety of constitutional issues related to education:

> All persons born or naturalized in the United States, and subject to the jurisdiction thereof, are citizens of the United States and of the State wherein they reside. No state shall make or enforce any law which shall abridge the privileges or immunities of citizens of the United States; nor shall any State deprive any person of life, liberty, or property without due process of law; nor deny to any person within its jurisdiction the equal protection of the laws.

These few lines have a great deal of meaning for state-provided and state-regulated schools. For instance, "no state shall make or enforce any law which shall abridge the privileges or immunities of citizens of the United

States" means that the courts can protect the constitutional rights of students and teachers particularly with regard to freedom of speech and issues related to religion. The line that reads, "nor shall any State deprive any person of life, liberty, or property without due process of law" is called the *Due Process Clause* and is invoked in cases involving student suspensions and teacher firings. Since states provide schools to all citizens, they cannot dismiss a student or teacher without due process. As we shall see later in this chapter, the courts established guidelines for student dismissals.

All the protections of the Fourteenth Amendment depend on the states making some provision for education. Once a state government provides a system for education, it must provide it equally to all people in the state. Thus, under the Fourteenth Amendment, the state cannot "deny to any person within its jurisdiction the equal protection of the laws." This is the *Equal Protection Clause* and it is invoked in cases involving equal educational opportunity. If a state provides an educational system it must provide equal opportunity for all citizens to use the schools.

The Equal Protection Clause is central to cases involving school segregation, non-English-speaking children, school finance, and children with special needs. You will recall from an earlier chapter that the famous *Brown* v. *Board of Education of Topeka* decision in 1954 centered on whether segregated schools were "equal." Prior to that decision, the Supreme Court had ruled that segregated schools were constitutional as long as they offered an equal education. The importance of the 1954 case was the decision that segregated schools were *inherently* unequal.

As you can see from the preceding discussion, the Fourteenth Amendment allows for constitutional protection in the schools. What is of considerable importance, and generates controversy, is the protection of the rights granted in the First Amendment:

> Congress shall make no law respecting an establishment of religion, or prohibiting the free exercise thereof; or abridging the freedom of speech, or of the press; or the right of the people peaceably to assemble, and to petition the Government for a redress of grievances.

The section of the First Amendment dealing with the establishment of religion, the *Establishment Clause*, plays an important role in decisions regarding school prayer and religious exercises in the schools. The section dealing with laws prohibiting the free exercise of religion, the *Free Exercise Clause*, is important when religious groups claim that public schools interfere with their religious practices or that public schools are teaching something that is offensive to their religious beliefs.

There is a thin line between not allowing the establishment of religion and interfering with the free exercise of religion. For instance, as we shall see later in this chapter, the U.S. Supreme Court prohibits school prayer because it involves the government in the establishment of religion. On the other hand, groups defending school prayer claim that the Court's decision interferes with their free exercise of religion.

The same problem plagues the issue of freedom of speech. On the one hand, the courts recognize the importance of protecting the free speech of students and teachers; on the other hand, the courts recognize the necessity for maintaining order in schools and for school boards to exercise control over teachers. This dilemma also exists in the interpretation of the Eighth Amendment, which reads: "Excessive bail shall not be required, nor excessive fines imposed, nor cruel and unusual punishments inflicted." But when does punishment of a student become "cruel and unusual" punishment? This, as we shall see later in the chapter, is a major issue in court cases dealing with corporal punishment. The first of these issues I will discuss is the tension between compulsory education and religious values.

COMPULSION AND RELIGION

Since their founding, public schools have been in conflict with religious groups. The Establishment Clause of the First Amendment to the U.S. Constitution states that "Congress shall make no law respecting an establishment of religion, or prohibiting the free exercise thereof." The problem is that many religions believe education cannot be separated from religion. Both education and religion are concerned with the moral and social development of the individual. Religion, education, and the First Amendment come into conflict when certain religious groups are forced to send their children to school and conform to the practices of the school, and when religious groups demand that the schools engage in certain religious practices, such as school prayer. In the first case, forced attendance and compliance with school regulations can be an infringement on an individual's right to practice religion, if school practices conflict with religious beliefs. In the second case, religious activities in public schools can mean that the government is giving support to particular religious practices.

The first major U.S. Supreme Court case dealing with the conflict between compulsory schooling and religious freedom is *Pierce* v. *Society of Sisters* (1925). The case originated in 1922 when Oregon passed the Compulsory Education Act, which required every parent, guardian, or other person having control or charge or custody of a child between 8 and 16 years of age to send the child to a public school. The act was clearly an attempt to close parochial schools by forcing all children to attend public schools. Two private schools in Oregon immediately obtained injunctions against Governor Pierce and Oregon state officials.

The First Amendment was not directly involved in the case because the law affected both religious and nonreligious private schools. The Supreme Court did indirectly support the guarantee of religious liberty, however, by maintaining the right to choose a religious school in preference to a public school. The Court stated that the "fundamental theory of liberty upon which all governments in this Union repose excludes any general power of the State to standardize its children by forcing them to accept instruction from public teachers only."

The Supreme Court ruling in *Pierce* v. *Society of Sisters* was based on an earlier ruling involving a Nebraska law requiring that all subjects in private and public schools be taught in the English language. The purpose of the law was to curb German nationalism during World War I by limiting the use of foreign languages. In *Meyer* v. *Nebraska*, the law was declared unconstitutional, but the court did recognize the right of the teacher "to teach and the right of parents to engage him so to instruct their children." The importance of the *Meyer* decision was the recognition of the parental right to direct the upbringing of their children within the reasonable limitations of the law.

In *Pierce* v. *Society of Sisters* these rights were again confirmed in declaring the 1922 Oregon law unconstitutional. The Court stated: "Under the doctrine of *Meyer* v. *Nebraska* . . . we think it entirely plain that the Act of 1922 unreasonably interferes with the liberty of parents and guardians to direct the up-bringing and education of children under their control." But the Court did not recognize the complete control of the parents and guardians over the education of their children. The Court very clearly defined the power of the states with regard to education.

Probably the most important part of the *Pierce* decision, besides declaring that children could not be forced to attend public schools, was the recognition of the power of the state to regulate education and compel students to attend school. The Court stated: "No question is raised concerning the power of the State reasonably to regulate all schools, to inspect, supervise and examine them, their teachers and pupils; to require that all children of proper age attend some school." Besides recognizing the right of regulation and requirements to attend, the Court also recognized the right of the state to certify teachers and regulate the curriculum with regard to citizenship studies. The Court ruled that the state had the right to require "that teachers shall be of good moral character and patriotic disposition, that certain studies plainly essential to good citizenship must be taught, and that nothing be taught which is manifestly inimical to the public welfare."

These qualifications to the *Pierce* decision placed important limitations on the right of parents and guardians to direct the education of their children. The state had the right to force attendance at an educational institution that met state requirements with regard to teachers, curriculum, and other reasonable standards. The only right recognized for parents was the choice between public and private schools, and this right was limited by the ability to pay for private schooling. The unresolved issue was what would happen if the state standards used to regulate public and private schools were in conflict with religious practices and the state required attendance at a state-accredited school. This is the problem that the Amish encountered.

The Amish are a subgroup of the Anabaptist-Mennonite tradition that has refused to be assimilated into the mainstream of American society and the modern urban and industrial world. They first came to America in the eighteenth century and settled in eastern Pennsylvania in compact communities. They retained in America their original European dress style of men wearing black clothes and wide-brimmed hats and women wearing capes and aprons. In areas of Pennsylvania, Ohio, Indiana, Iowa, and Wisconsin, communities of Amish continue to exist with traditional religious practices, clothes, and community living. The Amish continue to use horse-and-buggies for transportation and avoid the use of electricity and telephones.

One of the major threats to the Amish way of life is the public school and compulsory education. The public school threatens the destruction of the Amish community by the teaching of values contrary to its traditions and by the introduction of the children to modern styles of life. For the Amish, this threat can occur in areas that might seem unimportant to other people. For instance, one objection of Amish parents to compulsory high school attendance is the requirement that girls wear shorts for physical education, which is in serious violation of Amish beliefs. In the nineteenth century the Amish began to object to the rise of public schools. In an article entitled "From Erlanback to New Glarus" in a book he edited titled *Compulsory Education and the Amish*, Albert N. Keim quotes a nineteenth-century Amish leader: "The righteousness that counts before God is neither sought nor found in the public or free schools; they are interested only to impart worldly knowledge, to ensure earthly success and to make good citizens of the state."

The Amish particularly object to public high school because of its broader curriculum and preparation for a vocation or college. The Amish do their own vocational training within their communities. In addition, the Amish object to what is considered the modern education of the twentieth century. Amish education stresses following instructions, respecting authority, and mastering basic information. The Amish disapprove of education that stresses critical thinking and asking questions. Obedience to authority and tradition are seen as essential for the survival of the community.

New Glarus, Wisconsin, was the scene of the final confrontation between the Amish and compulsory-education laws. In 1968 public school authorities insisted that the Amish community comply with a Wisconsin law requiring school attendance until 16 years of age. The county court upheld the school authorities. The Amish appealed the case to the Wisconsin Supreme Court, which rejected the lower court's decision and ruled that compulsory schooling of Amish children beyond the eighth grade was a violation of the free exercise of religious rights. In 1972 the U.S. Supreme Court in *State of Wisconsin, Petitioner* v. *Jonas Yoder et al.* upheld the Wisconsin Supreme Court decision.

In the *Yoder* decision the U.S. Supreme Court placed some limitations upon the right of a state to compel school attendance, as recognized in *Pierce* v. *Society of Sisters*. The Court stated that in the *Pierce* decision there was recognition given that the "values of parental direction of the religious upbringing and education of their children in their early and formative years have a high place in our society." In addition the Court argued that a state's interest in universal education should not be at the sacrifice of other rights, specifically those of the First Amendment. In the words of the Court: "We can accept it as settled, therefore, that however strong the State's interest in universal compulsory education, it is by no means absolute to the exclusion or subordination of all other interests."

The *Yoder* decision also placed limitations on state educational require-ments. The Court stated that there were two primary arguments for maintain-ing a system of compulsory education. One argument was the necessity for citizens to be prepared to participate intelligently in an open political system. The other argument was that education was necessary to prepare people to be self-reliant and self-sufficient in society. The Court clearly stated with regard to these two arguments: "We accept these propositions." The Court then went on to argue that the requirement that the Amish attend school beyond the eighth grade did not aid in the achievement of the above educational goals. The Court stated that the Amish community was a highly successful social unit and its members were productive and law-abiding. Education within the community therefore appeared to fulfill the state interests in education.

The importance of the 1972 *Yoder* decision is in the placing of First Amendment religious freedoms above those of the state's interest in educa-tion. This would mean that in the future any conflict between religious practices and compulsory schooling would be decided in favor of individual religious freedom. The decision also requires that, in any future cases dealing with compulsory schooling, the state must show some relationship between its educational requirements and standards and its interest in educating self-sufficient and intelligent citizens. State standards cannot be arbitrary and unrelated to these objectives.

The U.S. Supreme Court also protects First Amendment rights when required practices in the schools come into conflict with religious beliefs. This decision involved objections of the Jehovah's Witnesses to saluting and pledging allegiance to the flag. The case began in the early 1940s, when the West Virginia Board of Education ordered that the flag salute become a regular part of the school program and that all teachers and pupils be required to salute the flag and say the Pledge of Allegiance. Refusal to participate was to be viewed as an act of insubordination, and pupils who failed to conform were to be expelled from school. Pupils expelled from school were considered delinquent and could possibly be sent to juvenile reformatories.

The Jehovah's Witnesses object to the flag ceremony because they believe that the obligations imposed by the law of God are superior to the laws of government. One of the laws of God taken literally by Jehovah's Witnesses is, "Thou shall not make unto thee any graven image, or any likeness of any-thing that is in heaven above, or that is in the earth beneath, or that is in the water under the earth; thou shalt not bow down thyself to them nor serve them." Jehovah's Witnesses believe that the flag is an image and refuse, for religious reasons, to salute it.

The U.S. Supreme Court ruling in *West Virginia State Board of Education* v. *Barnette* declared the West Virginia School Board ruling unconstitutional because of its abridgment of First Amendment freedoms. In its decision the Court went beyond the issue of protection of religious practices to the issue of protection within public schools of all constitutional privileges. The Court argued: "That they are educating the young for citizenship is reason for scrupulous protection of Constitutional freedoms of the individual, if we are not to strangle the free mind at its source and teach youth to discount important principles of our government as mere platitudes." Within the same framework, the Court emphasized that patriotic exercises should not be made compulsory. In the words of the Court: "To believe that patriotism will not flourish if patriotic ceremonies are voluntary and spontaneous instead of a compulsory routine is to make an unflattering estimate of the appeal of our institutions to free minds."

Another controversial issue is religious practices in schools. There is a great deal of pressure to introduce religious practice into schools in the form of Bible reading, prayer, and meditation. All three practices are in conflict with the Establishment Clause of the First Amendment.

School Prayer, Bible Reading, and Meditation

Many religious groups were outraged by the school-prayer decision in *Engel v. Vitale* (1962). The decision denied the right of a public school system to conduct prayer services within school buildings during regular school hours. Those groups of people who are angered by the decision argue that it made education godless, and they seek an amendment to the Constitution that would allow for prayer ceremonies in the school. The Court decision against school prayer was primarily based on the argument that school prayer involved the state in the establishment of religion. This is considered a violation of the Establishment Clause of the First Amendment.

The school-prayer case began in New York when a local school system was granted the right by the New York Board of Regents to have a brief prayer said in each class at the beginning of the school day. The prayer, considered to be denominationally neutral, read: "Almighty God, we acknowledge our dependence upon Thee, and we beg Thy blessings upon us, our parents, our teachers and our country." The New York courts granted the right of local school systems to use this prayer. The one requirement was that a student could not be compelled to say the prayer if the student or parents objected.

It was the decision of the New York courts against which the U.S. Supreme Court ruled in *Engel* v. *Vitale*. One of the major objections of the Court was the fact that government officials wrote the prayer. This seemed to put the government directly in the business of establishing religion. The Court stated that "in this country it is not part of the business of government to compose official prayers for any group of the American people to recite as a part of the religious program carried on by government." The Court reviewed the early history of the United States, and the struggle for religious freedom and the ending of government support of churches. The Court argued: "By the time of the adoption of the Constitution, our history shows that there was a widespread awareness among many Americans of the dangers of a union of

Church and State." The writing of a prayer by government officials ran counter to this long-standing struggle in the United States.

The Court rejected the argument that the school-prayer law did not violate any rights because it did not require students to recite the prayer and the prayer was nondenominational. The Court argued that this confused the right of free exercise of religion with the prohibition against the state establishing and supporting religion. Excusing students from reciting the prayer might protect their free exercise of religion, but the very existence of the prayer involved the establishment of religion. In the words of the Court: "The Establishment Clause, unlike the Free Exercise Clause, does not depend upon any showing of direct governmental compulsion and is violated by the enactment of laws which establish an official religion whether those laws operate directly to coerce nonobserving individuals or not."

The Court applied the same reasoning to the issue of Bible reading in the public schools. In *Abington School District* v. *Schempp* (1963), the issue was a Pennsylvania law that permitted the reading of ten verses from the Bible at the opening of each public school day. The verses were to be read without comment, and any child could be excused from reading the verses or attending the Bible reading, upon the written request of the parents or guardians. Like the school-prayer issue, the Court felt that a Bible-reading service of this type involved the state in the establishment of religion. The Court made it clear that it did not reject the idea of Bible reading as a part of a study of comparative religion or the history of religion. Nor did the Court exclude the possibility of studying the Bible as a piece of literature. What the Court objected to was the reading of the Bible as part of a religious exercise.

The courts are somewhat ambivalent on the issue of meditation in schools. Massachusetts passed a law requiring a moment of silence "for meditation or prayer" in public schools. In this case, the Court said that meditation could refer to any subject because the law used the word "or" which implied a secular intent for meditation. Therefore, a student might be expected to meditate on anything, including schoolwork or family life. In this situation, the law was not in violation of the Establishment Clause.

A Louisiana law allowing meditation was struck down as a violation of the Establishment Clause. In this case, the law included the permission for teachers to ask students if they were interested in praying. An Alabama law allowing for meditation or voluntary prayer and for teachers to lead classes in prayer was also ruled in violation of the Establishment Clause. The argument in this case was that the law lacked a secular purpose and that it was intended to support school prayers.

The test in all these cases is whether the intent is secular or religious. If the intention is found to be religious, then it is a violation of the Establishment Clause.

In 1992 the U.S. Supreme Court, in a dispute originating over prayers given by a Rabbi at a middle-school graduation in Providence, Rhode Island, ruled that prayers conducted at a public school graduation were unconstitutional. Writing for the majority of the Court in *Lee* v. *Weisman*, Supreme Court Justice Anthony Kennedy declared:

> The Constitution forbids the state to exact religious conformity from a student as the price of attending her own high school graduation.
>   No holding by this Court suggests that a school can persuade or compel a student to participate in a religious exercise. That is being done here, and it is forbidden by the Establishment Clause of the First Amendment.

PUBLIC AID TO PRIVATE SCHOOL STUDENTS

The U.S. Supreme Court cases dealing with religion and the schools touch on one of the most difficult aspects of establishing a public school system in a culturally and religiously diverse country. Most religious groups believe that religious instruction should be a part of the education of children and adolescents. But the public schools cannot open their doors to religious groups because not all religious groups are in agreement about basic beliefs and what should be taught. In addition to the practical problem of antagonistic religious beliefs in the schoolhouse, there are clear constitutional prohibitions against state support of religion and interference with religious practices.

But recognizing practical problems and constitutional prohibitions does not solve the problem for people who believe that religious instruction should be a part of education. The *Pierce* decision provides some relief by allowing parents to send their children to private schools. Private schools can conduct religious services and provide religious instruction. The major limitation on this right is that the family must be able to afford the cost of private schooling. If families cannot afford private schooling, and if they believe their children should be given a particular religious instruction, then their rights are limited by the fact that state-provided public schools offer the only free education that is available.

Those who want religion to be a part of education are put in a bind because of the constitutional prohibition against religious services and instruction in the public schools, and the prohibition against state support of private religious schools. There have been several attempts to provide indirect means to support private schools. The one method through which indirect support for private school students can be provided is called the "child-benefit theory."

The child-benefit theory was articulated by the U.S. Supreme Court in *Cochran* v. *Louisiana State Board of Education* (1930). At issue in this case was a Louisiana law permitting the purchase and distribution of textbooks to all schoolchildren. Under this law textbooks were provided to children attending private religious schools. The U.S. Supreme Court affirmed the Louisiana Supreme Court ruling that the law did not sanction the support of religious schools. Taxpayers' money was spent to purchase books that went directly to schoolchildren. The law existed for the benefit of children, not for the support of religious institutions.

The same reasoning was involved in the U.S. Supreme Court decision *Everson* v. *Board of Education* (1974), which allowed public support of school transportation for parochial students. In this case the support again went directly to the child and not to a religious institution. The Court stated: "We cannot say that the First Amendment prohibits . . . spending tax-raised funds to pay the bus fares of parochial school pupils as a part of a general program under which it pays fares of pupils attending public and other schools."

In a suprise decision in 1983, the U.S. Supreme Court made it possible for states to allow deductions from state income taxes for educational expenses including tuition, textbooks, and transportation. In the past, similar laws had been found to violate the Establishment Clause of the First Amendment. What was different in this particular situation was that the law recognized expenses for both public and private schools.

The decision, *Mueller* v. *Allen* (1983), concerned a Minnesota law that allowed state taxpayers to take deductions from gross income for expenses incurred for "tuition, textbooks, and transportation" for dependents attending elementary and secondary schools. The law allowed a $500 deduction for each dependent attending elementary schools and a $700 deduction for those attending junior and senior high schools.

The U.S. Supreme Court gave several reasons for its decision. First, the Court argued that the deductions were only one among many deductions. For instance, Minnesota law allowed taxpayers to deduct for medical expenses and charitable contributions. The Court stated, "The Minnesota legislature's judgment that a deduction for education expenses fairly equalizes the tax burden of its citizens and encourages desirable expenditures for educational purposes is entitled to substantial deference."

Second, and more important, the Court believed that the inclusion of public schools in the allowance for tax deductions avoided the pitfalls of previous attempts by states to provide aid to private schools. For instance, in *Committee for Public Education* v. *Nyquist* (1973) the Court found a New York law in violation of the Establishment Clause because it provided tuition grants only to parents of children in nonpublic schools. In the case of the Minnesota law, the Court noted, "Most importantly, the deduction is available for educational expenses incurred by *all* parents, including those whose children attend public schools and those whose children attend nonsectarian private schools or sectarian private schools." The fact that the law benefited a broad spectrum of groups, the Court felt, meant that it had a primarily secular effect.

Mueller v. *Allen* is important because it makes it possible for states to provide an indirect means of support to private schools. It also has important implications for state funding of public schools. It opens the door for local public-school systems to charge students for tuition and textbooks, with reimbursement for parents through state tax deductions. In some states this might be limited by state constitutions that require provision of free public education. The decision also might make it possible for the federal government to provide vouchers or tuition tax credits if they apply to both private and public schools.

Secular Humanism and the Religion of Public Schools

An interesting set of court cases in the 1970s and 1980s involved claims that the public schools taught a religion, *secular humanism,* which could be a violation of the rights of those not subscribing to secular-humanist values. The issue arose over state regulation of private schools. During the latter part of the 1970s and into the 1980s, the fastest-growing private schools were those identified as "Christian." These usually were associated with a fundamentalist Christian organization. At first, people outside the movement assumed the growth of Christian schools was a result of "white flight" from desegregated school systems. But when Christian schools began to multiply in rural areas of Wisconsin and Alaska, where segregation was not an issue, it became evident that the movement was a result of strongly held religious values.

Problems began in the Christian-school movement when state authorities demanded that the schools conform to state minimum educational standards. Most state minimum standards are not a small list of requirements but a vast set of statutes and regulations covering everything from the design of the water fountain to the curriculum. Christian schools did not have any problems with regulations related to the safety of school buildings, but they did object to curriculum requirements that interfered with the Christian objectives of their schools.

Of primary concern were state regulations that required the schools to teach ethical values that the Christian schools called *secular humanism.* The simplest definition of secular humanism is that it comprises a set of ethical standards that place primary emphasis on a person's ability to interpret and guide his or her own moral actions. This is in opposition to the Christian-fundamentalist viewpoint, which holds that the source of ethical and moral values should be the Bible and God. Secular humanism relies on the authority of human beings, while Christian fundamentalism relies on the authority of the Scriptures.

One of the earliest and most famous cases dealing with the issue was decided by the Ohio Supreme Court in 1976 in *State* v. *Whisner.* The case originated when Levi Whisner opened the doors of the Tabernacle Christian School in Bradford, Ohio, in 1973. The issue for Pastor Whisner was not whether the school met minimum state standards, but whether he should even apply for a charter from the state. Keep in mind the fact that compulsory-education laws in most states require attendance at a school approved by the state. If the student does not attend an approved school, the student can be considered truant and the parents and student held liable for the truancy.

James Carper of Tulane University reported in a paper delivered at the 1980 meeting of the American Educational Studies Association that after reading the 149-page *Minimum Standards for Ohio Elementary Schools, Revised 1970,* "Whisner and the governing board of the school concluded that as a matter of religious principle they could not conform to all of the standards and, therefore, decided not to initiate the prescribed procedures for obtaining a charter." The consequence of that action was immediately felt by the parents and their children when, within a month of the school's opening, the local probation officer sent out letters informing the parents that if their children did not attend a school that met minimum standards, a complaint against the parents would be filed in the local juvenile court. In November, two months after the opening of the school, fifteen parents were indicted by the county prosecutor's office for not sending their children to school. After some negotiation, the trial date was set for May 7, 1974.

Professor Carper wrote: "The trial court proceedings revealed again that to the state the primary issue was noncompliance with state law while the defendants believed that free exercise of religion was at the heart of the matter." One point revealed in the first trial was that the Ohio Department of Education required total compliance with state minimum standards and that one of those standards was a written statement of philosophy of education. The interesting question raised by this standard was how conflicts between a school's statement of philosophy and other department standards would be resolved. It was revealed during the trial that "if the statement of a school's philosophy of education, a mandated standard, ran counter to other minimum standards and made it impossible to fully embrace them, the department would not approve the school."

In August 1974, the trial court found the fifteen parents guilty; after an appeal, the Supreme Court of Ohio agreed to hear the case in October 1975. On July 28, 1976, the Supreme Court of Ohio reversed the lower court's decision and argued that Pastor Whisner and the appellants had "sustained their burden of establishing that the 'minimum standards' infringe upon the right guaranteed them by the First Amendment to the Constitution of the United States, and by Section 7 of the Ohio Constitution, to the free exercise of religion."

This decision gave legal recognition to the argument that the state minimum standards did require the teaching of a philosophy, secular humanism, which was in conflict with the religious values of the appellants. To understand this conflict it is best to review some of the specific points in the state's minimum standards objected to by Pastor Whisner.

Alan Grover, in his book *Ohio's Trojan Horse: A Warning to Christian Schools Everywhere,* provides a detailed summary of Whisner's objections to the minimum standards. For our purposes, I will deal with only a few of these objections, as a means of highlighting the issue of secular humanism. In Grover's words, "The 'Minimum Standards' philosophy points to the wisdom and self-sufficiency of man in finding solutions to all of society's problems." This, of course, is contrary to the belief that humans need the

Scriptures and God to deal with social problems. As examples of the Ohio minimum standards' emphasis on the wisdom and self-sufficiency of humans, Grover cited the following statements from the standards:

> Problems are solved by group discussion and decision. Man's comprehension of the present and his wisdom in planning for the future depend upon his understanding of the events of the past and of the various forces and agencies in society that influence the present. Through all time and in all regions of the world, man has worked to meet common basic human needs and to satisfy common human desires and aspirations. The health of the child is perhaps the greatest single factor in the development of a well-rounded personality. (The objection to this is the belief that the spiritual condition of the individual is more important.)

All statements quoted above were taken from the curriculum section of the state standards. What should be remembered is that the state required compliance with all standards and, consequently, Pastor Whisner considered compliance a violation of his religious beliefs. This particular case has opened the door to similar cases in other states and has made it possible to argue that compulsory attendance at a public school might be a violation of religious freedom. And it was certainly clear in the mind of Pastor Whisner that the public schools taught the religion of secular humanism.

In 1986, suit was brought by a group of parents against the Hawkins County School District in Tennessee for requiring students, on threat of suspension, to read from the Holt, Rinehart and Winston's basic reading series. Specifically, the parents objected to selections in the readers from *The Wizard of Oz, Rumpelstiltskin,* and *Macbeth.* The fundamentalist parents claimed that the textbook series contained explicit statements on secular humanism and taught values contrary to the religious beliefs of their children. In the words of presiding U.S. District Judge Thomas Gray Hull, "The plaintiffs believe that, after reading the entire Holt series, a child might adopt the views of a feminist, a humanist, a pacifist, an anti-Christian, a vegetarian, or an advocate of a 'one-world government.'"

In the decision, *Mozert et al.* v. *Hawkins County Public Schools* (1986), Judge Hull argued that the beliefs of the defendants were sincere and that by suspending the students the school district was denying them a right to an education because of the exercise of free speech. In addition, the school district provided no evidence of a compelling reason for requiring students to read the textbook series. In fact, the judge dismissed as bureaucratic the school district's argument that it was necessary for classroom instruction to require all students to use the same textbooks.

Consequently, he required the school district to allow students who were offended by the material in the textbook series not to participate in reading instruction. In his words, "During the normal reading period, the student-plaintiffs shall be excused from the classroom and provided with suitable space in the library or elsewhere for a study hall."

In 1987, a Sixth Circuit Court of Appeals reversed the decision by giving more emphasis to the state's interest in educating children as opposed to the students' right to free exercise of religion. This implies that any future cases will depend on whether participation in a particular part of a curriculum is necessary for achieving a compelling state interest. For instance, courts recognize a state's interest in teaching children how to read or preparing them for citizenship.

Cases dealing with secular humanism highlight the struggle over the values taught in public schools. In a broader framework, it is difficult to imagine how public schools could meet the conflicting demands of differing religious and ethical systems. The conflict over values in public schools places a burden on teachers. As I will discuss in the next section, there is often a conflict between the rights of teachers and the expectation of the school system that teachers will conform to community values.

TEACHERS' RIGHTS

During the nineteenth and early twentieth centuries, schoolteachers were expected to be models of purity. Pressure was placed on teachers to be circumspect outside the school with regard to dress, speech, religion, and types of friends. Within the school, a teacher's freedom of speech was abridged at the whim of the school administrator. Some school administrators allowed teachers to discuss controversial topics freely within the classrooms; others fired teachers who spoke of things within the classroom that were not approved by the administration. Very often, teachers were fired for their political beliefs and activities.

During the last several decades, court actions, the activities of teachers' associations, and state laws granting teachers tenure expanded academic freedom in the public schools and protected the free speech of teachers. The expansion of academic freedom in the United States first took place at the college level and later in elementary and secondary schools. The concept of academic freedom was brought to the United States in the latter part of the nineteenth century by scholars who received their training in Germany. The basic argument for academic freedom was that if scientific research was to advance civilization, scholars had to be free to do research and to lecture on anything they felt was important. The advancement of science depended on free inquiry. In Germany this was accomplished by appointing individuals to professorships for life.

The concept of academic freedom was not immediately accepted in institutions of higher education in the United States. Many professors were fired in the late nineteenth and early twentieth centuries for investigating certain economic problems and for backing reforms such as child labor laws. College professors found it necessary to organize the American Association of University Professors (AAUP), to fight for academic freedom. The major protection of academic freedom in American universities is provided by tenure. The idea behind tenure is that after individuals prove they are competent as teachers and scholars, they are guaranteed a position until retirement, as long as they do not commit some major act of misconduct.

Tenure and academic freedom are supported by the NEA and AFT as ways of protecting the free speech of public school teachers. Many states adopted tenure laws for the express purpose of protecting the rights of teachers. Court decisions also played an important role in extending academic freedom. But there are major differences between the way academic freedom functions at the university level and how it functions at the secondary and elementary levels. The organizational nature of public schools and the age of children in them places some important limitations on the extent of teachers' academic freedom.

Before they teach in the public schools, it is important for teachers to understand their rights and the limitations of their rights. There are three major types of rights about which teachers must be concerned. The first deals with the rights and limitations of speech and conduct of teachers in relationship to administrators and school boards. The second deals with rights and limitations of the speech of teachers in the classroom. And the third deals with the rights of teachers outside the school.

The most important U.S. Supreme Court decision dealing with the rights of teachers in relationship to school boards and administrators is *Pickering* v. *Board of Education of Township High School* (1967). The case involved an Illinois schoolteacher dismissed for writing a letter to the local school board criticizing the district superintendent and school board for the methods being used to raise money for the schools. The letter specifically attacked the way money was being allocated among academic and athletic programs, and stated that the superintendent was attempting to keep teachers from criticizing the proposed bond issue. In court it was proved that there were factually incorrect statements in the letter.

The U.S. Supreme Court ruled that teachers could not be dismissed for public criticism of their school system. In fact, the Court argued in *Pickering*: "Teachers are, as a class, the members of a community most likely to have informed and definite opinions as to how funds allotted to the operation of the schools should be spent. Accordingly, it is essential that they be able to speak out freely on such questions without fear of retaliatory dismissal." In this case, the participation of teachers in free and open debate on questions put to popular vote was considered "vital to informed decision making by the electorate."

The Court did not consider the factual errors in the public criticism grounds for dismissal; it did not find that erroneous public statements in any way interfered with the teacher's performance of daily classroom activities or hindered the regular operation of the school. "In these circumstances," the Court stated, "we conclude that the interest of the school administration in limiting teachers' opportunities to contribute to public debate is not significantly greater than its interest in limiting a similar contribution by any member of the general public."

The *Pickering* decision did place some important limitations on the rights of teachers to criticize their school system. The major limitation was on the right to criticize publicly immediate superiors in the school system. In the words of the Court, immediate superiors were those whom the teacher "would normally be in contact with in the course of his daily work." The Court, however, did not consider the teacher's employment relationship to the board of education or superintendent to be a close working relationship. One could imply from the decision that teachers could be dismissed for public criticism of their immediate supervisor or building principal. But what was meant by "close working relationship" was not clearly defined in the decision. The Court stated in a footnote: "Positions in public employment in which the relationship between superior and subordinate is of such a personal and intimate nature that certain forms of public criticism of the superior by the subordinate would seriously undermine the effectiveness of the working relationship between them can also be imagined."

There is a possible procedural limitation on a teacher's right to criticize a school system if the school system has a grievance procedure. This issue is dealt with in a very important book on teachers' rights published under the sponsorship of the American Civil Liberties Union (ACLU). The question is asked in David Rubin's *The Rights of Teachers:* "Does a teacher have the right to complain publicly about the operation of his school system even if a grievance procedure exists for processing such complaints?" The answer given by this ACLU handbook is "probably not." The handbook states that this issue has not been clarified by the courts, but there have been suggestions in court decisions that if a formal grievance procedure exists within the school system, a teacher must exhaust these procedures before making any public statements.

The Rights of Teachers also argues that a teacher is protected by the Constitution against dismissal for bringing problems in the school system to the attention of superiors. But, again, the teacher must first exhaust all grievance procedures. The example in the ACLU handbook was of a superintendent who dismissed a teacher because her second-grade class wrote a letter to the cafeteria supervisor asking that raw carrots be served rather than cooked carrots, because of the higher nutritional value of the raw vegetable. In addition, when the drinking fountain went unrepaired in her classroom, her students drew pictures of wilted flowers and of children begging for water, and presented them to the principal. The ACLU handbook states that the court decision found "the school policy was arbitrary and unreasonable and in violation of . . . First and Fourteenth Amendment rights of free speech and freedom peaceably to petition for redress of grievances."

With regard to freedom of speech in the classroom, one of the most important things for public elementary and secondary teachers to know is that the courts seem to recognize certain limitations. The three things that the courts consider is whether the material used in the classroom and the statements made by the teacher are *appropriate for the age of the students, related to the curriculum for the course, and approved by other members of the profession.*

An example of the courts considering the age of students, given by the ACLU in *The Rights of Teachers,* is a case in Alabama where a high school teacher had been dismissed for assigning Kurt Vonnegut's "Welcome to the

Monkey House" to her eleventh-grade English class. The principal and associate superintendent of the school called the story "literary garbage," and several disgruntled parents complained to the school. School officials told the teacher not to use the story in class. The teacher responded that she thought the story was a good literary work and felt she had a professional obligation to use the story in class. The school system dismissed her for insubordination. The first question asked by the Court was whether the story was appropriate reading material for eleventh-grade students. In its final decision, the Court found that the teacher's dismissal was a denial of First Amendment rights, since it had not been proved that the material was inappropriate for the grade level or that the story disrupted the educational processes of the school.

Another important issue is whether the classroom statements of a teacher are related to the subject matter being taught. One example given in *The Rights of Teachers* is of a teacher of a basic English class making statements about the Vietnam War and anti-Semitism, although the lessons dealt with language instruction. The Court found that his remarks had minimum relevance to the material being taught, but might have been appropriate in courses such as current events and political science. What is important for teachers to know is that their freedom of speech in the classroom is limited by the curriculum and subject being taught.

Whether the method used by the teacher is considered appropriate by other members of the teaching profession appears to be another consideration of the courts. In a case in Massachusetts, an eleventh-grade English teacher wrote an example of a taboo word on the board and asked the class for a socially acceptable definition. The teacher was dismissed for conduct unbecoming a teacher. The teacher went to court and argued that taboo words were an important topic in the curriculum and that eleventh-grade boys and girls were old enough to deal with the material. The ACLU handbook states that the court ruled that a teacher could be dismissed for using in good faith a teaching method "if he does not prove that it has the support of the preponderant opinion of the teaching profession or of the part of which he belongs."

In addition to the question of academic freedom regarding curriculum and instruction, there is the issue of teachers' freedom of conscience. For instance, a New York high school teacher was dismissed from her job for refusing to participate in a daily flag ceremony. The teacher stood silently while a fellow teacher conducted the ceremony. In *Russo* v. *Central School District No. 1* (1972), a federal circuit court ruled in favor of the teacher. The U.S. Supreme Court refused to review the case and, therefore, the circuit court decision was allowed to stand. The circuit court ruled that the teacher's actions were a matter of conscience and not disloyalty.

While teachers do not have to participate in flag ceremonies and or say the Pledge of Allegiance if it is a violation of their conscience, they cannot refuse to follow the curriculum of a school because of religious and personal beliefs. In *Palmer* v. *Board of Education* (1979), the U.S. Court of Appeals decided, and the decision was later upheld by the U.S. Supreme Court, that the Chicago public schools had the right to fire a teacher for refusing to follow the curriculum because of religious reasons. The teacher was a member of the Jehovah's Witnesses and she informed her principal that because of her religious beliefs she refused "to teach any subjects having to do with love of country, the flag or other patriotic matters in the prescribed curriculum." The Court declared, "the First Amendment was not a teacher license for uncontrolled expression at variance with established curricular content."

In summary, teachers do not lose their constitutional rights when they enter the classroom, but their employment does put certain limitations on those rights. Of fundamental importance is the requirement that teachers follow the prescribed curriculum of the school. Teachers have freedom of speech in the classroom as long as their comments are related to the curriculum. In addition, when exercising the right to freedom of speech teachers must consider whether their comments are appropriate for the age of the students and would be considered appropriate by other educational professionals. While teachers are required to follow a prescribed curriculum, they do not have to participate in flag ceremonies and other political ceremonies if it is a violation of their personal beliefs.

THE LIABILITY OF TEACHERS

Is a teacher liable for monetary damages if a student is seriously injured by rocks thrown by another student? The answer in some situations is yes! In the above example, Margaret Sheehan, an eighth-grade student, was taken along with other female students by their teacher to an athletic field. The teacher told them to sit on a log while she returned to school. During her absence, a group of boys began throwing rocks at the girls, resulting in serious injury to Margaret's eye. In *Sheehan* v. *St. Peter's Catholic School* (1971), the Minnesota Supreme Court declared: "It is the duty of a school to use ordinary care and to protect its students from injury resulting from the conduct of other students under circumstances where such conduct would reasonably have been foreseen and could have been prevented by the use of ordinary care."

The issue of teacher liability for student injuries is extremely important because of the potential for the teacher being sued for monetary damages. To protect themselves in these types of situations, it is important for teachers to carry some form of professional liability insurance. Often, this insurance coverage is provided by teachers' unions. In some cases, teachers might want to contact their insurance agents about coverage.

In *Teachers and the Law*, Louis Fischer, David Schimmel, and Cynthia Kelly state that teachers can be held liable for student injuries under the following conditions:

1. The teacher had a duty to not injure the student and to protect the student from injury;
2. The teacher did not use due care;
3. The teacher's carelessness caused the accident;
4. The student sustained provable injuries.

TEACHERS' PRIVATE LIVES

Another concern is teachers' activities outside the school. A controversial issue is whether a teacher's membership in a radical political organization is grounds for dismissal or denial of employment. The two most important U.S. Supreme Court decisions on this issue both originated in cases resulting from New York's Feinberg Law. The Feinberg Law was adopted in New York in 1949, during a period of hysteria about possible communist infiltration of public schools. The law ordered the New York Board of Regents to compile a list of organizations that taught or advocated the overthrow of the U.S. government by force or violence. The law authorized the Board of Regents to give notice that membership in any organization on the list would disqualify any person from membership or retention in any office or position in the school system.

The first decision concerning the Feinberg Law was given by the U.S. Supreme Court in *Adler* v. *Board of Education of New York* (1952). This ruling upheld the right of the state of New York to use membership in particular organizations as a basis for not hiring and for dismissal. The Court argued that New York had the right to establish reasonable terms for employment in its school system. The Court also recognized the right of a school system to screen its employees carefully because, as stated by the Court, "A teacher works in a sensitive area in a schoolroom. There he shapes the attitude of young minds toward the society in which they live. In this, the state has a vital concern." The Court went on to state that not only did schools have the right to screen employees with regard to professional qualifications but also, "the state may very properly inquire into the company they keep, and we know of no rule, constitutional or otherwise, that prevents the state, when determining the fitness and loyalty . . . from considering the organizations and persons with whom they associate."

The *Adler* decision underwent major modification when the Feinberg Law again came before the U.S. Supreme Court fifteen years later in *Keyishian* v. *Board of Regents of New York* (1967). In this case a teacher at the State University of New York at Buffalo refused to state in writing that he was not a communist. This time the Court decision declared the Feinberg Law unconstitutional. The reasoning of the Court was that membership in an organization did not mean that an individual subscribed to all the goals of the organization. The Court stated: "A law which applies to membership, without the specific intent to further the illegal aims of the organization, infringes unnecessarily on protected freedoms. It rests on the doctrine of guilt by association which has no place here."

The *Keyishian* decision did not deny the right of school systems to screen employees or to dismiss them if they personally advocated the overthrow of the U.S. government. What the *Keyishian* decision meant was that mere membership in an organization could not be the basis for denial of employment or for dismissal.

Whether a teacher's private life can be a basis for dismissal from a school system has not been clearly defined by the U.S. Supreme Court. The American Civil Liberties Union argues in *The Rights of Teachers* that courts are increasingly reluctant to uphold the right of school authorities to dismiss teachers because they disapprove of a teacher's private life. Examples given by the ACLU include an Ohio court ruling that a teacher could not be dismissed for using offensive language in a confidential letter to a former student. The Ohio court ruled that a teacher's private actions are not the concern of school authorities unless they interfere with the ability to teach. The California Supreme Court ruled that a teacher could not be dismissed because of a homosexual relationship with another teacher. The court could not find that the relationship hindered the ability to teach.

It would appear that the major concern of the courts is whether teachers' private lives interfere with their professional conduct as teachers. But the difficulty of establishing precise relationships between private actions and ability to teach allows for broad interpretation by different courts and school authorities. Teachers should be aware that there are no precise guidelines in this area. The best protection for teachers is to develop some form of agreement between their teachers' organization and their school district with regard to the use of private actions as a basis for dismissal and evaluation.

One of the limiting conditions applied by the U.S. Supreme Court to the actions of teachers and students is whether the activity interferes with normal school activities. For instance, in *Board of Education* v. *James* (1972) the U.S. Supreme Court upheld a lower court ruling that a teacher could not be dismissed for wearing an armband in class as a protest against the Vietnam War. The lower court reasoned that the wearing of the armband did not disrupt classroom activities and therefore, there was no reason for school authorities to limit a teacher's freedom of expression. The reasoning in this case was similar to that in the landmark case dealing with the rights of students, *Tinker* v. *Des Moines Independent School District* (1969), which will be discussed in the next section.

STUDENT RIGHTS

The *Tinker* case originated when a group of students decided to express their objections to the war in Vietnam by wearing black armbands. School authorities in Des Moines adopted a policy that any student wearing an armband would be suspended. When the case was decided by the U.S. Supreme Court, clear recognition was given to the constitutional rights of students. The Court stated that a student "may express his opinion, even on controversial subjects like the conflict in Vietnam. . . . Under our Constitution, free speech is not a right that is given only to be so circumscribed that it exists in principle but not in fact."

One extremely important condition is placed on the right of free speech of students and that is the possibility of disruption of the educational process. The Court does not provide any specific guidelines for interpreting this condition and limitation. What it means is that school authorities have an obligation to protect the constitutional rights of students and, at the same time, an obligation to assure that there is no interference with the normal activities of the school.

In recent years, student rights were limited by claims of interference with the educational purposes and activities of schools. A federal appellate court ruled that a school administration can disqualify a student campaigning for student body president because of remarks about the vice principal and school administration. The appellate court reasoned that the administration's educational concerns allowed it to censor comments that might hurt the feelings of others. This form of censorship taught students to respect others.

In *Hazelwood School District* v. *Kuhlemier* (1988), the Supreme Court ruled that school administrators have the right to control the content of school-sponsored publications because they are part of the curriculum. The case involved a newspaper published by the journalism class at Missouri's Hazelwood High School. The newspaper contained articles about student pregnancies and students from divorced families. False names were used to protect the students interviewed for the articles. The school's principal objected to the articles because the interviewed students might be identifiable to other students and he considered the sexual discussions inappropriate for high school students. The authors of the articles responded that both divorce and pregnancy were appropriate topics for modern youth and that they were widely discussed among students.

The right of school administrators to censor student publications was expanded to include all school activities. School administrators have the right to refuse to produce student plays, to prohibit student publication of articles that are poorly written and vulgar, and to ban student expression that advocates drugs, alcohol, and permissive sex. In censorship cases of this type, the legal test is whether or not the school administration's actions are based on legitimate educational concerns.

School authorities are also allowed to punish student speech that they consider to be "lewd and indecent." In *Bethel* v. *Fraser* (1986), the U.S. Supreme Court ruled that school administrators in the Bethel, Washington, school system could punish a high school senior, Matthew Fraser, for giving a nominating speech at a school assembly that used an "elaborate, graphic, and explicit sexual metaphor." The Court said that school officials have the right to determine what is vulgar and offensive in the classroom and at school activities, and to prohibit vulgar and offensive speech. This decision did not apply to speech about political, religious, educational, and public policy issues. It was limited to the issue of indecent speech.

In *Franklin* v. *Gwinnett* (1992), the U.S. Supreme Court ruled that students who were victimized by sexual harassment and other forms of sexual discrimination could sue for monetary damages. The case involved a Georgia high school student who was sexually harassed and abused by a teacher. This decision was made in the context of Title IX, which bars discrimination on the basis of gender. The school district was required to conform to Title IX. In making its decision, the U.S. Supreme Court relied on a previous decision barring supervisors from sexually harassing a subordinate. The Court extended this ruling to include teachers and students.

One of the more complicated First Amendment cases to be decided by the U.S. Supreme Court involved balancing the right of students to have access to books in the school library with the right of the school board to decide which books should be in the school library. The case, *Board of Island Union Free School District* v. *Steven A. Pico* (1982), involved the removal of books from the school library by the board of education because the content of the books was considered unsuitable for high school students. The issue originated when several members of the board of education attended a conference of a politically conservative organization of parents concerned with educational legislation in the state of New York. While they were at the conference the board members received a list of books considered morally and politically inappropriate for high school students. Upon returning from the conference the board members investigated the contents of their high school library and discovered nine books that had been on the list. Subsequently, the board ordered the removal of the books from the library shelves. The books included: *Best Short Stories of Negro Writers*, edited by Langston Hughes; *Down These Mean Streets*, by Piri Thomas; *The Fixer*, by Bernard Malamud; *Go Ask Alice*, of anonymous authorship; *A Hero Ain't Nothin but a Sandwich*, by Alice Childress; *Naked Ape*, by Desmond Morris; *A Reader for Writers*, by Jerome Archer; *Slaughterhouse Five*, by Kurt Vonnegut, Jr.; and *Soul on Ice*, by Eldridge Cleaver.

In rendering its decision the Supreme Court gave full recognition to the power of school boards to select books for the school library, and to the importance of avoiding judicial interference in the operation of local school systems. On the other hand, the Court recognized its obligation to assure that public institutions do not suppress ideas. In this particular case, there was a clear intention to suppress ideas by making decisions about book removal based upon a list from a political organization.

The Supreme Court's method of handling the above dilemma was to recognize the right of the school board to determine the content of the library, as long as its decisions on content were not based on partisan or political motives. In the words of the Court, "If a Democratic school board, motivated by party affiliation, ordered the removal of all books written by or in favor of Republicans, few would doubt that the order violated the constitutional rights of the students denied access to those books." In another illustration, the Court argued, "The same conclusion would surely apply if an all-white school board, motivated by racial animus, decided to remove all books authored by blacks or advocating racial equality and integration." Or, as the Court more simply stated, "Our Constitution does not permit the official suppression of ideas."

On the other hand, the Court argued that books could be removed if the decision were based solely on their "educational suitability." The Court also limited its decision to apply only to books removed from school library shelves, not to decisions about books added to the shelves. In summary, the Court stated, "We hold that local school boards may not remove books from school library shelves simply because they dislike the ideas contained in those books and seek by their removal to prescribe what shall be orthodox in politics, nationalism, religion, or other matters of opinion."

As I will discuss in the next section, students also have rights related to school attendance. These rights are tied to the concept of education as property.

SCHOOLING AS A PROPERTY RIGHT

A student's "property interest" in education is the result of a state statutory entitlement to a public education. The right to attend public schools is usually conferred on children by state law. This law, of course, can vary from state to state.

Property interest and the right to an education were major considerations of the U.S. Supreme Court in dealing with due process and suspensions from school in *Goss* v. *Lopez* (1975). This case dealt with suspensions from school of junior and senior high school students. The Court ruled that due process "requires, in connection with a suspension of 10 days or less, that the student be given oral or written notice of the charges against him and, if he denies them, an explanation of the evidence the authorities have and an opportunity to present his side of the story." The Court based its decision on "legitimate claims of entitlement to public education" as given in state law. What this meant was that a student's right to an education could not be taken away in an arbitrary manner.

The *Goss* decision established a precedent that due process is required before a school-dismissal decision. R. Lawrence Dessem, in a 1976 article in the *Journal of Law and Education,* "Student Due Process Rights in Academic Dismissals from the Public Schools," argues that in the future the due-process requirement might be applied to cases involving dismissal from school for academic reasons. The *Goss* decision dealt only with suspension for disciplinary reasons. In either case there seems to be a clear obligation upon school authorities to guarantee due process for all students.

Dessem outlines in his article the basic procedures that must take place to assure due process for students. First, there must be an attempt to make all decisions on the basis of fact. Second, there must be some provision to guarantee future review of any decisions. And third, just procedures must be followed in reaching any decisions.

In practice, these three procedures mean very specific things. A student must be provided with a notice detailing the charges, and the notice must be received in sufficient time for the student to prepare answers to the charges. A student must be given the chance to present answers to the charges in a hearing before an unbiased group. Dessem argues that schools cannot be required to have groups outside the school conduct the hearings because of the expense. Dessem states: "A hearing before a panel of disinterested teachers and school administrators would seem to strike an acceptable balance between the right of the student to an impartial arbitrator and the school's interest in keeping the expense and inconvenience of such hearings to a minimum." Students do have a right to have the decision based only on the evidence presented.

In *Goss*, the U.S. Supreme Court did place a limit on the procedural elements of due process by refusing to require that students be given the right to call witnesses and have legal counsel. "The Supreme Court's rationale," states Dessem, "for refusing to mandate this and several other procedures was that since 'brief disciplinary suspensions are almost countless, to impose in each such case even truncated trial type procedures might well overwhelm administrative facilities in many places.'"

The *Tinker* decision has provided some protection for the freedom of speech of students in public schools, and the *Goss* decision has provided protection from arbitrary dismissal of students from public schools. Both decisions represent the continuing expansion of civil liberties granted under the Constitution of the United States. Teachers and other school authorities have a duty and an obligation to ensure that these rights are protected. Teachers also have an obligation to protect their constitutional rights, thereby serving as models for students and setting an example for interpreting the meaning of civil liberties in the United States.

DO SCHOOL AUTHORITIES HAVE THE RIGHT TO BEAT CHILDREN?

Consider the following situations and compare your opinions with the decisions of the courts. Assume the following set of circumstances: The family of a child cannot afford private schooling. Due to compulsory-education laws, the family is forced to send the child to a local public school where the primary means of discipline is corporal punishment. The parents do not believe in the use of physical punishment, have never used physical punishment at home, and do not want the public school to use physical punishment on their child. In this situation, can school authorities spank the child? Can the child be forced to attend an institution that gives its personnel the right to use physical punishment, contrary to practices in the child's home?

Part of the answer to these questions was given in the U.S. Supreme Court decision *Ingraham* v. *Wright* (1977). A junior high school student, James Ingraham, in Dade County, Florida, refused to let the principal of his school, Willie Wright, paddle him for not leaving the stage of the school auditorium promptly. (Ingraham claimed that he had left the stage when requested by the principal.) When Ingraham refused to be paddled, Principal Wright called in his two assistant principals, who held Ingraham's legs and arms. The student was hit twenty times on the buttocks with a two-foot-long wooden paddle. His mother examined him when he arrived home and immediately took him to a local hospital, where the doctor prescribed pain pills, ice packs, and a laxative, and recommended that Ingraham stay home for a week.

At a Florida trial court hearing, many other students complained about beatings at the school. Children described being pushed up against urinals in the boys' bathroom and being beaten on the legs, back, and across the neck. One boy described how he refused to take a whipping because he felt he was innocent, and was beaten with a board across the head. Within a few days of the beating, the student underwent an operation to have a lump removed from his head; he claimed a subsequent loss of memory.

After a week-long trial, the Florida court granted the defense a motion for dismissal, arguing that there was no showing of severe punishment and that corporal punishment was not unacceptable according to the standards of contemporary society. This ruling was overturned by the Fifth Circuit Court of Appeals on the grounds that the punishment at the junior high school violated the Eighth Amendment's prohibition against "cruel and unusual punishment." A further appeal reversed this ruling and set the stage for a decision by the U.S. Supreme Court.

On April 19, 1977, the U.S. Supreme Court ruled that the Cruel and Unusual Punishment Clause of the Eighth Amendment does not apply to corporal punishment, nor does the Due Process Clause of the Fourteenth Amendment require that notice be given to students before they are subjected to corporal punishment. The Court argued that corporal punishment is the traditional means of maintaining discipline in the public schools, and that although public opinion is divided on the issue, there does not seem to be any trend to eliminate its use. The Court found no reason for extending the Eighth Amendment to the schools.

The Court felt that community pressure and common-law safeguards should be used to ensure that corporal punishment be used in a reasonable manner. This argument paralleled the lower court's argument that in this particular case, criminal charges could be brought against the junior high school principal and assistant principal. In other words, public school authorities can beat children, but the extent of the punishment must be reasonable.

Determining what is "reasonable" creates a difficult problem for courts and the community. A teacher or administrator who inflicts one or two spankings a year without causing any lasting physical damage would be considered "reasonable." But what about the teacher or principal who paddles so violently that students are left with black-and-blue marks? A principal of a Kentucky high school, in a recent lecture at my university, argued that administrators and teachers who use corporal punishment excessively exhibit behavior usually associated with child abusers.

But what if parents object to the use of corporal punishment? A decision regarding this issue was made by the Fourth Circuit Court of Appeals on May 9, 1980, in *Hall* v. *Tauney*. Thomas Flygare describes this case in the September 1980 issue of the *Phi Delta Kappan*. A West Virginia grade-school student was, in Flygare's words, "repeatedly and violently struck on the hip and thigh by a teacher using a homemade hard rubber paddle about five inches in width. She alleged that as a result of this paddling she was hospitalized for 10 days and has received the treatment of specialists for possible permanent injuries to the lower spine."

Since argument in terms of Eighth Amendment's Cruel and Unusual Punishment Clause had failed in the *Ingraham* case, Hall's lawyers decided to use a different tactic. The lawyers argued that the paddling, as Flygare states, "violated the right of her parents to determine the means by which she could be disciplined."

The Fourth Circuit Court ruled that parents had no constitutional right to exempt their children from corporal punishment in the schools. The statement of the court raised a whole host of issues regarding the power of parents versus the power of the school. Reflect on the statement by the court that "the state interest in maintaining order in the schools limits the rights of particular parents unilaterally to except their children from the regime to which other children are subject."

THE LANGUAGE OF THE SCHOOLS

As I discussed in Chapters 6 and 9, bilingual education is a political issue over which Republicans and Democrats are divided. Confusion over court decisions contributed to these political tensions. Some people feel that the court decisions opened the door for primary instruction to take place in a foreign language or "black English." This is not the case. Court rulings are quite clear that the primary task of the schools is to teach standard English, and that other languages and black English are to be used as a means to achieve that goal.

The landmark case is the 1974 U.S. Supreme Court decision in *Lau et al.* v. *Nichols et al.* The case was a class-action suit brought in behalf of non-English-speaking Chinese students in the San Francisco School District. The complaint was that no special instruction for learning standard English was provided to these students. The complaint did not ask for any specific instructional methods to remedy this situation. In the words of the Court decision: "Teaching English to the students of Chinese ancestry who do not speak the language is one choice. Giving instructions to this group in Chinese is another. There may be others." This point created a good deal of controversy in 1980, when the federal government issued regulations for a specific remedy to *Lau*. It was argued that specific remedies were not defined under the *Lau* decision. Those regulations were withdrawn in 1981.

The claim in *Lau* was that the lack of special instruction to help non-English-speaking students learn standard English provided unequal educational opportunity and therefore violated the Fourteenth Amendment to the Constitution. You will recall, from the beginning of this chapter and from Chapter 5 on school desegregation, that the Fourteenth Amendment guarantees all citizens equal protection under the laws.

The Court did not use the Fourteenth Amendment in its ruling, but relied on Title VI of the 1964 Civil Rights Act. This law bans discrimination based on "race, color, or national origin" in "any program or activity receiving Federal financial assistance." The Supreme Court ruled: "It seems obvious that the Chinese-speaking minority receives fewer benefits than the English-speaking majority from respondents' school system which denies them a meaningful opportunity to participate in the educational program—all earmarks of the discrimination banned by the regulations." Although the Court did not give a specific remedy to the situation, its ruling meant that all public school systems receiving any form of federal aid must ensure that children from non-English-speaking backgrounds be given some form of special help in learning standard English so that they may have equal educational opportunity.

The problem that was not addressed in *Lau* was that of specific remedies for the situation of children from nonstandard-English backgrounds. A decision regarding this issue was made by the U.S. District Court in 1979 in *Martin Luther King Junior Elementary School Children et al.* v. *Ann Arbor School District.* The court was quite clear that the case was "not an effort on the part of the plaintiffs to require that they be taught 'black English' or that a dual language program be provided."

As the court defined the problem, it was the ability to teach standard English to "children who, it is alleged, speak 'black English' as a matter of course at home and in their home community." The plaintiffs introduced into the case the testimony of expert witnesses who argued that attempts to teach standard English without appreciating the dialect used by the children at home and in the community could cause the children to be ashamed of their language and hinder their ability to learn standard English.

The court gave recognition to the existence of a bilingual culture within the African-American community, in which individuals would speak African-American English with peers and standard English with the larger community. In the words of the court, the African-American children "retain fluency in 'black English' to maintain status in the community and they become fluent in standard English to succeed in the general society."

After reviewing the evidence and the expert testimony, the court argued that there was a possible relationship between poor reading ability and the school's not taking into account the home language of the children. This prevented children from taking full advantage of their schooling and was a denial of equal educational opportunity. This argument was based on the reasonable premise that knowing how to read was one of the most important factors in achievement in school.

The court gave a very specific remedy to the situation, a remedy that might be used as a guide in future cases. The court directed the school system to develop within thirty days a plan that would "identify children speaking 'black English' and the language spoken as a home or community language." Second, the school system was directed to "use that knowledge in teaching such students how to read standard English."

The language of the school is one aspect of providing equal educational opportunity. Another aspect is equality of funding of schools.

SCHOOL FINANCES

You will recall that equality of educational opportunity means equal access to educational institutions. In terms of school finances, equality of educational opportunity is provided if equal amounts of public money are spent on each child's public schooling. The problem in many states is that the amount of money spent per public school student varies from one school district to another.

Resolving the problem of unequal financing of public schools does not necessarily provide complete equality of educational opportunity. As mentioned in Chapter 5, other important factors may get in the way of equality of opportunity, such as quality of teachers, type of curriculum, and instructional materials. Although these considerations are important in assessing the quality of schooling, one should not lose sight of the basic issue of justice. You can argue that it is unjust for the child of one taxpayer to have less public money spent on his or her education than is spent on the child of another taxpayer. It is unjust for the child of a taxpayer to be denied equal access to public institutions because of race. Like the issue of racial segregation, the issue of school financing is directly related to equality of educational opportunity.

Reliance on local property taxes can result in unequal support of schools because of differences between school districts in the value of the property to be taxed and the amount a community is willing to tax its property. For instance, some communities have several large industries and expensive residential and commercial areas that can be taxed for support of schools. Other communities are composed of modest residential areas and do not have any large industries. Both communities might levy equal taxes. This would not result in equal revenue, due to the unequal value of property in the two communities. This could mean, for instance, that a homeowner in one community could pay the same amount of taxes on a $40,000 house as a homeowner with a house of the same value in another community, but very different sums might be spent on the education of their children because of the disparity in total value of property between the two communities.

The disparities that exist between school systems in the same state is illustrated in a report in the March 5, 1990, issue of the *New York Times,* which compared the schools of East Orange and Millburn, New Jersey. Millburn spends $6,247 on each schoolchild while East Orange spends $4,867. The difference in per pupil expenditures is almost $1,400. The difference in expenditures reflects differences in property values. Millburn is a community of spacious homes and quaint country lanes. In 1988, the median sales price of a home in Millburn was $370,000. On the other hand, East Orange is an urban school district with a median sales price for a home in 1988 being $80,000.

The differences in school expenditures are evident in both systems. When Scott High School in East Orange needed a new library, a gymnasium was converted. Millburn built a new high school library in a large courtyard. East Orange's teachers average fourteen years experience and earn $35,000 a year.

Millburn's teachers average twenty years experience and earn $41,520 a year. The pupil-teacher ratio in East Orange averages 27 to 1, while in Millburn it is 18 to 1. Millburn offers fourteen advanced-placement courses and East Orange offers none. The *New York Times* explained that Millburn High has plenty of classroom space, but

> Scott High [East Orange], built here 52 years ago for 800 students, is bulging now with 1,200. The other day, Deborah Mayes's American history class was squeezed into the music room, next to the piano. Ester Lundy was teaching a freshman business course in the typing room as her students tried to balance their open texts atop typewriters.

Descriptions of this type highlight the inequality of educational opportunity that results from unequal financing of schools. The book that provided the basis for the original court cases against inequality of educational opportunity that is caused by the reliance upon property taxes to support education is *Private Wealth and Public Education*, by John E. Coons, William H. Clune, and Stephen Sugarman. This is a masterful study of the growth of school financing in the United States and the various attempts to solve these problems. The first part of the book presents a critical treatment of existing state aid to education plans and persuasively argues that existing attempts to equalize educational expenditures either have failed or have actually created greater inequalities. As a substitute for existing education-financing plans, the book offers a power-equalization formula that would equalize spending between school districts and between states and supposedly end inequality of educational resources between school districts. The study also presents a plan for implementing the power-equalization formula by using the judicial process to argue in court that the education of children should be considered under the Equal Protection Clause of the Fourteenth Amendment. One of the judicial techniques suggested is to compare the inequality of educational spending with those reapportionment decisions of the Supreme Court that led to the one-man, one-vote doctrine. It is the opinion of the book's authors that, in a democratic society, schooling should be considered equal in importance to voting.

The rationale given in the study for the need to support a power-equalization formula is directly related to equality of educational opportunity. The book argues that the United States is a competitive democracy in which a marketplace of talent is the prime determiner of individual success. As in other discussions about equality of opportunity, the primary concern is with assuring equal competition. The book states that "the sine qua non of a fair contest system . . . is equality of training. And that training is what public education is primarily about." The authors also recognize that the primary purpose of American education is preparation for a competitive job market. They state: "There are, we hope, loftier views of education that coexist, but in a competitive democracy those views represent dependent goals that can be realized only upon a foundation of training for basic competence in the market." Providing for equality in the financing of public education is necessary in order to make the operations of the marketplace fair and provide for the social mobility of the poor. The authors restate their faith in American education: "Social mobility as a value plays a potent role here, and public education must be seen in its special relation to the underclasses to whom it is the strongest hope for rising in the social scale."

The first major judicial decision dealing with school finances was made by the California Supreme Court in *Serrano* v. *Priest* (1971). This case involved the two sons of John Serrano, who lived in a poor, mainly Mexican-American, community in Los Angeles. The local school in the area had rapidly increasing class sizes and a consequent shortage of textbooks and supplies. Local school authorities told John Serrano that the financial situation in the schools would not improve. According to Charles Tesconi and Emanuel Hurwitz in their book, *Education for Whom?*, the family was forced to mortgage their property and move to another community to provide a better education for the two sons.

The case presented before the California Supreme Court put the situation of the Serrano family in the following terms: "Plaintiffs contend that the school financing system classifies on the basis of wealth. We find this proposition irrefutable. . . ." The court went on to assert that this was a direct result of the method of financing the schools. The example given by the court was of "Baldwin Park citizens, who paid a school tax of $5.48 per $100 of assessed valuation, were able to spend less than half as much on education as Beverly Hills residents, who were taxed only $2.38 per $100."

The California Supreme Court ruled in the *Serrano* case that the California school-financing system, with its dependence upon local property taxes, violated the Equal Protection Clause of the Fourteenth Amendment. The court stated: "We have determined that this funding scheme invidiously discriminates against the poor because it makes the quality of a child's education a function of the wealth of his parents and his neighbors."

Serrano was a landmark decision for action within state court systems. When the issue finally reached the U.S. Supreme Court, a major setback in the legal struggles occurred. In 1973 the Supreme Court ruled in one of the school-financing cases, *Rodriguez* v. *San Antonio Independent School District*, that the right to an education was not implicitly protected by the Fourteenth Amendment and was not entitled to constitutional protection. The Court declared: "The consideration and initiation of fundamental reforms with respect to state taxation and education are matters reserved for the legislative processes of the various states."

The *Rodriguez* decision meant that school-financing cases would have to be argued within the courts of each state in terms of state constitutions. This would mean a long struggle within each state to achieve a method of providing equal financial support to the schools. One cannot predict whether this will occur in all states in the country, but it is one important part of the attempt to achieve equality of educational opportunity in the United States.

In summary, the courts continue to play an essential role in protecting individual rights within the public schools. Because public schools attempt to educate a large population having a variety of backgrounds and beliefs, there is always the danger that minority rights will be lost or forgotten within the school. In addition, public schooling is a property right and in most states is compulsory. These conditions mean that some institutions must exercise vigilance in the protection of rights in education. This is the important role that the courts have assumed and will continue to assume in American education.

EXERCISES

1. Check with a local school district about their grievance procedures for teachers and students.
2. What provisions do local school districts in your area have for protecting teacher and student rights?
3. Investigate differences in expenditures for each student between school districts in your state.

SUGGESTED READINGS AND WORKS CITED IN CHAPTER

Coons, John E., William H. Clune, and Stephen Sugarman. *Private Wealth and Public Education*. Cambridge, Mass.: Harvard University Press, 1970. This is the book that provided the basic arguments for the school finance cases.

Dessem, Lawrence. "Student Due Process Rights in Academic Dismissals from the Public Schools." *Journal of Law and Education* 5, no. 3 (July 1976).

Fischer, Louis, et al. *Teachers and the Law*. White Plains, N.Y.: Longman, 1990. Written in a question-and-answer format, this is a very useful and up-to-date guide to laws affecting the teaching profession.

Flygare, Thomas. "Schools and the Law." *Phi Delta Kappan*. This monthly column provides one of the best guides to recent court cases related to education. It is highly recommended for any person involved in the educational system.

Grover, Alan. *Ohio's Trojan Horse: A Warning to Christian Schools Everywhere*. Greenville, S.C.: Bob Jones University Press, 1977. The book contains a description of the *Whisner* case and the arguments regarding secular humanism.

Hanley, Robert. "New Jersey Schools: Rich, Poor, Unequal." *New York Times* (5 March 1990): B1, B4. This article describes the disparities between the school systems of Millburn and East Orange, New Jersey.

Keim, Albert N., ed. *Compulsory Education and the Amish*. Boston: Beacon 1972. This book contains articles about the Amish and their struggle against compulsory education.

Lapati, Americo. *Education and the Federal Government*. New York: Mason/Chapter, 1975. The last section of this book reviews all the major U.S. Supreme Court cases regarding education.

Lehne, Richard. *The Quest for Justice: The Politics of School Finance Reform.* New York and London: Longman, 1978. An excellent analysis of the movement for equitably sharing the cost of school finances.

Rubin, David. *The Rights of Teachers.* New York: Avon, 1972. This is the American Civil Liberties Union handbook of teachers' rights.

Tesconi, Charles, and Emanuel Hurwitz. *Education for Whom?* New York: Dodd, Mead, 1974. This book contains essays about the school-finance cases.

Walsh, Mark. "High Court's Ban on Graduation Prayers Disappoints Districts." *Education Week* (5 August 1992): 1, 41–43. This article discusses the U.S. Supreme Court case *Lee* v. *Weisman* (1992) which banned prayers from public school graduation services. The article contains lengthy excerpts from the decision.

————. "Students Claiming Sex Harassment Win Right to Sue." *Education Week* (4 March 1992): 1, 24. This article discusses the U.S. Supreme Court ruling in *Franklin* v. *Gwinnett County Public Schools* (1992) which provides students with protection from sexual harassment by teachers.

Index